dove

dove

THE FREEDOM SERIES: BOOK ONE

M.H. Salter

DAYTIME MOON PUBLISHING

Dove is a work of fiction. Names, characters, places, and incidents either are the product of the author's imagination or are used fictitiously. Any resemblance to actual persons, living or dead, events, or locales is entirely coincidental.

Copyright © 2016 by M.H. Salter

Song lyrics copyright © 2016 by James Lee Stanley

Excerpts from the novel *The Dharma Bums* copyright © 2000 by Jack Kerouac

Book and CD Cover design by Damonza

Edited by Gary Smailes at BubbleCow and Paul Hines

eBook ISBN: 978-0-9925267-2-6

Print Edition ISBN: 978-0-9925267-3-3

First published 2016 by Daytime Moon Publishing

Contact the author at: www.mhsalter.com or mhsalter@daytimemoon.com.au

All rights reserved

the author

also by m.h. salter

Doorways
A Rose By Any Other Name

coming soon

Becoming Smoke – The Freedom Series: Book Two

about the author

Melanie Hyland Salter lives in Adelaide with her husband, three children, two dogs, and an army of cats.

The novel, *Dove*, was shortlised for the Impress Prize for New Writers, and received an Honourable Mention in the PeaceWriting Awards. Her short story, *Mountain Man* (retitled *Frozen Souls*), was published in Dark Edifice #2, and was Highly Commended by the Australian Community Writers Inc. Her short story, *Sunrise Lake*, won first prize in the Away With Words Short Story Competition and was published in the accompanying anthology. Her short story, *The Saving Grace*, was Highly Commended by the NYC Midnight Short Story Challenge.

Melanie has a BA in Writing, and a Diploma of Professional Writing. She is registered on the Australian Society of Authors as a Mentor for fiction writers.

the dove soundtrack

the music

This novel contains songs written and performed by James Lee Stanley, who features in the story as a fictional version of himself. Listening to the music, therefore, brings something live and tactile to an experience that normally only happens in the mind of the reader. The soundtrack is available for purchase or download through iTunes, Amazon, www.jamesleestanley.com/store or www.mhsalter.com/store

1. *I Knead You*
2. *Growing Panes*
3. *Natural Sugar*
4. *Political Party*
5. *Stolen Season*
6. *Wishing Well*
7. *Jericho Wind*
8. *Flowers For the Living*
9. *Wait For the Summertime*
10. *Three Monkeys*
11. *No Trace*
12. *Every Minute*

Words & music by James Lee Stanley, except *Political Party* by Larry Good, *Wait for the Summertime* co-written by Ralph Porzilli, *Three Monkeys* by Michael Smith, and *Every Minute* by Stephen Bishop. Produced, arranged, performed, and engineered by James Lee Stanley for Beachwood Recordings.

the music man

James Lee Stanley is an American folk-singer/songwriter with 27 albums released nationally. He established his first recording contract through Cass Elliot and since then has worked with artists such as Peter Tork, John Densmore, Bones Howe, Michael Smith, John Batdorf, Cliff Eberhart, Bonnie Raitt, Robin Williams, and author Tom Robbins. He was also a regular on *Star Trek: Deep Space Nine* and *Star Trek: Voyager* playing, among other things, the singing Klingon and the most attractive Romulan ever.

He currently records with Beachwood Recordings, and tours the USA with over 300 shows per year.

acknowledgements

Firstly, to Gerri Monckton. If this 155,000 word novel contained only the word "thanks" printed over and over, it would still not be said enough to convey the gratitude felt by myself, and my mother, for everything you did for her. Mum said to me, *"Once I'm better, I want to do something special for Gerri. She's been amazing through this and there's no way I'd still be here now if it weren't for her. And I mean that."* I told her I'd think of something. So, to Gerri, because Mum can't say these words to you herself, I hope this published immortalization of her feelings, and appreciation of what you did for her, will suffice. Remember that friendship, just like a mother's love, is eternal.

To every single soul who has ever stood up for the freedom of others: to the people who marched, to the people who fought, to the people who died, and to the people left behind, I offer you these two humble words and hope they are adequate: bless you.

If you have never heard James Lee Stanley sing, I urge you to do so now. Right now. It will change your life, I promise. I first met this amazing soul in 2004 when I traded my house deposit for a plane ticket from Australia to America in order to fulfil a fantasy and see Peter Tork of The Monkees – a man who owned my heart (sorry Jason). Little did I know my heart was about to be stolen by another (sorry Jason). I can honestly say that James Lee Stanley is the biggest gentleman on this earth (sorry Jason!). Much love, appreciation, and fan-gushing goes out to James for allowing me the privilege of attaching his beautiful voice to my work, and for allowing me to bring him down through the ether. James, you are no longer a god, but a friend.

A huge thank you goes out to Alan Canfora, a survivor of the Kent State Massacre, who allowed me to experience that traumatic day through his memories. Alan was the brave soul waving that iconic black flag in memory and tribute of his childhood friend killed in Vietnam, whose funeral Alan had attended ten days earlier. With that bold flag waving just feet away from the National Guardsmen and their loaded rifles, Alan was an easy target who was shot through the right wrist. He may have dropped his black flag of grief in that terrifying moment, but he picked up a new flag of justice and truth, one which he continues to wave today. Through this book, I hope I have made a new generation aware of that tragic day in May. I hope I have helped to keep the memory alive of those we lost: Allison Krause, Jeffrey Miller, Sandra Scheuer, and William Schroeder. And I hope I have honored the injured: Alan Canfora, John Cleary, Thomas Grace, Dean Kahler, Joseph Lewis, Donald McKenzie, James Russell, Robert Stamps, and Douglas Wrentmore. For more information about the Kent State Shootings, the Jackson State Shootings, or Alan Canfora's memoir, please visit www.alancanfora.com.

To Laurel Krause, I send my love across the water. Thank you for your words, your thoughts, and for introducing me to your beautiful sister, Allison, who was shot and killed on that sunny, spring day in May. Laurel and her family have never stopped in their search for restorative justice over the death of Allison, and the others killed and injured. In 2013, Laurel took the case before the United Nations Human Rights Committee, in Geneva, seeking an independent, impartial investigation into the May 4th Kent State Massacre. Such an investigation has never been conducted. In 2014, the US Department of Justice finally proclaimed, "In 1970, four students were killed, were murdered." This is the first time in over 40 years the truth of *murder* has been admitted. Healing can only come with truth, and the truth *will* come in time. Laurel is the co-founder and director of the Kent State Truth Tribunal, as well as The Allison Center For Peace, which is dedicated to fostering peace in America. Both are non-profit organizations. For more information or to make a donation toward the fight for truth and restorative justice, please visit www.truthtribunal.org.

To the Scribblers, Anne Mountford, Faline Williams, and Vikki Holstein, I love you guys more than words, which is why it is not necessary to say any more.

With love and thanks to Raine Johnston-Salter for his totally hilarious toilet joke, which I promised to include in this book.

I am so very grateful to all of you who helped with the accuracy of my research: Stan Cocheo, Dorothy Barchok Sindel, Roy Skellenger, and Gary Lockwood. Thank you for correcting my stars. And to my editors, Gary Smailes, and Paul and Kelly Hines.

To Jason. Thank you for believing in me, and in this book, and for knocking me up, and for using this book in your marriage proposal. With our tradition of doing everything out of order – pregnancy, engagement, proposal, wedding – I would now like to use this book to answer your question. So: "Yes, Jay, I will be your wife."

And finally, to my mother, Glenda Rowe. I hope they have bookstores in heaven.

For love.

For peace.

For freedom.

And for the one person who gives me all three ...

For Jay.

may

What's the matter with peace?
Flowers are better than bullets!

~ Allison Krause, Honors student, Kent State University

chapter one

ray

Fear can inspire you to fight, or to fly, in order to survive a threat.

We flew.

We flapped our wings as hard and as fast as we could to escape the country that wanted to kill us. And, with every down-stroke, I prayed we weren't leaving a trail of white feathers in our wake. We hovered somewhere south of the Tennessee-Kentucky state line, on a barren highway with no shade, in the late afternoon. It was just another day really – the first day in May 1970 – just another day in which I hitched the strap of Japhy's guitar higher on my aching shoulder and dragged my throbbing feet along this empty road and wondered how the hell we would ever get all the way through Tennessee, Kentucky, Indiana, Michigan, and across the border to freedom, to safety, to Canada.

The back of Japhy's neck was sunburned red, gritty with dirt, and I wanted to lean forward and press my lips against his skin. To breathe in his Japhyness and feel the delicious ache that accompanied it. Wiping my forehead, I smiled at the image of our two shadows side by side on this earth, like two lovers stretched out on a bed.

Fisting my fingers, I gripped the urge to touch his cheek. I couldn't give in; I knew where that would lead us – running for your life has a damn erotic edge to it (hell, just ask my lost virginity) – and we didn't have time for that right now.

Scratching the stubble on his cheek, Japhy turned to me. Sun glowed through his whiskers, tiny fires dancing on his skin. "Is today the first?" he asked.

I nodded.

"So, I'm officially a delinquent, then?"

I nodded again, as if that very thought hadn't been bouncing around against the inside of my skull all day, hammering at my brain all day, making me wince with each blow all day.

"You're doing the right thing," I said.

"You reckon my dad called the cops?"

"Course not."

Japhy shrugged. "Said he would."

"He *won't*!"

Japhy glanced at me and raised his eyebrows.

"He was angry, that's all," I said. "Deep down, he's relieved you won't be going ... Over There."

"You can say the words, you know." He smiled. "You can say *Viet Nam*. It's not a jinx."

"Don't care." I dipped my head, and walked on. "I'm not taking any chances."

I would not let a mere slip of paper remove this man from my world; I would fight anybody who tried to take him away. I may not look threatening (just a girl standing five-three in heels, with a flower in her hair and a peace sign around her neck) but, boy, I'll scratch out eyes if I have to.

I keep catching myself in these moments of ferocious protection over this person I've only known for a matter of weeks. I keep catching myself and wondering if I'm doing the right thing in giving up the future I'd so carefully planned. And I keep catching myself in the knowledge that nothing makes love grab hold of your heart more forcefully than the threat of it being taken from you. So, was I doing the right thing? Oh hell, yes!

Japhy would gladly sacrifice himself to save all the faceless people this war in Viet Nam was supposedly being fought for. I, on the other hand, would gladly sacrifice all those faceless strangers – and even myself – in order to save him and his big, stupid heart. Maybe that makes me a monster? Perhaps. But it is people like Japhy that this world needs. It is people like Japhy that will one day save us all. Therefore, it is people like Japhy that need us to save them from their own stupid goodness.

I stared as Japhy's boots kicked up clouds of dust that clung to his jeans with each forward step. I stared as silver shards of light speared the dust cloud, thrown there through bullet holes in a murdered 55 Mile road sign. I stared as folk singer James Lee Stanley climbed aboard my brain like a little bum climbing into the car of a moving freight train. He winked and smiled at my look of surprise, and then sat with his back against the wall of my skull, tapped his tiny foot against my spongy brain, and strummed his matchstick-sized guitar.

Japhy strode in rhythm to the beat of James's song, the tap of James's toe, the pluck of James's strings. The crunches of gravel underfoot drummed a perfect four-four melody. Crunch. Crunch. Crunch. Crunch.

"*Well, I don't need no mighty mountain shining silver in the sun. I don't need to reach its highest peak before my days are done. I don't need the name of fame hung up on everything I do. But I need you.*"

Crunch. Crunch.

"*Oh, honey, I need you.*"

Crunch. Crunch.

"*Well, I don't need no milk-white mansion, or no shiny limousine. Don't need to see my face hung up on some huge movie screen. Don't need the Nobel Peace Prize for some deed that I might do, but I need you. Oh, honey, I need you.*"

Focusing all my attention on James's performance, I meditated on this prayer-of-sorts the musician handed me.

"*Well the birds still need the sky for flying, and the fish still need the sea. Abercrombie still needs Fitch, and I need you.*"

I just grooved away, pretended that everything was cool and I wasn't worried about the F.B.I. tracking our footsteps, or arresting Japhy, or forcing him to the frontlines of a war with nothing to shield himself but a loaded gun. Nope, I wasn't worried about nothing. Nothing at all.

"*I don't know just how it happened – why I love you like I do. What you got that keeps me singing – what you got that sees me through all the bad times and the good times, baby, the times between the two. I need you.*"

Bouncing against our backs in time with our footsteps ("*Oh, honey, I need you*") was Japhy's acoustic, which twang-thumped against my back with every step, and our rucksack, on whose front pocket winked the small, blue button I'd given to Japhy on the morning we left everything behind. The words printed across it said: *James Lee Stanley for President!* I remembered his smile as he'd read it. "If only," he'd said. "If only."

Inside this single rucksack was all we had left of home: some clothes – which were all dirty and stinky these days – the *Dove* album by James Lee Stanley, *The Dharma Bums* by Jack Kerouac. We'd given up everything, said goodbye to everything, all because some fat politician had shoved his hand into a glass container where his sausage fingers death-gripped a blue plastic ball with *SEP 14* painted on it.

A car engine buzzed in my ear like the drone of a hovering insect.

My stomach clenched and my heart stuttered and my legs tensed, ready to run.

But I didn't run. I lifted my chin toward the shiny carapace, a shimmering phantom on the horizon.

Taking a breath, I managed to keep my voice steady. "Your turn," I said.

Japhy squinted at the nearing vehicle, the sunlight reflecting off it in dazzling splinters of gold. "Dove."

As the car drew near, we held out our thumbs and watched the Mustang convertible with a gray-haired suit blur past.

"Aha! Hawk!" I grinned, and prayed that particular hawk wasn't a narc. What if he stopped at the next payphone and told the feds there was a draft-aged hitchhiker on this road …

"How'd you know he's a hawk?" Japhy asked. "Just because he wore a suit and drove a fancy car doesn't make him pro-war. You can't judge people on their physical appearances or possessions."

I squinted at him. "Well, he seemed like part of the Establishment to me. And stop trying to weasel your way out of it! The only reason you don't like this game is because you and your optimism are losing. Another point to me. Thank you."

"Maybe we should get off these back roads?" said Japhy, staring first in one direction, and then in the other. "No one's going to pick us up out here."

"Maybe not," I said. "But that also means no one is going to catch us, either. Come on."

There's a rhythm to walking, much like music. Once you find it and hear the four-four beat inside your head (*crunch, crunch, crunch, crunch*), nothing else matters. Not the burn of your calves, not the ache of your feet, not the stink of your sweat. We'd become true Dharma Bums: sleeping on the ground, pissing in the grass, fucking 'neath the stars, needing nothing else in the world but each other. I could walk for a thousand years as long as I had Japhy's shadow beside mine in the dirt.

God. I was so lucky to have someone like him love me. And, God, how I really didn't deserve it. Monsters don't deserve to be loved by angels.

And yet here I was, a monster, adored by this beautiful beautiful angel.

Of course, I'd never told him about what I'd done. He didn't know that my soul was shredded. He didn't know that killing someone rips a hole right through you. And if I have anything to do with it, he will *never* know how it feels to have somebody else's death ingrained into your very being, as much a part of you as blood cells, and eyelids, and yesterdays.

He will never know that every night – in that second when the real world gives out beneath you and your naked soul has nothing with which to shield itself – the truth looms, with its blazing red eyes and its accusatory finger pointing right at your heart, and its fetid breath whispering "murderer" in your ear.

He will never know that, for every day of your continued

existence, you will see the face of the person whose existence has ended because of you. Snuffed out as easily and effortlessly as blowing out a candle flame. And with that light extinguished, your world is shrouded by a darkness that no amount of brightness can, or will, ever undim.

They say that killing during war is heroic, but you can't mend a shredded soul with a war medal. You couldn't mend a shredded soul with anything, really. I knew about these things. And because I knew about them, I would make sure that Japhy *never* had to; his soul would stay as pure and white as mine had been, once upon a time.

"A lonely highway," said Japhy. "Sunlight blinds ... from a windscreen."

"Huh?" I blinked at him, and he nodded at another car rising up over the horizon like a phoenix. "That was my Kerouacian haiku."

I smiled. A Kerouacian haiku: a flash in the mind, a glimpse at enlightenment, no rules, no form, just what-the-hell-ever, man.

We held out our thumbs again.

"Dove," said Japhy.

"It's not your turn!"

"Okay, fine, you call it then." He raised an eyebrow. A challenge.

I raised both eyebrows back at him. "Hawk."

The car was one of those ugly station wagons with fake wood paneling, and it slowed ahead of us, its engine grumbling like a hungry stomach. I shook off my surprise, ran up to the car and grinned at the three frat boys inside. They all looked different – one wore a blue cap, one had a shiny white scalp, and one had dark red hair. And yet they all looked the same – sky-blue eyes complete with storm-black pupils, shark-white teeth in pink gums, and chips on their shoulders bigger than their feet.

Biceps bulged the sleeves of their letter jackets, which were similar to those worn at Berkeley. Blue and Yellow. I took a breath against images of green lawns, and student-filled commons, and sorority houses. Images I would never see for myself. Not now. My acceptance letter for the University of California – which I'd kept beneath my pillow to enhance my dreams – was in a crumpled ball in my waste paper basket. Beside Japhy's crumpled draft notice and my crumpled hopes.

It wasn't fair.

For weeks, a hot balloon of pride and accomplishment had inflated inside my ribcage and kept my feet off the ground. We were going to Berkeley. Berkeley Fucking University! Just like Jack Kerouac. I was going to *be* somebody. I was going to *make something* of my life. And wouldn't that just shock the shit out of my folks!

And then, in a glinting, sharp-as-a-pin instant, my dreams had burst and I was left with an empty cavity where that balloon of pride had swelled.

But giving all that up had been *my* choice. I'd convinced Japhy to drop everything and go to Canada. I'd convinced him Berkeley wasn't that important to me. I'd convinced him I had no regrets.

I'd convinced *him* ... but me?

"Hey, man, thanks for stopping." Japhy leaned down to the car window. "You're a lifesaver!" and smiled in at the driver.

Hearing Japhy's words, a little of my emptiness closed over.

"A real lifesaver." He smiled.

And, with his smile, a little of my icy regret thawed.

"Our pleasure." The driver's words popped free from his chewing gum, and his oily gaze slid down my body and back up again.

"Three new strangers," I mumbled to Japhy, "give relief ... to my sore feet."

The backseat was littered with scrunched potato chip bags, chocolate-smeared candy-bar wrappers, and empty beer bottles, which the frat in the back cleared with one sweep of his giant arm.

Japhy and I crawled in beside him, pushing our rucksack and guitar over the back on to their pile of bags. Before we could sit down properly, we slammed into our seats as the car rocketed on to the road.

From the radio, the familiar four-four beat of James Lee

Stanley's introduction began, and I grinned and leaned into Japhy, tapping my foot and nodding my head. It was a sign. A sign that everything would be fine now.

"Well, I don't need no mighty mountain shining silver in the sun ..."

"Hate this song!" The frat behind the wheel – the one with the cleanly shaved head – leaned over and clicked the knob.

"Hey!" I sat up. "I was listening to that."

White Scalp laughed, shrugged, and stared at the road ahead.

"I'm starving!" groaned the red-headed frat beside me. "Can we stop soon and get some beers?" Two huge front teeth collided with his words, which hobbled from his mouth in an injured lisp.

"You're hungry for *beer*?" I didn't mean to snap at him, but something about all of these guys just crawled right under my skin and lodged heavy and cold in the pit of my gut.

Maybe I should have paid more attention to that feeling.

Instead, I inched away from him as far as I could go, pressing in against the warmth and protection of Japhy's arm.

"We've got some wine in our bag, if you'd like some," said Japhy, spinning around and reaching for our pack. He pulled out the half-empty stoppered bottle of red, as well as the cheese and bread we'd bought three days ago in Nashville before the long, foot-aching walk that had gotten us to this point.

I glared at Japhy as he offered up our only food and drink to these idiots, but he ignored me.

Beside me, Red Hair snatched the cheese, bread, and wine from Japhy and handed it through to the blue-capped, freckle-faced frat in the front passenger seat, who broke the food into three pieces and dispersed it all evenly between them, before tossing the empty bottle back to us.

I clenched my fists and opened my mouth to call them all selfish pigs, but I felt Japhy's hot breath whispering Kerouac into my ear: "Practice charity without holding in mind any conceptions about charity, for charity after all is just a word." He put his arm around me and pulled me against him, as if physically restraining me would cool the burning in my throat where my volcanic words bubbled.

"So," he asked, "where're you cats headed?"

"Road trip," said Blue Cap. "Last taste of freedom for a while."

"Yeah." Red Hair turned to us. "Start our army training in a few days."

My eyes bulged and my jaw dropped. "But you don't have to enlist, and you won't be drafted: you're students."

"We *were* students." Red Hair grinned. "Now, we're *soldiers!*"

All three frats barked and grunted like a pack of wild animals.

So, was this the reason for my instant dislike, then? Had I somehow felt their hawkishness, their desire for violence, their bad karma like a fourth presence in the car? "You're actually going Over There of your own free will to kill innocent people?" I lurched out of Japhy's hold. "What the hell have they ever done to you?"

"Innocent?" Red Hair looked at me with pupils the size of plates. "Don't you watch the news? Those Gooks ain't innocent!"

"They're just as innocent as our side are!" I said.

"North Viet Nam are nothing but communist bullies!" said Red Hair. "If we don't make a stand against them, and help defend South Viet Nam, *our* country could be taken over by communism as well. It's the Domino Effect. You should be *thanking* us! We are fighting for *your* freedom! For peace!"

I crossed my arms. "Oh, don't give me that line. Fighting for peace! It's bullshit! It's the biggest oxymoron there is. People are *dying* and you are *defending* it!"

"Yes, I'm defending it," said Red Hair. "I think this war is good, but not because people are dying over there. It's good because we are helping other people to *live*."

I laughed. "Save your breath, buddy. You'll need it later to blow up your date!"

The two frats in the front let out a long, "Oooh!"

Japhy bit back a laugh and put his hand on my knee. "Ray, come on. Cool out, huh?"

"No, Japhy, it's a free country, I have a right to say how I feel. War is stupid and pointless, and anyone who believes it's *not* stupid is stupid too! No wonder the world is so screwed up, with these idiot-sticks running around!"

Red Hair leaned past me to look at Japhy. "Hey, you'd better tell your girlfriend to shut her mouth."

"Or what?" I said. "You can't tell me what to do. The only reason you don't want to hear my opinion is because you know I'm right. You feel guilty because the Establishment forced you into doing something you don't want to do!"

"Ray ..." Japhy groaned.

"They aren't *forcing* us!" Red Hair said.

I wiped his spit off my cheek and fired straight back at him. "Bullshit! You are scared shitless of being drafted, so by joining of your own choice you've tricked yourselves into thinking what you're doing is right, even though you know it's not!"

"No, that's not–"

"There's no way you'd have the balls to do what Japhy is doing!"

"But, I–"

"He has been drafted, but instead of selling his soul to Nixon and compromising his beliefs, as you have done ..."

"No we–"

"... He is going to Canada!"

In the rear-vision mirror, White Scalp's eyes narrowed at Japhy. "You're a draft dodger, huh?"

A voice in my head started shouting at me, Shut up! Shut up! Shut up! What if they are narcs? They are about to go right to the damn Induction Board; do not piss them off! But, instead of listening, I smirked back at the driver's reflection. "You're damn right he's dodging!"

And then I slammed into Japhy as the car made a fast, sharp turn off the highway onto a dirt road. He cried out as his head hit the window. Bottles clinked at our feet. The surrounding trees became so dense only thin trickles of sunlight filtered through the canopy of branches above, and the sky turned its back on us.

"Why have we turned off the highway?" asked Japhy, rubbing his head.

"Shortcut," muttered White Scalp.

"You know the *one* thing I like about you long-hairs?" Red Hair lisped. He put his hand on my knee and slid it up my thigh. "The chicks always put out."

I slapped his hand away. "Not with you, honey."

"Hey, man, what is this?" Japhy asked.

"What this is, *man*, is something that don't concern you. So back off," said Blue Cap.

The car shuddered to a stop in a sunlit clearing as bright as the fear in Japhy's eyes.

And all three frat boys turned to face me.

chapter two

japhy

All three frat boys turn and face Ray with hungry-wolf smiles and full-moon eyes.

Their gazes are fingers of optic nerves unbuttoning her shirt and caressing her skin.

While she crosses her arms and stares right back – jaw clenched, lips tight, eyes fierce – all I can do to protect her is stammer like a jerk. "Uh, listen, I think there's been a misunderstanding. Thanks for the ride, but we'll just get out here …"

"Oh, come on, we only want to be educated a little in the hippie culture," says the driver.

"Free love?" says the passenger.

The slimeball beside us touches Ray's leg again.

I stare at his hand. At his fingers skittering up Ray's inner thigh like a spider. And I can't move. I can't speak. I can't breathe.

Do something! I scream at myself. Fucking do something!

But I just continue to stare and blink and stare.

"Is it true you hippie chicks don't wear bras?" And then those dirty fingers are blurring up and under Ray's shirt. Touching her smooth, soft skin in a place where nobody else but I have ever touched her.

She slaps him in the face and he grabs her wrist.

That crisp *clap* of skin on skin snaps me into action. "Take your hands off her!" I push against his brick-wall chest as hard as I can.

Nothing happens. I can't budge him. He just smiles at me.

And then I fall backwards.

Thick forearms rope around my middle and pull me out into the bright sunshine. My sneakers leave twin grooves in the dirt as I kick and twist. The last I see of Ray is a green flash of her eyes, their whites bright in the darkness. The disgusting, red-headed imbecile shadows over her, pulls the door closed, and she is trapped in there with his hungry smile, and filthy hands.

"Ray!" I cry out her name to let the gods, or the universe, or karma know that she needs help.

Help that I cannot provide.

But the gods, or the universe, or karma do not reply. Or, on other hand, maybe they do ...

Crack!

The noise is so loud that at first I think a tree limb has fallen behind me. But then, as my head jerks sideways and pain shoots through my skull, I realize the sound came from inside my own jaw.

Crack!

My head jerks sideways again as another giant, beefy fist slams into my chin. I flop my head forward in the only act of self-protection I can manage. I try to curl inside my own chest cavity, where the armor of my ribcage will keep me safe. With my useless hands pinned behind me, I collapse backwards against the jerkball holding me up, and I watch the other one lift his knee and with a loud grunt drive his foot all the way through my stomach and out the other side.

I double over, gasping for breath. Tears blind me.

"Ray." I breathe her name. A talisman. A prayer. "Ray." With my own eyes scrunched tight, I see her; another man's hand on the skin that I love so much, a sob escaping the lips that I love so much, fear in the eyes that I love so much.

She haunts me.

"Get that ring off him," one of them says. "Looks like real gold."

"No," I murmur, fisting my left hand to protect the gold band my grandfather gave me after graduation.

The frats try to pry open my fingers, but the only way they are going to slide that piece of metal off my hand is when it goes limp in death.

"Hey, stand him up," snickers the voice behind me. "Let's make him watch!"

As laughter bruises my skin, arms tighten around my chest again and I am lifted back on my feet.

"Check it out, bud," one of them whispers in my ear. "Your girlfriend is totally into it!"

"Ray?" I open my eyes and see straight in through the car window. Her fingers lace in the short red hair of the wolf, pulling his face to hers. She kisses him, then pulls away, dips her head, and laughs.

I smile.

Her strength warms me.

"Yeah!" shouts the frat boy behind me. He releases my hand and raises his arm to punch the air in triumph. "Go, Sam, go!"

I wrench free. Spin. Smash my fist into anything I can find.

Teeth cut my knuckles.

The driver, the one who's been holding me, staggers back a step. Spits blood on the ground. Snarls. Then launches himself like a missile, his shoulder in my sternum.

I fold like a flower beneath a foot, driven deep into the dirt.

"You fucker!" the other frat screams in a high-pitched wail.

With his body pinning me down, the driver punches and punches. Then he lifts himself up and dusts himself off. That's when the kicking begins.

Curling in on myself, I think, Oh, well, at least I got one punch in. And then I rise up, out of my body to hover above the clearing and watch it all take place through the eyes of a third person ...

Japhy's head rolls from side to side on a floppy neck – left, right, left – in rhythm to each kick, kick, kick. He huddles somewhere in the freezing cold caverns of his own unconsciousness, with teeth chattering and lips blue. He does not feel the blows that fall upon his body. He does not taste the blood, salty on his tongue. And he does not see the car door open, does not see Ray kick the red-haired man directly in his shriveling ego, does not see her stumble out onto the dirt, landing on her hands and knees.

"Japhy!"

The sound of her voice, however – the voice that he loves so much – punches down through the freezing depths to wherever he crouches, and it drags him back to the surface of full consciousness ...

"Japhy!"

"Ray?" I unfurl myself and lift my head, turning toward her; a flower seeking sunlight. Her eyes are puffy, her neck is swollen red, and she wears nothing but her shoes and shreds of a torn shirt. She stands there, staring at me. She just fucking stands there with her breasts, her ass, and her triangle of dark hair, shining like a neon sign. Like an invitation.

"Run!" I scream. "Go!"

But she doesn't run.

She takes a step toward me.

Only one step, though, because the frat on the ground stops whimpering, stops clenching his balls, and his hand clenches instead around her ankle. He rips her balance away and she hits the dirt with her face.

"Ray!" I scream.

A boot connects with my exposed face and I feel the edges of my world flicker and start to fade again.

chapter three

ray

In the dirt beneath Red Hair I twisted and kicked and scratched and punched until I was free from his grip and up and running and surrounded by trees and all alone.

I turned in a circle. The trunks were so dense and so exactly-the-same that I didn't know my way back to Japhy. But then I took a breath, cleared my head, and sound filtered in. Cries of pain. Grunts of exertion. Thuds of boots on skin. Laughter. Smashing. An engine. Tires on gravel. And then nothing.

The silence called me forward. Trees blurred as I ran until I was in the open, with sunshine touching my face, cupping me in its warm, loving hands and asking, "Are you all right, my child?"

Grabbing a dress that had been flung in a bush, I slid inside its softness, and looked around the clearing. There was our sleeping bag: road-kill with a muddy tire track down the middle. There was Japhy's guitar: a stack of splinters and wire. There were our clothes: a trail of colored material. There was our rucksack: a discarded skin. And there was Japhy: a pile of crumpled, dirty, and bloodstained clothing.

"Japhy?" I fell to my knees beside him. "Japhy oh my God are you okay please be okay you have to be okay I'm so sorry are you all right are you breathing speak to me please please say something speak for Christ's sake Japhy speak to me!"

"Well, if you'd let me get a word in ..." His voice was a pain-filled whisper, but that was good enough for me.

"I'm sorry," I said. "I'm so sorry."

"It wasn't your fault." Japhy groaned as he sat up, and his eyes widened when he saw me. "What did he do?" Japhy gasped. "What did that son-of-a-bitch do?"

I pressed my fingers to my swollen neck where Red Hair had squeezed me into silence and stillness. "It's nothing."

"Nothing?" He pulled my hand away and gently ran his fingertips over my bruises. "Oh, Ray ..."

"I'm sorry, Japhy. I should've kept my mouth shut."

"Well, yeah, maybe. But voicing your opinion isn't why this happened; I'd say they planned it right from the start." He glanced along the dirt road, wincing as he turned his neck. "We'd better get out of here in case they come back."

"Can you get up?"

He held his hand out, and I helped him stand. With just that small amount of movement, a thin veil of perspiration shone on his skin. He stood bent over, hands on knees, gasping for air.

"Is anything broken?"

"Not sure ... everything hurts."

"Just rest there for a minute; I'll collect our stuff."

"Do I look like ... I'm ... going anywhere?"

Our cooking pots, plastic utensils, cans, and packs of dried food were littered around the clearing. Japhy's notebook was mud-caked. The James Lee Stanley album cover had been torn right down the middle; the record glittered in jagged pieces. At the end of this trail was *The Dharma Bums*, which lay half-in, half-out of a shallow puddle, the pages soaking up brown water. Its jacket – which had been ripped completely off – lay dry and clean a few yards away. Ignoring the useless broken corpse of the guitar, I opened our rucksack and looked inside, hoping that the fat envelope of cash might still be there.

"Damn," I mumbled, stuffing our clothes inside and rolling up the sleeping bag.

I soaked up a puddle with my ruined shirt and wiped Japhy's face with the damp material. Then he leaned on me and we hobbled into the dense thicket of trees until we found a clearing to crash in for the night, far away from anywhere, where no one would find us. I set Japhy down on a fallen tree, then I rousted about for little pieces of wood to last the night while Japhy got a fire started. We opened a can of beans and a can of cheese macaroni and sat them in the red-hot hollows to heat.

A small stream tinkled through our clearing and I stripped naked and waded into the knee-high water, dunking down, scooping up water and letting the chill seep all the way down into my bones and cleanse my soul. Scraping clods of mud from the bed, I scoured my skin until it welted.

"Well, Ray," I mumbled, "you've done it again."

Why couldn't I just shut the hell up? Why did I have to push people so much? And why was I surprised when they pushed back? Maybe this is what I deserved?

I bit down on my bottom lip, using the pain to hold back the tears that so desperately wanted to escape my molested body. I couldn't cry; I couldn't let Japhy see.

Hold it in, hold it in, hold it in.

Cupping my palms into a bowl, I splashed water on my cheeks to camouflage any tears that broke through my barricade.

Japhy slumped on a log in the red-fire glow, watching me, shaking his head every so often, and then wincing and hissing in a breath.

Hold it in, I thought. Hold. It. In.

"You should get dry," he called. "You're shivering like crazy in there."

Standing up, he held out my damp, ripped shirt to use as a towel. "Come here, baby. We can't afford for you to catch pneumonia right now."

I splashed toward him and he draped the dirty material over my trembling shoulders, and then he wrapped his solid arms around me like a blanket.

I wanted to melt into him. Wanted to be absorbed into his skin. Then, maybe, I wouldn't have to be inside mine anymore.

Hold it in, Ray!

"Thank you," I whispered.

He let out a soft laugh. "Don't thank me; I didn't do anything."

"You're *warm*," I said.

"Oh. Right." Another laugh. But not a happy one. "Let's eat, huh?"

Nodding, I dressed in a pair of Japhy's tracksuit pants and oversized top, offering my own, ruined shirt to the fire. The flame disappeared beneath the weight of the damp fabric that was now woven with sweat, tears, and memories of this day. I thought the fire was about to die, to give up and leave us cold and alone. But, after a moment, light glimmered at the edges and, in a sudden burst of smoke, the flames blazed once again, using the very material that had threatened its existence as fuel to burn even brighter than before.

Japhy and I huddled together on the fireside log. I'd only been able to find one of our spoons, so we took turns to dig down into the two tasty cans that had heated in the coals, spooning up mouthfuls of hot beans, or macaroni with its cheese sauce still bubbling away on the spoon, and little clumps of dirt mixed in.

I wasn't hungry, but I ate.

It tasted good, too. I was surprised I enjoyed it. But that's life, right?

The ground beside the fire was soft with a heavy layer of moss and dry pine needles. After we'd eaten, and I'd washed our solitary spoon in the stream, I lay our waterproof mat and tire-marked sleeping bag down, and Japhy and I snuggled into it, and into each other. Nestled in the crook of Japhy's shoulder, I asked again if he was okay. His left eyebrow was cut and swelling with every minute; a purple bruise darkened his jaw; his bottom lip was split, and twice its normal size; and his hair was sticky with blood.

"Ray?" Japhy frowned down at me, but then he closed his eyes and looked away. "Did he ... did that guy ...?" There was a soft gurgle in his throat as the rest of his question drowned in anger.

"No." I bit my lip. "Loser came on my leg. Couldn't even get it in."

He let out a breath, a sob, and kissed my forehead. When he brushed a strand of hair off my cheek, I stared at his red, swollen knuckles, and I saw again – with a fierce stab of pride – his fist cracking across White Scalp's cheekbone.

"If I ever see those guys again ..." He whispered so softy I had to hold my breath to hear him. "... I swear, I'll kill them."

It was more like a vow spoken to the universe.

"I'm sorry," I said. "I'm so sorry."

"Geez, it wasn't *your* fault!"

"I left you there, Japhy. They were beating the life out of you, and I just ... left you! I should've done something; I should've tried to stop them, tried to help you, but I just ran away like a coward."

I took a slow breath, tried to gather myself; my edges were unraveling and the thread kept slipping through my fingertips.

Hold yourself together!

"Ray," said Japhy, "by running away from them, you *did* stop them. It was *you* they wanted, not me. Once you were gone, they left."

"Not before they almost killed you!"

"I'm fine." He shook his head. "Just a few bruises. But I'm the one who should be sorry, not you. I shouldn't have let that happen. I should've been there to protect you, and I wasn't." He scrunched his eyes closed. "Actually, I *was* there to protect you, and it happened anyway." Shaking his head again, he touched his fingers to my cheek. "That's even worse."

I placed my hand on his hand. "It happened and we can't change that. We just have to move forward."

"You sound like me." He tried to smile. "Oh, by the way, you get another point."

"What?" I asked.

"You called Hawk didn't you? Well I think you guessed that one, Ray."

Snuggling into the warmth of his body, my arms hugging

his waist, my head against his chest, I whispered, "Love you, Japhy."

"Love you, Ray," he answered, pronouncing it a long-drawn-out R-a-a-y. It made me smile. It always made me smile.

"Soldier trees stand guard," he whispered. "Two warriors smile ... with bruised faces."

"Oh ... that reminds me." I pulled out the soggy copy of *The Dharma Bums* to show him. "Look what the bastards did."

"It'll dry." He shrugged. "And we can tape the cover back on."

I sighed. There he was. Same old optimistic Japhy.

What will it take to break you? I wondered as I looked into his eyes. But I already knew the answer. That was, after all, why we were heading for Canada.

I nuzzled closer to him and he kissed my hair.

"You cold?" he asked. "You're still shivering."

I shook my head but he held me tighter anyway as we lay in silence, just being thankful for the solidness of each other.

Slowly, the sun tiptoed over the horizon and the darkness in the woods thickened into velvet. Silver pins of moonlight stitched a pattern through the branches, and I stared up at the stars – into a universe of dark and diamonds.

"*Imagine we're alone in the mountains*," he whispered the line of my favorite James Lee Stanley song, "*and I'll be there just loving you*." And then his voice faded away into a soft snore.

I closed my eyes, stopped my mind, and concentrated on the eternal multiswarm of electrical energy on the backs of my eyelids. There is nothing in the world, Ray Smith says in *The Dharma Bums*, but the mind itself, and therefore anything is possible, including the suppression of suffering.

But I wasn't so sure I believed Ray Smith anymore.

The suppression of suffering? The possibility of anything? Really?

Sobs rocked me until my bones clacked together so loudly I thought the noise would rouse Japhy from unconsciousness. Tears flooded my body, sweeping on their tide the memories of being locked inside that car.

Was anything possible? Really, was it? Could I keep Japhy safe, and alive, and in one piece? I couldn't even protect myself.

The universe was so much bigger than little old me – so much stronger than my fragile, twiggy fingers – and if it wanted to snap them off and steal Japhy from my grasp, then there was not a thing I could do to stop it.

Not a single God damned thing.

By the time I finally fell asleep, the sky was purpling at the edges. A new day crept up to us and stood hulking over our two forms huddled on the ground. Before I gave in to drowsiness, I wrapped my arms around Japhy, and clenched those fragile, twiggy fingers as tight as I could.

Whatever you have planned for Japhy – I sent my thought out to this new day – you will have to break through me to get to him. You will have to break me to pieces.

chapter four

japhy

The heaviness of Ray's arms around my chest wakes me. I grit my teeth against the sharp pain in my ribs, but I don't move her off me. I just lie there, still.

It's only pain. It's endurable. A small price to pay for her touch.

Resting my chin against her hair, I stare up at the bruise-colored sky through the intricate pattern of twigs above. Against this canvas of morning I see the previous afternoon projected there, like a movie screen of memory, in full and glorious color: the white and brown Ford LTD skids to a stop in the sunny clearing. The trees all lean forward, craning their branches, and whipping each other out of the way for a better view. Two frat boys jump out of the front seat, and speak to each other in hysterical voices, and they fling open the back door. But this time, when I am ripped out of the car and I see Ray's frightened eyes begging me to help, I do not fail her. I pull my arms free from the frat boys' hold. I trip them and they crash to the ground. I stomp on their ribs and kick their faces. They cry, beg me to stop. But I keep going. I love the feel of their soft flesh beneath my heels. Love the way it *gives* slightly every time I drive my foot down. I kick again and again until they no longer scream and my sneakers turn crimson. Back at the station wagon, I lean into the back seat. The third frat has his dirty fingers on Ray's leg, and I grip his hand and squeeze it until the cracking of bone echoes through the car. Then I scrunch the material of his shirt in my fist and I push him backwards so hard his coppery head smashes through the window. Tiny shards of glass tinkle to the ground with a musical trilling like victory bells.

As I help a still-clothed Ray out of the car, she stretches up on her toes and kisses me with depth and gratitude and need. Her arms cling so tight around my neck that I can't pull away from her, and I know she doesn't want me to.

"Thank you," she whispers in my ear. "My hero."

"Well done, Andrew."

I turn at this new voice and see my father, who for some reason is standing in the tree line.

He steps out into the light and walks toward me. "Way to show those jerks who's boss. I'm proud of you, son." And he smiles at me in the same way he smiled at Bill O'Malley, the neighbor's kid, who returned from Nam last month with only one leg.

I look down and scuff my shoe in the dirt.

"You're a real hero." The same words spoken to Bill O'Malley. And he slaps me on the back. Just like with Bill O'Malley.

"Thanks, Dad." I lift my gaze from my toes, but he's gone.

Just the trees nod and sway gently at the edge of the clearing.

I close my eyes and hear his words again. The low timbre of his voice relaxes me, the way it used to when I was a boy and he'd tell me there were no monsters under my bed.

He'd been right about that. The monsters weren't hiding under my bed at all.

I gaze up through the trees again.

If I hadn't listened to Ray – if I had followed my father's orders to go to that induction appointment – where would I be right now? On a bus somewhere, heading to an army barracks, probably. Instead, I'm out here, in the free world, with my best girl on my arm.

I'm free, yes, but covered in bruises and dried blood, while Ray – if she is telling the truth – had some potential rapist ejaculate on her leg. But she *has* to be telling the truth about that, because if that's *not* what really happened ... if that asshole actually managed to ...

I shake my head and imagine his face once again covered in blood and pieces of broken window.

Ugh, why am I such a pussy?

Maybe the army would be good for me? Might harden me the fuck up. Might change me into a son that a father can be proud of. A man that a girlfriend can depend on.

But I sigh. It isn't going to happen.

Ray frowns in her sleep, wrinkling her forehead and pursing her lips. I know that look. That's her *don't-tell-me-what-to-do* face. That's her *I'm-right-so-don't-bother-arguing* face. That's the face she was making the moment I realized I loved her.

I press my lips to her hair and inhale the scent of dirt and sweat and Ray. I want to stay here forever – safe, with no one else but her anywhere near – but, unable to take the agony in my chest for another second, I shift, and she snaps into a sitting position.

My skin chills with the sudden absence of her skin.

"What's wrong?" she asks. Her face is puffy and her eyes are bloodshot.

"Sorry," I whisper. "Go back to sleep; it's still early."

"No." She rubs her eyes and squints around the campsite. "I won't be getting a wink of sleep until you are safely tucked away in Canada somewhere." Crawling out of the sleeping bag, she gathers our things. "Let's get going."

*

Huge elm trees wave their welcomes as we cross onto crisp, green lawns, and cream picket fences, and flagpoles flapping with red, white, and blue.

"What time is it?" I ask.

"I thought you said you didn't need time anymore."

"I don't." I shrug. "Just asking."

"Maybe you shouldn't have given your watch away," she says.

"That couple needed it more than I did. They looked like they hadn't eaten in a few days. Besides, time means nothing to those who live in the moment."

"Well, obviously," says Ray, rolling up the oversized sleeve to uncover her own watch beneath the folds, "even those who live in the moment still need to know the time! It's almost noon."

"I'm starving," I say.

"Well," she grins at me, "I guess we could've used your watch now, huh?"

"Nah." I shrug. "We've still got yours!"

Her mouth gapes. "This was a sweet sixteen present!"

"Yeah, from your *parents*."

She frowns and crosses her arms, coming to a dead stop right there in the street. "So?"

"So?" I frown back. "Since when are you sentimental about your folks?"

"I'm not selling my watch, Japhy!"

"Okay." I put my arm around her shoulder and draw her in for a hug. "You all right?"

"Fine." She fake-smiles up at me.

"All right," I say.

The main street of this little hamlet is just as neat and clean as the outskirts. No litter blows along the gutters. No dirt browns the car wheels that roll smoothly by. No cracks spider-web the footpaths. The women wear their hair in perfect up-swept do's.

"This place is creepy," whispers Ray. "Let's just eat and get out of here before they find our bodies in six months, bricked up in somebody's wall!"

An old couple approaches us, the woman smiling from her perfect face as she passes.

"Spare some change?" I ask.

The woman frowns then, and her face cracks.

"Why don't you get a job!" barks her husband, leading his wife away quickly.

We turn to see a suit unfolding himself from a shiny car.

"Spare some change, man?" Ray asks.

He ignores us and crosses to the other side of the road.

"Thank you!" Ray calls after him.

Another businessman comes around the corner, swinging an umbrella on his arm, even though the sky above is the kind of clear blue that hurts your eyes.

"Spare some change?" asks Ray.

"Pardon?" He looks down at her and blinks.

"Can you spare some change?" she says again. "All of our money was stolen."

His gray eyebrows shoot up into his hat. "Really?"

"Yes." She folds her arms across her chest. "It was awful. Terrifying, actually."

"Where did this happen?"

"Oh, a few towns over," says Ray. "I'm not sure of the–"

"Not in *this* town, though?"

Ray shakes her head.

"That's a relief!" The man digs into his coat pocket and coins jingle in his palm. "This is all I have on me."

"Oh, thank you, sir! You are very kind."

The man smiles and off he walks, twirling his umbrella once again and whistling out of tune.

With our handful of shiny dimes and quarters, we enter a small diner where the smell of frying fat sticks to everything.

The lady behind the counter stands in silence, watching as we read the menu behind her on the wall. Her disapproving eyes flick over our bruised faces, dirty clothes, and tangled hair. Her nose wrinkles.

Hamburgers, steak, bacon, chicken, fish: the words are painted blood-red.

Looking down from the menu, I watch Ray count the small pile of silver coins in her hand, her lips moving silently.

Then she looks up. "How much for a burger with the lot, hold the dead, rotting cow?"

"Same as one *with* the dead, rotting cow," says the lady, with a roll of her blue-shadowed eyes.

A man, hunching at the counter with a burger of his own, snorts through his nose. He is the first person we've seen who doesn't fit into this perfectly manicured town. His shirt barely covers his bulging stomach, and the belt on his jeans fails in keeping his pants hiked up over his backside.

Ray frowns at him, a small wrinkle forming between her eyes, and then she turns back to the woman behind the counter. "But the meat is the most expensive thing."

"Well, then, get the meat too," says the lady.

The man sniggers again.

Ray stiffens and her hands fist around the coins.

And I wait for it. I wait for sharp words to slice the air. I know what she is about to say: slaughtering innocent animals for food is nothing less than cold-blooded and cold-hearted murder. Humans can live a perfectly healthy lifestyle without meat in their diet, so eating animals is unnecessary and selfish!

But she blinks. Her forehead smooths. She says nothing.

Wow.

"We'll take one, please." She smiles.

"These too." I stammer, and hold up two colas. Opening one for myself, I take a long, loud swallow.

The waitress writes our order on a pad and mumbles, "Burger with the lot, no burger." Then she looks up at Ray and says, "To *go*."

Ray's frown returns and she opens her mouth, and I almost reach out to her. Almost place a gentle hand on her arm. Almost.

But she closes her mouth, swallows her words, and smacks the coins down on the counter. "Thank you very much," she says, and then gives the woman a broad, friendly smile.

Wow again.

I stare at Ray, and she turns to me and winks.

When our burger is ready, Ray silently takes it from the lady's hand and walks out the door.

"I'm impressed," I say when we are outside on that immaculate street.

"I can't go around preaching to everyone all the time," she says. "It pisses them off." Ray sits on a wooden bench and, as I sit beside her, she halves our burger and hands me my share.

"Baby, what happened yesterday wasn't your fault," I say.

She shrugs and bites her lip, keeping her eyes away from mine.

"Don't change who you are, Ray. Don't ever change who you are; I love that girl. I love that she always speaks her mind. I love that she stands up for herself. I love that she is the strongest person I've ever met."

"You think I'm *strong*?" she whispers.

I nod and take her hand. "I wish I were as strong as you, Ray. I really do."

"What are you talking about?" She frowns up at me. "You can restrain yourself so easily. People dislike me because I snap at them. They think I'm rude and selfish. They tread on eggshells around me in case they accidentally say the wrong thing! Can you imagine how it feels ..." she whispers, "... to be a disappointment?"

I squint up at the clear blue sky, but all I see are my father's eyes.

Do I know how it feels to be a dissapointment?

I close my eyes and I clear my throat and I say nothing.

chapter five

ray

It was after midnight when we finally dragged our aching feet over that invisible line between Tennessee and Kentucky. Between yesterday and today. Between our past and our future.

I imagined that line painted in shimmering gold. I imagined stepping over it. And I imagined it cleansing me, magically trapping within its boundary everything that had happened there, so even the memory of the backseat of that car could not follow me, could not cross the line, could not hurt me anymore.

"Kentucky!" I clapped my hands and jumped up and down. "Another state closer to home, baby!"

"Great," muttered Japhy. "Can we sleep now?" He dropped the bag on the side of the road and plopped onto it.

"Come on, Japh. You can't stop there. You'll get squished by a truck!" I held out my hand and he sighed, then reached up, groaning as I pulled him to his feet.

After a pause, he turned away and shuffled off up the road.

"Japhy?" I called. "Hey!"

But he simply flapped his hand at me to follow.

A few hundred feet ahead, a bridge rose up over a small creek, and Japhy crawled beneath it, unrolled the sleeping bag, and was totally crashed out before I cuddled up beside him.

I woke the next morning to the rumble of a truck overhead. A light film of dew coated my face. Wrapped in a cozy blanket of drowsiness, I rolled over and curled my body to fit perfectly with the curve of Japhy's; his chest hard against my back; his arm draped around my stomach; his hand warm and cupping my breast.

"Love you, Japhy," I heard my voice in the void that's highly embraceable during sleep.

"Love you, Ra-a-ay," he mumbled back.

I smiled. *"Imagine we're alone in the mountains ..."*

"... And I'll be there just loving you," he finished.

I lay there in his arms, shut out all the noise generated by the plastic world, and meditated on the sounds of nature: birds singing, wind rustling through the trees and grass, Japhy's light breathing in my ear. I shivered from the heat of his breath on my neck and I snuggled into him.

"Mmmm," he groaned as I moved my hips against his waist. "Good morning!" There was a smile inside his words.

I snuggled in closer. Closer. As close as I could get until we became one person, sharing the same heat and heartbeat. I rolled over to seek his lips. They were soft, like women's lips, and, with each kiss, a wave of giddiness enveloped me, making everything outside our shared sleeping bag fuzzy. As we kissed with growing hunger and need and force, the cut on his lip split again and I tasted his blood on my tongue. Salt and copper and heat. Every movement, every thrust, another ache. The pain in our joined bodies made everything more intense. I was alive. He was alive. And what better way was there to reassure your existence than the combination of pleasure and pain?

But then he froze and lifted himself off me. "Um ... is this okay?"

"What?" I breathed.

"*This*," he said again, moving his hips. "Is *this* okay?"

"Of course," I laughed. "Since when do you need reassurance?"

"Well, since ... you know ..."

"I told you, nothing happened in that car."

"Maybe not," he said. "But it *almost* did."

"You know what?" I pushed him away, rolling onto my side so I couldn't see him – and so he couldn't see me. "Nothing spoils the mood for a girl quite like discussing her *almost* rape!"

"Shit. I'm sorry." He draped his arm around my shoulder. "I'm just worried about you."

"Well, don't be," I muttered. "I'm fine!"

"All right." He kissed the back of my neck. "If you say so." He kissed the back of my neck again. "You're fine." Again. "Fine." And then he moved his lips around to my ear, where he breathed, "fine."

Damn him.

I rolled over and let his lips fall on mine. I let him cover my skin with his skin so his body became my body. I clutched at him as we both let go of reality and all that existed were two mingled souls in a sleeping bag.

*

Japhy fished a shirt from the rucksack and as he slipped it over his head we heard a soft clinking in the pocket. Eyes wide with remembered knowledge, he dove his hand into the fold of material on his chest, and then unfurled his fingers to reveal three brass washers with scotch tape covering their holes. They jingled nonchalantly against the meat of his palm as if saying: You dumbheads, how could you have forgotten about *us*?

"Breakfast, then?" said Japhy, clenching his fingers around this treasure. "My shout." And we headed off to put our three jingling friends to good use.

In the busy town square, we were carried on a river of people. It washed us along on its tide of arms and legs until – like water around a stone – the river of limbs parted around a lone busker.

Unknowing, unhearing, uncaring about anything beside his music, the busker just grooved away to his own flow. Even with a gray goatee, and lines on his face created over a long life, he radiated youth. He was exactly the same as us. Pure dove.

He winked at me as I splashed by, and chills crackled

through my soul as his fingers began to pick the guitar strings in a familiar rhythm.

"Well, I don't need no mighty mountain," he sang, "shining silver in the sun ..."

No way!

Japhy and I stopped in the stream of people, and we sat down right there at his feet so that the current of legs now surged around all three of us until the song was over. We had nothing to give him but a simple yellow dandelion that grew up through a crack in the pavement; I dropped the flower into the man's open guitar case. He nodded his gratitude and we walked away with our feet floating just a little way above the ground.

Across the square, a newspaper vending machine hungrily swallowed our hippie dimes and Japhy scooped out all issues from its belly. We walked up and down the street, selling them for a dime each.

When our pockets tinkled heavily, a diner crooked its finger and beckoned our empty stomachs forward.

The stares that greeted us as we entered the busy café were the usual beady-eyed, hawk-like stares, but I just shrugged them off like water off a dove's back.

The tables and booths along the window were almost all occupied. A counter ran down the center of the room with a row of stools and a jukebox against the far wall. By the door, a cashier sat filling out a newspaper crossword puzzle and smoking a cigarette. She didn't look up or acknowledge our "Good morning, ma'am" as we passed her to sit at the last unoccupied booth.

The air swirled with the scent of tobacco and coffee and deep-frying oil, the plonk of glasses being set down on tables, and the incessant white-noise of monotonous conversation.

We didn't have to wait long before our waitress arrived. Her nametag introduced her as Ahn.

She was tiny. Beautiful. And Vietnamese.

I glanced down at the table so as not to stare at her.

It was because of this woman's people that my life had been turned completely upside down. It was because of this woman's people that the Government were after a piece of my heart. It was because of this woman's people that everything had turned to shit.

But then I looked up, couldn't help myself, looked right up into her face.

She smiled at me, a genuine smile, the kind that makes the eyes sparkle with authenticity. It made such a nice change that I smiled right back at her in the same genuine manner.

Behind her eyes, behind the light of her smile – right in the back, near her retinas – shadows were trapped in cages. The delicate eyelid skin was creased, as if for a long time her eyes had been scrunched closed. Perhaps it was the images she hadn't been able to block that now paced like angry tigers at the back of her eyes.

"Good morning to you," she said, handing us a red, plastic-covered menu. "Would you like some time to decide what can I get for you?"

Japhy clanked our coins proudly onto the table. "Can we please have a cup of coffee to share, and however many flapjacks this will buy us?"

Ahn did not move. Her haunted eyes took in the pile of coins, then traveled across Japhy's and my bruises, coming to rest on our rucksack, which sat perched between us like a third diner. Finally, she collected the money piece by piece, counting it slowly before dropping it into the front pocket of her apron. Then she bowed. "I am right back."

"Thank you," said Japhy, smiling and spreading out the last copy of the *Lexington Herald-Leader* between us like a tablecloth. We both stared down at the front page where the great round face of Nixon, the Big Dick, smirked up at us beneath the headline: *GIs Attack in Cambodia*.

"Oh, you've got to be kidding me," mumbled Japhy. "Last week, Dick was pulling troops *out* of Nam; he was *ending* the war. Now all of a sudden, we're invading Cambodia? He's *extending* the war, not stopping it!"

I shook my head and wrapped my arms around my chest. "There'll be protests, no doubt."

"Yeah!" He grinned. "We'll make a big noise over this one;

he'll *have* to listen. The war will be over before we know it! Just think, we could go home again."

Home? I tried to smile, to mirror his enthusiasm. That *would* be a dream.

Ahn returned to the table and set down a steaming coffee decanter and two cups, clinkingly balanced atop one another.

As she filled both our mugs with rich-scented brew, she glanced down at the paper and her eyes shone as she read the headline. "Cambodia now? That's good. I hope this makes them realize they can't win."

"Who can't win?" I asked.

"The Viet Cong," she said. "We are showing them we are stronger. They cannot push us around, or bully us anymore."

"I don't mean to be rude, Miss," said Japhy, "but are you saying you think this war is a good thing?"

"Of course it is a good thing." She frowned at us. "You think that the war – it is bad because people are dying over there, yes?"

"Yes," I answered, returning the same confused frown.

She smiled at me, and I felt myself soften. "The war is good," she said, "not because people are dying over there, but because it is helping other people to live. The Viet Cong killed my sister and her baby because her husband joined the South Vietnamese army, because he wanted to fight against communism. They made us watch the murders. There was nothing we could do."

The smell of coffee blended with the images in my head, creating a sludge of horrific, brown empathy that made me want to vomit.

"But I was lucky." Her tender voice didn't give in, didn't break from the force of all her anger. "My husband's father had moved to America years ago, and now has a very financial business. He flew us out here, where we are safe. But my parents, my brothers, and their families, they are still over there and I wait to hear bad news of them every day." Nodding her head toward our rucksack, Ahn sighed. "It is hard to leave your family, your home, your country. One day soon, all these troubles will be finished and I can go home again to my loved ones. But there would be no chance at all of this, I am sure, if you and your United States were not helping us to *win* our freedom. I am very, very grateful for this." She bowed her head to Japhy and then me. "And I hope that you will get to go home soon, too. No one should be forced to do what they don't want to."

I gaped at her.

"Your breakfast will be ready soon. And your coffees are on the house," she whispered, glancing over to the cigarette-smoking woman at the register who had ignored us earlier; she was still bent over her newspaper and taking no notice of us, or our waitress.

"Thank you so much," breathed Japhy, clasping his palms together as if in prayer. "But we don't want to get you in any trouble."

"Oh, shush." She waved at us. "I can see you two have been through some terrors. I know what that is like."

"You're very kind," said Japhy.

"No." She shrugged. "I am sympathy."

I watched Ahn as she wove her way through the tables, smiling at every single customer. And then I turned back to see Japhy sitting forward with his face in his hands, hair curtaining his eyes.

"What's wrong?" I asked.

"I'm scared." His words were barely a whisper, but they boomed loudly in my ears. Even over the scraping cutlery, I could hear his fear. "I'm so scared, Heather."

Heather? He hadn't used my real name since the night we left our innocence and our old selves wrapped up together on my bedroom floor.

I sighed and leaned back against the booth, which was suddenly as hard as truth beneath me, and I squirmed uncomfortably upon it. "I know," I said, and took his hand in mine. "I'm scared, too."

"What do you have to worry about?" He peeked up at me. "It isn't your neck they're after; it's mine. I'm the one that's been drafted!"

"Because, you idiot, if I lost you, I'd lose myself. You *are* my life!"

"I don't want to go to Nam," he hissed. "More than anything else in the world, I don't want that. I don't want to die." He turned to face me directly then, and I saw his eyes glisten. "But I feel so *guilty*. These people are suffering. I should be doing something to help them. Instead, I'm just running away and protecting myself. I'm a *coward*."

"No!" I squeezed his hand. "A coward is someone who stands at the threshold of something terrifying and then runs in the opposite direction."

He widened his eyes at me. "That's exactly what I'm doing!"

"Are you?" I asked. "It's not as if you are taking the easy way out! You are giving up your entire world. We both are. We are leaving our home, our friends, our family, and we can never come home. Never. Those boys who go Over There, it may be hell for them, but at least, once it's over, they can come back. They can see their families again. We can't. We are sacrificing our whole lives in order to *save* them. Don't you think, for one second, that you are a coward, Andy. You are *not* running away from terror, but toward a whole *new* terror. That is not cowardice; that is heroism! As far as I'm concerned," I leaned into him, "you're the bravest person I know."

"Here you are!" Ahn placed a jug of syrup and a plate of flapjacks on the table. "And if there is anything else I can get for you," she said, "anything at all, please let me know."

I looked up at her through the steam that rose like courage between us. "Thank you." I smiled. "You have given us everything we need."

chapter six

japhy

"You hear that?" I squint at the horizon, narrowing my eyes, not because the sun is bright, but because I don't want Ray to see the fear thrilling through me. She's already seen me get beat, she's already seen me cry, she's already seen that I cannot protect her. I can't let her see that will probably never change.

She nods. "Another car."

"It's your pick this time," I say, wincing at the sharp pinch in my ribs as I lift my arm and hold my thumb out and try to keep it from shaking.

"Hawk." She squints, too. "I just hope I'm wrong."

So do I, I think.

An orange van crunches over the gravel and rolls to a stop beside us. The peace sign painted on its door slides open. Two dark eyes and a crescent-moon smile grin from a black-as-night face. "You cats need a ride?"

I'd never met a Negro before, but he couldn't be any worse than a car full of frat boys.

I hesitate, but Ray is already climbing aboard, grinning at this giant black man, who places a huge hand on Ray's back, steadying her. Seeing his fingers splayed wide across the back of her ribs, gentle as a caress, yet firm and guiding, makes my mouth go dry.

I should be the one helping her up. I should be the one who ensures she doesn't fall. But, instead, I'm the one standing back, watching her disappear into another back seat.

Lurching forward, I vault inside the van, but as I pass him, the black guy with the smiling mouth places one of those huge, steadying hands on my back, too. And it's a nice-as-hell feeling knowing that I am not going to fall.

"Thanks, man," I say.

"Any time." His voice is deep, comforting, friendly. And I find myself hoping that he truly means what he just said.

A mattress covers half of the van's interior. There's a small sink and a fridge. Cushions dot the remainder of the floor, and colorful scarves hang over the windows, tinting the inside of the van in reds and blues and yellows. I lean back into a cushion beside Ray, and she winks at me.

It's okay, I tell myself, as I watch the biggest man I have ever seen in my whole life slide the door closed with a jolt. It's okay, I tell myself, thinking of the peace sign that adorns the other side of that door. It's okay, I tell myself, because these are my people.

Extending his hand out to Ray first, and then to me, the black cat says, in a smooth voice laced with a Jamaican accent, "What's happening? Glad you could join us." Even sitting crossed-legged, he towers over me. He must be, what, six-six if he's an inch? His black hair worn in an afro like an aura about his face gives the illusion of even more height.

When my palm touches his palm, and his fingers enclose around my fingers in a gentle but firm grip, his eyes connect with mine, and in their warm depths I recognize the golden hue of friendship.

Then he sits back into the swallowing embrace of a red cushion. "This is my old lady," he says, sweeping his hand toward the driver's seat. "Or should I say, my wife?"

She giggles. "You love saying that, don't you?"

"Of course I do! I'm proud to tell the world this lovely woman is all mine, till death do us part."

I turn toward the driver, surprised for some dumbass reason that there is another person in here.

She swivels around. "Newlyweds." Her soft voice floats back like a cloud of smoke, and when it hits me I inhale deeply. She is stunning. Her eyes are the color of a desert oasis – the perfect mixture of green and blue – and are fringed by a forest of thick, golden lashes. When she smiles – although her lips only curve slightly at the edges – those eyes beam a smile as big and warm as the sun itself.

A pair of white sunglasses hold her fire-orange hair off her face, which is as creamy-white as her husband's is chocolate-black. Together they form a perfect Yin Yang of matrimony.

I blink when I realize I'm staring.

"Anyway." She turns her attention to the never-ending blacktop and the van sails us back onto the road. "I'm Lauren."

I hear a soft gasp beside me from Afro, but when I look at him, he just smiles at me.

"Thanks a lot for stopping," I say, wriggling around to get comfortable on some cushions.

"Oh, it's no beef," calls back Lauren. "You guys look like you could use a break."

I touch my swollen face. "Yeah, well, we ran into some trouble."

"Face first, by the looks of you," says Afro.

"I just wish we could offer you something for your troubles," I tell them. "Some gas money, maybe, but we just had all of our bread stolen."

"That's terrible!" cries Lauren. "Did you go to the police?"

"No!" Ray and I both say in unison.

There is a beat of silence.

"I mean," I stammer, "there's nothing they could've done anyhow; those guys are long gone by now."

"So, this is an awesome van," says Ray.

"Yeah, thanks," says Afro, taking up her obvious change of subject. "I always wanted one of these, but could never afford it. I wanted one so bad, I used to pray to God!"

"God works in mysterious ways!" calls Lauren.

"He sure does," Afro nods his head. "Although, when I realized that God wasn't Santa, I just stole the van and asked for forgiveness instead!" He laughs. A deep, jolly laugh. "Heh!

Heh! Heh!" It rises up from his feet and reverberates through his entire body. "Heh! Heh! Heh!" The kind of laugh that seeps through your skin and makes your whole soul grin.

"He's kidding," says Lauren. "He does that a lot."

"Well, if God is really watching me all the time," he says, "the least I can do is be entertaining!" And then, with all the finesse of a magician, Afro slides a thin, hand-rolled joint from out of his hair.

I stare at it.

The white cigarette paper contrasts brilliantly with his black fingertips.

I close my eyes against the brightness. The image of the joint strobes and flashes in my head. My chest reverberates with the deep bass drum *boom* of my heart and the harp-like *plink* of my taut nerves.

"Need some pain relief, brother?" Afro grins another contrast: a row of bright white teeth against dark skin.

He is so contagious; I smile back. "Sure."

And he hands me the joint, which I scissor between middle and forefinger, the way I've seen Uncle Fred hold his smokes.

"Nah, man," Afro says. "Like this." He pinches thumb to forefinger.

Holding the joint the way he shows me, I bring it to my lips, fat end first.

"Heh! Heh!" Afro shakes his head. "Other way, brother."

"Yeah, I know," I say, fumbling with the cigarette. "I know."

"You ever smoked before?"

"What?" I scoff. "Of course!"

Ray leans forward. "When have you had marijuana?" she says. "And why didn't you share it with me?"

"Oh, well, it was before we were together."

"Oh." She grins and rolls her eyes. "Right."

Striking a match, I hold my breath. The whole world pauses inside that long second before combustion. And then the match hisses into a white ball of light and heat. The paper tip of the joint whooshes and crackles and my mouth fills with dry fire. I try to inhale, but my lungs are crushed by my thudding heart, and I cough and cough and cough.

"Are you two hungry?" Lauren asks. "We have food in the cupboard below the sink. Help yourselves."

Ray opens the pantry and throws a bag of potato chips at me.

Afro leans in and whispers loudly, "She *never* stops eating!"

"Hey, I heard that!" says Lauren.

And then that wonderful laugh echoes out again – "Heh! Heh! Heh!" – as a squeal of delight rings out from the front seat: "James!" and the volume of the radio rises to the roof. Lauren drums on the steering wheel as the familiar bass riff of James Lee Stanley's *Growing Panes* gathers momentum, grooving down the scale with a funky blap blap blap blap, and the van fills with the smell of burning and freedom.

Curls of blue smoke drift up to where James's guitar chords hover. The swirling cloud seems to absorb the energy from the music. Then everything pauses, waits, teases, as James steps up and begins to sing in that heart-halting voice that makes me tingle every time. Now, I'm not a homosexual by any means, but this man's voice? Well. He could seduce anyone, I swear.

"*I'm a stranger in the mirror. A lover in a crowd.*"

Lauren joins him, with a clear, strong harmony: "*A heat wave in December. I'm the lost that ain't been found.*" Then she points to Afro and calls out, "Hey, babe, take it!"

He comes in on the next line: "*I've been running down the road, moving fast the other way.*"

Ray and I look at each other and grin as they sing together: "*And all I hear when I get there, baby: Should have been here yesterday!*"

Afro passes the joint to Ray in a ceremonious way, bowing his head to her. She bows back, takes a long suck on the joint as if she's been doing it for years – and maybe she has; how would I know? – and offers it back to me.

"*I am still growing,*" sing James and Lauren, with Afro's background vocal: "*Feeling just a bit confused.*"

James and Lauren: "*Oh, growing.*"

Afro: "*Ain't got nothing left to lose.*"

And then I can't take it anymore and I throw my head back and arms wide. "'*Cos the pain is slowing me down.*"

Afro: "*And I don't know where I'm going.*"

Me: "*I'm still growing, but I'm taking the long way around.*"

This song, and its perfectly timed entrance, has me bursting out of my body, has the ends of my hair sizzling.

"*Pennies on my eyelids. There's nickels in my ears. The dimes are in my loafers, but my dollar disappeared.*"

The joint comes around again for its final circulation as we all wail and howl out the words, "*No, I don't mind this burning if it's what it takes to shine,*" with arms outstretched and Ray singing and wiping tears of gladness, "*No one knows what's mine!*" before the song ties itself up, neat as a ribbon, and the volume again becomes soft as smoke.

"So you guys like James Lee Stanley too?" I ask.

"He's outta sight," says Afro. "Although not as good as my favorite band, Dog Whistle, but you've probably never heard them."

"We've been fans of James since we heard him at Altamont last year," says Lauren.

"No way." I turn and drape an arm over the front seat. "You saw him *live?*"

"Uh ..." In the rearview mirror, Lauren's cheeks flush pink. "We didn't actually *see* him, no. But his songs were beautiful. That voice!" She sighs.

"One of the best moments of my life," says Afro, and Lauren flushes even more.

"So, you guys have names, or what?" she asks.

"Oh, yeah." My voice is so far away from myself I snort a laugh, and soon we are all laughing at nothing but each other's laughter. With an aching jaw, I finally manage the introductions. "I'm Japhy," I say. "And this is my beautiful Ray."

"As in Raelene?" asks Lauren.

"Nope," says Ray. "As in Ray."

"But that's a man's name!"

"Says who?" asks Ray.

"I don't know." Lauren shrugs. "Men named *Ray?*"

"You only think of it as a man's name," says Ray, "because society has taught you to think it's a man's name."

"Yeah." Lauren shrugs again. "I guess that's true."

"It could be Ray, like, rays from the sun." Afro lights a second joint, and a cloud of smoke drifts out of his grinning mouth as he speaks.

"Oooh, I *like* that!" Ray glows. "I'm going to say that from now on. 'Hi, I'm Ray, as in the sun.' Far out. But they're not our real names. Nope," says Ray, taking the offered joint from Afro. "We changed them when we dropped out. Have you read *The Dharma Bums*?"

"That's Kerouac, isn't it?" asks Afro.

"Yeah, don't you just dig the beat writers!"

"Oh, yeah," he says, "I dig them, she digs them, you cats dig them, we all dig them! They're very *deep* books."

"We were supposed to read *On The Road* this year for English," says Lauren. "I never got around to it."

"Well, in *The Dharma Bums*, you have the two main characters," she points to me and then to herself, "Raphy and Jay." As her words float around and into her ears, she claps a hand over her mouth and snorts with laughter.

"Ray Smith is the novel's narrator," I explain, while Ray sobs with laughter. "He follows, learns from, and is in constant awe of Japhy Ryder, the enlightened poet and number one bum of them all."

"You think I am in constant awe of you?" asks Ray, grinning and wiping her eyes.

"I don't *think* that; it's a well-known *fact*!"

"A fact, huh?" Then she just shrugs and nods. In those two simple movements my heart expands and fills up my entire chest.

"So you named yourselves after these characters," says Afro. "You must really dig the book."

"There is no other book," says Ray.

"Yeah, it's just these two people bumming around living as free as you please."

"Like Lauren and me," says Afro. "We are just blowing around this country like leaves on a breeze, man."

"So, you're a leaf?" Ray takes another drag.

"Yeah." He nods. "Yeah, man. *Leaf*. That's me. Call me Leaf. So, where you two cats headed, anyway?"

Ray's smile droops at the edges and she looks at me quickly, then away again.

"Uh …" I run a hand through my hair. "Toronto."

"Canada, huh? You a draft-resister?"

I say nothing.

"Hear that, lovely?" Leaf calls to the front seat. "We're harboring a fugitive!"

Lauren's laughter trills back to us.

"Hey, don't be ashamed, brother," Leaf says. "We're all against the draft, man."

"Yeah," says Lauren. "It sucks."

"Sucks!" says Leaf. "But remember, if the world *didn't* suck … we'd all fall off!"

"Thanks," I smile and I shuffle around on my cushion, keeping my eyes averted and blinking as wet gratitude stings my lids.

"We can take you as far as Ohio," Leaf says.

"Great!" I say, "Thank you so much."

"Where are you headed after that?" asks Ray. She isn't smiling anymore. In fact, she looks disappointed.

"Don't know yet," answers Leaf. "Wherever the wind takes us." And now he is the one averting his gaze. "Just so long as we keep on moving."

"Why?" asks Ray. "Is someone chasing you?"

Lauren's eyes flick to Leaf in the rearview mirror and they narrow slightly before returning to the road.

"Just The Man," Leaf says. His voice is flat and clean and stripped of all humor. "Just The fucking Man."

chapter seven

ray

It was dark when we crossed the Ohio River and entered this new state – another one down – and Leaf took over Lauren's shift at the wheel. He drove one-handed, with his arm around her shoulders while she leaned against him and slept.

God, they were cool. Freedom oozed from their pores, making them shine, and I wanted to shine like that. I wanted to be like them.

Japhy and I curled together on the mattress inside this orange shell of safety that shot us across the country like a cannonball. The peace sign on the van's door was a circle of salt, protecting us, preventing evil fate from sneaking in and snatching my Japhy away so soon after he'd come into my life.

"I was just lucky, I guess," Leaf said to Japhy. "The draft missed me; my number didn't come up until the end when no one was really listening anymore."

"Yeah, well, I heard mine, all right. Christ." Japhy shook his head. "Still remember the way everything kind of just stopped when I saw my date come out of that damn bowl."

"So," said Leaf, "what if your plan fails and you don't make it to Canada?"

Japhy sighed hot breath in my ear. "I guess I go to jail. What's five years out of a long life?"

"You wouldn't just join the army? Get it over with in one year, and then get on with your long life?"

"I couldn't," said Japhy. "Even if I did go to Nam, there is no way I could shoot someone. I wouldn't be able to live with myself."

"But what if you *had* to?" asked Leaf. "What if it was kill or be killed? If it was him and you, both aiming guns at each other: either you shoot, or you die?"

"It wouldn't matter," said Japhy. "Either way, I'd be dead."

I cringed against the wall of his body as he spoke. Either way, I thought, we'd *both* be dead.

"But no matter what," Japhy continued, "this draft has forced me to give up my life. No matter what choice I made, or will make, my whole life has had to change. It's not fair! Why should they have the power to take away people's freedom, all in the name of freedom?"

"Maybe you're looking at this whole scene from the wrong angle, you dig?" said Leaf. "I mean, it's all about perspective, really; I'll bet all the live lobsters in the kitchen of the Titanic didn't view its sinking as a tragedy! See? Perspective, man! If you never got drafted, you'd never have met me!"

The road under us changed from the shush of smooth tarmac to the crunch of bumpy gravel, and I sat up to look forward through the window. As we rounded a bend in what I realized was not a road but a long driveway, I saw a large farmhouse appear out of the darkness.

Leaf parked the van next to a small collection of other cars and a motorcycle.

Lauren lifted her head. "Where are we?" she yawned.

"Our new home." Leaf kissed the top of her head. "Welcome to *Utopia*."

"Oh, thank God," she sighed. "I need to pee so bad."

Leaf smiled at her. "Bladder to be safe than sorry!"

I slid the peace-sign door open with a whoosh, letting cold air and fate rush in and tousle my hair as I stared out at this house: a two-story weatherboard, painted crisp white with shutters in every color of the rainbow. Jumping down with a solid crunch of boots I put my hands on my hips and stood tall as the front door opened and out filed the kinds of people I had only seen in news footage about San Francisco and flower children and Woodstock. All tie-dyes and beads and bare feet.

"It's a kind of half-way house for students," said Leaf.

"Like a dorm?" I asked.

"I guess so, yeah."

As these strangers approached, they hugged me, welcoming me like old friends, long-lost family.

I am home, I thought, as they gathered us up and herded us into the house, where I stopped and gaped and sighed: I am home.

The living room floor was covered in cushions and beanbags, which were in turn covered by bodies. Scented candles lit the room. Shadows played across the walls, sliding over faces and bare skin as the flames flickered and danced atop wax podiums. The air dripped with sandalwood incense, and it soaked into my soul.

Hell, yes! I thought. This is where we belong.

"Cool, huh?" said Lauren.

"I've never seen anything like this place!" I grinned. "I *love* it."

She nodded as we sat at a long wooden table in the kitchen. Bowls of steaming soup and crusty rolls were plonked in front of us by a chick in a sarong with a daisy behind one ear.

As I slopped up my soup with chunks of freshly baked bread, I watched Lauren and Leaf at the other end of the table. He had returned his arm around her shoulder, and they seemed unable to break the invisible seal between them. Like magnets.

"I love you so much," whispered Leaf.

"I know," she grinned.

"Don't you ever leave me, lovely!" he said, and then smiled. "I'll never let you go, anyway!"

Lauren rolled her eyes at him and then looked away.

Glancing at Japhy then, I leaned in close. "Hey," I whispered. "You realize, we don't know anything about those two, and yet we are trusting them with our future."

"What do you need to know?" he whispered back.

"Well, for a start," I shrugged, "we don't even know Leaf's real name."

Japhy laughed softly. "They don't know ours, either. I think it's awesome! A completely clean slate."

"Mmm." I slurped my soup.

"Do you *like* them?" he asked.

"Yeah," I said. And I did. "I liked them right away. Leaf is an absolute gas, and Lauren is so damn sweet, I just want to bundle her up! Not to mention the fact that these two people have been in the same vicinity as James Lee Effing Stanley! I mean, could you imagine that?"

Japhy leaned back and grinned at me.

Again, I glanced over at Leaf and Lauren, who dipped bread in each other's bowls and laughed to themselves. Yes, Japhy was right: so I didn't really know much about them, or what they'd done, or who they were, so what? What I *did* know was: they were my people. They were everything I wanted to become. They were freedom wrapped in black and white skin.

I finished my soup just as a delicate hand dropped a flier onto the table in front of me. The words were typed in blue ink on a sheet of cream paper:

PIGS OFF CAMPUS!
12:00 NOON MONDAY MAY 4
K.S.U. COMMONS IN FRONT OF THE VICTORY BELL.

"So, you guys want to be a part of history, or what?"

I looked up from the poster into the face of a tall beauty: her hair was dark and velvety, her olive skin looked equally soft, and her almond-shaped eyes glittered and burned with a passion brighter than any star.

"I'm Allison," she said, taking the seat beside me, and then nodded to the guy behind her. "This is Barry."

"Hey," he said.

"You're students?" I asked.

"Yep," said Barry. "At Kent State."

"Kent?" I frowned at them. "But isn't that about an hour away?"

"Two, actually," he said.

"So why are you handing these out *here*?"

"Everyone here goes to schools all over Ohio," said Allison. "Mainly Antioch, over in Yellow Springs, Ohio State University in Athens, as well as Kent State. Kent is a commuter school; most of us freshman stay on campus during the week, and then head back home or out of town on weekends. Me, for instance," said Allison. "I'm originally from Maryland, but my family has just moved to Pittsburgh. And Barry's family are in New York."

"Why did you want to go to Kent?" I asked them. "I mean, if you're going to an out-of-state college, you could go anywhere! You could have gone to Berkeley! Why Kent State?" I felt Japhy's eyes on me, warm against my skin like he was physically touching me, but still I could not look away from this girl; she was living my life.

"Well," she sighed. "I've wanted to go there since I was five years old. It's a beautiful campus, especially right now with the lilacs in full bloom." Allison paused, and a glow built inside her until she illuminated the whole room. "Did you ever see something, or feel something, and for an unexplained reason, you just *know* that it's going to be part of your future, part of your fate? That no matter what you do, it's going to happen anyway, so why fight it?"

"Yeah," I said. "I know exactly what you mean."

The corner of her mouth lifted into a smile. "We want peace now. We're demanding it. And we're going to make it happen, for everyone, no matter what."

I squinted away from her brightness and looked down at the flier she'd dropped on the table. "So what's all this about?" Handing it across to the others, I asked, "A peace rally?"

"Not exactly," she said. "We already had one of those on Friday."

"This is a response to their response to our response!" Barry smiled at me and dropped into another free chair at the table. His words were as soft as his aura and I understood exactly why these two people had been drawn together.

"Right on!" Allison laughed, and turned to me. "You know

how Nixon announced on Thursday night that US troops would be sent into Cambodia? Well, we held a campus rally on Friday to protest. I mean everyone is pissed about it. Nixon's nothing but a damn liar! He didn't even bother consulting Congress or the people of the United States, he just usurped power and pulled a *coup d'état*!"

Who the hell is this chick? I thought, and stared at her, fascinated, as she used words like *usurp power*, and *coup d'état*, while at the same time, looked like a goddess in a beige military jacket. I mean, shit, she was *cool*.

"In essence," she continued, "President Nixon made a mockery of his job to represent law and order; he *murdered* the Constitution! Therefore, in recognition of the deceased ..." Allison placed her hand over her heart, while Barry bent his head in solace, "... we committed the Constitution to the earth."

"Ashes to ashes," said Barry. "Dust to dust."

"You buried it?" I grinned.

"Hell, yeah, we did! Anyway, in town later, after the *wake*, the cops were forcing the bars to close early and throwing everyone out, into the streets. Fires were getting lit in trashcans, and some store windows got smashed, which is totally not cool, but that's what happened. I don't know who was doing this stuff, none of the students were involved, but anyway, by yesterday morning, all these rumors were swirling around town that there was going to be an even bigger disturbance last night, so the Ohio Governor sends in the National Guard – can you believe it? – to protect the town! Totally unnecessary. I mean, yeah, okay, we did have another anti-war rally on the Commons, and we did march around the campus beckoning for more students to join us, and yeah, okay, we did throw some shit at the ROTC building ..."

"What's that?" I asked.

"The Reserve Officers Training Corps building," Allison said. "It's where students can sign up for the army. Campuses all across the nation are torching them! So, yeah, we did light it on fire, but so what? It was an *anti-war* rally! And our decrepit old thing was scheduled to be demolished soon anyway. I mean, the campus cops didn't even give a shit about what we were doing! Eventually, the fire department came, and the fire was put out, so we marched off, gathering more students, but when we got back the ROTC was completely engulfed in flames! And the National Guard were surrounding it. Man, what a sight, huh?"

Barry nodded. "Yeah, they were all just these black silhouettes against the fire. Bayonets fixed and raised. Total trip, man. Total trip."

"But now," continued Allison, "Governor Rhodes is trying to blame us for the thing burning down, when we weren't even there!"

"It was probably Norman the Narc," muttered Barry.

"And you know why Rhodes is so concerned with the precious town of Kent all of a sudden?" Allison asked.

"No," I leaned forward, addicted to this woman's words, and story, and passion, and life! "Why?"

"It's election time, isn't it? The primary is only two days away! Rhodes is running for the Senate on a law and order ticket; he's trying to score points. And guess who was choppered into Kent this morning, acting all official, and shaking his head at the poor, charred ruins of the precious ROTC building? Apparently Rhodes had some big meeting today with the National Guard leaders and federal officials about how dangerous it is to allow all these anti-war protests to continue, and they need to 'remedy the situation' and blah, blah. I mean, come on! We're students, not snipers. We want peace, not guns. Can you believe this guy? He's worse than Nixon. Well, no, maybe not! Anyway," Allison took a breath and pointed to the poster that Leaf now read, "we just want to get these damn pigs off our damn campus so we can get back to our damn studies in peace!"

"We'll be there!" I said, glancing first at Japhy, and then at Leaf and Lauren. "Won't we?"

"I don't know if that's such a good idea," said Japhy.

"Yeah," said Lauren. "What if they get a little rough? The *National Guard* is involved, for Pete's sake!"

"Yeah, and if they start *arresting* people ..." Japhy raised his eyebrows.

"But, Japhy, this is our first protest!" I said. "A chance to make a difference, and be a part of the solution! And anyway, they won't give us trouble because it's a *peaceful* protest."

"Well ..." Tucking a strand of orange hair behind her ear, Lauren shrugged and looked at Leaf. "What's the worst that can happen?"

"Great!" Allison clapped her hands and stood. "Meet us on the Commons at the Victory Bell. Right now, though, we better get back; it's almost curfew!"

Allison and Barry left the small kitchen, and the walls deflated, as if the very presence of those two spirits had forced the wooden house to balloon out around them, as if their combined energies were so powerful that the universe bowed down in awe. And tomorrow, I would become one of them.

"For you and you." The blond woman with daisies in her hair handed us each a plastic cup full of orange juice.

"Is this ...?" I whispered to Japhy, who stared down at the orange liquid in his cup. "Is this *acid*?"

He answered with a flash of teeth, and clunked his cup against mine. "Glug a slug from the jug, Ray!"

"*Japhy?*" I gasped as he tipped his head back and drank the juice in one giant swallow.

Hesitating, I looked down into my cup again. Inside this plastic container was a promise of enlightenment. To tune in. To become part of the growing social consciousness. All of us joining together, merging, forming one entity in the search for peace and the fight to obtain it. A chance to expand my mind. To see God.

Or worse. The future?

I blinked up at Japhy again, and he nodded at me.

"Go on!"

Well, I thought, what the hell? What have I got to lose besides my sanity? And I brought the cup full of oranges and LSD to my lips.

We stood from the kitchen table, and followed Leaf and Lauren into the adjoining living room. Then, in case my legs suddenly turned into jelly, I sat cross-legged on the floor beside Japhy and leaned into him, waiting for something to happen.

How long does it take? I thought. What will it feel like? What if I have a bad trip?

"Hey." Lauren leaned in close so I could hear her over all the music and talking. "You okay?"

"Yes!" I nodded. "Of course."

"Is this your first time?" she asked, and smiled.

"What? No!" And I laughed and waved my hand in the air. "I've done this a million times."

"Cool." She leaned back again and candlelight reflected off a small silver cross nestled comfortably in her cleavage. The shards of light shot off the silver chain and darted around the room like tiny, speeding fish with gleaming scales.

"Are you Christian?" I asked, pointing at the necklace.

"Catholic." She closed her hand around the crucifix, and a small fish of light wriggled in between her fingers. "I got this at my first communion. I never take it off." She lifted the cross to her lips and kissed it. "It protects me."

"Oh," I said.

"*Oh.*" She mimicked me, and laughed. "You don't believe in God?"

"A god, not *the* God." I shifted on the floor. "We study Buddhism, actually."

"That's okay," she shrugged. "It's all the same principles: love and forgiveness."

Love and forgiveness, I thought. Yes, that's nice. Everyone should practice those beliefs. The whole world should worship at the idol of Love and Forgiveness. Then there would be no hate. No anger. No stupid-as-all-hell war, that's for sure. Everyone would just love and forgive. It was so simple. Why did no one else get it? Maybe it was *too* simple?

I opened my mouth to tell Lauren the meaning of life, but my tongue was suddenly all fuzzy and I wanted a drink. That's when I noticed her cup of juice was still full. I stared at it, confused, and she followed my gaze.

"I prefer a natural high," she said, and placed a hand on her stomach, which I suddenly realized was full and round.

"Oh! Wow, congratulations!" I said. How had I missed *that?* "How far along are you?"

"Five months." Grabbing my hand, she placed it on the swell of her stomach. "He's kicking. Can you feel him?"

"Him?" I asked, feeling nothing but her hard, round belly.

"It's much more intimate to say *him* and *her* instead of *it*. Don't you think?"

As if the baby knew we were talking about him, he kicked again. I felt him, or her, and I couldn't speak; it blew me away. The miracle of what I felt moving inside Lauren was overwhelming; my mind whirled in awe of the universe.

The tall, blond chick, the one with the daisy, hovered over the turntable, flicked through albums, and swayed slowly to a song that played only in her head.

"Play some Dog Whistle," yelled Japhy, and Leaf snorted a laugh.

When she slid out her choice from the rack, I recognized the cover and smiled Yes! She dropped the needle onto the vinyl. Static crackled before the teasing guitar riff and rising bass leaked from the speakers. James Lee Stanley snuck up behind me with his wailing "ooh" note, and I felt his presence throb from the speakers straight into my soul. I lifted my face toward the roof and absorbed the music like a light summer rain falling on my skin.

"*Natural sugar,*" sang James, "*sure is sweet. Keeps me happy, keeps me off the street.*"

And then, as if to add to the moment, as if to add to my wonderment over the creation of life, two people in the shadowed corner of the room began making love. Right there in front of us! Naked skin and tongues and patches of hair and oh my God.

Lauren watched me watching them, and she laughed softly.

"*Natural sugar – natural high – all I need to get me by.*"

"Relax, huh?" Lauren leaned forward and pressed her lips against my lips. "Just go with it." She smiled. "Just be natural!" Then she turned her aqua eyes onto Leaf, who stretched out beside us. He tugged at her arm and she slipped her dress over her head and lay down with him.

I stared. I couldn't move. My lips burned where she had kissed me. My heart buzzed, it was beating so damn fast.

People were having sex around me. Sex! It felt wrong to watch, but it felt just as wrong *not* to watch.

"*Oooh – we're gonna get happy! Ooh – we're gonna feel good!*"

The air thickened with love. It wove in and out of the smoke as if sewing itself into a quilt. And then it *was* a quilt. I could see all the different colored patches of smoke that the weaving love had sewn together. I felt Japhy's hand on my hand and I interlaced my fingers with his and the throb of his pulse against my palm and every beat of his heart sent a surge of electricity through me. Zap-zap! Zap-zap!

"*Natural sugar is mighty fine – only use the natural kind.*"

James Lee Stanley's guitar and bass licks were air-soft hands that made love to us gently, while at the same time, rough and hard and good.

More people shed their clothes like old skins, revealing their true selves underneath. Some of them were up and moving. With their eyes closed and their arms floating ribbons, they *became* the music. They no longer *danced*; they were inside the song, dressed in the beat of it, marionettes moving by the strings of groove.

"*It's a natural me and a natural she.*"

I'd never taken my clothes off in front of anyone besides Japhy (I didn't count what happened in that back seat – I didn't want to even think about what happened in that back seat, thank you very much, brain!), but at that moment I didn't give a God damn hoot and holler. I wanted these beautiful people, these hippies, to accept me as one of them, so I let Japhy unbutton my shirt and peel the soft material back over my shoulders, and I shed not just old skin, but my old self. My skin smiled with exhibitionism.

We lay down naked beside Leaf and Lauren, and I felt the quilt of love tuck itself around us as it fell over everyone in the room.

"*Natural goodness – you know it's good as good can be.*"

One of Japhy's hands scrunched in my hair; the other pressed on the small of my back, moving lower, pulling my hips harder against his own. Grinding himself against me, rhythmically, with the music.

"*Ooh – we're gonna get happy! Ooh – we're gonna feel good!*"

And then his faced morphed into a monster's.

His deep brown eyes blinked into searing sky blue. His dark blond curls glowed fire red. And he grinned with pointy, shark-like teeth that stabbed out over his lips at crooked angles.

I gasped as I stared up into the face of the frat boy, who once again pressed down on me. Once again lisped into my ear: "I'm sorry about this, but I'll never live it down otherwise ..." Once again my own answering breath: "It's okay, I won't fight you. Make love, not war, right?" And once again I smiled as I kissed him and tensed my muscles and prepared to drive my knee into his hard softness.

Pinning my eyelids closed, I pressed my face against Japhy's skin. I inhaled him deep within my bones, and the monster vanished like a wisp of clearing smoke.

I sighed at the gentle swirls of colors on the back of my eyelids as my skin tingled beneath Japhy's fingertips. Butterflies of changing designs fluttered in my vision. And I realized that none of this was real – it was an illusion, just as Ray Smith had been telling me in chapter five of *The Dharma Bums*. Every day my six senses trick me into believing that I actually have six senses, and that I am making contact with an actual world. If it wasn't for my eyes, I wouldn't see Japhy in front of me. If it wasn't for my ears, I wouldn't hear the deep, shiver-inducing voice of James Lee Stanley. If it wasn't for my nose, I wouldn't smell the sandalwood incense. If it wasn't for my tongue, I wouldn't taste the orange juice on Japhy's lips. If it wasn't for my body, I wouldn't feel his fingertips. But, there is no me, no James Lee Stanley, no mind, no Japhy, no nothing!

"*Natural sugar is all I need to straighten out my head – natural sugar even keeps me warm at night in bed.*"

Beneath the woven sheets of guitar and vocals, the sound of a wet harmonica slid around all over the place. I wrapped myself around Japhy, opened myself up, and felt him brush between my legs. Oh God. The ache of it throbbed into my bones.

"*It's a natural me – natural she.*"

My body felt three-feet thick, numb with sexual sensitivity.

"*Natural goodness – you know it's good as good ...*"

My hands buzzed and with my eyes still closed I ran my fingertips over skin and carpet and hair, and I absorbed it all, everything, through my pores, until I became the carpet and someone else's hair, and someone else's skin. With both of Japhy's hands on my body, I felt a jolting thrill as a third hand, a stranger's hand, a hand that was *not* Japhy's, curled around my own seeking fingers, a third hand smoothed up from my wrist, along my arm, and another body pressed into me from behind, fitting against the curve of my back like we were three pieces in a jigsaw puzzle. I opened my eyes and looked down at the dark skin that contrasted so beautifully against my own.

I froze. My body tensed, rigid and ready to attack. My hands fisted. My knee bent. My mouth opened to scream. But there were no icy-blue irises this time. No hungry white teeth. Just Leaf. Just my new, sweet, beautiful friend. And this vibrating feeling of desire. Which swelled within my skin at his touch. Which had swelled inside me the moment I had first touched him. Which made my pores forget they'd ever been touched by anyone besides Japhy. Which cleansed me of ... what? In this moment, I couldn't remember what had happened in the back seat of that car. In *this* moment, *that* moment never even existed.

"Your hands ..." I muttered to Leaf. "You're a healer!" And I kissed him. And I put both my hands on him. And I let him bless me.

Because, after all, this was what they all did. These hippies. These beautiful people. These peace-freaks that I so wanted to be like. They healed the whole God damn world.

Facing Japhy again, I whispered: "Is this okay?"

He looked at Leaf and he blinked and then said, "Yeah, it's fine, babe, it's just like yabyum."

And I whispered, "Yabyum, yabyum, yabyum."

"Yabyum?" Leaf murmured in my ear. "What's that?"

I ran a hand down the length of his shiny body and let it rest on his hip. "Don't you know about yabyum?" As I tilted my head around to Leaf's chocolate lips and strawberry tongue, tasted their sweetness, Japhy's heavy breaths in my ear took me right up to the edge, and I couldn't believe what I was doing. And yet I *could* believe it, because nothing had ever felt so right.

"Here's what yabyum is," said Japhy. He sat up and crossed his legs, feet on knees, and looked right down into my eyes as I lowered myself onto him with my arms around his neck. "This is what they do in the temples of Tibet. It's a holy ceremony, done just like this in front of chanting priests." Japhy let out a soft groan; I felt the pressure of him push inside me. "People pray and recite Om Mani Padme Hum, which means Amen the Thunderbolt in the Dark Void." He groaned again, louder. "I'm the Thunderbolt and she is the Dark Void, you see?"

I closed my eyes. Pinwheels of colored suns exploded on the screen of my eyelids, bursting in rhythm to the motion of Japhy pulsing forward and back, chanting softly, "Om Mani Padme Hum, Om Mani Padme Hum," as he aligned his chakras with mine and our energies surged together.

The song of James Lee Stanley faded behind the music that we made. That we all made. Funky and orgasmic. Faster and faster. Up and up and up. Lost in the crescendo of ecstasy that permeated the smoky air, Japhy and I rode the group-shared orgasm to its peak. It crashed over us in a ripple of foamy, bubble-tickling bliss, leaving us gasping for air.

Leaf sat up, pretzeled his legs and lifted me onto his lap; I took all of him inside me. His big hands held my hips and he rocked me in a slow rhythm, and as we began to chant *Om Mani Padme Hum*, I felt the wave begin to swell under me once more.

There was a click as the turntable needle lifted and dropped back on the vinyl and, under the heavy breathing and groans from around the room, I heard that familiar soft hiss and crackle. The sound of pure anticipation. I held my breath, and waited ...

chapter eight

japhy

I open my eyes to a morning of brighter colors and softer edges. My muscles ache and I am newborn. Cleansed. I sit up and grin wider than my face.

Ray still sleeps beside me, wrapped all around in a pink and blue quilt. I trace a finger along the line of her chin and she smiles as she dreams.

God, I love this woman.

Lauren walks in and leans over Leaf. "Wake up, sleepyhead."

"It's too early," he groans.

"The early bird catches the worm, remember?" she says.

"Yes," he says, "but the second mouse gets the cheese."

"Come on," she calls over her shoulder. "Breakfast is ready."

A clinking drifts out from the kitchen on the low muffle of voices. I follow my bare feet to where Lauren helps three other women with a growing stack of flapjacks. She meets my eyes and then looks away as her cheeks flush and her entire face turns the same shade as her hair.

I smile as I feel my own cheeks heating up and I sit beside a cat wearing nothing but an American flag headband. At the long dining table, two other men and one woman are partially or completely naked.

"Our nudity doesn't make you uncomfortable does it, Japh?" asks the guy beside me.

"No, not at all," I answer, and am surprised to find I'm not lying. It doesn't bother me. They are so comfortable in their own skin that their comfort projects into me, and I'm the one who suddenly feels awkward for wearing shorts.

After last night, I am *one* with all these people. I took part in an entire group ritual. A ceremony. And now, filled with peacefulness and belonging, I don't want to leave here.

Ever.

The mouth-watering fragrance of flapjacks, scrambled eggs, and fried tomatoes drifts into the living room and shakes the sleep out of the rest of the commune, filling the kitchen with more dressed, and not dressed, people.

Leaf appears in the doorway with Ray holding on to his arm, and I am suddenly struck by how small she really is. I always saw her as this huge personality that filled my entire world, and as I see her standing there now, dwarfed by Leaf's height, I shake my head, awed by how a body so tiny can contain such magnitude, such power over me.

With her hair sticking out in all directions and the quilt still wrapped around her shoulders, she scans the room and chews her bottom lip. Her eyes are wide; I can see all of the whites around her green pupils. They flick quickly, left then right, across the faces at the table. But then she spots me, and slumps into herself a little. She shrugs off the quilt – wearing nothing beneath but my boxers, shirt, and a shy smile – and folds it, placing it on the bench seat beside me. I lift my arm to her and she slides in under it, nestling against me.

Through the doorway bounces Sunshine, as bright as her namesake. She wears fresh daisies in her hair, and a pink sarong wrapped around her like a towel. "Morning, Japh," she says, "Ray." And kisses us both on the cheek as she passes, greeting every single person in the same fashion. By the time breakfast is served, she has made her way around the entire table. And if anyone comes in late, Sunshine calls them over to kiss their cheek and wish them a good morning.

This is what we want. This life. This family. This freedom. Just *this*.

I chew a tomato with cheek-aching happiness.

Opposite us, Lauren sits and bows her head and clasps her hands and then, mouthing a quick "Amen", she piles her plate. She keeps her eyes on her food the whole time and doesn't look up even when Ray whispers her name.

After breakfast, Ray grabs my hand and pulls me outside.

I stumble after her down the wooden porch steps and we walk hand in hand, in silence, around the house. Nothing but blue sky, and green grass, and wire fences, and chickens, and cows, and yes yes yes!

The sun on my skin feels different than it ever has before. "Do you feel that?" I stop and tilt my face upward.

"What?" she asks.

"The sun," I say.

She smiles and looks up at the sky. "Yes, Japhy, I can feel the sun."

"No," I shake my head. "I mean ... can you feel ... that *feeling* ..."

"Are you still stoned?"

I sit and cross my bare legs. The grass is warm and dry beneath my skin, and the soft blades tickle my toes. "Listen," I say. "Do you hear it?"

"What?" Ray sits beside me and tilts her head. "I can't hear anything."

"Exactly! It's so quiet out here; it's like being inside heaven."

"It is pretty amazing."

"Um, I was thinking," I say, plucking a strand of grass and rolling it between my fingers. "Maybe we could live *here* instead. Just go underground; hide out from the rest of the world, you know?"

Ray shakes her head. One single shake. And there it is: that puckered mouth, and that frown, and that gorgeous forehead wrinkle. "Still too risky," she says. "What if the place is ever raided?"

I laugh. "And what are the chances of that?"

"The chances are *none*, because we won't be taking them!"

"But ..." I shrug and look away across the paddocks. "We could stay in America! We could go *home* every now and then. I could check in on Mom. While she's still ..." The word *alive* fills my mouth but I can't get it past my lips. "Healthy," I finish.

Ray takes my hand and squeezes it. "I know you're worried about Nora, but the doctors said she would be fine after the operation, didn't they? They said they were confident they would get it all."

"Yeah. But if we just stay here–"

"No, Japhy!" she says, squeezing my hand so hard this time that I wince. "I'm not going to risk that. And Nora wouldn't want you to risk it either."

My head falls, weighed by truth. I remember when we told my mother we planned to leave for the border. I remember the soft, sighed "Thank you" she'd handed to Ray, as precious as a kiss.

"And what about Lauren and Leaf?" asks Ray, sweeping the hair up off her face into a ponytail.

"What about them?"

She huffs, and lets her hair fall back around her face. "We've just met these two great people – real hippies, real free spirits – and *they* won't stop here for long," she says. "I get the impression they can't stay in one place for too long."

"Yeah." I pluck some more grass. "I got that vibe, too."

Ray leans forward. "What do you think they are running from?"

"Dunno."

"Do you think it's something ..." Ray leans closer. "Bad?"

"Would it matter?"

"No." Ray shrugs. "I don't think it would; I'm just curious. I mean, what if they *killed* someone?"

I smile. And then I laugh.

"What?" Ray crosses her arms. "I'm serious. You never know who could be capable of that."

"Yeah, maybe Lauren bludgeoned someone with her pregnant stomach!"

"Okay, maybe they're not murderers, but they're definitely running from something."

"So are *we*!" I say.

"Maybe I'll just ask them what their deal is."

It's my turn to frown. "No, Ray."

"Why not?"

"Because it's none of our business. If they decide to tell us, then great. If they decide *not* to tell us, then that's great, too. And if we really are their friends, then it won't matter either way. Right?"

She pouts at me and I just want to kiss her.

"Right?" I ask again.

"Fine. Okay. I won't ask them."

A shadow falls over us. I turn but all I see is a silhouette, an independent shadow. The sun glows a holy nimbus around a head with the unmistakable shape of an Afro.

"Won't ask who, what?" asks Leaf as he folds himself beside us, all long legs and pointy elbows and Jamaican inflections.

"Nothing!" I look at Ray and she grins at me. "We were just saying how we want to find a place like this in Canada."

"Yeah?" Leaf nods. "I know of a few."

"Really?"

He pulls a crumpled piece of paper from his pants pocket, unfolds it, and points at the scribbled writing. "Someone gave me this list of places; there are a couple on here we could check out."

"Wait ..." Ray tips her head to the side. "You said *we*? I thought you two were staying here."

Leaf smiles and licks a finger, holding it up in the air. "Yes, well, I think the wind is blowing in that direction, you dig?"

"Oh, far out!" she says, clapping her hands. "Wow, life really is like a great park, with pathways crisscrossing everywhere, and you never know which path you'll end up on, or who'll you'll end up on it with."

"I think life is like a big jigsaw puzzle," I say, "but someone has lost the box so you don't know what the final picture is meant to look like."

"Well, I think," says Leaf, "life is like an analogy." And he leans back in the grass, staring up the passing clouds as if, for him, making this decision is no harder than choosing which color shirt to wear. As if, for him, it really is no big deal.

But then again, who says it is? Right?

chapter nine

ray

Lauren slept, curled like a child in the window seat of the living room, with one freckled arm flopped over her face, exposing the blooming, orange flower of her underarm hair.

A copy of Sylvia Plath's *The Bell Jar* lay open on her chest. It rose and fell and rose and fell. Sunlight stroked her smooth face with its gentle fingers, and I felt my own fingers grow hot. I balled them into fists and sat on my hands to stop them reaching out to replace that lucky ray of sunshine.

Now, I'd never been attracted to women. I mean, hell, I wasn't one of *those*! I liked men! I had a boyfriend whose penis I enjoyed, and I wanted to marry him someday and have hundreds of his babies by using that very penis. So, you see, I couldn't be ... you know ...

But I kept seeing her lean toward me. Kept feeling her lips hot against mine. Kept smelling the muskiness of her sweat mixed with rose perfume oil.

And I couldn't wait to tell her she didn't have to worry anymore – about whatever it was that worried her – and that she could settle down with us, and raise her baby with us, and be safe and happy with us.

That we would all protect her.

Lauren sighed in her sleep, and I heard myself sigh too.

Her long, blond eyelashes batted like a kitten's paw at the unraveling string of her dreams, and I wondered what she dreamed of. I wondered *whom* she dreamed of. I wondered if she would ever dream about ...

"Ray?" Her eyes opened and she looked right into my heart. "Everything okay?"

"Oh, what? Yes! Everything's just groovy."

"Great," she smiled, stretching her arms over her head.

"Hey," I said. "Can I ask you something?"

"Of course."

"How do you feel about Leaf ... contributing ... in things like last night?"

"You mean the Be-In?" Sighing, she turned her eyes to the window. "It's just sex, right?"

"So it doesn't ..." I pointed to the silver crucifix around her neck. "It doesn't bother you?"

"Why? Because I'm Catholic?" Lauren shrugged and fingered the chain at her neck. "Sex is a beautiful thing; we need as much beauty in the world as we can get."

Behind her, sunlight fluttered against the window, a white moth.

"Is Japhy the only guy you've ever been with," Lauren asked. "Before last night, I mean?"

I cleared my throat. "Yeah."

"So, how do *you* feel now?"

I smiled. "I thought I would feel awkward, you know? Or ... dirty. But I don't. In fact, I feel ... liberated! Or purified. I feel so free that I don't think my skin will hold me in much longer. I feel like nothing can ever bring me back down to earth. I was going to have a bath this morning, but," I shook my head, "I'm too scared I might wash off whatever this is. That I might scour it out of my soul. Does that sound crazy?"

"Not at all." Lauren released her necklace and it dropped back into the crevice between her breasts. "God works in mysterious ways."

"God?" I said. But then I nodded, squinting as the sunlight played across my cheeks like soft fingertips. Perhaps that's exactly what it was.

"You know," Lauren tipped her head to the side, "the first time I met ... uh ... *Leaf*," she smiled, "I was absolutely terrified of him! I mean, he is so tall, and, well, I'd never met a *black* person before. I didn't know where to look or what to say. Even though I just wanted to hide from him, I couldn't. I was fascinated. Awestruck. But at the same time, I was scared to death! And that fascinating fear was ..." She shook her head. "Addictive! I think it's like what that Allison chick said last night about recognizing your fate in something. Or some*one*. I couldn't get away even if I wanted to." She leaned so close I felt her breath on my lips. "And that, my dear friend, is *God*."

"No," I whispered. "That's *love*!"

"Yes," she said. "Exactly."

Love, I thought, God, fate. Call it whatever you want. Or don't call it anything at all. Because, no matter what you do, it's going to happen anyway, so why fight it?

"Japhy and I were just outside, talking to Leaf," I said.

"Oh, did he ask you?"

"Ask us what?"

"About Canada!"

I frowned. "What about Canada?"

"Well, the thing is," she said, "I'm not really supposed to talk about this too much, but I've been missing my sister a super lot lately. She's so great. You remind me of her, actually."

"Your *sister*?" Something bloomed hot in my solar plexus and I couldn't tell if it was pride or guilt.

"Yeah. The first time I saw you, I got the same vibe from you. You seem to have the same ... I don't know ... fire inside."

I dipped my head, letting my hair cover my cheeks. "Thanks."

"Anyway, I was talking to Leaf about everything, and we decided that we'd like to come with you and Japhy. To Canada." She put a hand on my leg. "If you'll have us, of course."

"Wait." I steadied my breathing and stared at her fingers on my skin. "*You* were going to ask *us*?"

"Uh huh." She let her head tip to the side and the corner of her lip formed a smile. "So? What do you say?"

I placed my hands on her stomach and leaned forward. "Baby?" I called. "This is your Aunty Ray! From this moment on, I want you to know I'll always be there for you!"

Two tiny movements pushed Lauren's dress outward like a heart beating beneath gauze, and I rested my palm there, as if holding hands with our future.

As if making peace with my past.

*

"Here we are, kids!" Leaf called back to us, as the van rolled into the parking lot of Kent State University. "Get your dancing shoes on!"

"Whoa." Japhy leaned his head out the window as I slid open the door and stepped onto the asphalt, stretching my arms high. "Allison wasn't wrong."

The grassy area by the parking lot was packed full of students that jittered around each other like marbles in a shaking jar. Some gripped banners, some waved flags, some just held determination in their fists.

"I'll see if I can find her," said Leaf as he jumped out of the van and looked around. "You guys want to wait here?"

"Sure," said Lauren.

Leaf kissed her, and touched her cheek, before disappearing among the gathered students.

Sitting in the van's open doorway, with her feet dangling out, swinging back and forth through the warm spring air, Lauren looked like a patient child waiting for her parents to return. She looked like a little kid.

Or perhaps, I smiled, like a little sister.

She sucked on a red lollipop and she blew a kiss at me with stained lips, before her eyes flicked back toward the crowd, searching, waiting for the one person in the world she would do anything for.

Looking up at the campus and dorm buildings of Kent State University, I imagined all the classes and lectures that were, right at that moment, being conducted within its orange brick walls. And all these people – I thought, as I turned my gaze toward the students around me – all these people have what I want more than anything. They have what I gave up.

What I gave up for my one person.

Japhy still sat in the passenger seat of the van, frowning through the window.

"You okay?" I tapped on the window, startling him.

Then he hung his elbow out and smiled at me and nodded. "You?"

"I'm okay." I dropped my arms from my chest, and let them hang useless at my sides, before crossing them over my chest once more. "I'm good! I'm great! Why wouldn't I be?"

"You know why." He looked up at the campus building. "I'm really sorry, Ray."

But I waved his words away before they could perch in my soul. "There's nothing to be sorry for."

"All right." He nodded again. "If you say so."

"There they are!" Lauren pointed across the lot at Leaf, who waved to us from the edge of a large group of students.

They gathered around a small brick wall with a brass railroad bell, by the side of a football field.

"Hey, guys!" Allison peace-signed at us as we approached, and I was struck again by the sheer force of her – she had some potent mix of beauty and compassion and power swirling inside her. Was she even a mortal? People naturally gravitated toward her, like planets around a sun, and she warmed us all in her rays of friendliness.

"The vibe around this place is electric!" Japhy said.

Barry nodded. "It's great to see the jocks and the freaks all coming together for once. But the National Guard are trying to shut us down before we even start!"

"Hey!" A student yelled somewhere off to my left. "Pigs off campus! Pigs off campus!"

I turned to see a guy, who surely couldn't have been much older than me. His face was smooth and handsome, with electric blue eyes that pierced me like a bullet. As he passed, he offered us a small smile, and a shrug, and if it hadn't been for his green uniform and his combat gear and his M1 rifle, I would have assumed he was, in fact, just one of us.

"Pigs off campus!" The student yelled at him again as another student strode toward him and stuck the long stem of a lilac right down the barrel of his gun.

"Thank you." The guardsman smiled. "Now my rifle matches my mother's curtains!" When he laughed, in those genuine notes that flowed from his throat, I heard the distinct catch of doubt as he surely thought: What the hell am I doing here?

"What are you doin' here, man?" Allison asked him. Unlike some of the other students, who snarled and snapped behind us, Allison spoke to him with gentle compassion, rather than accusatory hatred.

He smiled at her. "I don't *want* to be here, doing this. I mean, hell, this is just a school!"

"So, why don't you leave, then?"

His blue eyes darkened like a storm, his cheeks bloomed pink, he looked down at the toe of his shoe and gave a shrug. "Can't."

Allison frowned and touched a hand to his shoulder. "Of course you can, man. Just put down that gun and walk away."

When the guardsman finally looked at her, I swear he was about to tell her some great secret. "It's not that easy," he said. "It's either this or Nam, and I don't want to be in the middle of a war zone!"

I felt the heat of Japhy's eyes burning into my skin; this could just as easily have been him.

"Um, maybe when this is all over ..." the guardsman smiled down at Allison. "Could I take you out sometime?"

"Take me out?" she laughed. "Sounds like a deadly military command!"

"You know what I mean."

"I'm sure that would be a gas, but I don't think my boyfriend would really dig it." Allison nodded over her shoulder to where Barry gave a small wave. "But thanks for the offer."

"What the hell are you doing, boy?"

We all turned to see a second guardsman stalking toward us. He was older and his face was set in a frown, his square jaw jutted forward, and his eyebrows drew down in the middle.

The young guardsman's casual stance snapped tight. His back straightened. His shoulders lifted. His jaw clenched.

The officer pointed to the lilac at the end of the gun. "Do you think that is funny?"

"No, sir," the young guardsman stammered and shook his head.

"Doesn't your division have target practice next week?"

"Yes, sir."

"Will you be going there with that silly flower?"

"No, sir."

"Then what is it doing in your rifle barrel?"

"It was a gift, sir."

The officer held out his hand. "And what are you going to do with it?"

The young guardsman sighed, and his eyes flicked so quickly toward Allison I wondered if I'd imagined it. He reached for the flower and winced as he slid it out, like a splinter from flesh, like it physically hurt him to do so.

"That's better!" The officer snatched the lilac. "Now straighten up. Start acting like a soldier. Forget all this peace stuff!"

He threw the flower at their feet, and Allison lunged forward, glaring at him.

She lifted the lilac, gently, as if that very flower was in fact youthful innocence made tangible, rather than just a symbol for it. "What's the matter with peace?" she asked the officer. "Flowers are better than bullets!"

The officer narrowed his eyes; he seemed to take in everything about her from her dark ponytail, to her T-shirt, to her blue sneakers. Finally, he turned, muttering something to the young guardsmen. As they both walked away across the commons, the young guardsman looked over his shoulder and winked one of those amazing blue eyes at Allison.

"Yeah, that's right!" someone shouted after them. "Get the fuck out of our school!"

Allison raised her hand, two fingers held up in a salute of peace, and then she shook her head. "How nice the *individual* National Guardsmen are."

"Yeah," said Leaf, "but never underestimate the power of stupid people in large numbers!"

I saw them all on the other side of the Commons. All of them. The sheer number of them. Easily over a thousand. Maybe two. Campus police, state police, the army, jeeps, tanks, and media with cameras flashing. And right out front, staring us down, the Ohio National Guard. Lined up, shoulder to shoulder. Dressed in full combat gear, gas masks, M1 rifles, bayonets, grenade launchers. They stopped my heart. Stopped my breath. They were aliens, in total alien dress, with piggish alien faces, ready to take over the world. Plastic goggles stared right at me. Plastic nostrils flared green. And those ugly rifles with their glinting bayonets. Not plastic. Not plastic in the slightest. Behind them, the blackened ruins of the ROTC building stuck up like the bones of a charred skeleton. As a frightened coed hugged her textbooks to her chest and hurried by them to get to her next class, I drew in a breath. Because this was, after all, just a school. A *school*! It was not a war zone, no matter how much it resembled one.

A jeep rolled by, and from it boomed a bull-horned voice that rang with the high-pitched squeal of feedback. "Disperse! Disperse! Leave, for your own safety!"

"*You* leave!" someone shouted at the jeep.

"This is *our* school!"

"If anyone should disperse, it's all you assholes!"

"Pigs off campus! Pigs off campus!"

"For your own safety," the amplified voice continued, metallic and cold, "all bystanders and innocent people, please clear the area!"

"Pigs off campus!"

A rock flew through the air, punctuating our cries with a clatter as it bounced off the jeep's tire, and pure anger rose up from my stomach to fill me completely.

How dare they! This was a public campus, and this was America, a free country, and we had a constitutional right to free assembly! A right to state our beliefs! A right to dissent in this free country of ours!

And it all became clear. We'd become too powerful for them! And they were scared of us.

They were *scared*.

Because flowers were better than bullets.

Because peace was better than war.

Because freedom was better than force.

And we forced them to listen to us now.

My body tingled. I could feel *change* settling on my skin like a silk veil dropping from the heavens. This was the moment the world would change. And I was right in the middle of it.

"They will *have* to start listening now," I said. "They can't ignore us anymore. I mean; they *must* be worried if they've sent in the National Guard!"

It was all starting to unravel – the war, the draft, the Establishment – and I gripped tightly to one of those woven silken threads and yanked until my arms ached.

I'm ready, I thought, I am ready to shout, to be heard, to make a difference. I am ready to change the God damned world. Hell, yes!

Japhy leaned down and shouted in my ear. "How many of us do you think are here?"

"Dunno." I looked around.

"Two thousand, I'd say," said Lauren.

My breath came in gasps, filling my lungs and stomach with fluttery nerves.

All these people whose hearts all beat, right now, with the same peaceful purpose.

And I was one of them.

I heard a shutter click and turned to see a man in a tan coat that was too big for his wiry frame. He held a camera up to his face while a gas mask swung from his belt.

"Get out of it, Norman," said Allison. She shooed at him as if he were a fly. "Go brown-nose somewhere else, will you?"

"Who is he?" I asked, as the photographer sloped away.

"Terry Norman," said Allison. "He's a junior, but I swear he's an undercover FBI agent or something!"

"He's such a narc," said Barry. "Always taking pictures of us for the campus cops."

The bell clanged and there was a roar as I saw that line of military men move toward us.

"They're coming!" said Japhy. "Move back!"

As the Guard glided toward us, one entity, we backed away, one entity. Like magnets, repelling each other, keeping a safe buffer of about a hundred feet. They herded us like the sheep they wanted us to be, funneling us all away from the Commons, in between two buildings, up the hill, up, up, up.

I was swept backwards, away from the Guard, on a wall of sound and moving shoes and fists punching sky. At the front of the crowd, Allison swore at the troops and flipped the bird and shone like the sun.

"Yeah!" I screamed, letting go of Japhy's hand to raise my fist in the air, and then I took a breath, and then I could no longer breathe, and then I could no longer see as white clouds of tear gas clapped their ethereal hands over our noses and mouths and eyes.

We coughed and cried and ran up the hill between the buildings to a pagoda made of wood and concrete, where the air was clean and crisp and crackling with our energy.

To the marching of our feet, I could hear the James Lee Stanley song *Political Party* loud and clear inside my mind. The volume knob turned clockwise by the tangible fingers of energy rising from the crowd, and I stomped in time with the beat and sang the words under my breath.

"*It's a couple of well-placed phone calls. It's a notably empty chair. Secret agenda. Unwritten rules. You don't even have to play fair, 'cos we're having a party! A political party!*"

The Guard sliced forward between the two buildings and split us right down the middle. As we ran past the pagoda and down the hill, I held tight to Lauren's hand, because in the blindness of the gas clouds I'd lost everyone else but her.

The students chanted "One, two, three, four, we don't want your fucking war!" and "Peace now! Pigs off campus!", while the raw vocals of James Lee Stanley chanted, "*Fat cats!*

Bureaucrats! Fat cats! Bureaucrats!" in my head as we watched the Guard circle around and stop on a football field.

The two split groups of kids joined together again, because we were strong, and nothing was going to come between us or our message. Nope, not today! Because we were the strong ones here! And the Guard were now trapped on that field, with us on one side, and a chain-link fence on the other.

"*Laughing people carry on in undertone of panic. Those who have the most to lose are grossly diplomatic.*"

I scanned the faces around me, but could not see Japhy and Leaf, or Allison and Barry. Just the strength of our message.

Yeah, I thought.

Hell, fucking yeah!

I flipped off the guardsmen, and everybody flipped them off, and they flipped us off right back.

"*Recruiting happens instantly with a handshake or a kiss. A fingerprint or a photo is gonna get you on the list, 'cos we're having a party!*"

"Pigs off campus!" I shouted. "Pigs off campus! Fat cats! Bureaucrats!"

Students threw stones, but they all hit the grass and didn't come close to reaching any of the Guard.

"*We're having a party ...*"

With a whistle, a smoking canister flew toward me, and I heard someone cry out: "Tear gas!"

Lauren clutched at my arm and stared around with eyes so wide I worried they would pop from her skull and fall to the grass and get stomped on by the fleeing demonstrators, and more white clouds rose like ghosts, and my eyes watered, and my throat melted. Coughing, I lifted my shirt over my mouth to breathe through the material but it didn't help.

Blinded again, I grabbed for Lauren's hand and we ran.

"Can you see where Leaf went?" she shouted.

I squinted around with bleary and burning eyes, but couldn't see him anywhere. And Japhy? Where the hell was Japhy?

"It's okay." I gripped tight to Lauren's hand. "We'll meet up with them afterwards."

A student beside us grabbed one of the tear gas canisters and threw it back at the Guard and we all cheered. When it flew at us again, the same student, laughing now, sent it hurling away, and then waited, grinning, for the match to continue.

"Yes!" I screamed. "Pigs off campus!"

"Just you, me, and them. The hostess knows who I am. Be sure and mind your manners so they ask us back again."

We threw more rocks, and they threw rocks back at us.

"Don't come empty handed if you want to make some friends, 'cos we're having a party!"

My heart was beating now in a military drum roll. This was so real, so powerful, so terrifying, so exciting!

We were showing them! We wouldn't just sit around anymore and let the Government bully us, or order us to join their army, or fight their war, or die for them. We had rights! Free speech, man. Freedom of assembly. Freedom to dissent.

Just freedom!

Take our message back to Nixon: Hell, no, we won't go!

Up ahead, students ran closer to the guards to shout at them; I wondered if Leaf and Allison and Barry were up there somewhere, screaming "Fuck you!" in their faces.

On the football field, the Guard converged into a huddle, and then several of them turned, kneeled, and aimed their rifles at us; I wondered if Leaf and Allison and Barry were up there somewhere, screaming "Fuck you!" in their faces.

Ha!

Because, were those guns supposed to scare us? Because, it's not like they were loaded. Because, surely it's illegal to carry live ammo on a campus. Because, we were unarmed and posing no threat, just a few rocks, and spiky words. Sticks and stones, man, sticks and stones.

The kneeling troops stood, turned, and marched back up the hill toward the pagoda, that structure that symbolized peace and freedom and prayer.

They were retreating! We had won! Pigs off campus!

The Victory Bell still clanged away, victorious and clear.

Because we had won. And it was over. And soon it would *all* be over. All of it! The draft, the war, the pointless deaths.

The revolution was now, and I was here, right in the smack-bang center!

"*All for one, one for all; best intentions got. Until someone's rainbow crashing down sweetens up the pot ...*"

When a rock hit me in the shoulder, I staggered backwards and grabbed my stinging arm, ducking as a second rock flew toward me. I pulled Lauren out of its way and looked to where it came from. With his hand raising again, and his too-large brown coat, that Norman kid, the narc, the FBI lover, grunted as he let fly a piece of broken concrete. He checked his watch, and then again his arm bent, released, threw another rock. At *us*. At the *students*.

"What the hell ...?" Lauren muttered.

A flash of metal blinded me for a second, shiny and silver, and I thought it must have reflected from the camera he wore around his neck. But then a flood of words washed all understanding from my brain.

"He's got a pistol!"

"Get that motherfucker!"

The music in my mind clicked off. It didn't make sense. Why would *he* have a gun? He was one of us? Wasn't he? There must be a mistake. A misunderstanding. My eyes were sore from the tear gas; I must have seen something else in his fist.

But then I saw his fingers curling around the barrel of a gleaming pistol, saw him lift it straight up and fire into the sky.

Crack!

I'd never heard a gunshot before, but when I did, there was no mistaking it. The single shot – sharp and pointed and clean – cut the air right down the middle.

"Kill the pig!" someone shouted.

"Stick the pig!"

Two male students flew at Norman and fists cracked against his face. One of them grabbed his arm and the other tried to wrench the camera off his neck, but Norman twisted away from them, and smashed the butt of the gun into one of their faces. More bodies surged forward like a tide and dragged Norman under so I could see nothing of him beneath the angry frothing of fists.

"Back off!" Norman screamed in a high-pitched voice, and just as quickly as the angry students had descended on him, they flowed away again, revealing Norman crouched low like a cornered, frightened animal. "Back off or you're going to get it!" The gun flashed silver in the sunshine again.

Crack! Crack! Crack!

Two fountains of dirt sprayed into the air like geysers as he fired into the ground at his feet. The students fell backwards, their arms covering their heads.

I fell back.

And Lauren fell, too.

Then Norman ran.

And all was calm again.

"Jesus," I muttered, shocked at what I'd just witnessed.

My heart pounded, and my hands shook, and I felt laughter bubble up inside me at the ridiculousness of what had just happened, at how close I'd been to a gun – a real, live gun with real, live bullets – and how close, therefore, I'd been to getting shot.

Actually *shot*!

I could have *died*!

Maybe a minute went by as I froze in that terrifying realization. I continued to stare in the direction Norman had gone just to make sure that he wasn't skulking back to us with his pistol pointed right at me.

Finally, I looked back up the hill to where the National Guard officers – who I'd actually forgotten about for that long minute! – had been retreating.

Had been.

Because, as I turned to look at them, a voice called out, "Guard!" and they turned, too.

One moment they were marching away, and it was all over. This political party was over. The next moment, they all spun, like choreographed dancers: twenty-eight members of the Ohio National Guard twirling around and floating down onto one knee in a graceful and flawless pirouette.

Time stopped.

Although that bell kept right on ringing.

"All right, prepare to fire ..."
Rifles lifted.
Someone near me screamed, "Get down!"
But I couldn't get down. I couldn't move. Panic thickened the air around me and I knew if I breathed it in, I would surely drown.
"Guard ..."
Then one syllable cracked through the suddenly still air.
Just one syllable.
A broken word cut in half by its very own meaning.
"Fi–"
And all the while, that bell. That bell. That beautiful bell.

chapter ten

japhy

The loud crack of that first gunshot cuts through my mind, and I drop, flat down on my face on the grass.
    Crack!
    American troops won't open fire on American students, I think. Not with real bullets.
    Crack! Crack! Crack-crack-crack-crack!
    I lift my head.
    Bodies zigzag.
    Run for cover.
    Hunch forward with their hands over their heads.
    Fall.
    Crack! Crack! Crack!
    Where is Ray?
    I taste dirt as a something thunks into the ground beside me.
    Where is Ray?
    I drive my face back down, covering it with my arms.
    Where is Ray?
    Even though they are just rubber pellets, they will hurt like a son-of-a-bitch if they hit me. I need to move. Now.
    And where the fuck is Ray!
    I count three and I am up and running to a small oak and

sitting with my back against it breathing hard as bullets bounce off the flesh of the tree – bullets that would have bounced off *my* flesh – and clumps of grass and dirt and bits of tree explode up into the air.

Crack! Crack! Crack!

Are they seriously aiming at me? I wonder. Why? What did I do to them? Jesus Christ, we waved a few flags, threw a few rocks, that's all!

I smell grass and gunpowder and copper.

I hear screams.

I hear: "I'm hit!"

I hear: "I've been shot!"

"Stay down, Tom!" someone yells. "Stay down, it's only buckshot!"

And then: "They're *not* blank! *They're not blank!*"

Not blank? I think. But that would mean ... no, surely not.

Crack-crack-crack!

And somewhere, a bell clangs on and on and on, and the shots keep on firing forever.

Until there is peace. Until silence encases us all in a soundproof shell of frozen disbelief. Until it shatters into glittering shards of reality. Screams ricochet throughout the University grounds. And on the heels of this rushes the shocking and horrible truth.

"Ray?" Pushing myself away from the tree, I run. "Ray!" Toward the parking lot. "Ray?" I jump over students on the ground, writhing, sobbing, bleeding. I ache to stop, to kneel, to tell them help is coming and they will be fine. But I make my feet move on. Hating myself for leaving them.

As I cross a service road, my feet stagger, and my stomach rolls, and I see death for the first time in my life. The man lays on his stomach, his feet neatly askew, his head facing right, a river of blood surging from his open mouth in a gruesome tribute to all the future words he will never speak. A young girl drops to her knees beside him and screams. She looks right at me and pleads for help, but what can I do?

This can't be real. This is a nightmare. This is *my*

nightmare. This is a war zone. This is everything I've been running from.

"Help!" the girl screams, and her eyes fix on something right behind me.

I turn and see National Guard troops running for us.

I see their uniforms and helmets and concerned eyes.

I see their rifles.

And then I see nothing but rage.

"Murderers!" I scream. And I am not the only one.

Students rush forward, forming a wall of protection around the man on the ground, and cry, "Haven't you done enough?"

The troops hesitate, unable to push through this wall of violent words. They turn. They disappear. They retreat from the bodies of the injured students, leaving them to bleed on the grass.

At the edge of the parking lot, Allison slumps in Barry's arms. Her pale face is a white moon against the backdrop of dark hair. I don't plan on stopping because, after all, she has Barry, and she is fine anyway, and we will *all* be fine anyway, and this is just some sick joke or a nightmare or a bad trip. Just some elaborately staged lesson from the Government to put all of us squawking doves back into our cages. But when I hear Allison's whispered words, they scream through me and my legs just stop moving.

"I'm hit," she gasps.

"What do you mean?" Barry frowns at her, but Allison's eyes close and she doesn't answer him. "Alli?" He traces a thumb gently across her cheek. It is a gesture he must have done a hundred times, a million. A gesture that conveys tenderness, and fragility, and all-out awe that this stunning and vibrant woman chose to be with *him* over every other man in the world. And it is a gesture that never before left a red streak of blood in its wake.

Barry freezes, staring at the bright smear that slashes Allison's skin like war paint. Staring at his blood-covered fingers, he realizes at the same moment I do that the blood has come from Allison's side, from the place where he caught her as she fell.

A green station wagon with a red cross on its side shudders across the lot, swerving around students, and I run for it, slapping my hand on the window until the glass slides down, although the driver does not stop.

"There's a girl over here!" I shout, jogging along beside the car. "She's hit!"

The driver shakes his head. "Sorry, kid. I got orders. We're to treat the National Guard only."

"But … she is *dying!*"

"I got orders!" he says again, as if that is an acceptable reason. "We can't treat no one until the officers are looked at."

I stammer at him and then scream my words, because at least raising my voice makes me feel good: "What sort of injuries can any of them have that are more important than kids who have holes blown through their bodies?"

"I'm sorry." He blinks at me with heavy lids, and then accelerates. As he pulls away, I wonder how long he will survive with guilt so heavy pressing down on him. How long until it crushes him to death?

Looking back at Allison, I send her a prayer, but can do no more, because where the fuck is Ray?

Circles of arms form around the fallen. Healing circles. Protection circles. Students hold hands and cry and daze around and shake as they surround the ones who lie on the grass, the ones who won't get treatment, the ones who are bleeding out while we watch.

The ones who only wanted peace.

Fucking peace!

What is so wrong with peace? I recall the words Allison said to that officer not half an hour ago. Flowers are better than bullets, she'd said. And I recall the look on that commanding officer's face, the way he'd studied her as if committing her features to memory. And I recall what may have been her last words ever spoken, I'm hit, and her look of shock before it drained away, along with all her color and her consciousness, and I wonder if that is exactly what that fucking officer had wanted. To shut her up. To shut us all up.

And then, with a gasp, I see her.

Ray is crouching. Huddled over. And covered in blood.

No.

I run faster.

Oh, please, no, not Ray. Please, anyone but her! Anyone.

Skidding to my knees, I grab her by the shoulder and turn her around. She stares at me. Her eyes so full of horror and tears. "Japhy?" she breathes. "Help."

"Where are you hurt, baby?" I say, looking down at her bloody shirt.

"Help *her!*" she gasps.

"*Her?*" And then I blink and the world is once again populated with other people besides Ray.

Lauren looks so tiny lying there in the grass. Like a child's doll. Like a dying bird. She sobs, clutching the swell of her stomach. Her fingers slip and slide in the red liquid that coats her skin.

"Help her!" Ray says again, and I realize she is not the one injured.

Oh, thank God, I think. Thank God.

"I'm okay," Lauren says and she smiles. She *smiles!* "I'm not hit. If I was hit I would be able to feel it, right? Well, I can't. I can't feel it. So I'm okay. I'm okay."

And then suddenly, Leaf. Leaf is all around her like a tornado.

"Oh, shit! Oh, Lauren, oh, shit!" He falls to the ground and takes her hand.

"We have to get her an ambulance, now," Ray says. "Right now."

"Can't," I shake my head. "They won't treat us until they've treated *them.*"

"Well, go and call another one!"

"Right!" I stand and run toward the closest building, and as I enter the doors, I see a small crowd of students already gathered by a phone. They stare at the receiver. Hang up. Lift it. Listen again. As if their shock has wiped away all knowledge of how to use a fucking telephone.

"We need ambulances!" I shout. "Someone call for ambulances."

But one of them turns to me. Her face is white and her eyes are watery. "The phones are dead."

Her words don't make sense. No, I think, the kids are dead, not the phones. The kids.

Back outside again, I run to where Lauren waits for medical treatment that will not be coming.

"The phones are down," I gasp to Leaf.

"Then *we'll* drive her to the God damn hospital and I'll treat her myself if I have to!" he says.

"No!" Lauren clutches at Leaf's shirt, and she speaks in a whisper. "No, I can't! We can't go there!"

"Got no choice, honey."

I reach out and grab Leaf's arm. "Don't move her!"

"But she's bleeding!" he sobs.

"Do you know where the hospital is?" I ask. "Because I have no idea where to take her."

Ray's eyes flick from Leaf's to mine, then she is up and grabbing hold of passing shirt sleeves. "How do we get to the hospital?" she shouts. "Where is the hospital?" But even though some students pause, and some even look like they understand what she is saying, no one gives us an answer.

And so we wait.

And we watch Lauren grow paler with every passing minute.

And we sink into the ground that grows muddy with her blood.

And we hold our breaths every time she exhales, praying that her chest will rise again in a second or two.

And then we hear it. Finally. A siren's song in the distance.

Leaf lifts Lauren off the ground, scooping her up like she weighs no more than a feather pillow.

With every jolt of Leaf's running feet, she screams.

The sound rips my soul.

And then she doesn't scream anymore, and Leaf runs

faster, and the tattered shreds of my soul rip even more in her sudden silence.

Students with ashen faces are scattered around the asphalt. Some crying, some screaming, some staring up at the sky with blank, watery eyes, saying nothing at all. One girl weeps over the body of a woman; blood pools from a neck wound and stains the scattered pile of textbooks beside her.

I wrap an arm around Ray and hug her to me as we run. She leans in and starts to sob. Hard, wracking sobs that jolt my bones. I stop, lift her in my arms and just keep on running toward the sound of the ambulance.

Anger nips at my exposed skin and I tingle with the need for an explanation. Why are *two* of my innocent friends – and who knows how many others – currently bleeding from fucking bullet wounds? This is America, and *they* are Americans! This is not the war. We are not in the Vietnamese jungles. We are in a school. A *school*! These are just kids!

What the fuck?

The shouts around me escalate. The students have become sharks. Blood has been spilled in their ocean, and that red sweetness now blooms within them. They want *more* blood. They want National Guard blood. And they are hungry.

But above the din of gnashing teeth is a single, pleading voice that falls over the students like a warm blanket. "I don't care whether you've never listened to anyone before in your lives!" it shouts, "I am begging you right now, if you don't disperse, they're going to move in and it can only be a *slaughter*! Would you *please* listen to me? Jesus Christ, I don't want to be a part of this …"

The ambulances shriek over the hill, past that fucking pagoda, and into the parking lot. Their doors fly open and a gurney streaks toward us. Leaf flops Lauren onto it. The white flash of skin on the inside of her forearm gleams as her arm slides off the stretcher. It hangs, loose as a broken wing, as she is pushed inside the van.

Leaf climbs in beside her and clasps onto her hand like it is the only thing keeping him tethered to this world. He looks out at me. He doesn't speak. But then, he doesn't have to.

I give him a small nod, and then I am moved aside as a second gurney is loaded into the ambulance, and I barely even recognize the face of the woman on it; this beautiful soul – who could have been Gandhi, or Martin Luther King, or Jesus Christ – was now not even *Allison* anymore.

"She'll be just fine," an orderly says to Barry, who climbs in and mirrors Leaf by grabbing for Allison's hand.

As the doors slam shut and both Lauren and Allison are blocked from my sight, I can't shake a dreaded feeling that both of those luminescent young lives have been dimmed too much. That there is only enough light left within to make up *one* living soul. That perhaps, one will draw from the other. One will give, so the other can live. And I thank God that I'm not the one who must decide which one that will be.

"Come on," Ray says. Grabbing my hand, she pulls me away. "We have to follow them."

The last image I have as I reach the van, is a group of shocked and traumatized students, writhing together on the commons where it all started. And above, on the upper slopes, completely surrounding this tear-stained gathering, is a line of National Guard captured in perfect silhouette. Standing shoulder to shoulder. Guns raised. Bayonets pointed at the sky.

And, Jesus Christ, I don't want to be a part of this.

I slide behind the wheel, start the engine, and finally allow my knees to buckle under the weight of whatever the fuck just happened.

"Go!" she yells.

We speed out of the lot, on the tail of that ambulance, squealing into the Emergency Only section of the Robinson Memorial Hospital, eight hour-long minutes later.

The hospital is an ants' nest that's been poked with a stick.

By the time we find a park, the ambulance we followed is empty.

I head for the glass doors of the hospital, but Ray grabs my arm, halting me.

"Maybe we should just hang here for a bit," she says. "The cops will be all over the place soon."

So I nod, and get back in the van, and stare out the window.

Over to my right, a man hugs a bleeding wrist against his chest. I recognize him as the guy who'd waved a black flag during the protest. He'd been right there, right out at the front. Right in their faces.

This guy has balls, I'd thought, as I'd watched him scream into the barrels of all those cocked rifles. This guy has real balls. And I'd wished for a moment that I could be like him. So I had walked forward through the students. And then I had dropped to the dirt.

I watch him again now, with his face no longer angry-red but white, as he stops and stares through the open doors of an ambulance. He takes a small step forward and says in a soft voice, "Jeff? Jeff, man, you okay?"

Inside the ambulance, I see man on a stretcher. His face is covered in blood, and I wonder why the doctors have just left him in there when he obviously needs help.

But then the man with the bleeding wrist turns and hangs his head and drips past me through the glass doors of the hospital.

"Is this my fault?" Ray whispers.

"What?" I gape at her. "Why would this be *your* fault?"

She bites her lip and blinks as tears spill down her cheeks. "It was my idea to come. She didn't want to. I made her join in. She would have been *safe* if it weren't for me wanting to be a part of a stupid peace rally!"

I squeeze her shoulder. "If this is anyone's fault," I say, "it's mine."

"How?"

I take a breath and look out the window; I can't meet her eyes, can't let her see the monster inside me. "When I saw you on the ground, covered in blood, I wished for it to be *anyone but you*. I was glad, Ray. I was fucking *glad* when that wish came true."

"No," she says. "Stop it!"

How? I think. How do I stop this guilt? I *don't* stop it, that's how. This guilt is my punishment, and I will take it gladly if it means that Lauren and her baby, and Allison, and all the others, will get through this.

"I can't just sit out here any longer," I say, removing the keys and opening the van door. "I need to know if she is alive."

Ray grabs for my arm. "But the police are questioning people in there!"

"Fuck the cops." I pull away. "I want to make sure my friends are okay."

Her lips press into a line, but then she nods, and follows me because, really, what other choice does she have?

When I storm through the doors of the hospital, I hold my head high and march right by the thousands of military uniforms that turn to look at me. The very same uniforms that I am trying to escape.

Do they know who I am? Do they know *what* I am? Do they know that some of them are, probably right this second, searching for me: Andrew Michael Mack, draft dodger, felon?

Ray squeezes my hand and I squeeze hers right back.

We walk by a man and woman who are being told by one of these uniformed men that their child has been injured in the crossfire.

Crossfire? What fucking crossfire?

Leaning against a wall, two more people shake their heads and say things like, "... brought this on themselves, then!" and "... should have killed more of them!"

Ray stops in the corridor and stares at them, but I pull her on.

"Don't," I whisper. "Just don't."

The lady at reception directs us to a waiting room with bursting seams, where all the Kent State kids and confused family members are gathering. Through the packed tight and fidgeting bodies, we see Leaf staring through the large window. Slumped in a seat, Barry raises a hand to his cheek to wipe at tears that flood from him.

We hurry over.

"Lauren's in the Operating Room," Leaf says. "I kept asking them if she is gonna make it and they wouldn't answer me. They wouldn't answer me! It's been ages. She'd better not die."

Barry flinches at these words.

Ray hugs Leaf and shushes like a mother in his ear.

All three of them start to shake as she chants: "She's gonna be fine, she's gonna be fine, she's gonna be fine."

Time is a funny thing when warped by grief. I can't tell you how long we sit there in that room. Maybe only minutes pass. Or maybe we are in there for days. Everything is blurred at the edges, foggy, slippery. It slides from my grasp the same way dreams slip farther away the harder you try to hold onto them, and you are left wondering what is real.

Like Barry, for instance.

Because I saw his mouth open and lips move but the words were too fantastical.

Did he really just tell me that Allison died on the way to the hospital?

And did American soldiers really just open fire on American students for absolutely no fucking reason at all?

Beside me, Ray rocks back and forth, shaking her head and whispering Allison's name, as if hearing it aloud will make her believe what Barry has told us. Allison. Allison. Allison.

And if that is really true, if Allison's light really did go out inside the walls of that ambulance, does it mean then that Lauren's light grew brighter?

I watch Leaf – his face empty – watching a man in green scrubs cross the room toward us.

"Donald Black?" asks the doctor.

"Yes! Here." Leaf stands.

"Your wife will be fine."

Leaf gushes out a breath and he laughs. "Oh God, thank you, God."

"The bullet merely grazed her, skimmed over her stomach. She was lucky. Very lucky. Unfortunately, the wound sent her body into shock. We did all we could, but I'm sorry, sir, the baby did not survive." He places a hand on Leaf's shoulder. "I'm so sorry."

"No!" Leaf groans as his legs crumple and he falls onto the seat behind him.

"Can we see her?" Ray asks.

The doctor nods. "One at a time."

Leaf wobbles upright, turns to us, and places a hand on my shoulder. "You still got the keys, man?"

I nod, fishing in my pocket.

"Take the van," he says. "Get to the border. We'll meet up with you at Mandala when we can." He shoves the piece of the paper with the commune's address into Ray's hand. "Mandala," he says, again.

"But we can't go now?" Ray blinks at him. "What about Lauren? We can't just leave you here!"

"I'll go back to Utopia. I'll be fine. But he," Leaf nods at me, "needs to get out of here."

"Are you sure?" I stare right into his eyes; I know he is running from The Man too, and is he sure, is he really sure?

Leaf inclines his head. "Just go."

"But ..." Ray is shaking her head at him and as she starts to speak, a uniform strides past; she shrinks backwards. Then she throws her arms around Leaf's neck and kisses him. "Thank you."

"We'll see you both soon," I say.

Leaf nods stiffly at my words, and I wish I'd just said: "We'll see you soon," instead of, "We'll see you *both* soon." For that was all he and Lauren were now: the *both* of them, the *two* of them, rather than the *three* they had been when this day had begun, a *family* that would now never be.

Then I look down at Barry and I have no idea what to say to him. But he meets my eyes and just shrugs one shoulder; after all, there is nothing to say. No words exist. And really, none are needed anyway. Because when your world has completely fallen away, and everything you believed in is proven to be false, all you have left is shared truths, shared experiences, and the knowledge that these building blocks will somehow, someday, rebuild the whole universe. That with truth will come peace. That with truth will come justice. And with truth will come the promise that tragedy and betrayal – such as we witnessed on this day – will never occur again.

Surely, never again.

chapter eleven

ray

The hospital grew smaller and smaller in my side mirror, as Japhy and I sped away from Leaf and Lauren. Poor, sweet Lauren, who was lying on a hospital bed with a hole in her stomach where her baby should be. The baby I'd vowed to protect.

My mouth started to water. "Stop the van."

"What?" Japhy glanced at me. "I can't stop *now*! You crazy?"

"I'm going to be sick."

The van veered onto the side of the road and I jumped out, hunching over on the shoulder of the highway. When I vomited, I expected blood from my razor-sharp claws of shame, but there was none. Japhy held the hair off my face, and when my wave of nausea ebbed, he pulled me into his arms. I cried on his shoulder for precious minutes, but he didn't hurry me. He just stood, holding me until I was okay.

"You can't blame yourself for this," he said.

How does he know me so well?

He kissed my hair. "What happened, happened. It would've happened whether you said anything to her or not. We can't change it. It wasn't your fault."

I nodded and climbed into the back of the van to wash my face in the little sink, and rinse the acrid taste of bile out of my mouth. We changed out of our stained clothes and washed the blood off our skin, and then we returned to the front seats and kept driving, both staring out the windshield, lost in the horrific maze of our own memories.

As we flew across the earth, he looked over at me, waited until I met his gaze, and then he smiled.

And just like that, for a fleeting second, everything was fine again.

How does he do that? I wondered. How does he just eclipse out all the shit in my world with a simple pull of his mouth and flash of his teeth?

Closing my eyes, I tried to sleep, but every time I did, I heard gunshots, and I saw again as Lauren staggered and fell to one knee, and stared up at me with her eyes so wide and pleading, and I just stared back, helpless, as her white dress blossomed in the center with a great black rose, its bloody petals unfurling wide. Too wide.

The color of the blood. And the color of her eyes. And the color of my fear.

All three so, so black.

Black as night. Black as eternity. Black as death.

And finally, as black as sleep ...

Two states and four hours later, Japhy's hand on my leg jolted me awake.

"Look." He pointed out the window and I squinted my sleepy eyes.

"Oh shit," I whispered as a green road sign raced toward us. "Oh shit."

The bright white lettering leered at me and screamed right into my face: INTERNATIONAL BOUNDARY 2 MILES.

Japhy wasn't smiling at me anymore.

"Oh shit." I took his hand and locked my fingers around his bones.

Here we fucking go.

chapter twelve

japhy

I pull the car over, breathing deeply and gripping the wheel like it's the only thing linking me with the real world.

"Oh shit," Ray says again. "Oh shit."

She stares through the window at the pinking sky, her eyes wide, her cheeks a little sunken, her mouth a flat line. She grips my hand, pressing her fingertips into my skin, holding on so tight as if she expects something to swoop down and snatch me from her.

Prizing her fingers away, I lean across, open the glove compartment, and take out a crumpled packet of cigarettes. I offer her one but she shakes her head.

"Well." I light the smoke and inhale its heat into my lungs. "This is it."

"Yep." Ray says. "Shit." And she takes my hand again.

We sit there, watching the sun go down over the United States of America for the very last time. By the time the sun rises tomorrow, I think, I will either be in Canada or in jail. A prison either way. And either way, I will never see the sun like this again.

When the red glow of my Marlboro burns down to the filter, I flick the butt out the open window. Caught by a breath of wind, it blows onto the road in front of us, somersaulting in a pinwheel of red-orange sparks, before coming to a stop, its ember quenched by liquid night that drops down suddenly, as thick and heavy as a blanket falling over our heads.

"Ready?" I spit on my hand and run my fingers through my hair, combing it back off my face. Then I tuck my shirt into my jeans. "Show time."

"Wait." Ray swivels in her seat and leans forward. She takes a deep breath and stares at me, her face all serious lines and deep creases. Minutes pass, and she doesn't speak, and I don't speak either. I study her just as closely as she does me. Finally, she nods and I start the engine again and we are off and moving toward our fate.

Trees crowd and jostle on the bend in the road ahead. Their green heads sway, their wooden necks crane for the best view, as they watch us approach. And then suddenly, as one, they all step back and there it is: the border, lit up bright as day. And once we pass them, the trees lean out behind us again in their perverse curiosity, waiting to see whether or not we will make it over the line.

Three gray booths are spaced out across the road. A man in a dark uniform directs the queue of cars with a flitting white beam that slices the night. I pull up in the left lane, behind a black Studebaker, and we wait with heavy breaths and dizzy heads.

"Maybe we should find a back way through?" Ray whispers, her words coming out so quickly they crash into each other. "I didn't think it would be this ... this ..." She sighs and shakes her head. "I can't do this!"

But, in front of us, the red brake lights of the Studebaker wink out as it drives forward into Canada, and the dancing flashlight beam waves at us.

"Shit, shit, shit, Japhy, shit!"

"If we turn around now," I tell her, "it will look too suspicious. We have to keep going."

Ray's hand is in mine again as we pull alongside the booth and I wind my window down all the way.

"You're an American Citizen." The man inside the booth

speaks in a monotonous drawl, like he is stating the fact that we are Americans rather than asking us.

"Yes, sir," I say, and Ray echoes me.

"Where were you born."

"Liberation, Alabama," we both answer.

"What is your reason for entering Canada."

Ray leans over me. "We're just passing through. Going to visit my sister in Alaska. She's getting married."

"May I have a look in the back of the vehicle." The man leaves his booth and comes to the van before we can answer.

"Of course." I jump out and slide open the back door.

The man looks in – left, right, left – and nods. "IDs, please."

We hand over our driver's licenses. Part of me hopes he will look at my name and then look up at my face and say: Andrew Michael Mack? You can't come in here! Go back home where you belong! Go and face your fate like a real man!

But he glances at our ID so quickly I don't know why he bothered.

"Fine. Go on through. Have yourselves a nice night."

Ray stares at him through the open door. "You mean, that's it? We can go? Just like that?"

But the man has already stepped back into his booth and is no longer interested in us. He raises his hand to Flashlight Man, who waves to a new pair of headlights that come slinking in behind us.

I stand at the open car door, gaping like a fish in the cold froth of the headlights.

"Come on!" Ray hisses at me. "Get in the damn car!"

I can't feel my fingers as I climb back behind the wheel, and close the door, and accelerate forward, and drive onto Canadian soil for the first time.

The tires hum over the road, whispering *freedom, freedom, freedom*, and with every syllable I feel my fear fall away, bouncing and squirming on the tarmac behind me.

And then Ray whispers, "Oh shit!"

"Can you believe that?" I grin at her. "Can you fucking *believe* that?" I punch the steering wheel and holler out, "Woo hoo!"

"We did it!" Ray wraps her arms around me, and I veer onto the side of the road, laughing. "Sorry!" she says. "But shit, Japh, we actually did it. We're here. We're in Canada, and you're safe, and you're never going Over There. You are never going to Nam!"

"Never," I say, as I watch the border in the rearview mirror. I see that invisible line, over which I can never cross again. Over which lies my whole life and everyone I will never see again.

But I made it. We made it. We accomplished exactly what we had set out to do.

So, now what? I wonder. Now what?

*

The Mandala commune is a small farmhouse with wild roses creeping over one side, and an old rotting porch that slants all the way to the ground. A beautiful old tree in the front yard would be perfect to sit beneath and meditate on cool, perfect, starry nights beneath the cool, perfect, Canadian skies. In a giant garden beside the house, rows of tomato plants climb along the fence and everything smells of mint. Naked children run about, squealing and laughing, as they chase two little dogs in circles. A handful of adults watch from the porch, bathing in the yellow glow of a bulb and flapping away at moths and mosquitoes.

"So?" Parked in the front yard, beside the other cars, I squint at all this through the windscreen. "What do you think?" I ask.

And I can feel Ray's smile heating up the empty space between us. "I think it looks like home," she whispers.

"Let's go home, then."

As we approach the house, a man stands from a rocking chair on the porch and then jumps down the steps to greet us, landing on both feet. He wears dirty jeans and a faded purple shirt, unbuttoned, that reveals a tuft of gray hair on his exposed chest. His shoulder-length brown and gray hair is held off his forehead by a thin plaited headband the same color as his shirt. His eyes are bloodshot, his pupils huge, and between his eyebrows a dime-sized birthmark stains his white skin.

With his right thumb hooked around the longneck of a beer, and with his index and middle fingers of the same hand spread wide in hippie salute, he introduces himself.

"Hey there, I'm Guru. Can I help you?"

"Hi, Guru. I'm Japhy. This is my girlfriend, Ray. We were wondering if we could ..." I shift my feet on the gravel. "Could we stay? Here? With you?"

"You want to join?" he frowns, but then smiles.

"Yes," says Ray, and she straightens up. "Yes, please."

"Well, yeah!" Guru spreads his arms wide. "Yeah, man, it's cool. All are welcome here. Come! Meet the family." And he spins in the dirt and runs up the porch steps.

I follow him up the stairs, but Ray halts. She is staring, grinning at a sparrow hopping along the porch railing, leaving tiny sparrow footprints behind it.

"The sparrow hops along the veranda," she whispers, "with wet feet." And she tugs at my sleeve and points and repeats herself. "The sparrow hops along the veranda with wet feet!"

According to Japhy Ryder in *The Dharma Bums*, this is the greatest pop haiku of all time. And it is right here in front of us, welcoming us into our new life.

A dog barks, and our little sparrow – who should've been tucked up in his nest by now anyway – flies off in a blur of brown and gray, as quick as an omen, and I wonder if it had really been there at all.

"This is my wife, Marcia," Guru points to a short-haired, crinkle-eyed woman who smiles up at us from the porch with all the grace of a true Bodhisattva. "And this is Belle and Jones." Beside Marcia, a pretty girl with John Lennon eyes and a baby suction-cupped to her left breast, smiles and waves as her boyfriend stands to shake my hand and pull Ray into a fierce hug.

They are all huddled around a small wireless radio, and in between the quick, halting words of welcome, I hear the tinny, crisp voice of a radio announcer ("... *Kent State University* ...")

and I feel my insides flinch ("... *four students were killed and nine injured ...*"), feel my stomach twist itself into a knot.

Four dead. Four people died? Four people I had stood with only a few hours ago. People like Allison who were so full of life that it spilled from them.

Gone.

Those people, Lauren included, are already no longer people, but statistics.

"You hear about the shootings at Kent State today?" asks Guru, tipping his head toward the bodiless voice on the radio.

I nod. "Our friend was shot. We knew one of the girls killed, too. We were traveling here together – all four of us wanted to come to Mandala."

"You mean, you guys were actually *there*?" asks Belle. "That's so heavy. Will she be okay?"

I sit down and lean my back against the balcony railing. I feel the warmth of Ray as she sits beside me.

"She was pregnant," Ray whispers. "She lost the baby."

"Oh." Belle hugs the infant at her breast. "That's so ..." She shakes her head.

"Must have been horrible," Guru says. "Bad enough just hearing about it."

Marcia crawls over to Ray, who I suddenly realize is sobbing. The woman cups Ray's face and kisses her forehead. Then she stands up and holds out both her hands. "You two look hungry. Come and eat something; you'll feel better." One by one, she pulls Ray and then me to our feet, drags us into the kitchen, and pushes us toward a wooden table.

"Sit!"

Ray swipes at a tear as she drops into a chair.

Seated at the other end of the table is a young girl, about fifteen. She looks at me quickly from beneath a curtain of blond hair, and squeaks a whispered hello before hiding her face behind a dog-eared copy of Robert Heinlein's *Stranger in a Strange Land*.

"Good book?" I ask.

She raises the cover higher so I can't see her face.

"Don't bother talking to Jenny." A tall, skeletal man leans

against an arched doorway, through which couches and cushions are visible. He smiles with his skull-like face, his sunken eyes crinkling at the corners. "You won't get much conversation out of her."

"*Tais-toi!*" Jenny whispers.

"Oooh." The stick-man laughs and pulls out the chair beside Ray, turning it around to straddle. "They call me Needles, by the way. Nice to meet you."

"Ray," says Ray.

"Like the sun?" he asks, offering her a grin.

She nods but doesn't return his smile.

"Hey, man," I say, holding out my hand. "I'm Japhy."

"Cool, cool," says Needles, turning back to Ray.

I drop my hand to my side.

"What brings you here, Ray?"

She looks up at me, and I clear my throat. "She came with *me*. She's *my* girlfriend." I sit and wrap my arm around her shoulder.

"So, why are you here, then?" Needles asks.

"I was drafted."

"Oh." He rolls his eyes. "Another resister."

"Another?"

"We've had a few come and go."

Marcia appears beside me with two large slices of vegetable pie and orange juice. She sets the plates and cups on the table with a *clink-scrape*.

"Do you have a telephone?" Ray asks Marcia. "I'd like to call the hospital and check on our friend. I want to make sure she's okay."

Marcia points to the wall, where a pale green telephone is mounted beside the fridge.

"You don't mind ...?"

"Go right ahead, honey."

Nodding a thank you, Ray leaves the table. I hear her speaking quietly to the operator.

"So, will you two stay on?" asks Needles. "Or you just passing through?"

"We'd like to stay on," I direct my words to Marcia. "If you'll have us."

"We'll vote on it after a while." Sitting opposite me, Marcia laces her fingers together. "But you two seem like you'll fit in just fine." She nods her head toward my plate. "Eat!"

When Ray hangs up the phone, she ignores the empty chair between me and Needles and sits down on the other side of the table, beside Marcia. "They wouldn't let me speak to Lauren, but Leaf was there," she says, dragging her plate and juice across the table toward her. "He says her injuries were not too severe. Just a shallow flesh wound. But they are a bit worried about her mental state. They had to sedate her after she was told about … when she realized she lost …" Ray swallows. "They're keeping her in for observation for a week, he thinks. He sounds pretty upset about it, but says they'll catch a bus and be here as soon as they can."

I sigh, and stab the last piece of pie on my plate.

Marcia stacks up our empty dishes as quickly as my mother used to do. At home, I'd barely returned my fork to the plate before it would be swept out from under me, rinsed in the sink, dried, and put away neatly in the cupboard.

"Marcia?" I ask. "Do you mind if I make a call?"

She shakes her head, and I stand.

With the receiver clenched in my fist, I dial home and pray that my father won't get to the hallway first.

"Mack residence?" he says.

Damn it.

"Hi, Dad." I swallow a sudden lump in my throat. "It's me."

I hear the clatter of the phone being placed on the table and the muffled sound of his voice as he calls out my mother's name. "Nora? Your son is on the phone!"

Your son. I sigh.

"Andy?" My mother is breathless. "Honey, are you all right?"

And suddenly that lump in my throat is bigger and swelling by the second. "Mmm hmm."

"Did you make it?"

"Yes."

"Oh, sweetheart." She breathes.

I want to tell her that I was almost killed today, and that I stared into the black pupils of Death, and that I was so close I could have kissed him.

I want to tell her, even though we made it to Canada and I will now be safe from the draft and the army and the war, that I don't want to be here.

I want to tell her that I'm so scared.

But instead I just breathe. And I swallow and I breathe. "How are you?" I ask.

"I'm fine, honey. I'm just fine. I'm booked in for the mastectomy in three weeks. May twenty-fifth. But don't worry about me, you hear?"

I nod. And I breathe. And I swallow. "I'm sorry, Mom," I whisper. "I should be there. I'm sorry."

"Don't be silly! I'm fine," she says. Her voice softens. "I'll be fine whether you are here or not. Besides, I have your father."

I scoff at that.

"Come on, now." She sighs.

I imagine her sitting forward on the small wooden stool by the telephone table, winding the phone cord around and around her index finger.

"How much money do you have left? I don't want you taking advantage of anyone's hospitality."

"It's gone," I say, wincing.

"All of it?"

"Yeah. Long story."

"That was most of my savings!"

"I know. I'm sorry."

She sighs. "Well, if it's gone, it's gone. I'll wire you some more first thing tomorrow."

"No! Mom, really, we don't need ..."

"How are you going to eat? To live?"

"I don't know. I'll get a job. I'll earn my way."

"Of course you will, but until then, I'm sending you money, and you will just shut up and accept it!"

I smile. "Miss you, Mom."

"I know you do, honey. And I know that what you've done

isn't easy. But just remember that a *country* doesn't make you who you are; it's what you are willing to give up that truly matters."

I nod into the receiver.

"And, Andy?" she says.

"Yes?"

"I am so very *proud* of you."

I turn my face to the wall and press my forehead against the cool brick, so no one but this big, sturdy house knows that I am crying.

chapter thirteen

ray

"All fine at home," Japhy muttered. His teeth flashed, and his cheeks puffed with a smile, but his eyes hid from mine. No one else would notice his eyelashes had turned a single shade darker with tears.

"Ray?" Marcia said. "Do you need to call your parents to let them know you are safe?"

What would be the point of that? I wondered.

"That's okay," I said. "Maybe tomorrow."

"Yes, I'm sorry! You two must be so tired." Marcia stood from the table and pushed in her chair. It scraped across the floorboards. "Come with me; I'll show you the rooms we have empty at the moment; you can choose which one you like."

"Which *one*?" I asked.

"Sure." Marcia shrugged. "We only have *two* free, and I assume your friends will be needing the other one, once they arrive, and if they decide to stay."

Japhy and I would be sharing a room?

Now I *did* want to call my parents just so I could say: Hey, Momma? Guess what I am about to do! And there's absolutely *nothing* you can do to stop me!

We grinned at each other. Japhy's cheeks did that adorable

pinking thing that drove me crazy, and any ghosts I'd thought I'd seen in his face moments before were gone now.

Our own room, I thought. *Ours.* Far effing out!

Hand in hand, Japhy and I followed Marcia up the stairs to the second-floor landing.

"This is Jones and Belle's room." She pointed to a closed door. "And their kids are in there, across the hall."

Through an open doorway, I glimpsed a rocking horse and chest of drawers with clothes lolling out like colored tongues that licked at the floor.

"Guru and I sleep on the third floor. Jenny is are up there as well. And Needles lives in the basement."

Thank God, I thought, thinking of that creep being safely two floors away from me.

"So, you can choose between these two rooms," Marcia said, pointing to two open doorways. "Both beds are made up, and there are towels and toiletries in the adjoining bathroom. Make yourselves at home."

"Thank you, Marcia," said Japhy.

She shrugged and nodded. Then she clasped her hands. "Namaste and goodnight."

"Namaste," I called, as she floated back downstairs.

The first room we entered was ours. I didn't need to look at the second one; I didn't care if it was bigger, or the bed was more comfortable, or the curtains were thicker.

This. Was. Ours.

Mine and Japhy's.

Ours.

The bed was a brass-headed double with a white embossed cover and red pillows. When we flicked the light switch, two mismatched lamps glowed on the bedside tables, which were just two stacked piles of encyclopedias. Against one wall stood a beaten, wooden wardrobe, with its doors open as wide as a hug. And on the wall opposite the large window was a mural: a single white feather, suspended in mid-fall, above a pool of glistening red blood. I stared at this painting. The details so crisp – each barb of the white feather so defined despite the same shade of white wall behind it. And even though this beautiful, pure entity seemed headed for that horrible, gory wetness below, it would *never* land, would *never* become stained in red, because it had been frozen in this moment. It was *safe* in this moment. And it would *always* be safe in this moment. No matter what.

The bathroom, which connected our room to what would soon be Leaf and Lauren's, was tiled in descending shades of blue; azure sky at the ceiling, midnight at the floor. The walls met sandy floor tiles, which glowed beneath a great, yellow orb light shade. Mobiles of colorful glass fish swam on the roof, and green towels hung like seaweed on wall hooks.

Japhy sat on our bed, kicked off his shoes and stared at the picture of the falling-but-not-falling feather, while I brushed my teeth in this room at the bottom of the ocean. We had made it through the portal into a whole new world where gravity didn't exist, where we could breathe underwater, and where nothing would ever threaten us again.

My wrist flicked up and down, my mouth foamed, and I spat into the sink.

So normal. So mundane. And so wonderful.

*

The next morning, I ripped back the curtains and the sun splashed orange and pink streaks across the eternally falling, never landing, white feather on the wall. Opening the window, I breathed deep. The air smelled newborn and tickled my cheeks with chilly fingertips.

Crawling back under the warm nest of bedclothes, I rested my face on Japhy's back. His skin smelled musty and unclean and I drank him in as deeply as I could. "Good morning."

"Is it?" Japhy groaned and buried his head beneath the pillow. "Close the curtains, will you?"

"No," I said, shaking his shoulder. "It's time to get up and start the first day of our new lives!"

He groaned again.

"Fine," I said. "I'll meet you downstairs."

Before I left the room, I drew the curtains once again, and the shadows crept forward to cover Japhy in darkness.

Belle and Jones were on breakfast duty and they had spread the kitchen table with food: pancakes, a mountain of scrambled eggs, tomatoes, sliced chunks of bread, and a plate of blistered sausages. I stared at the pile of greasy meat. My nose crinkled as the smell of seared flesh raped my nostrils, but I bit my tongue and fisted my hands and held back my words.

"See what made the front page today?" Guru slid a newspaper across the table, and I leaned over it.

In black and white pixels, a young man lay face down. His feet askew. His arm folded beneath him. Something dark stained the ground and flowed away from his head in a straight line: a black river. A woman crouched over his body, her hand frozen in the air, her mouth open in an eternal scream, which echoed inside my bones as I read the article.

Four Dead In Ohio

Three days of riots and destruction at Kent State, Ohio, came to a bloody end yesterday when four students were shot dead, and nine others wounded. The Ohio National Guard were called to Kent on Saturday after out-of-control students smashed and looted downtown stores, and burned down the university's ROTC building. National Guard leader, Robert Canterbury, said the guards became fearful for their lives yesterday. They were forced to open fire on the students, who ignored orders to stop the noon protest and had become increasingly violent toward the Guardsmen. The students' unruly behavior escalated from bad language and shocking insults to rock throwing and threats with knives and other dangerous weapons, culminating in gunshots from both sides.

When asked to comment on the shootings, President Nixon said yesterday, "When dissent turns to violence, it invites tragedy."

One Kent resident was quoted: "When trouble-makers have long hair, use bad language and go barefoot and even destroy property, they have to be stopped."

Another simply stated: "More should have been killed."

The names of the deceased have not yet been released. It is rumored that two of the four students killed were not participating in the demonstration but were simply making their way through the university's parking lot when the shots were fired; however, this claim has not yet been verified. The number of wounded Guardsmen, and the severity of their injuries, is still, at this stage, unknown.

"Their injuries are unknown because they weren't injured!" I threw the paper down in a rustling heap on the table. "Those bastards are blaming the students? Nixon is blaming *us*? They make it sound as if we *deserved* to be shot, wounded, killed. And even if we *had* deserved it, the stupid journalist is missing the point: four innocent people are dead. Shot *dead* for trying to stop violence that is killing innocent people in other countries!" I covered my face with my hands. "Ugh!"

I wanted to scream at someone. I wanted to punch something. I wanted to curl into a ball of arms and limbs and tears. But instead, I took a deep breath and pushed my full plate away.

Marcia had been watching me with narrowed eyes, and now she stood and said it was time for chores, and did I want to come with her?

I nodded, grateful, and stood, following her around the side of the house and into the vegie garden.

"You looked like you needed some fresh air after that news article," she said, her words puffing out as hot, white clouds in the cold space around us. "Would you like to talk about it?"

I shook my head.

"Well, I want you to know, you can come to me. About anything. Anytime."

I smiled and nodded and wiped at a tear before she could see.

Then, Marcia opened the waist-high wooden gate and gestured me through. "Welcome to the Garden of Eden."

In the cool morning breeze, a signpost waved; wooden arrows swung from it. Burnt into these arrows were the words *Fruit* (pointing left), *Vegies* (straight ahead), and *Flowers and*

Herbs (right). Each arrow pointed along a dirt path: little roads inside this metropolis of produce.

"Wow." My mouth hung open. "This is huge!"

"It's a trip, huh?" She handed me a plastic basket from the stack by the gate. "Come on. We have to be ready to leave in an hour if we want to get a good stall at the market this morning. I assume you're tagging along today? See how we make our living?"

"Yeah!" I felt like a little kid at Christmas, being asked if I wanted to see Santa's Workshop. "I'd love that!"

I followed Marcia through the scent of wet dirt, a watering can slopping and splashing against my leg. "So, this is your place, then?" I asked. "Yours and Guru's, I mean?"

Marcia nodded. "It used to belong to Guru's grandmother. She left it to him when she died, shortly after we married, and we moved in with the expectation of filling every single room with our children. We tried. But ..." She shrugged. "Ah well. You know the saying: when life gives you lemons ..."

"You make lemonade," I finished, and thought that Marcia would have been a great mother.

"Nope." Her smile was as big as the entire universe, and her eyes twinkled with a million stars. "You squeeze juice in life's eye, and then go and buy some damn tequila!"

As we watered, weeded, and picked, I thought about Japhy's mother, Nora, and the small herb garden she grew under the kitchen window. She loved pottering in the dirt, and I never understood the attraction. I understood it now, though. And I wished she could see this place. It was like being on another planet.

This whole place was another planet! All these people, beautiful alien beings.

And, despite everything I had been through, everything I had given up, I was now one very contented alien.

I was happy.

And Japhy was happy.

And therefore, what else did I need in life?

chapter fourteen

japhy

I am not happy here.

Needles's sneakers are caked in an inch or two of mud as he treks across the yard to the chicken coop, and I follow him, staring as his feet kick up clods of muck. The breeze ruffles his wispy, blond hair out in straight lines behind him, like fingers reaching for me. I drop back a step.

To my left, I see Ray in the veggie patch with Marcia. Even from this distance, the whites of her teeth flash to me as she smiles. She raises her arms out from her sides and spins in a circle. Her laughter unspools from her throat and floats to me, wrapping itself around my neck like a tightening ribbon. And then she stops, and waves.

I raise my hand, let it fall, and turn back to the chickens clucking happily in their eternal search for worms. Lucky bastards.

During this last week of travel, my head was so packed full of worries about getting across the damn border and avoiding the damn draft that I didn't give a damn thought to what would happen once we actually made it here.

And why not? I sigh. Because I hoped that we *wouldn't* make it.

"The egg baskets are kept in here," says Needles. He stops at a small shed attached to the coop.

The scent of straw and grain and mice seeps out from the darkness. I stick my head through the door and make out, in the dimness, shelves lined with plastic containers, hessian bags of hay, three or four spades, a stacked pile of steel buckets, and an axe.

"In here's the food," says Needles, "and everything you'll need to muck out all the chicken shit, which you can scoop into these," he points to the buckets. "And then scatter it onto the vegetable patch."

"Right," I say, taking the spade he hands me.

The coop is made from an old children's cubby house. It was once painted white with a pink door and matching shutters. Now the paint peels off it in curls, revealing gray wood beneath like bone under skin. Through the black holes of the open windows, I see shapes of straw-filled boxes, from where ghostly white chickens watch me with beady eyes. Attached to this decaying structure is a large, wired-off courtyard, where chickens strut and scratch and screech.

Needles and I hunch and duck our heads as I open the door and step inside, and he closes it behind us. My shoes sink down a few inches into the mud and wet straw and shit.

Great. Just perfect.

The birds squawk and run around me in wide circles as I slide my spade across the ground and then dump its load into the waiting bucket.

Slide, lift, splat.

Slide, lift, splat.

"You know, chickens are very intuitive animals," says Needles. "If a chicken don't trust you ..." He shakes his head. "You're not worth trusting, I think."

"That so?" I say.

"Yup." He squats down and holds out his palm. Three chickens peck his skin and he laughs.

"Hey, Needles?"

"Mmm?"

"Can I ask you something, man?"

"Sure." He stands up and reaches for his spade.
"You happy here?"
He nods. "This place is the best."
"Why did you decide to live here?"
"At Mandala?" He sighs, and leans forward on his spade handle. "That's easy. The chicks!"
I frown, and look around me.
"Nah, dude. The *women* that come through here."
"Oh."
"Hippie chicks, dude. Pussy. With this whole women's lib trip they're all on, they give it out to *everyone*!"
"Huh." I slide my spade and wish I hadn't said anything.
"Even chicks who have boyfriends give it away. They say they don't believe in being owned by a guy. They can do whatever they want!" He snorts a laugh. "Or *whoever* they want, am I right?"
I ignore him and dump more shit in the bucket.
"Don't s'pose Ray feels that way, does she?"
"What? No!" I frown at him. "She's my girlfriend, man!"
"Okay, peace." He holds his hands in the air. "Just asking. Good to know the boundaries, that's all."
I stoop and grab my bucket and move away from Needles to the door of the cubby house.
What a friggin cheese-weasel!
Slide, lift, splat.
Wants to know the boundaries! Christ.
Slide, lift, splat.
As Needles works, he whistles through his teeth. I don't recognize the tune. The hisses of air and high-pitched chirping scratch down my soul and I grit my teeth and try not to hear him.
Slide. Lift. Splat.
And then I freeze.
"Oh Christ! Needles?" I call to him.
"Yeah, man?" He turns to me. "What is it?"
I point at the shadowed doorway through which I can see feathers in the dirt. So many feathers. The ones near my feet

are white and lovely. The ones surrounding the body on the ground, however, are stained red.

"Shit," Needles mumbles, as he leans down to look closer at the dead chicken. "This is Matilda. God damn that damn fox!"

He averts his eyes from mine, but not before I see them well with tears. He shuffles past me, snatches his spade, and disappears around the corner of the shed. A metal blade cuts into soft earth, and I imagine the growing hole, the grave, widening at Needles's feet like a mouth.

I remain with Matilda, watching over her, offering the silent protection she no longer needs, until Needles shuffles back in. He crouches down and gently lifts the mauled corpse into his arms. "Come on, sweetheart," he whispers, and carries her away.

Following Needles, I lean against the wall of the shed and hang my head as he places the chicken softly in the deep, black maw of dirt. Beside the grave, I notice a tree stump and think it might act as a nice marker for this poor chicken who has met such a horrific and untimely death. But then I notice the feathers ingrained in the wood. And the stains on the flat bed of the stump. The way it looks black in the centre. I think about the axe leaning against the wall of the shed. And as I watch the irony of this man crying over a dead chicken that he would have eventually killed anyway, I think about the mural on my bedroom wall. The way that feather falls, and will eventually be covered in blood. No matter what.

Needles fills the hole with dirt, pats it down with the flat of the shovel, and sniffs.

It doesn't matter what we do, it doesn't matter who we befriend, it doesn't matter where we hide; eventually, one way or another, we all end up covered in blood.

*

After our first full day in this new – unwanted – life, Ray and I sit on the front porch and watch the sky as it reddens into our second day.

"Bloody welts of bent light scratch across clouds," I whisper. "Bleeding rain is coming."

"Nice." She nods and tips her head to the side, sucks on her bottom lip. "Fairy floss ceiling of spun-sugar clouds ... Life is sweet."

I wonder if she knows she is smiling, or if it is unconscious. And I wonder, too, if perhaps I am unconsciously frowning. I take a deep breath and relax the muscles in my face, smooth out any lines that may crinkle the happiness mask behind which I'm hiding.

"Japhy?" she whispers.

"Mmm?"

"Thank you."

"For what?"

"Getting drafted."

"What?" I feel my mask crack across my forehead.

"Well," she says, sitting up and facing me. "If you hadn't been drafted, we would never have come here, would we? I'd still be in school, worrying about stupid stuff like exams and prom dresses and graduation speeches ... and my college acceptance letter."

"Yeah," I say, "which was something you'd been dreaming about for months before I came along and jived it all up for you."

She shrugs, and turns her eyes back to the sky. "Dreams are funny things. While you're in them, it's all you can see, it's all you know. But you don't realize how pale and insubstantial that dream world is until you wake up and feel the strength of reality beneath you." She leans her head against my shoulder. "I'm awake now, though. And the colors are so much brighter!"

"What if *this* is the dream?" I ask her.

She gives a soft laugh and a sigh that presses heavily against my chest. "If this is the dream," she says, "then please never wake me up."

I kiss the top of her head, glad that from this angle she does not see my happiness mask splinter and fall to pieces in my lap.

chapter fifteen

ray

I paced the arrivals section of the Toronto Coach Terminal, a great, gray building. My nerves and my excitement at seeing Leaf and Lauren again kept me twitching back and forth past the row of chairs where Japhy sat, biting a thumbnail, and following me with only his eyes.

"Will you sit down!" he said. "You're making my head hurt."

"I can't." I stopped in front of him and hugged my chest. "What if she doesn't forgive me? What if they both hate me now?"

"Then they wouldn't be coming here, would they?"

"Maybe they're only coming to get the van!"

"You said Leaf sounded fine on the phone this morning."

"He *did* ..."

When Leaf called to say they'd be arriving this afternoon, the receiver had shaken in my hand with the reverberation of his laughter. "Heh! Heh! Heh!" His laugh, which no one could refuse to laugh right along with. His laugh, which I had missed so very much. His damn laugh, to which (I realized at that very moment) I was addicted.

"This is them, isn't it?" Japhy nodded toward a Greyhound that pulled into the parking bay. "Bus three-five-zero?"

I looked at the palm of my hand, even though I knew perfectly well what the smudged numbers I had written there said. I looked down, not to verify that three-five-zero was indeed correct, but to give myself an excuse to look away, to not have to meet her eyes when she came down those steps.

But like a child unable to look away from an eclipse despite the danger to her retinas, I felt my head pull upwards and my eyes search for hers.

First, her shoes. Crisp white sneakers with three blue lines on the side. And a brown star-shaped splatter of dried blood on the left toe. Right foot down, then feet together. Right foot down, then feet together.

And then her face. And finally her eyes, which locked directly on mine, and I couldn't blink.

I gasped at the deep lines in her face, the black hollows under her eyes, the emptiness in her stare. Despite her childlike movements, she looked elderly. Ancient. Undead.

Like she had endured all the horrors of an entire life in only three days.

Before Lauren landed both feet together on the ground, Leaf had jumped down the bus stairs in one go and wrapped an arm around her shoulders. Protecting her from harmful outside forces, perhaps? Or holding her together while internal forces tried to smash their way out?

She stumbled under his weight, and then she pushed him away. "I said I was fine!"

"Okay." He held up his hands and stepped back. "I'm sorry."

Here goes, I thought, as Japhy and I walked toward them. Forcing a smile into my voice, I called out, "Hey, you cats need a ride?"

To which I heard the wonderful and uplifting response of: "Heh! Heh! Heh!"

I gravitated toward that sound. My safety net. And I let myself fall, face first, into it.

Once I had kissed, hugged, and done the "Oh, man, I missed you" thing with Leaf, I turned to face Lauren.

Her wide, blue-green eyes gazed up at me.

Accusingly?

"It's so good to see you both again," she whispered, and held her arms out to me.

And I folded inside them. The swollen bump of her now-empty stomach pressed against me.

Why is she still so big?

In all my visualizations of this moment, she was flat-stomached; I never imagined this physical reminder of loss would throb between us like a beating heart.

"I'm so sorry." With my face pressed against the soft curve of her neck, I could still smell hospital on her skin. Or maybe that was the stench of guilt.

She held me tight and shushed into my ear. Oh, she would have made an excellent mother.

Would have.

"So sorry," I said again.

I felt a hand press on my shoulder and Leaf said, "Come on guys, let's get out of this nightclub."

I coughed out a small laugh, sniffed, and wiped my nose with the back of my hand.

"How are you feeling?" asked Japhy, taking hold of Lauren's arm.

She stiffened and, for a second, glared at him. But then her whole being softened, and she kind of leaned onto him like a crutch as we helped her through the busy terminal, bent forward and feet shuffling.

"I'm still sore," she told Japhy, and then grinned. "But I'm nicely medicated."

"Lucky you," he muttered.

I glanced at him, but he looked away.

In the parking lot, we helped Lauren into the van. With every painful groan or sharp intake of breath, I cringed. My fault. My fault.

"Lay down in the bed, honey," said Leaf, starting the engine. "Just rest up, okay?"

She rolled her eyes. "I don't *need* to rest. All I've been doing is resting."

"Well, then, just take it easy."

"What do you expect I'm going to be doing back here? Cartwheels?"

Leaf sighed, but then smiled as he ran his hand over the steering wheel. "Hello, old girl," he whispered. "I missed you! Heh! Heh!" He started the engine, and drove us back toward Mandala, while Japhy navigated beside him.

Lauren crawled over to the cupboard below the sink and pulled out cups and bowls and plates, stacking them in a tower beside her.

"What are you doing?" I asked.

"Looking."

"For what?"

"Aha!" She sat back on her feet and grinned and raised a small silver box above her head. Flipping the lid up with her thumb, she pinched a joint between two fingers and lifted it to her lips in one fluid movement.

"I thought you weren't into the whole drug scene," I said as she hissed a match to life and brought it up to ignite the rolled paper.

It whooshed alight and she breathed in. "Doesn't really matter now, does it?" She spoke with tight words as she kept the breath in her lungs for as long as she could manage. Then she blew out more words that hovered in smoky clouds above my head. "I was only staying straight because of the baby." Her hand fluttered to her neckline, searching, but found only bare skin.

"Where's your necklace?" I asked her.

"Oh." She shrugged and looked out the window. "Threw it away. Piece of junk."

"But it was really special to you, Lauren."

"Well, I thought I was really special to Jesus as well, but I guess I was wrong. And, by the way, it's not *Lauren* anymore; my name is *Poppy* now."

Poppy? I looked toward Leaf, who met my eyes in the rear-vision mirror. His shoulders lifted and fell.

"If all of you can rename yourselves and start over with clean slates, why not me?" she asked.

Poppy, I thought. The flower of remembrance and

consolation. Was she turning herself into a living memorial for that poor baby? And an eternal reminder of what she lost.

Great.

But I met her eyes, and I smiled. "It's nice to meet you, Poppy."

She took my hand and squeezed it. "Thanks, Ray," she whispered. "Thank you."

Leaf soon pulled the van to a stop at Mandala and leaned forward to gaze at the farmhouse through the windscreen. "So this is the famous Mandala commune, huh?"

"Yep." Japhy nodded, staring out at the building. "This is ..." he swallowed. "This is *home* now."

"What do you think, lovely?" Leaf called back.

But Poppy was asleep, curled in on herself so tightly there was nothing left but arms and legs.

"Is she okay?" I whispered.

"She's fine." Leaf slid out from behind the wheel and opened the sliding van door. He stared at the knotted form on the mattress and then scooped his arms underneath, lifting Poppy into his chest. "She is just perfectly fine."

chapter sixteen

japhy

Leaf lifts the sleeping Poppy from the van and heads toward the farmhouse. I trot up beside him and clap him on the shoulder. "Come on, I'll show you to your room."

"Thanks."

Stepping backwards over the threshold of the kitchen doorway, I ask him, "So, you had no ... uh ... issues getting across the border, then?"

He meets my eyes as he steps past me into the kitchen. "Why would we?" he says. And then he winks.

"No reason." I smile, and nod. "No reason at all."

And as he follows me up to the second-floor, his feet clunking on the steps behind me, I understand that here in this solid old farmhouse, in this new and welcoming country, he is just as safe as I am. Like me, he no longer needs to run.

But I wonder if, like me, he still *wants* to. Whether, for Leaf, the need to be running and *home* is greater than the need to be safe and *lost*?

Home is where the heart is. That's what they say.

Well, what the fuck do *they* know? They probably didn't have to leave their home soil.

I lean against the doorframe as Leaf lays Poppy down on their bed and pulls the blue covers up to her chin. In sleep, she is not Poppy, but Lauren again. I can imagine her eyes full of innocence and desire to see the world, rose-petal lips curled into a smile of delight, and freckled cheeks pink with all the wonders the future will bring.

He kisses her forehead. Lingers there for an extra second, and then silently crosses the room.

"How is she?" I whisper. "Really."

"Uh." Leaf chews his bottom lip as he steps into the hall and pulls the door shut behind him. "She's not great. But she *will* be. She's still in shock, I think. We all are. But the hospital isn't where she needed to be, you dig? I had to get her out of that place."

"So, you convinced them to release her early?"

Leaf grins. "Something like that! Now." He claps his hands together. "I understand I have a welcome party to attend?"

I nod and head toward the stairs. "It's out the back; come on." But at the landing, I stop and turn. "Hey, Leaf?"

"Hmm?"

"You ever feel like, I don't know, you aren't sure if you've made the right decision ..."

"Oh, sure, all the time! I used to be so indecisive. These days, though?" He tips his head to the side, thinking. "I'm not so sure."

I feel the smile's warmth in my core, but it doesn't spread any further. What is my problem? I'm in a great place, with people I like. This is my life now. Why do I have to get all harsh on it, why can't I just enjoy the vibe? Move on from all the shit that's happened. Fresh start. Clean slate.

Fuck.

"I think," says Leaf, "you need to take life with a grain of salt, my friend." He smiles. "A grain of salt, a wedge of lemon and a shot of tequila!"

I turn toward the steps.

"Oh, and Japhy?"

Pausing with my hand on the banister, I turn back to face him.

"I was just wondering ..." He reaches into his back pocket

and pulls out an envelope. "How do you feel about the name *Gus*?"

"Huh?"

"Gus Cooper?" He is smiling. Those huge teeth blinding in the dimness.

"Why?"

"Well, see, I know a guy, who knows a guy, who has this friend."

"Called Gus?" I ask.

"Heh! Heh! Heh! No. Not exactly."

I face him fully on the stairs, frowning up as he grins down at me.

"Here." He hands me the envelope.

It's thick. Folded. "What's this?" I ask. "Is it from this Gus guy?"

"Nope." Leaf slaps a heavy hand on my shoulder. "*Gus* is already here."

I open the envelope and slide out a Canadian birth certificate and driver's license with my old school yearbook picture grinning up at me.

"What?" I gasp. The walls in the stairwell shrink in against my throat. "How did you … Where did you …?"

"You're now an official Canadian!" Leaf sidesteps by me and hops down the remaining stairs. "Come on, *Gus*, let's go celebrate! Heh! Heh!"

I stare down at the papers that shake in my hands, and I grit my teeth against the desire to make a fist and crumple this new life that I have absolutely no control over.

"Leaf!" I hear Ray's voice float up the stairwell. "There you are!" Her words are fuzzy at the edges, just like my vision. "Everyone is waiting to meet you!"

"Ray!" he says, and his voice slowly fades as he walks away. "I was just wondering, how do you feel about the name Georgia?"

The envelope slips through my fingers, my knees disappear, and I clunk into a sitting position with my hands holding up my head while my entire world spins around me. Up, down, around. Up, down, around. A Ferris wheel, spinning hearts and minds up, down, and around.

I have to tell her, I think, forcing myself to stand.

I have to tell Ray that I am going home. And that, once again, she'll have to give up her dreams for me.

chapter seventeen

ray

The wine flowed, the drugs kicked in, and everyone was where they wanted to be: eight miles high, baby, and I was a different person.

I was Mrs. Georgia Cooper, to be exact.

"Where's Japhy?" I asked Leaf as he accepted a handshake and a beer from Guru.

"He was right behind me on the stairs," Leaf said, shrugging.

Around the growing bonfire, the children danced like little Indians, while music filled the air, booming from the speakers placed on the living room windowsill. I nodded my head to the tapping-foot beat, the stripped-naked guitar, the finger-sliding squeal of strings, and the silk-woven vocal chords of James Lee Stanley's *Stolen Season*.

"*In our stolen season, feet won't touch the ground. It's a Ferris wheel that's spinning hearts and minds around.*"

I sat and drank and watched as Leaf was handed around the circle like a new toy, and his laugh hung a continuous note in the air like the harmonic ringing of a Tibetan Singing Bowl.

"*And the heights will make you dizzy, take your breath away. In our secret stolen season, there is just today.*"

"Ray?" A topless Belle skipped toward me with body paint

and some brushes; her milk-full breasts, painted with matching peace signs, swayed back and forth with each step. She held the brush out toward me, an offering.

"Oh, no, I couldn't," I said, folding my arms across my chest.

"Why not?" she asked me.

Yeah, why not? I asked myself.

"It's just skin," said Belle. "And we all have it."

I looked across the bonfire to where Needles sat with his head bent in conversation with Leaf, and turned my back on them.

"Well ..." I bit my lip.

"Come on!" Belle jumped up and down. "Trust me!" She held up the brush again. "I'll free you."

How could I say no to that?

I closed my eyes and stripped naked.

"*But when you're lost in loving, time will not stand still. Each hour seems a second, each shadow touch a thrill.*"

The cool night air licked at my skin and a line of goose bumps rose in its wake. But then they smoothed under the heat of the bonfire and my own red-hot courage.

"*And each kiss will leave us breathless as our two hearts beat as one.*"

Belle redressed me so completely in a clothing of beads and painted butterflies and daisies and peace signs and the word DOVE in rainbow letters across my forearm that I only knew I was nude by the breath of wind on my bare skin.

"*In our secret, stolen season, in the shadows of the sun.*"

Was it wrong for me to be enjoying myself out here? Was it wrong for me to be laughing while, inside, Poppy mourned a baby whose death I had caused?

"Would you *stop* it?"

Japhy's sudden words in my ear made me jump.

I placed a hand on my chest. "Where'd you come from?"

"Where are your clothes?" he said.

"It's just skin, Japhy." I rolled my eyes. "And we all have it!"

I heard Belle laugh somewhere off to my right.

"Come with me." He took my hand. "I need to tell you something."

As Japhy led me away from everybody, out into the field, James Lee Stanley's voice grew softer with distance.

Softer, but not silent.

"In our stolen season, our world within a world."

"I know what you're going to say!" I grinned. "Leaf already told me we're married!"

"It's a simple act of love between a boy and girl."

"What?" Japhy stared at me. "We're *what*?"

"I'm *Mrs.* Georgia Cooper."

"What?" Japhy frowned.

"I'm the wife of Mr. Gus Cooper." I placed my hand softly on his chest and felt his heart about to bash its way through bone and into my palm, and I knew exactly how he felt. "I'm your wife."

"But ..." He shook his head. "No."

"No?" My hand dropped to my side and I tilted my head forward so hair covered my suddenly burning cheeks. "Oh."

"No, wait, Ray, that's not what I meant." He reached for my chin and tried to lift my eyes to his, but I turned my back on him, and on what I couldn't face there.

"No yesterdays can find us, and tomorrows don't exist."

"What did you want to say to me, Japhy?" I said. "You dragged me all the way over here, so it must have been important."

Japhy stepped around me, tried to bend forward, to see in under my hair, but I turned away again, and he sighed.

"Just say it," I whispered, "so I can get back to the party."

A yellow dandelion danced at our feet, flicking its petals from me to Japhy and back again as it followed our conversation and bopped along to the background music.

"Ray ..." Although Japhy's voice was a whisper, it boomed through the air.

My ears rang with its echo of my name and everything I heard within it.

"I know you love it here and everything ..." he said, "I mean,

I know you think this is a wonderful life for us and everything ... but ... but I just ..."

"*But all too soon it's over and the world falls back in place.*"

"But *what?*" I clenched my teeth down, squashing my words, wishing like hell that he would *not* answer that question. My stomach churned: I knew what was coming.

"*From our secret, stolen season, from our state of grace ...*"

He didn't speak.

And I didn't breathe.

We both waited.

"*And into every day and night some magic weaves its spell.*"

Then he gave a great sigh. Like a man heaving the weight of the world onto his shoulders. The kind of sigh that transferred from him to me, into my lungs, into my heart. The heaviness of it pinned me down. I wanted to turn and run away from the moment that was coming. The moment in which he ripped my heart in two. But I couldn't move, so I just stood there, trembling, like the condemned convict waiting for the trapdoor to swing and the noose to snap tight.

"*It's a secret, stolen season, and we can not tell ...*"

"Hey," he said. "Hey!" And he dug his fingers into my shoulders and turned me forcefully around to face him, to stare right down into my eyes so I couldn't look away. "Since you're already my wife, I guess I already know the answer to this question ... but ..."

Japhy bent down and plucked the little dandelion from the dirt. Making a small hole in the stem, he threaded it through itself to form a circle. Then, he took my left hand and slipped the ring on my finger. I stared at the bright yellow petals that glinted like the golden sun of a brand new day.

"Ray?" Then he smiled. "Georgia Cooper, will you–"

"YES!" Completely weightless, I flew at him, wrapped my legs around his waist, and we half-fell, half-lay back into the cradle of the paddock's grass.

"Love you, Ra-a-ay," he said.

"I love you, Japhy."

"*If there's a way of knowing what is lost and what is gained in our secret, stolen season, where our hearts remain.*"

*

I stared at the screen of the little television set in the corner of the living room, unable to understand exactly what I saw. Pockmarked brick walls. Windows peppered with black holes or otherwise completely shattered. Faces peering out through the blown-out glass; their eyes wide. I'd seen eyes like those before, lids flung open in disbelief and horror.

"Jesus Christ," Japhy whispered beside me. "They've done it again."

"As the war in Viet Nam escalates," said the newsreader, "so too does the war in America, as it becomes a country divided. In this latest instance of pro and anti-war disagreement, the Mississippi State Police opened fire last night on a women's dormitory at Jackson State University after a small group of anti-war protesters failed to disperse. Twelve people were injured and two have been killed."

Two photographs filled the screen as my eyes filled with tears. Their faces blurred and I blinked furiously, trying to focus on their features, wanting to acknowledge these two men and the bright lives that had been snuffed out; that small gift of tribute was all I could offer. That and the silent promise I made to remember their names.

"Phillip Gibbs, a twenty-one-year-old junior pre-law major, was shot four times. And James Green, a senior at Jim Hill High School, was hit in the chest while walking past the University on his way home from work; he was only seventeen.

"In response to the growing opposition to America's involvement in the war, President Nixon maintains US troops will soon be withdrawn."

Nixon's smug face pressed against the television screen, and when he started speaking, my hands balled into fists. "The new mission of our soldiers is to train the South Vietnamese Army to fight their own combat missions, to strengthen their own soldiers against the enemy in everything from numbers, to equipment, to leadership. At the same time we will be steadily reducing the number of troops that we send over there."

Big Dick's face was replaced by a street of marching people with their fingers held up in V's and signs begging for peace.

"Despite this promise by President Nixon," said the newsreader, "two weeks ago, American troops crossed the border of Viet Nam and invaded Cambodia and Laos. Angry Americans took to the streets as a result, and on May four, the National Guard fired live ammunition into a group of anti-war demonstrators at Kent State University, killing four students and wounding nine others. This tragedy set off a nation-wide protest, with over four million students going on strike, four hundred and fifty campuses across the United States shutting down, and thirty ROTC buildings going up in smoke. In Washington and San Francisco, anti-war protestors numbering one hundred thousand, and one hundred and fifty thousand respectively, have taken to the streets in protest."

"This is big," whispered Japhy. "This is really big. Surely they can't ignore us now! They'll be pulling our troops out any day." He nodded. "Any day now, and the war will be over, and they won't even care that I refused induction, and we can go home and get on with our lives and start cleaning up all their mess!"

And I nodded too, because I wanted to believe him. I wanted to believe the words painted on a white banner hanging from a New York University's third-story window: *They can't kill us all.*

No, I thought, they *can't* kill us all. But it seems like they will give it a damn good try.

chapter eighteen

japhy

I sit on a branch in a large oak tree in the corner of the goat pen, legs crossed on the strong bough. I've been coming up here every evening for the last two weeks. Two weeks! Up here, I can meditate. I can look at my life from a different angle. I can convince myself that life is good. No, great even! Because up here, I feel like a Bikkhu, like a monk, like a poet, like Kerouac's Japhy Ryder.

Up here, where my feet don't touch the ground, I can look down on everyone like a ghost, like someone who doesn't really exist, like Kerouac's Japhy Ryder.

As the sun slides behind the horizon, the brilliant oranges and pinks and deep reds surround me; an aura that goes out from me, in all directions, in every direction, toward infinity. I watch the small group of hippies in the distance, dancing around a bonfire. I hear their laughter. I hear *her* laughter. And I force myself to laugh, too.

But I can't laugh.

Damn it, I can't.

I punch the thick tree branch and wince in pain.

Why?

I punch again.

Leaves fall and clatter onto my skin before they spin to the ground.

What is *wrong* with me? Why can't I be happy here? Why can't I accept this life? There are thousands who would kill to be in my shoes. Thousands who, in fact, *are* killing in Nam and would give anything to be out of that hell and sitting in a tree above a group of peace-loving hippies.

But not me! Nope, not the wonderful Japhy. Not Andy Mack. Not even Gus Conner, or Cooper, or whatever-the-fuck my new name is.

I punch the tree a third time, and the skin on my middle knuckle splits open. I hiss a breath over my bottom lip and press the cut to my mouth. The crisp, coppery burst of blood cuts into my tongue. I lick it, like a dog healing a wound. And then I look down again when I hear Ray's laughter fluting across the field; it curls through the air, and ties itself around my heart like a beautiful ribbon wrapping a gift.

With the saltiness of my own life still fresh in my mouth, I force myself to laugh again.

It bubbles in my stomach, rising like a gas. And then, finally, bursting from my chest like a great bird freed from a cage, my laughter soars through the sky. With wings wide, eyes closed, it feels the rush of air caress its face and knows that it will never let itself become trapped again.

Never again.

I slide my leg over the bough of the tree and I fall through the sky, arms wide, eyes closed, while the air caresses my face.

And when my feet thud-thud onto solid earth, I stride toward the light of the bonfire with a true smile on my face.

"There you are!" Ray calls to me as I get closer. "Where have you been?"

I don't know, I think. But I'm back now, Ray. I'm back now.

chapter nineteen

ray

Flames reached orange arms toward the indigo sky, grabbing at the first stars of the evening with fiery fingertips and using them to point and spotlight on Japhy as he rounded the corner of the house. His face was bright and open and lovely. His eyes did not stray from me once as he strode forward with such purpose and need that my heart skipped a little. The way it used to when I saw him unexpectedly around the corner of a school building. The way it used to when I heard his dad's borrowed car rumbling in my driveway. The way it used to at the mere mention of his name.

"Where have you been?" I asked, but he didn't answer. Just grabbed my face in both his hands and kissed me so deeply that I forgot who I was for a second. And then I remembered. I remembered exactly who I was: I was *his*.

He stroked my cheek and looked into my eyes as if he hadn't seen me in weeks. "Hello."

"Hi," I laughed. "Are you okay?"

"Yes," he said. "Yes, I'm fine now." Again, he kissed me. And again, I was gone.

"Hey, Japhy's back!" Leaf bongoed at us from across the circle. His long fingers popped against the small drum in a frantic, funky beat, his head dipping to the sound of his own music.

And I realized with a start that Poppy swayed beside him. Her arms were crossed over her chest and she stared at her bare toes instead of smiling around her at all the beautiful people. But still, she was *here*. She was out of bed. She was outside. After two weeks of refusing to leave her room, she was here, at Leaf's side, as if she had never been absent at all.

How long has she been out here without me even noticing her? I wondered. Has she seen me smiling, and laughing, and enjoying life?

Shit.

Maybe it was the firelight on her pale face, maybe it was the loss visible in her eyes, or maybe it was the morphine tablets that were dissolving in her bloodstream – but she looked so *young*. She looked like an innocent girl, no older than fourteen, fifteen tops, who had gone up against the big, bad world, and lost.

"Poppy!" Leaf smiled up at her, still banging away. "Take the solo, babe!"

She glanced down at him, shook her head, and looked away.

"Okay!" said Leaf, his fingers tapping louder. "Just leave it there, then. I'll get it later."

"Can everybody gather around the fire, please?" Guru called out, his smooth voice carrying easily over the whoosh of the flame.

Leaf put down the bongo and stood, draping his arm around Poppy's shoulder and rubbing, like he was drying her with an invisible towel, trying to warm her, to shine some life into her.

She just kept staring at her feet.

"It has come to my attention recently," Guru called out, "that two of our newest Mandalans, Ray and Japhy, have decided to join their souls as husband and wife."

I felt Japhy's shoulder nudge me, playfully, but I couldn't look away from Poppy.

"So," said Guru, "I thought, why wait? How about a little unofficial ceremony, huh?"

A wave of applause washed around the circle.

Japhy took my hand and squeezed it.

Leaf let out a loud, "Yeah!"

But Poppy kept her head down. Her eyes down. The corners of her mouth down.

Nausea sloshed in my stomach.

Damn it all.

This was a *moment* for me. This was a real moment that I would remember for the rest of my life and I would *not* let it become tainted by my own guilt.

I turned, angling myself so Poppy's demons no longer sneered at me, and I focused everything that I was on Japhy. On right now. On breathing in only this second, and then breathing out this second. Now, now, now.

"What do you think?" I asked, grinning, and biting my lip. "Should we ..." And suddenly I just wanted to laugh out loud. Felt as if something wanted to burst outward from my chest and fly free. Could this really be happening to me? Could I really be about to marry Japhy? The boy I had dreamed about forever. The boy who'd been a year in front of me in school and never knew I existed. The boy who shocked me when, six weeks ago, he'd reached for the same book as me in a store, smiled, and said, "You're Heather Wren, right?" The boy who had wanted me just as badly, all along.

Now, I told myself.

He took my hands and – *now* – he looked at me so seriously that – *now* – my laughter faded. Again, he transported me back into that girl who sits in her pink bedroom, dreaming about this boy while her heart dances to the syllables of his name spoken out loud.

"Marry me?" he whispered. "Right now."

"Now?" And I swear, my heart almost gave up right then. "Okay," I said. At least, I think I said it; the rush of blood was so forceful in my ears, I couldn't hear my own voice.

In the fire, a log broke apart with a fountain of orange

sparks and a gunshot *crack*. Poppy jumped and pressed her face into Leaf's shoulder.

Through the smoke, Leaf's calm brown eyes reached out and soothed me.

This was not my fault. This was not his fault. Or Japhy's, or Poppy's, or God's. We did not pull those triggers. The Government had bloody hands and stained souls. Not us. Not me.

I closed my eyes. Returned to now. Now. Now. Now.

Guru took our hands so we three formed a circle.

"Ray," he said, "repeat these words to Japhy." He whispered in my ear the words I was to say, and I looked deep into Japhy's brown eyes.

Now.

I somehow kept my voice strong and clear. "You are my husband, my lover. My heart shall beat because of you. My mind shall think because of you. And I shall love because of you."

His hands were shaking in mine. Or was it me who shook?

Then Japhy began, "You are my wife, my lover ..." But his words choked off and stopped. He bit his lip, shook his head, held his breath.

And so did I.

Until I saw his chest bloom out, and his shoulders hitch back, and his chin rise up, proud.

"My heart shall beat because of you," he said. "My mind shall think because of you. And I shall love because of you."

Guru placed a hand on each of our shoulders, linking us all. "May you remain long in this life together, and when the sun sets on this union, may you meet again in the one place that is sacred to both of you."

The one place sacred to us both? I wondered. Where would that be?

"Matterhorn?" Japhy whispered, as if reading my thoughts.

"Yes." I nodded. "Matterhorn."

"*Imagine we're alone in the mountains ...*" he smiled.

"And I'll be there," I said, "*just loving you.*"

Guru stepped away to retrieve something from the edge of

the circle. "And now the fun part." He held up a long Indian peace pipe wrapped in snakeskin; two mottled feathers hung from it, dancing and spinning on a breath of wind. "Let us bless this union!"

"Wait just one minute, Guru!" Belle stepped forward, her hand in the air. A tie-dyed papoose was draped across her chest; with the fire glowing behind them, the rounded weight of the sleeping infant gave her the silhouette of a heavily pregnant woman. "Before anyone goes and gets blessed off their heads, Jones and I have something we'd like to say." She nodded at her old man, who came forward and took her hand. Belle then beckoned for Marcia to join them.

"Is everything all right?" Marcia bounced Belle's daughter, Skylar, on her shoulders, and the little girl giggled and waved down at her parents.

"Actually, no." Jones shrugged. "We do have *one* little problem."

"Marcia," said Belle, "ever since we arrived here, you and Guru have made *our* family, *your* family. And ... well ..." She sighed. "It's come to a point now where something needs to change."

"What?" Marcia frowned as she lifted the child off her shoulders and hugged her. "What are you saying? You're not leaving Mandala?"

"Is it something that we've done?" asked Guru. He knelt down and wrapped an arm around the little boy, Dylan, who tugged at Marcia's skirt.

"More like something you *haven't* done," said Belle.

The fire cracked as another log split and fountained orange sparks into the air. A yellow glow flickered on Guru and Marcia's faces, making them look sick, anemic, scared as hell.

"But we love you all so much," whispered Marcia, smoothing the hair of the little girl in her arms. "Please don't go. Please don't take these beautiful beings from our home!"

"Marcia." Belle smiled and she placed a hand gently on the older woman's shoulder. "The problem we have is: you never had the chance to have your *own* children."

"If I've been too clingy, then I'm sorry, it's just that ..."

"Jones and I want to *give you a baby*," said Belle.

The fire cracked again as everyone stared. Mouths opened and closed. Foreheads crinkled in confusion. And eyes sparkled with shocked comprehension.

"You mean ..." Marcia gulped in a breath and her hand rose to clutch at her throat.

"I would like to offer you my uterus." Belle grinned. "Let me give you a baby."

"Oh my God ..." muttered Guru. "Oh wow, oh God. Really?"

"Yes." Jones reached out his hand to Guru, and they shook. "If you'll let us?"

"Let you?" Marcia gasped. "Oh, Belle! Jones! Oh!"

Tears stung my eyes as I watched these people embrace and laugh and cry with happiness, and I gripped Japhy's hand, and smiled over at Leaf and Poppy.

But Leaf stood alone, staring at the house, and when I turned my head I saw the porch door close like an eye.

"This really *is* a cause for celebration now!" called Guru. "To *family!*" Putting the pipe to his lips, Guru lit it, drew back, and then passed it to me.

I took the pipe gently, unsure exactly what to do, but Guru nodded to me, and Japhy nodded to me, so I held the end to my lips and inhaled, and held the harsh, plastic-tasting smoke in my lungs as long as I could. My throat burned. What the hell was this stuff? When I breathed out, I felt time slow down almost to nothing and I watched my hand, moving as if through water, passing the pipe on to Japhy, my beloved spiritual husband.

I floated to the ground and lay back, staring wide-eyed at the sky, at the clouds that sped past like darting fish.

Wow, good shit, I thought and laughed to myself.

Then, the sound of a bell jingled in my ear. Clear. Pure. Beautiful.

I cracked open my eyelids to see the living room floor sway beneath me.

Living room? When had we come inside?

Slanted beams of solid gold ran from the window to the

carpet, holding the walls up. Everything glowed. Someone stood, Needles I think, and passed through one of the golden beams and I realized they were not solid beams at all but rays of morning sunlight shining through the window.

Where had the night gone?

I closed my eyes again and let the wonder of the new day kiss my eyelids hello.

The ringing stopped and Needles called out to Japhy: "Phone, man."

I sat up as Japhy crawled away from me. My head felt full of rocks, but I managed to balance it on my shoulders and wobble behind him into the kitchen. I poured myself some juice to wash away the stale taste of cigarettes and alcohol, and then leaned with my elbows on the kitchen bench, as Japhy lifted the handset.

"Hello?" His eyes brightened at the sound of a familiar voice.

I grinned at his childlike glee, and had I known it was the last time I would see him smile like that, I would have memorized everything: the exact amount of wrinkles at the corners of his wide mouth; the depth of the dimple in his right cheek; the number of perfect teeth displayed; the light inside him that made his eyes shine and his face beam.

His slow change from that beacon of radiant happiness to this vacant darkness brought me to his side in an instant.

"What is it?" I asked, and squeezed his arm. "Who is it?"

His eyes were dull and empty. No light shone there now. His skin was pale and waxy.

"Is it Nora?" I said. "Was it the operation?"

But he just stared at me as the receiver dropped from his limp fingers, clapping once upon the floor like the final beat of a heart.

chapter twenty

japhy

Are you happy now? I ask myself. You got what you wanted. You got what you've been wishing for.

We are going home.

Ray crosses through my vision, back and forth, from the wardrobe to the bed, stuffing clothes, item by item, into the duffle bag. Sunlight slants through the window and highlights every feature. She glows like an angel. Like the most precious jewel in the universe.

"I know what you're going to say," she says, "but are you *sure* this is the best decision?"

She's right. She *does* know what I'm going to say. Which is why I don't even bother saying it. I just flick my eyes to her, blink once, and then look back at the feather on the wall. The fucking feather that can never escape the bloody fate waiting below it.

None of us can.

"You are not expected to be there," she adds, as if this is supposed to make me feel better. "Your mom would want you to stay here. To stay *safe*."

I ignore her.

She sighs and stuffs more clothes.

"Are you sure you don't want to borrow the van?" asks

Leaf. He sits against the doorway to our shared bathroom, picking at a loose piece of cotton on his pants. "You'll get there faster. Less stops than a bus."

I shake my head, but I don't look at him; I can't take my eyes from the bright pool of red on the wall. No, if we drive the van to Alabama, we'll have to come back here to return it. And that's a promise that I just can't make right now. Returning.

"Japhy's right," says Ray. "At least on a bus, we don't have to concentrate on the journey. Besides, we've only got four days until the ..."

She stops, but I hear the word she tried to protect me from: *funeral*. I hear it loud and clear.

Fuck.

"... Until we need to be there," she finishes. "So the timetable is perfect. We'll be getting into Liberation tomorrow. If," she says and stuffs some more clothes in the bag, "we make this morning's bus."

"Well ..." Leaf shrugs. "If there's anything I can do ..."

"We know," says Ray. "Thank you." Her words are waterlogged and she stares at Leaf, trembling. "See you soon?"

It's a question. Not a statement.

And it's so full of hope that it fills the room.

"See you soon," he answers her, his voice as heavy as a promise.

I clench my jaw and look down at my shoes, praying they won't want me to say those words back.

Lifting the full bag onto her shoulder, Ray turns to me and holds out a hand. "You ready?"

Am I ready?

I laugh at the stupidity of that question. No. Of course I'm not ready! I'm eighteen years old; would you be ready to go and bury one of your parents at only eighteen years of age? No. No, you would not. And neither am I, thank you very much.

But I suck in breath, and I take her hand, and I hold on to it like she's the only thing that still exists for me on this whole empty earth. I hold on to it to make sure that I don't lose her as well.

I hold on to it all the way to the bus station, and as we board the bus, and as we cross the border with our brand new Mr. and Mrs. Cooper IDs. I hold on to it as we pass through state after state, as we drift through the night and the next morning, and finally roll into the town in which I was born.

I am home.

After all this time wishing I could come back, home is now the last place in the world I want to be.

The cream walls of the Liberation Station are peeling, like skin off a corpse. Out in the yard, old train carcasses rust and clang into pieces on the ground; birds build nests amidst these metal skeletons.

New life inside the bones of death.

I step off the bus and hear Ray hiss in a breath as I grip her hand even tighter. But I don't relax my hold. I can't. What if she slips through my fingers like a ghost? What if she disappears like a memory? What if she stops holding me together like skin?

The smell of petrol and oil and dirt rushes at me. Underneath it all is the scent of stale wine and urine. Suddenly a memory rises up from the dust and I am five years old again, walking with my father, my hand lost in his giant palm as we cross the platform to our waiting train. I don't remember where he was taking me that day, but I do remember the face of the homeless man. He leered out at me from the shadows, his teeth brown, the whites of his eyes terrifyingly bright in contrast to his grimy skin. I pressed my face against my dad's hip and felt him steer me away to safety.

"There!" Ray says.

I blink and my five-year-old self is gone, is somewhere lost in the past, on a train with my father and the solid-real warmth of his hand.

Ray points to a bench in the center of the walkway.

I freeze when I see the person waiting there for us.

My mother's hair is glossy and golden, swept up, bouffant style, with not a single hair, or bobby pin, out of place. Her cheeks are pink with fresh rouge, her lips a subtle rose. And her clothes are neat and recently pressed.

All normal.

But then ...

An apron is tied around her waist; just two days ago, she'd never have been caught outside the house wearing such a wifey thing. A fat wedding band glints on a thin gold chain around her neck; her left hand flutters up to touch it as if the small matching ring on her finger keeps seeking out its mate.

And her eyes. Oh, her eyes ...

The only things that betray when you wear a mask out into the world.

You can slap a smile onto a face that just wants to frown. You can paint color onto cheeks that are otherwise pale with grief. You can wrap the gown of a strong body around muscles that curl in on themselves.

But eyes? The eyes reflect the heart. And if that breaks, then there is no way to disguise it.

My breath hitches in my throat and I let go of Ray's hand.

I walk. And then I run. And then I am holding tightly to the only other someone who needs to be held together even more than I do.

chapter twenty-one

ray

It looked exactly the same and yet completely different.

The driveway was the same dull gray flagstone, with the same paint stain from where I'd knocked over a tin of whitewash when I was five and Dad taught me to ride without training wheels and my mother had yelled at me.

The same prize petunias grinned up at me from their perfect soil, hardly a petal different from the ones that had crunched at my feet when I was ten and I'd taken a shortcut through the bed and my mother had yelled at me.

Unchanged too was the crisp white trellis, which perfectly matched the crisp white picket fence and the crisp white window shutters. Like bones through broken skin, white wood peeked through green ivy that crept silently up to my second-story bedroom window, the same way Japhy had crept silently up there and tapped on the glass with a fingernail. Back when he had still been Andy. Back when we had planned our lives to be nothing like they were turning out.

I closed my eyes and again I heard the soft clicking of Andy's fingernail on my windowpane, and then I was sucked backwards through time ....

Tick tick tick and blood rushes like a river in my ears as I grin and slide up the frame with a whoosh, and he falls inside, onto me, onto the floor, tangled together. We press our palms to our lips to keep laughter from sinking through my floor to my parents' bedroom beneath.

Not that they would care about what I was doing up here anyway.

"Mind if I come in?" he whispers.

His breath touches my cheek, and it heats every part of me. "What are you doing here?" I ask, wishing I'd worn the short, lacey nightgown instead of the hideous full-length floral thing my grandmother had given me for Christmas three years ago. This was a child's nightgown. And I didn't want him to think of me as a child.

He sits up and pulls something from his shirt pocket. It's a piece of paper, folded three times with sharp lines and black typeface that cuts me into pieces. "It's here. Came this morning."

"No ..." I shake my head and snatch the letter. "Are you sure it's yours? Maybe there's been a mistake?"

"Heather ..." He shakes his head, and then he shrugs. "We knew it was on its way."

No, I think. No, they can't take him away from me. He is mine. Don't they understand that? Mine. And so newly mine that it's just not fair.

"So ... so ... so ..." I can't speak. Can only stammer.

"I don't want to die ..." he whispers.

Pressing my palm to his cheek, I discover it's warm and wet with fear. I want to tell him we have to run. I want to tell him everything will be okay. I want to tell him I'll protect him. But the words do not come.

I frown and fist my hands and open my mouth to tell him to fuck this army, to fuck this Government, to fuck this war; but instead, the words that finally do fall from my tongue and land on the floor between us shock me as much as they do him. "Fuck me?" It's a whisper, as soft as a caress.

His eyes hold me tight. Squeeze me around the chest to the point of pain. Neither one of us moves.

Time holds its breath. Then exhales in a whoosh.

His hand is in my hair, and his lips are on my lips, and his tongue is on my tongue. I fall backwards, and he drapes over me. We do not separate. We will never separate again.

I hear his belt clinking as it slides through the buckle. I hear his zipper clacking down along each interlocking tooth. I hear cotton thread snapping as I tug at the buttons on his shirt. I hear the pores of my palm humming against his smooth, bare chest. And I hear a clear, ringing bell – a piercing, trilling note – at the precise moment he buries himself inside me. It is the one place where he can hide from the world and from the people that hunt him. The one place where he can never be found by anyone but me.

He pushes deeper and I feel skin pulling, ripping free, giving way beneath him. Pain splits me open from the inside out, but I grit my teeth, and I close my eyes to these falling tears, and I gladly accept this sharp discomfort. I will gladly take any pain if it means Andy will be spared.

When he is done, I stroke the back of his neck as he sobs and sobs and sobs, and my hair and skin absorb his tears.

We stay there, on the floor of my bedroom, for the entire night. And, for the entire night, he remains safely hidden by the folds of my flesh. Whenever we wake – returning to the real world and the horrible truth it brings – we nudge and burrow and use each other's bodies until we are lost and hidden and safe once again.

The very next day, we change our names, we pack our bag, and we leave our innocence behind us on the bedroom floor, shivering alongside my virginity and my little girl's nightgown.

I blinked away the memories and returned to now. Four weeks had passed since that night. Four weeks? No way ... An entire lifetime had passed since that night.

Sex, rape, orgies.

Protests, gunshots, marriage.

L.S.D and P.C.P and Y.E.S.

And let's not forget death, death, death.

An entire lifetime, and yet the home in which I had lived out my previous existence hadn't aged a single day. Hadn't changed at all. How was it possible for a structure to appear so strong on the outside, completely belying the destruction that cancers its insides?

I took a deep breath as I stepped up to the front door and raised my hand to knock.

Should I knock? I wondered. Or should I use the spare key I knew was hidden under the third rock from the left in the garden bed?

I held my breath as my knuckles fell against the wood, knocking softly. How many times had I opened this door to see strangers, hesitant and wide-eyed, on this very stoop? A hundred? A million? In all those times, throughout all those years, I never thought the world would flip and I would be the one, hesitant and wide-eyed, on the wrong side of the threshold.

Footsteps thudded heavy and slow on the tile in the entrance hall, and I couldn't tell whose feet they belonged to. I used to be able to discern my mother's steps from my father's, but that had been a whole lifetime ago, after all.

The knob turned and clicked, and the hinges creaked, and the door moved away from me, and I stood face-to-face with eyes full of pain. Eyes exactly like my own.

I expected her to squint at me, to search my face for some flicker of familiarity, because surely, during this last month, I had changed so dramatically that not even my own mother would recognize me. But no. She just crossed her thick forearms over her giant bust and coughed.

"Well, you're back then, are you? I told you it was stupid to go running off with a boy you'd only just met." Her arms remained pretzeled over her chest, a cage over her heart. "What?" Her eyes narrowed at me. "You look like you want something."

Yes, I thought, I want my mother. I want my father. Is that so much to ask?

I thought of Japhy, sitting at home beside Nora and no one else. I wanted to be the one who still had *both* her parents.

I spun and ran down the driveway, staining the flagstones with my tears, and I did not stop when she called after me, her present-day words drowned out by the memory of her screaming at me to never come back again.

chapter twenty-two

japhy

"I just can't believe he's gone." Mom sits on the porch swing, staring down at the very spot on the deck where my dad had taken his last breaths. "We were just sitting out here." She tells me this story for the third time, as if the more she says the words out loud, the easier it will be for her to accept. Or to stop the pain. Or to bring him back. "I only went inside for a minute, just a minute, to get us something to drink. And when I returned he was lying face-down on the floor. Right there. He hadn't made a sound. He wasn't …" Her voice tightens and she pauses, waiting for the grief to release its grip on her vocal cords. "He wasn't breathing. When the paramedics got here they revived him, but I think he was gone even then. It was only his body that was still alive."

She takes a deep breath and looks at me. "He was only thirty-eight."

Her eyes contain the same level of pain as they'd had before; this story, therefore, had no soothing effect, no balm-like qualities. So why does she keep speaking? Why does she keep describing the moment my father died? Does she think I really want to hear this? Because I don't! Or does she want me to live, and relive the moment too, because maybe … just maybe ... if I had been here ... if I had not left home ... then this would not have happened?

"I feel him around me still," she says. "I'll be speaking to him, and I'll look up when he doesn't answer. And then I remember and I just ... I just can't believe he's gone ..." She takes a breath and starts all over again as I stand up and walk into the house.

"Honey?" she calls out.

But I keep walking.

Behind me, the screen door slaps against the frame like a hand striking a cheek.

*

The cemetery is bright with lush, green grass. As we drive slowly by the communal garden beside the packed parking area, a myriad of colorful flowers and trees sway gently as if nodding their condolences. A place so full of death yet so busy with life.

Men in suits and women in veils get out of their cars and head toward us, holding out their sympathy to my mother, and telling her they are so very sorry for her loss, telling her that Michael had been a wonderful man, telling her it wasn't right to lose someone so young, telling her how he always spoke so lovingly about his family.

I wonder if he'd talked about me recently. If he'd told any of these well-dressed strangers how I'd shamed his family name, how I was such a coward, and how he couldn't care less if he never saw me again.

Hunching away from these people and their accusing eyes, I squirm beside the empty hearse, which has no doubt been used to transport the body of my father here today. Peering through the windows at the silver casket racks, I notice a single flower that has come away from its bouquet. I think it's a lily. White petals curl like cupped fingers, beckoning me to rescue it from an otherwise slow death, all alone, where it will wait and wilt and turn brown.

Mom slides her arm through mine then; she flashes me a wide smile as if we are about to go to the theater, rather than attend her husband's funeral. "You ready?"

Why does everyone keep asking me that?

Ray slides an arm around my mother's waist, ready to catch her if she stumbles beneath the weight of that fake smile. She jumps at Ray's gentle touch.

"You all right, Mrs. Mack?"

"It's Nora." She stretches her lips even wider. "And yes, I'm just fine."

I wonder if anyone else notices the way she favors her left side, the way she holds her arm up, protectively, across her chest, or the way she keeps pressing two fingers to her breastbone the way you press a bruise to see if it still hurts. I wonder if anyone else here knows she postponed her mastectomy in order to bury her husband today. And I wonder if she wonders how it will feel to have yet *another* piece of herself taken away.

We file toward the open grave, a long line of black suits and veils and running mascara, to white plastic chairs arranged in a semicircle for the immediate family.

I wish more than anything – more than *anything* – that those chairs were not waiting for my mother and me. I wish more than anything I had not let Ray convince me to leave Liberation in the first place. I wish more than anything my father's words of shame had not been the last words ever spoken between us.

The crowd of mourners parts as we approach. They move aside like thick black curtains, revealing the empty space beside my father's freshly dug plot. The grass there waves and dances in the cool breeze and I kneel to press my palm into the earth. It is as soft and inviting as a blanket. My fingers shake as I trace an invisible headstone and the name that will one day be all that is left of whoever lies here, an eternal neighbor for my dad.

There is a saying that when you shiver, someone has just walked over your grave. But when *you* are the one to walk over that future grave, your body does more than just shiver.

In fact, it does not actually *shiver* at all. Instead, a calmness drops over you, like a veil. A calmness, because now you know exactly how much time you have left to live. Because you have seen your life reduced to just letters and dates. Because, all of a sudden, you understand that you cannot escape your own death.

No matter what.

So what is the damn point of trying?

"Japhy?" Ray kneels beside me and drapes a hot arm around my shoulder.

When I meet her eyes, I feel my calmness-veil shift, like a breeze has just blown over my face.

What is the point of trying to escape death? I think, as I touch her cheek.

She is! I answer myself. *She* is the God damn point. She is the point of everything! I will fight my fate for her; I will win for her; I will live for her. I will not be laid to rest here, an eternal neighbor for my dad.

As I stand – and she stands beside me, gripping my arm – I wipe a hand across my face, removing those gauzy cobwebs of acceptance from my skin.

We walk to the rows of chairs and I sit between my mother and Ray.

I stare at the coffin, unable to convince myself that inside it lies the body of my father. He can't be gone. He has always, *always* been there. How can he just disappear like that? How can someone like him, someone who is so loved and needed, just cease to be? I want to open the coffin lid, to prove to myself that he is really in there, that he is really dead. I grit my teeth and scrunch my eyes closed so tight they hurt. Then I open them again, and stare at the pine box through white stars that flash inside my vision.

A pine box.

In my memory, I hear myself screaming to him. "Would you rather I go to Canada and live safely, or to Nam and come home in a pine box? Or would that be okay with you, since I'll get a military funeral and you can tell everyone that your son died a hero?"

"How *dare* you!" He spat the words at me. "How dare you think I'd care about that over the life of my *son*? I love you, Andrew!" But when he spoke, he kept his eyes fixed to a spot above my head.

I waited, but he refused to meet my stare, and I refused to say those words back to him.

"I am not *you*, Dad," I said. "And this is *not* Korea. You can't fulfill your dreams vicariously through me. It's not *my* fault the army didn't accept you! It's not *my* fault you never got to kill someone!"

And that's when he had finally looked at me. Those big blue eyes, which I had always sought out for comfort, were now cold and hard and unfamiliar. "Go to Canada," he hissed. "And don't *ever* come back here." He closed his eyes and turned away, walking down the hallway with his hand pressing along the wall as if to hold himself up.

Now, as his pine box lowers into the earth, I stand on numb legs and follow my mother's feet to the gaping hole that has swallowed the man I'd always wanted to become. Taking a handful of dirt, I throw it into the grave and hear it rattle against the wooden lid, so loud in this otherwise silent garden. And as those particles of earth fall through my fingertips, I imagine each grain is a word, shouted across the ether.

I love you.

I miss you.

Forgive me.

Please.

"It isn't your fault," Ray whispers to me, and that's when I realize I have spoken out loud.

"Andrew Mack?"

The voice behind me is deep and not unlike my father's.

As I turn and blink the sun out of my eyes, I wonder if perhaps my father heard me after all, if perhaps he is answering me somehow.

"Oh shit!" Ray's voice hitches in the middle as she looks up at the man who has spoken my name, and her fingernails puncture my skin.

chapter twenty-three

ray

No, no, no, no, no ... This can't be happening. Oh, please, no.

"Andrew Michael Mack?" the man asked again.

Japhy just nodded his head.

In the palm of my hand, his fingers slackened. Beside me, his body drooped. He was giving up.

No!

After all the running. After all the fighting. After all the smeared blood, and spilled tears, and lost innocence, Japhy was waving a white flag in this man's smug face.

God damn it, no!

The two men were dressed in ordinary, everyday suits – one brown with a green tie, the other gray with a blue tie. Even though they were not in uniform, you could just tell they were detectives. Maybe it was the way they set their jaws. Or the way they looked down at us. Or the way they smirked with arrogance.

Or maybe it was the guns on their hips.

Whatever. These two assholes believed they were superior to us, and by God they wanted to make sure we believed it too.

Well, screw them.

I stepped in front of Japhy, tried to block out his entire six-foot frame with my own five-foot-two inches of fury. "Do you realize this is a *funeral?*" I shouted.

"Miss, I am Detective Floyd with the F.B.I. and–"

"I don't give a goddamn *who* you are. Have some respect, why don't you! This man's father has just died. Or don't you care?" I laughed then. Couldn't help it. "Of course you don't care; you're just a fucking badge!"

"Ray," Japhy hissed in my ear. "Cool out."

Detective Floyd looked over my head at Japhy. "Andrew Mack, I am placing you under arrest for failure to report for armed forces physical examination on May first."

"Please, Officer?" Nora wobbled forward and held out a hand to the detective as if offering him an invisible bunch of flowers. "Please ... not today. I've just buried my husband. Don't take my son from me as well."

"I'm sorry for your loss, ma'am, I really am."

I snorted.

"But," he continued, "I am required by law to take this man with me right now."

"Law?" I said. "And does the *law* require you to stoop so low as to gatecrash a funeral to catch a draft resister? This country is fucking high!"

"Miss," said the officer, "please stand back."

I stepped toward him. My hands fisted. Forehead wrinkled. "Fuck you."

He grabbed hold of my arm. "I said, please stand back."

"And I said, fuck you." I shrugged his hand away, but he grabbed me again. "Take your hand off me."

But he didn't.

"Take your God damn hands off me!" My voice rose into the high-pitched realm of fear.

His fingers squeezed, dug into the flesh of my bicep. And for a second, this hand did not belong to an officer of the law, but to a frat boy, and his face wavered behind a sudden and traitorous veil of tears.

Beside me, Japhy shook his head as if dislodging a shroud. His shoulders lifted. He stepped forward, and said, "Let go of her fucking arm." His voice was as dry as the handfuls of dirt that had scuffed the top of his father's coffin a hundred lifetimes ago, and then there was a flash of skin and a sound that ripped through my whole body with a shocking jolt of awe, and the asshole cop finally released his hold on me.

There was silence then, the world struck dumb by the *crack* of fist on bone that froze hearts and breaths for miles around.

Detective Floyd's eyes were cool and calm. He still wore a smirk like a fucking badge – although now the corner of his mouth was bleeding where Japhy's punch had landed.

As the two officers took him to his knees and snapped the cuffs around his wrists, Japhy blinked up at me. His eyes wide as plates and full of something that gleamed as bright and warm as the sun.

As the officers wrenched him to his feet and marched him away, he looked back over his shoulder and mouthed two words at me.

The same exact words I wanted to say to him.

I'm sorry.

chapter twenty-four

japhy

So, it seems like nothing gets you out of a criminal charge better than sympathy. The two jerkball detectives dropped the charges of Resisting Arrest and Assaulting an Officer, as I am suffering obvious emotional trauma. So, thanks, Dad, wherever you are. Thank you for dying.

A dead father, however, can *not* get me out of my Failure to Report charge.

Damn.

At least the jerkball detectives are satisfied with the choice I have made. Maybe that's why they let me off? Maybe it had nothing to do with you, Dad.

Whatever.

It's all over red rover. My goose is well and truly cooked. My clean, white feather finally landed in that pool of waiting blood.

The gray cinder blocks of the holding cell bruise my spine and chill my skin through my clothes as I sit on the cement floor. With my forehead on my knees, my pants slowly soak up tears I don't want the old drunk next to me to see.

Why didn't I just stay at Mandala? Ray was right: no one *expected* me to be here. Mom would have been fine without me. She could have gotten through this day, buried her husband of almost twenty years, and then gone home, alone, to an empty house ...

Shit.

And now what? She will have to do that anyway! And she will have to take herself to hospital next week. And get herself home again after surgery. And take care of herself while the gaping hole in her chest scars over and heals.

"Japh?"

I don't lift my face at the sound of Ray's voice.

"Japhy, you can come home now."

"No." My voice is croaky and thick. I shake my head. "I can't."

"Yes," she says. "You've been released into your mom's care. You're free."

Free? I sigh and finally look up.

She takes a step back when she sees my eyes.

"I've been charged with draft evasion, and I have two choices." I stick out my index finger. "Pay a ten-thousand-dollar fine, and serve a five-year jail sentence ..." Then I stick out my middle finger and my hand forms a peace sign. "... Or I can fight." Balling my fingers into a fist, I push up off the floor. "So I'm going to fight."

"What?" Ray steps back again, shakes her head, and then launches forward, grabbing the bars of my cell. "No!"

"I'm going to Nam. That's what he wanted."

"Baby, listen, okay?" She reaches for me and snatches my hand and squeezes. "Your dad died of a heart attack. It wasn't your fault. It wasn't. He had a bad heart. Don't do this to yourself. Don't blame yourself. Don't punish yourself."

"Knew you wouldn't understand." I try to turn, try to pull my hand from hers, but she holds on and will not let me go.

"Okay," she says, "you're right. You *do* have to fight. *We* have to fight, but not Over There. We have to fight *here*. We have to fight against the Establishment, against the war, against what happened to Poppy and Allison. They got the guns, but we got the numbers, right? You always told me that if someone is going to change their beliefs it has to be because *they* want to, not because someone else wants them to. So, you have to fight for what you believe in, not for what *he* wanted you to believe in; otherwise you are fighting for the wrong reasons. For empty beliefs. You have to stay true to yourself, Japhy." She swallows and blinks her beautiful green eyes at me. "You have to stay true to Andy."

Damn her.

"Stay true to the man I love."

I close my eyes, but I still see her pleading face.

"Please don't leave me?" she whispers and I feel her warm lips press against my fingers. The heat of her wraps around my memories, and the cold jail cell morphs into her bedroom. I smell sage incense and clean carpet and lemon laundry detergent. And I smell her. God damn it, I smell her so vividly my eyes water. Patchouli oil and sweat and *woman*. The saltiness of sex is on my tongue, and the softness of her skin is everywhere. And her voice: *Fuck me?* A question, not a statement. An offering. A door to a whole new world.

Jesus.

One year, I tell myself. It's only one year in Nam, and I can come home and put all this behind me forever.

The drunk guy in the corner lifts his head. "If he's leaving you, sweetheart, you can have me!"

I pull my hand from hers and blink up at the ceiling. "I leave tomorrow morning."

"Tomorrow!" Her hand grabs at her throat as if that word chokes the life from her. "No, no, wait, we can still get you out of this. You can apply for Conscientious Objector, or we can work out how to get the money for the fine, or we can have a baby; they won't take you if we start a family ..."

I want so desperately to take her hand, to feel her warmth, to see her smile. I want to say: yes, okay, we'll work this out somehow and I won't go Over There, and everything will be fine. I want so desperately to see pleasure and happiness in her eyes. A glimpse of my future in their clear emerald depths.

But instead, I grit my teeth against all of that, and I laugh and say: "Us? Have a baby? Jeez, that's the *last* the thing we need right now! In fact, a baby is the last thing I want *ever*!"

"You don't want to have a baby with me?" Her voice is small.

"I can't fathom how anyone, in good conscience, can bring a child into a world that is falling to pieces. It's nothing less than cruel. I *refuse* to make a child and then watch it suffer through whatever future is coming for us all, because, if it's anything like our present, it will not be good!"

I turn away from the pain in her eyes. I turn my back on everything that I want. Because, after all, where did chasing my dreams get me anyway? Here, in this fucking jail cell, facing the very thing I had run from in the first place.

"But ..." she whispers, "but ... we could ..."

"No! Fuck's sake, Heather, would you *listen* to me for once!" My voice bounces off the cold stone walls, and she shrinks back as my hard consonants slap her. "I am going to Nam. I *want* to go. I want to fight. Want to shoot some Cong."

Blinking at me, her eyes shining, she raises a hand to her red cheeks. Then her lips peel back from her teeth and she stabs a finger at me through the bars. "What the *fuck* is wrong with you? Can you hear yourself? This is not you, Andy. You don't talk like this, and you certainly don't think like this. I know you better than you know yourself – or at least I used to."

A slimy laugh wriggles out of my throat. "You always do this!" I snarl at her. "You always have to be the one in control. Well, I'm not going to do what you say this time."

She looks so hurt and I want to shut up, just shut the hell up, but I see her weakness and I go right for it. "You told me to leave the country, to go with you to Canada, so I did; and my dad died. You told me to avoid the draft, to run, so I did; and I'm in a holding cell. No more, Heather. I won't do what you tell me anymore."

"So, that's it, then?" she asks. Her words break. "It's over?"

And I shrug.

I shrug, because if I speak I know I will say: yes, okay, we'll work this out somehow, and I won't go Over There, and everything will be fine.

I shrug, because it is the only way I'm able to lie to her.

I shrug, because I am suddenly too terrified to do anything else.

chapter twenty-five

ray

Japhy's cell unlocked with a click and scrape to swing open like a giant birdcage. He flew by me in a whoosh of freezing air, its chill surrounding me in a cloud as cold as truth: Japhy was leaving me.

As I walked away from the holding cells, the man who reeked of whisky called out: "My offer still stands, sweetheart! Just call the station and ask for Joey; I'm a regular here!"

I curled into myself on the short drive home, and when we arrived at the house, I ran to the safety of the guest room, where I'd been sleeping since we arrived. Sliding down with my back pressed against the door, I ignored the footsteps in the hall. Heard him stop at my threshold, sigh, and then walk away again.

Good.

Go.

I can't face you.

You are leaving me.

Pushing my face against my knees, I bit down as hard as I could handle, leaving a trail of dashes and dots on my leg. Morse code. SOS.

During the evening, I snuck out of my room a few times to use the bathroom, and the sweet waft of casseroles brought over by the neighbors almost drew me out into the living room, but no, I just couldn't bear it. I couldn't see his face this way, with his eyes full of goodbye and his lips puckering to say that one word I couldn't afford to hear.

Behind my locked door, my only companion was the night as it slowly fell and drew itself over my crouched form like a blanket. Black and comforting. It waited with me as I listened to the sounds of the house: to Japhy and Nora saying goodnight; to the toilet flushing; to feet stopping at my door and a gentle fingernail's *tap-tap-tap* on the wood; to those bare feet sliding away again.

The darkness wrapped me up as I gasped for breath, choked on a sob, and shook with pain. It covered me in its velvety folds as I stood and unlocked my door. It shielded me from Japhy's eyes as I glided into his room and into his bed and into his arms.

My fingernails ripped him. Scratched him. Welted him. My teeth pinched skin, and when I heard him gasp in my ear, I bit down harder. I pulled his hair and he pulled mine and the blessed sting in my scalp took away my pain. Pressing him down onto the mattress, my tears soothing his wounds, I wrapped my legs around his waist, guiding him, filling my whole body with his heat and his strength.

A low rumble rose in his throat, a wild growl. He lifted me in clawed hands and flipped me onto my back, rising over me like a hungry animal. Now he bit. Now he scratched. Now he drove me deep into the mattress with each thrust. His hips cracked against mine, bruising me, bruising him.

And then with both my hands I brought his face slowly to mine. His lips. His tongue. His breath.

His kiss.

It was too much. Just too damn fucking much.

With the heels of my hands I shoved at his chest and pushed him onto the floor with a crash.

"Fuck you," I whispered, slipping beneath the cloak of darkness again and opening the bedroom door.

"Fuck you too, Ra-a-ay," he whispered back.

The sound of my name wrapped its familiarity around my

shoulders, and a smile pulled at me. But I sank my teeth down until I could taste my own blood and the pain in my lip blurred out everything else.

*

The car ride to the bus station the next morning was silent, but full of so many words that hung in the air and made it too thick to breathe. Words I wanted to say. Words I wanted him to say. Words I wished had never been said in the first place.

And among them, the one word – that one fucking word – waited for me.

Goodbye.

I chewed my bruised bottom lip and stared out the window.

Was goodbye easier to hear when you knew it was coming? Or harder, because you felt the grief even before the person had gone?

Goodbye.

What a lie. There was nothing good about it.

I wanted to reach across the back seat and take Japhy's hand. I wanted to bury my face in his neck. I wanted to dig my nails into his arm and leave half-moon imprints of myself in his skin. I wanted to climb into his breast pocket and curl up there with my whole body pressed against the bass drum of his heart, and I wanted to stay there for the rest of my life where it was warm and safe and smelled of him.

Snap!

A large bug plinked against the windscreen, smearing the glass with its transparent yellow insides. Nora flicked the water on and the wiper blade flip-flapped back and forth like a pendulum until the glass was clean again; there was no trace that poor, unfortunate bug had ever existed in this beautifully cruel world.

Looking over at Japhy, I froze. His eyes were right on me. Why the hell had I not been looking at these eyes as much as possible during the last few hours?

Idiot!

He reached out across the void to take my hand but I grabbed his fingertips and pressed his nails into my arm. He didn't pull away, afraid of hurting me; instead he clenched his hand down on my skin, hard. Until I bled. He carved me. Left a trace of himself in my skin. A piece I could keep, always. Proof that he had existed in this beautifully cruel world.

Just in case.

"Here," he said, pulling a gold band from his ring finger.

"What?" I stared at the ring he held out to me. "Japhy, I can't take that. I know how special it is to you. It was from your grandfather."

"I'm not giving it to you," he said, placing it in my palm and folding my fingers over it. "I'm asking you to hold it for me until I come home."

"And then I'll give it back," I said.

"And then you'll give it back."

I nodded and looked down at the ring in the palm of my hand – the only goodbye I was going to get. But really, wasn't that the best kind?

"Ray?" he whispered. "Will you promise me something?"

"What?"

"Don't write me."

"What? No, that's crazy! Of course I'm going to write!"

He shook his head. "If you write me that you are well and happy and missing me, then I'm going to want to come home all the more. And if you write me that you are struggling and that your life sucks, then I'm going to want to come home all the more. So I think it's better for me to concentrate on not getting shot ..."

I flinched.

He ignored me and continued. "It's better imagining that everything is just as I left it and will still be that way when I get back."

"No." I frowned at him and shook my head. "Absolutely not."

"Please, Ray?" he asked. "It's the only way I think I can get through this year."

My lips formed the silent word *fine*, and I wondered if my agreement really counted if it wasn't spoken aloud.

chapter twenty-six

japhy

I press my forehead against the cool glass of the bus window; the vibrations rattle my brain, stilling all thought. Outside, the two biggest people in my world shrink smaller and smaller as I am carried farther and farther away. Ray's face burrows into the shoulder of my mother, whose body jolts with sobs. And then I turn the corner and they are wiped from my life as quickly as a bug from a windscreen.

Leaning back against the seat, I draw a long breath and hold it trapped in my lungs.

What am I doing?

I must be insane.

Jesus, what the fuck am I doing?

"*Insanity's train is long and slick, with yawning wide open doors.*"

My breath bursts free as the bus driver turns the radio up, and the voice of James Lee Stanley hovers above me like the reassuring hand of a god.

"*Humanity's queued to take the trick and there's always room for one more.*"

What if I pay the fine? Ten thousand dollars isn't really that much money, is it? Surely, Mom could come up with that, right? She already got a loan to pay for the surgery; surely she could get another one? But could she pay that back? Or would the bank take the house?

"*It's a nightmare on wheels and it's moving. Ride a spell. Cyclic hell.*"

Shit.

"*Here we go 'round evolution, a monkey's parade to the wishing well.*"

And five years in jail ... that wouldn't be so bad. At least I'd come out *alive* at the end of it. Probably. I'd only be 23. I could marry Ray, and settle down, and start a family. With no college degree. With no job. With a prison record.

"*Pilate, well, he's a friend of mine. Feeding, bleeding the flames. He'll take me flying anytime I cop to the crucifix fame.*"

Shit.

"*He's a nightmare in drag and he's cruisin'. Ride a spell. Cyclic hell. Here we go 'round evolution.*"

One year, I think. Just one year. I can do this.

"*A monkey's parade to the wishing well.*"

One year and then I'll be free and clear. I could still go to college, still become a man who has the means to provide for his family.

So what if I come home with a bloodstained soul? At least Mom will still have her house, and Ray will still have a worthy husband. Right?

Oh, Ray. Shit, shit, shit.

I wrap my arms around the empty cage of my chest, and I imagine the hard bones and warm flesh beneath my fingers is not mine, but hers.

Why did we waste our time after coming home from the courthouse yesterday? Why did we retreat to our separate corners of the universe? Why did I not clutch on to her fiercely, and stare and stare and stare at her face, and make love to her over and over and over again? Why was I such a dick?

Why did I not even tell her I love her?

Because, I thought, I wouldn't have been able to let her go.

"*Inside of each coach, conductors smile; they won't betray overloads, but prey to a cross of wires while embracing a contact they know.*"

As tears sting my eyes, I cup my hands over my ears and try to block the music, the vocal, the voice of this man who has always soothed me. Always calmed me. Always made me feel like the world was on my side. He'd appear, like an omen, whenever I needed him, as if to reassure me that all is okay. That fate has got my back. That whatever may be happening to me is happening for a reason. Well, no! Not now! I don't want his reassurance this time. Surely, this is not where I'm supposed to go? Surely, fate has fucked up somewhere along the line? Surely, I'm not supposed to be on this fucking insanity train?

"*It's a nightmare on wheels and it's moving. Ride a spell. Cyclical. Here we go 'round evolution ...*"

I hunch forward, my head between my knees, picturing the road through the floor of the bus, blurring as it speeds my life away. As it speeds me away from her.

With my fingers to my lips, I kiss the only piece of Ray I have left – the microscopic particles of her skin beneath my nails – and I sit up straight and stare at my lonely reflection in the glass. Trees whip by behind the ghostly image of this man who looks tired, and maybe a little bit old. Dark bags hang beneath his eyes like bruises from a bleeding soul. Alone in the company of himself, he holds out his hand in greeting. Holds out his hand in wonder. Is this face really mine? I return his stare from the bus window. Not smiling. Not hiding.

I press my forehead against the cool glass of the bus window; the vibrations rattle through my brain, stilling all thought. I let my eyelids close. Let the rumble of the engine lull me to sleep, where terrifying monsters wait to pounce on me with sharp teeth and razor claws. I roll on my back without fear, and expose my belly and throat to these hungry demons. Because with these devils, I am safe. Because I am now safer here in my nightmares than I ever will be in my new hellish reality.

*

Inside the Army Induction building at Fort Gordon, Georgia, the air is hot as Satan's breath on my neck. And all sound echoes around me like taunting laughter as I stand naked, cupping myself with shaking hands in a circle of other naked boys who are all cupping themselves with shaking hands.

We are cattle. Pieces of potential soldier-meat inspected for slaughter.

I cough. I run on the spot. I urinate in a jar.

I am weighed. I am X-rayed. I am pricked.

My skin and ears and eyes are examined with bright lights.

A cold rubber finger probes inside my mouth and up my ass and between my toes.

My brain is picked over for germinating seeds of crazy.

And then I wait for that rubber stamp to slam down. 4F or 1A. Fail or pass. Rotten meat or top-quality soldier-steak.

Maybe the injuries from those frat boys will come back to bless me. Maybe the shrink can see into my head and glimpse the slowly fraying ropes of sanity. Maybe my piss will show up all the substances in my system, because who wants a fucking stoner firing an M-16?

Maybe it will all be okay? Maybe I will go home after all. No Canada, no jail, no fine. Nothing but perfect physical and mental failure.

"Andrew Michael Mack?"

I step forward.

"The Army Induction Board on this day has looked at your *physical* capabilities in relation to serving in the United States Army. We find you able."

Shit.

"The Army Induction Board on this day has looked at your *mental* capabilities in relation to serving in the United States Army. We find you able."

I sigh and my head droops, too full of thoughts and heavy with fear to stay upright.

"The Army Induction Board on this day has looked at your

psychological capabilities in relation to serving in the United States Army. We find you incapable."

Incapable?

"This examination has revealed strong pacifist beliefs, and we feel that these beliefs will interfere with your ability to carry out orders assigned to you in combat."

Holy shit ...

My head is light, a helium balloon, and it rises up and up until I am bumping against the ceiling.

I am free.

I am *free*!

I want to laugh, and cry, and scream.

Incapable!

Never has one word held so much exhilaration.

The rubber stamp rises above my papers and it comes down with an almighty *crash* that ricochets off the naked chests of the all the men in line beside me who are not as incapable as I am.

I can go home. I can go on with my life. I can *live*.

I press my lips flat, squashing the smile that just wants to burst off my face. I hold it in and feel it building inside my chest until my skin stretches so taut with the pressure, I am surely about to burst apart like the grenades that I will never have to throw.

"Andrew Michael Mack?"

Again I nod.

"As stated, the Army Induction Board on this day has looked at you, and at your overall abilities to serve in the United States Army. We have found you psychologically incapable to serve." My papers are lifted in chubby fingers, banged against the table top to get all sheets aligned, and then placed on a stack of papers. The same stack that all the others were placed on.

"Had you *not* attempted to break the law, had you *not* avoided reporting for this examination, you would be free to return home this afternoon. Andrew Michael Mack, as a physically and mentally able citizen of the United States, you will be sworn into the United States Army this afternoon."

His lips peel away from his pointy teeth in a grimace. "Congratulations, soldier."

chapter twenty-seven

ray

I twisted Japhy's gold ring around and around on my thumb. What If I'd done everything differently? Would I still be here, alone, with my face pressed deep into Japhy's pillow?

I sighed and rolled onto my back. Tears trickled and tickled my skin as they slid over my cheekbones and soaked the hair at my temples.

When did this plan go so wrong? We were fine. We were free. We were safe. But then Death smiled seductively, and crooked his finger at us, and we ran straight into his outstretched arms.

Damn.

Damn, damn, damn it all.

I threw the pillow across the room and it knocked into Japhy's stereo. The needle dropped and bounced, and James Lee Stanley cleared his throat and reached out to me. Because he knew. He *always* knew.

"*It's a picture still and gray of a winter's day, and the icy rain hangs heavy on the wire. The sleet has turned to snow and there's miles more to go to the comfort of a warm and friendly fire.*"

He knew what I was going through; his voice, his words, his soul dripped with loss. He knew how it felt for your whole world to freeze solid, while all around you the disrespectful world just kept right on turning with the smooth ease of life.

"*And the frozen sun don't care if you ever make it there. No, the frozen sun won't pay you any mind. Behind those clouds of gray, he just looks the other way. Doesn't even know he's leaving you behind.*"

Yeah, I thought. My sun had definitely left me behind.

"*And that Jericho wind is howling again.*"

I wanted to howl. Oh man, I wanted it so bad.

"*Howling like a thousand times before.*"

I wanted to throw my head back and cry and let my pain echo around the world.

"*And it won't leave you alone 'til it chills you to the bone, and you're lost there on the cold side of the door.*"

Why? I asked James. No, not why; how? How does life thaw out, and go on, at a time like this?

"*Nobody knows, when that cold wind blows, how it finds its way so deep inside your heart. And it freezes all your dreams, they're so brittle that it seems the slightest moon could shatter them apart. When that Jericho wind comes wailing again and you're walking, every step can seem a mile.*"

I wish I could go back. I wish I could do it all over again.

"*With your fingers going numb, as you hold out your thumb by that icy highway sign, glacial in denial.*"

I wish I was at the beginning again, with Japhy's shadow beside mine in the dirt as we thumbed for cars, and shivered together through the night.

"*They say don't look back. They say don't look down. They say look both ways when you cross.*"

The door squeaked open.

"*Who cares what they say when you're holding the coins that they toss.*"

The bed heaved as Nora sat on the edge and stroked my hair. "Heather, honey, are you okay?"

"I'm fine," I said, and my face contorted.

What is it about the question: Are you okay? Before you answer, you are fine, but as soon as you speak the words, I'm fine, you lose hold of every part of yourself. You crack and crumble beneath your very fingers, and fall in a heap at your own feet.

Maybe it's the lie that unravels you. The lie: I'm fine. You can say it to anyone out loud, but never to yourself. Because if you try, the truth goes ape at you, and it rips you into pieces.

"Oh, sweetheart." Nora's thawing arms gathered me and fitted me back together. "I know this is hard. Trust me," she laughed dryly. "I know. But hey." She leaned back. "You've got me."

But she was not the one I needed.

"Can I tell you a story?" she asked. "On my first date with Michael, a Friday night, he arrived on the doorstep with a bouquet of seven daylilies," Nora smiled. "One for each day of the week, he told me. They were the most beautiful flowers I'd ever seen. I put them in my mother's best crystal vase in my bedroom, and I watched them slowly die, flower by flower. I was devastated! I remember thinking that they were symbolic somehow, and that this wonderful man I'd just met, and the romance that was only just beginning, would die out just as easily and quickly as those seven flowers. My heart broke as I threw those wilted, dead flowers into the trash the following Friday. But then, that night, Michael came around again with a new bunch of seven more. Every Friday after that, he would buy me a bunch of seven daylilies. Every single Friday for twenty years. He never missed one. Until last week. And this morning, I had to throw away the last bouquet he ever bought me. I thought it would make me sad. I thought I would feel his loss then, more than ever. But you know what?" She shrugged. "I felt his presence and his love more at that moment than I ever have before. The flowers didn't mean anything. They never did, not really. It is the love that matters. The love that blooms within us will never wilt, or drop its leaves, or die."

My stomach flip-flopped around like a fish on a wooden pier. I was shaky and dizzy. My head ached from crying and I was exhausted from feeling exhausted. Why was she telling me this? Did she think it would make me feel better? What a horribly depressing story! I mean, Christ! I don't want to hold on to the love that blooms within me! Screw that. I want to hold on to Japhy. I want to feel his skin, his muscle, his tangibility. I want him here. I want him safe. I want him now.

"I made you some sandwiches," said Nora as she combed my hair with her fingers.

I groaned and rolled my head from side to side.

"Don't be silly now; you have to eat something. You've hardly eaten anything over the last few days, and you've had nothing at all today. It's a wonder you aren't fading away."

Maybe she's right, I thought. I feel empty. Hollow. Missing half of myself. Maybe food will help to fill that void? Salvation in a sandwich?

"It's peanut butter and pickles. Your favorite, right?"

"How did you know?"

She smiled. "Andy mentioned something about it once. He was amazed that someone so beautiful could ingest something so disgusting."

"He said that?"

"He said it at the kitchen table." Nora grinned. "While he made himself eat an entire pickle and peanut butter sandwich."

"He never told me that!"

"I remember, he said, 'Mom, I want to know everything about this girl. I want to experience all of her experiences.' And that's the moment I realized I would have to share my little boy with another woman."

"He wasn't your little boy anymore, huh?"

"Oh, Heather." Nora shook her head. "When you're a mother, you'll realize just how absurd that notion is." Pressing the plate in my hands, she kissed my forehead. "Thank you for being here with me. It's nice to have some company. Your parents don't mind, do they?"

"Nope." I took a bite of the bread. My parents didn't know I was even here; story of my life, really.

The smooth peanut butter stuck to the roof of my mouth. The texture made me gag. At the sourness of the pickles, my salivary glands freaked out and filled my mouth with spit.

Why did this taste so different to normal?

Does grief lace even your taste buds with bitterness?

Just chew and swallow, I told myself. Just one bite. Chew and swallow. Get it down.

I felt the mouthful slide down my dry throat. Felt it land in the empty cavern of my gut. Felt the mushed-up ball of bread, peanuts, and pickles sit in my stomach like a heavy, wet sack until my body rejected it.

Rolling from Nora's embrace, I ran to the bathroom with my hand over my mouth.

My stomach clenched like the hand of an invisible giant, squeezing out the food.

Nora followed, held my hair away from my face with one hand, and rubbed my back with the other, mumbling soothing words, and I thought: So, this is what a mother does?

When I had purged so much there was nothing left inside me but a dry skeleton, Nora handed me a wet towel.

I pressed the cool material against my face and sobbed.

"I'm sorry, honey; I shouldn't have forced that food on you. I'm just worried about you, you know?" she said. "You're getting yourself too worked up."

Her husband of twenty years had just died. Her only son had been whisked away to prepare for a war from which he might not return. She was scheduled to undergo surgery to remove her left breast, which was growing cancer like an incubator. But instead of grieving over her lost spouse, and worrying about her child, or her own health, she fussed over *me*. Me!

Selfless, just like her son.

She handed me a glass of water, which I took gratefully and gulped down in between sobs and gasps for air. But as soon as the water reached the pit of my stomach, it bounced and came straight back up, pouring cold and thin out of my throat as I curled back over the toilet bowl.

"Take a couple of deep breaths," Nora said. "Think about Andy. That'll make you feel better."

I groaned and leaned my cheek against the cold plastic seat and prayed for this all to be over. I begged. I offered to give up everything I had. All my past. All my dreams. All my memories of him. Just to have the real thing back by my side.

And, from down the hallway, James's ghostly voice whispered to me: "*As memories return you've got just the walls to burn to keep you warm here on the cold side of the door ...*"

My memories are torture, I thought as I hocked and spat. And yet, James Lee Stanley was right, was always right: my memories were the only things providing warmth.

After they'd chilled me to the bone in the first place.

chapter twenty-eight

japhy

Thirteen stripes of red. Thirteen stripes of white. Fifty white stars on a blue square. When you look at it this way, when you break it down into these individual components, it's all just a whole bunch of geometry shoved side by side. Rectangles and stars and a square, all forced together whether they chose to be there or not. Forced to come together for the greater good; to form the symbol of freedom and bravery and glory.

I did a project on the American flag in the eighth grade. I know the white symbolizes purity and innocence; the red symbolizes valor and bravery; the blue symbolizes tenacity and justice.

Justice?

Is it *just* to enlist men against their will and force guns into their hands, and make them kill other men who had guns forced into their hands, too?

Is it *just* to punish those men who refused to take the guns? Who refused to kill?

Justice?

Perhaps this flag should stand for hypocrisy.

I stare up at the brass pole on which the American flag hangs limp, and I feel the marionette strings tighten around my wrist; my arm lifts up and my fingers press to my forehead in salute.

An officer steps forward. On his barrel chest, little gold medals gleam and wink at the place where his heart should be. "When I say your name," he calls, "please step forward and repeat the oath."

Boy after boy in the line beside me steps forward and declares allegiance to this country and this army and this fucking war. And with each boy after boy, it draws closer to being my turn.

What if I refuse to speak? Can I go home?

What if I lie? Will they know? Will they care?

Atop the flagpole perches a brass eagle. Its clawed beak shines in the bright lights. Its eyes flash at me.

Say the words, it squawks. Become one of us. Say the words.

"Andrew Michael Mack!"

I sigh. I step forward. I open my mouth.

And I say them. I say the words.

"I, Andrew Michael Mack, do solemnly swear that I will support and defend the Constitution of the United States against all enemies, foreign and domestic; that I will bear true faith and allegiance to the same; and that I will obey the orders of the President of the United States and the orders of the officers appointed over me, according to regulations and the Uniform Code of Military Justice. So help me, God."

There. I've said it. It is out there, out in the universe. And, so help me, God, I feel lighter somehow. As if the burden of responsibility for any deaths I may cause has been taken off my shoulders; I no longer have choices, and therefore, I will no longer suffer any consequence that any of my future actions may cause.

I may be caged, but I feel freer than ever.

I take a breath and my feet rise off the floor.

Jesus, I think. I *like* this feeling of weightlessness.

Oh ... so help me, God. Please, please, please help me.

*

Layer by layer, my skin is peeled from my bones, leaving a bare skeleton standing in a line of fifty other skeletons, all waiting to be dressed in their new outer coverings.

My familiar folds of blue denim, paisley print cotton and high-top sneakers are stuffed into a bag stamped with the words ANDREW MICHAEL MACK: the name of the person to whom those clothes had belonged.

Dressed now in army greens and big, shiny boots, I shuffle into a room lined with mirrors and a row of plastic chairs.

The electric razor buzzes in my ear like a poisonous wasp as my head is stripped of all my remaining Japhyness and the chill of the air on my naked scalp burns like cleansing fire. I close my eyes to the man who pleads at me from the mirror.

What do you want me to do? I say to him. I can't help you now; I'm sorry.

Rising from the chair like a phoenix, my severed hair lapping at my heels, I leave Japhy behind to be swept up off the floor with a broom and dustpan.

Out in the bright light of day, with silver dog tags jingling against my chest, I wonder, who the hell am I now?

Not Japhy. Not Andy. Not me.

I am a number in the system.

I am 13-9-19-50.

Pleased to meet you.

*

The definition of survival is continuing to exist in spite of an accident or difficulty.

So. I breathe.

No big deal, right? I can survive this.

I will survive this!

At the foot of a white, metal, unmade bed, I stand, I exist, I survive.

Beside me, the other guys look terrified to be standing in

these army barracks, at the feet of these unmade beds, wearing greens and black boots and bald heads under fab new green hats.

Yeah, some of them chose this. Some of them proudly enlisted. Some of them look forward to what awaits us. But all of us, the enlisted and the drafted, are scared fucking shitless.

Gritting my teeth, I unfold my blankets and sheets and make sharp hospital corners and pull the covers tight at perfect right angles, and the other boys are still just standing there, staring at the naked stripes on their mattresses.

Yes, I can get through this.

I can survive this.

The pale guy beside me hugs his blankets to his chest like a shield.

"You all right, man?" I ask him.

He turns his head and frowns at my neatly made bed, as if unable to comprehend how mine looks so different to his. "I'm not supposed to be here!" he whispers, taking a step closer. "This wasn't supposed to happen." And his eyes glimmer and shine as he blinks at me. "I'm not supposed to be here."

"Can I give you a hand with that?" I take the bedding from him and open the sheet out with a crisp *snap*. It hangs in the air and then falls slowly like a clean, white feather.

"I'm Timothy." He shoves his hands in his pockets as the sheet lands on the mattress with a sigh.

"I'm ..." I pause.

Who am I now?

I remember the face of the bald-headed stranger in the mirror. As I shove Timothy's pillow into its starched case, I think about another definition of survival: to remain alive longer than someone else. To persist. To succeed. To endure.

To never give up.

So, who am I?

Well, I am the one who will never give up.

No matter what they take from me, I will never fucking give up.

I run a hand over my bald head and smile. "I am Japhy. Pleased to meet you."

*

The rest of my Induction Week as a soldier of the United States Army is edged in a white glow that ebbs and flows at the corners of my vision. As if, at any moment, I will faint dead away. As if this is all, in fact, just a dream as insubstantial as the gauzy threads of reality that float and sway in my peripheral vision. As if I am not really here at all.

Day after day after day, I make small talk with Timothy, but as soon as words are spoken between us, they evaporate and I have no idea what either of us just said. I notice the look of confused concentration on his face too, and on the faces of other boys who introduce themselves and then watch their words disappear instantly into the ether.

Following a pair of shiny boots into the mess hall, I sit and fork a mound of mash potato around on my tray during the six-or-so minutes we have in which to stuff the food down before the next platoon comes through for their six-or-so minutes. Maybe I eat. Who the hell cares?

With food in their stomachs, some of the other cats in my barracks snap out of their dazes. Conversations are handed out from one person to the next, to the next.

"Where are you from?"

"Wasn't the food terrible?"

"Are you a Jets fan?"

"When do we get our guns?"

I crawl into bed, pull exhaustion over my head, and wait for blessed unconsciousness to rescue me from this place.

One week down. Only eight more to go.

And if I *do* survive all eight weeks of Basic Training, and then the next eight weeks of Advanced Individual Training, then I can spend another fifty-two weeks dodging bullets in Nam.

So. One week down, sixty-eight to go. I can do this.

As the lights blink out, a slow, wailing bugle song drifts through the camp.

Ba-baaah.

Each note is as heavy as a human soul, and thick with grief, and sacrifice, and reverence, and gratitude, and patriotism.

Ba-baaah.

I know this song; it played at my grandfather's funeral. By the final note every eye in the cemetery that day had been wet, as if this song alone had the power to bestow upon every listener the truth of their own flimsy mortality.

Baaah-ba ba-baaah-baaah.

And *this* is the song the army chooses to play for us to signal lights out? This death song? This funeral dirge? So, as we all drift away into dreams, we can imagine the day when these wailing bugle notes will hover over the hanging heads of our grieving loved ones.

Ba-baaah.

Welcome to the United States Army: goodnight, sweet dreams, and don't forget that this may very well kill you. But, sleep tight, and don't let the bedbugs bite.

Ba-baaah.

The song ends and the silence grabs me by the throat. Darkness shields every one of us in a blanket of anonymity. I listen to the deep sighs of relief that draw out into something much deeper, and I wonder if it is Timothy crying into his pillow beside me, or if it is, in fact, just me.

*

It is Saturday, May 30, just two days until I begin training to become a soldier who will be shipped over to a war in a meagre 16 weeks' time. We stand before the flagpole and watch as the American flag is raised briskly to the top. But before it has time to flap and snap proudly in the wind, it is lowered again, to half-mast.

I cannot look away.

A voice speaks into a microphone, the words amplified and echoing a second later.

"With an eloquence uniquely its own among our national observances, Memorial Day conveys for us the message of the price and pain of freedom. The fallen heroes we honor on this occasion rest in nearly every corner of our nation and world. And their silence testifies that there were Americans in every crisis of our history who placed their country above themselves and their own safety and comfort.

"We remember their spirit as the timeless one through which our freedoms have endured these nearly two centuries of our nationhood. From these heroes' faith, from their example, we gain strength, courage, and inspiration to continue to build an even better nation and society. This is an inspiration for human decency and must be our greatest heritage from them.

"Memorial Day, coming in the spring as it does, and with its emphasis on flowers, has strong ties with nature's process of renewal. And the very season, with its expression of hope, also would seem to suggest that mankind renew its eternal search for peace with freedom and the guarantee of human dignity. When the quest is successful, the men and women, like those whom we honor in this hallowed moment, will no longer need to know the total hell of war.

"As a speaker for the American Legion on this occasion, I want to return to an earlier thought in this talk. That thought is that, from these heroes' demonstration of faith in America, we gain the strength, the courage, and the inspiration to continue to build an even better nation and society. America belongs to each of us, to you and me. We share her failures, her triumphs, and her responsibilities. We share individual responsibility to make America all we want and hope for her to be. There can be no delegation of that responsibility. Our hopes and our aims for America can be broad or dangerously narrow. Above all, and no matter what our age, let us make America's business our business, and her interests our interests.

"And here each of us must utter a prayer that God grant us the continued vision ... the wisdom ... to see always the big picture, the grand and decent scheme of things. Let us strive always for the ideal, not the selfish comfort of the moment. Let this resolve begin in the minds and hearts of young, as well as older Americans, on this day of tribute to those who found America worthy of their deepest possible expression of faith: their lives.

"Thank you for you kind attention. It was a pleasure to represent The American Legion before you."

As his words end and his voice melts from the bright sunshine that beats down on our shoulders and caps, I finally turn my gaze away from the square cloth of stripes and stars for which so many had fought and died. Had died for peace. For freedom. For the big picture.

I watch this man as he steps down off the podium and salutes the flag, and I think how easy it must be for him to come out here and talk about how we cannot delegate responsibility. Yet he will probably go home this evening to his lovely wife and his messy children. He will sigh and stack his fat, slippered feet up on the coffee table, cluck his tongue at the nightly news and the horrific images that are being projected from South East Asia, and he will feel content, and perhaps even satisfied, that he is doing his part for peace and freedom and, what had he said? The guarantee of human dignity? Jesus Christ. And what is his contribution to all this? A speech. A fucking Memorial Day speech! Well, fuck him. He isn't the one who has been delegated the responsibility to go to Nam and shoot other human beings through their beating hearts. He isn't the one who is placing his country above his own safety and comfort. If it had been *his* freedom of choice that was snatched away during the draft lottery, I bet that fucking speech of his would have been very different.

The flag makes its way slowly back up to the top of the pole again, and I wonder if, next Memorial Day, it will be *my* memory that is held in the bowed heads of every man, woman, and child in this fair country. Will I be one of the fallen heroes?

No.

Because isn't a hero someone who faces their own death willingly and without fear?

june

Tin soldiers and Nixon coming.
We're finally on our own.
This summer I hear the drumming.
Four dead in Ohio.

~ Neil Young, Ohio

chapter twenty-nine

ray

The edges of the curtains had only just started to glow with the first rays of a summer morning when the crash and tinkle of smashing glass jolted me into a sitting position on Japhy's bed.

"Nora?" I opened the bedroom door and flinched as another crash, and then another, bounced off the hallway walls.

Walking softly along the corridor, I froze at the kitchen doorway.

The floor was strewn with packages of mincemeat, a frozen leg of lamb, a pack of bacon rashers. A carton of eggs lay on its side, yolk oozing from one cracked shell. Three packets of unopened American cheese were stacked one atop the next like a child's building blocks, and I pressed a hand to my mouth as Nora kicked them across the room and they thudded against the cupboard doors.

In the center of the kitchen sat the trashcan, filled with everything from the pantry and fridge, including three full milk bottles that had shattered on impact and soaked into all the cardboard boxes beneath.

From the first time I set foot in this house, this kitchen had been a haven for me; such a contrast to my own parents' sterile house that had no heart. This room was always warm, you could feel the life thudding through it as soon as you walked in the door. Its orange countertops as bright as the dawn sky, the yellow tiles on the walls threaded with daisies, the brown diamond-pattern linoleum worn down by a lifetime of growing feet. And a vase of fresh lilies. Always lilies. Now ...

"Nora?" I squeaked.

She turned to me and flashed a toothy smile. "Oh great! You're just in time!" Scooping up all the meat and dairy that littered the floor, Nora pressed them down into the overflowing bin, which she grunted up into her arms. "Follow me!"

Grabbing one side of the garbage can, I was led out the back door, into the dawn light, to a corner of the yard where a shovel leaned against the fence.

"What's going on?" I asked, setting the bin down. "Are you all right?"

"There will be no more death!" she said, stabbing the blade of the shovel into the ground again and again and again. "No more death." *Stab.* "In my house." *Stab.* "Thank you very much!" Her face reddened with effort and her perfect hair fell, strand by sweaty strand, down her back as the hole grew wide as a grave.

"There!" Letting the shovel fall to the grass, Nora clapped her hands together.

Item by item, she snatched food from the bin and dropped it into the hole. The lamb, the beef, the bacon. Eggs and cheese. Packets of cake mix. White sugar.

"No more death?" I asked her. "What does that mean?"

"It means," she said, "my husband had a heart attack. And I have cancer. And my son is going to war. So I got to thinking: Why did these things happen? Karma, that's why! Karma! Ouch!" She snatched her hand away from the trash and hugged it to her chest. Blood ran in a thin stream from her palm, down her arm, to drip off her bent elbow. "Shit. See?" And then she turned and ran back into the house.

Like a horror version of *Hansel and Gretel*, I followed the trail of blood droplets to the house, and when I got to the back door my hand hovered over the handle. Inside was a sound even worse and more surprising than the smashing of glass had been.

Wet sobs. They hitched and gurgled, drowning in the very grief they tried to flush out. Pain so intense it formed like condensation in my own throat.

Nora rocked on the kitchen floor, with her knees drawn to her chest, her arms around her legs. Her shoulders shook so violently they rattled the whole house until the walls around me – walls I had thought to be so solid – started to crumble and fall to pieces on the floor.

When I touched a hand to her arm, she stilled, and then looked up slowly. Her eyes were stormy oceans of sadness, but she smiled through the gray clouds like golden beams of sunlight. "Oh, Heather. I'm sorry."

"What for?"

"You don't need to see me this way," she said.

"Are you kidding? Of course I do!" I sat beside her and drew my own knees up for a hug. "It means you are human after all."

"Human?" she mumbled, touching a finger to her left breast. "You mean, *mortal*."

Then she sniffed, stood and walked down the hallway with her head high and shoulders back. Her bedroom door closed as softly as a sigh, and soon I heard her shower running.

I imagined her in there: head bowed, staring at a body that would not look the same tonight as it did now. No wonder she had just lost her mind.

How would it feel to dry that breast for the last time; to cup it with a bra for the last time; to see a symmetrical body in the mirror for the very last time?

And what on earth could I possibly say to this woman that would make this day less terrible?

It was seven AM. We had to be at the hospital in one hour. In two hours, the muscle and fat that swelled above Nora's heart would be gone. A part of her that her husband had surely stroked and kissed a million times during their relationship. A part of her that had nourished and comforted her suckling son.

A part of her that had become evil and malicious and needed to be exorcised.

Where does dead tissue go? I wondered, as I picked my way through the kitchen and switched on the percolator. Does it go to the same place as our soul? Would Michael be waiting with tingling fingers to hold this small, ethereal piece of his wife, to slip it into his ghostly pocket like an amulet to get him by until the day Nora finally leaves this world and enters his completely?

I opened a new trash bag and began to clean up. The only things left intact were the items Nora had purchased yesterday: a year's supply of oatmeal; four huge boxes of fruit and vegetables; organic coffee; and the biggest juicing machine I'd ever seen in my life. When she'd walked into the house, weighed down with all this stuff, I'd thought nothing of it. I'd thought she was into buying bulk. But it turned out she was just having a good old-fashioned breakdown.

Steam rose as the coffee machine hissed and spat and dribbled brown liquid into the pot. The smell of the ridiculously expensive organic coffee was bitter; it filled the whole room, the whole house, surely the whole street, and stuck to the back of my throat like mud. I swallowed but couldn't dislodge it. And then the familiar rolling of nausea hit me.

Hunching over the kitchen sink, I heaved and heaved, but nothing came up. I wiped at my watering eyes and splashed water on my face.

"Are you still not well?" Wrapped in her husband's bathrobe, Nora leaned against the doorframe, watching me with her head to the side.

"I'm fine," I groaned. "How are *you* feeling? About ... you know ... later?"

"If you mean the surgery?" Nora waved a hand in the air. "That's canceled."

"It's *what?*" I stood up straighter.

"Canceled." Nora lifted the glass coffee percolator and smelled it. "Ah. That's *good*." She didn't pour it into a mug to drink; instead she poured it into a small pot and set it on the stove to boil. "I'm so jealous of my colon right now."

"What do you mean, the surgery is canceled?"

"I mean it's no longer going ahead." She shrugged. "Oatmeal?"

"What? No, I don't want oatmeal. Why have you canceled?"

"Because it's not necessary." Nora took a second pot from under the cupboard and scooped in some grain from the ginormous bag of oatmeal. "The major flaw in today's medical society," said Nora, taking out some apples, carrots, and a handful of kale, "is that it only treats the *symptoms* of a disease. 'Oh, you got cancer, Mrs. Mack? No problems, we'll cut that nastiness right out of there. And, just to make sure we got it all, we'll pump your body full of deadly chemicals to kill any leftover nasties and make all your hair fall out!' It's just unnecessary when the human body is quite capable of healing itself by treating the *cause* of the disease with a plant-based, organic diet, natural supplements, coffee enemas, and," she said, flicking a switch on the monstrous juicing machine that took up almost all the bench space beside the stovetop, "hourly glasses of raw juice."

"Wait." I gaped at her. "Coffee *what?*"

"Coffee enemas," she said, as if we were discussing the loveliness of the weather this morning. "Coffee taken rectally," she explained, "reduces toxins from the liver."

So ..." I frowned and shook my head. "You are planning on putting that ridiculously expensive coffee up your ... uh ..."

"Ass?" She smiled. "Well, of course. I wouldn't put a *cheap* brand up there, now, would I?" Taking my hand, she led me around the counter to the bar stools. "You look like you're about to fall down. Sit. I'll make you some breakfast."

"No, I don't want to eat."

"Just sit, will you!"

As I climbed onto a stool, I had a sudden memory of Japhy doing this exact thing every day after he picked me up from school: we'd sat at this bench eating Nora's muffins while I flicked through the latest *Rolling Stone* and Japhy quizzed me for an upcoming math test. But that had been a whole different life.

"So, what's the deal with all these funny names y'all are using?" Nora asked as she stirred water through the pot of oatmeal over a low flame. "Ray and Japhy. And these people you mentioned: Leaf and Poppy. I don't get it."

"Uh ..." I shook my head. "When you drop out, you are kind of re-born, so you re-name yourself. But I still don't understand why you've canceled the ..."

"Drop out?" she said. "What's that mean?"

"You drop out of the mold that society wants you to live in. Nora, why have you canceled the surgery? I mean, okay, sure, I can dig that you want to be healthy and all, but aren't you being a little bit ..." I shrugged. "Insane!"

She faced me then, and her eyes searched mine, dug around inside my brain for some kind of answer. "I don't know who I'm supposed to *be* now. I guess I was always defined by what I was, not who I was. A housewife, not a person. But what am I *now*? A widow with cancer." A single tear slid down her cheek and she smiled sadly. "I don't want to be defined by that."

"No," I said, reaching over the counter and taking her hand. "You're a *mother* and a *survivor*."

"Yes." Nora nodded. "That's exactly right."

Thank God, I thought. "So, you'll have the surgery?"

"Heather, I've lost my husband. I may lose my son." She tapped the wooden spoon twice against the side of the pan and the chimes rang through the empty house. "I am in charge of my own destiny now. And no one will be taking another piece of me away."

chapter thirty

japhy

Music blares through my dreams. A bugle horn. Tinny and screeching.

I was eleven years old at the racetrack with my father. The grass flicked in the breeze, bright green and spongy beneath my shoes. A line of rippling thoroughbreds with bright, colorful jockeys atop them lined up at the starting gate, snorting and pawing the ground, and all the while that damn bugle kept right on screeching.

My father smiled down at me, and then he screams, "Wake the fuck up!"

The horses, and the track, and my father vanish in a sudden flash of white, and I'm covered in sweat and florescent lights.

"Morning, girls!"

Clang! Clang!

I squint into the brightness. A broad-shouldered man in a hat like a park ranger's bangs something metal against the foot of our beds as he struts down the center of the room.

Clang! Clang!

The sound hangs in the air above us like a threat.

Behind him, the naked windows are still black with unconsciousness, the same color as this man's skin. He stops and turns, slowly, in a full circle, smiling into the silence as we all sit up in our beds and rub our eyes and blink at him.

"What the fuck," he screams, "are you all doing? Get out of those fucking beds! Get to your fucking feet! Form a fucking line! NOW! NOW! Fucking now!"

CLANG! CLANG! CLANG! CLANG!

Shit.

I scrabble off the bed and stand in my boxers and socks in a line beside all the other sleep-swaying boys. The air rings with the metallic note of fear and throbs with the bass drum beats of our hearts.

"My name," says the man, "is Sergeant Ash. And you will call me Drill Sergeant." *CLANG!* "Is that clear?"

"Yes, Drill Sergeant!" we say.

"I can't fucking hear you!" *CLANG! CLANG! CLANG!*

"YES, DRILL SERGEANT!"

He nods. "It is my unfortunate job to take you sorry sons-of-bitches and teach you exactly how NOT to get fucking KILLED! You will listen to my every word. You will obey my every word. And you will damn well NOT get yourselves fucking KILLED! Clear?"

"YES, DRILL SERGEANT!"

"All right." His dark lips peel back, revealing bright pink gums. "Let the fucking fun begin."

*

These boots are so damn heavy. Every lift and fall burns up my calves and into my thighs like an electric shock.

Left, right, left, right.

I say the words in my head. Meditate on the sounds they make as they bounce off the glowing, red pain centers in my brain.

Left, right.

The sun is all the way up now and it sears hot lips against my face and hands and neck.

Left, right.

My gigantic boots scale up and over a brick wall higher than my own head. My boots left-right-left through a pathway of car tires, cobblestoned together in a zigzag. They stand solid and fixed as I squat, stand, squat, and then star-jump, and push-up, and wheeze, and left-right-fucking-left, and I start the course all over a-God-damned-gain.

Ahead of me, someone goes down in a pile of dust and army greens.

As I left-right-left closer, I see it is Timothy. He sprawls, face in the dirt, with the toe of his boot caught in the lip of the last tire, while the other guys weave through the course and jump over the crumpled body. He cowers beneath the flying boots that land so close to his face.

Drill Sergeant Ash bends double, screaming in Timothy's face to get up, get up, get the fuck up, Private, and Timothy's lip trembles as he ducks under another pair of muddy black boots, and rolls and struggles to free himself.

I slow down as my big heavy boots bounce me from tire to tire, and when I finally reach Timothy, I stop.

"What the fuck are you doing, Private?" Ash shouts at me. "Move! Move! Move!"

But I don't move move move.

I crouch and grab Timothy's foot and wrench it free.

He scrabbles like a crab, through the mud, away from the ferocity of Ash's words, and then he is up, and nodding a thank you, and getting as far away as he can.

Standing still, the muscles in my legs tick, and my lungs melt from the hot speed of my breaths. Ash narrows his eyes at me as I blow and huff and gasp.

"Get down, Private!" he screams.

No, I think. Oh, please God, no. I can't ... I just can't.

"Get the fuck down in this mud and push up until I tell you to stop!"

"Yes, Drill Sergeant!"

I fall, landing on my hands, and gritting my teeth as I straighten and bend and straighten my arms, and cry out with effort.

"Maybe next time," he shouts right down in my ear, "you

will listen when I give you an order! You will obey when I give you an order!"

"Yes, sir!"

"Do *not* call me, sir! I am *not* an officer! I am a drill sergeant and I have to work for a living!"

"Yes, Drill Sergeant!"

"What is your name, Private?"

"Andrew Mack, Drill Sergeant!"

"Fall in!" He calls, and the thudding of boots on the ground grows loud around me. "All of you assholes can drop too!"

I hear grunts and hands hitting dirt as they all rise and fall in time with me. "Why the fuck," he screams as he walks the line, "did no one else stop to help Private Murdoch? Why was Private Mack the only one whose balls were big enough to go against me, and help a fallen soldier?" His boots stop at my face. So shiny I can see my bright red skin reflected in their curves. "Is it because these two have some kind of sweetheart romance going on?"

A rattle of laughter rasps along the line.

"No, it's not! It's because Private Mack here has something that I will be forcing down all your throats over the coming weeks. I will rape your mouths with it until you swallow so much that your skin bulges. He has shown *selfless service*. And *that* is what it takes to be a fucking soldier! Private Mack, at ease! The rest of you, drop!"

My chest thuds to the earth and I lie there, gasping for air, while all around me I hear whimpers and groans and a breath of my name uttered in anger.

Turning my face to the left, I see glaring dark eyes and snarling lips. They call him Lion. Judging by the ferocity in his gaze, it's a fitting name.

I mouth the word *sorry* to him.

He narrows his eyes. "You will be," he spits.

"The rest of you sons-of-bitches," shouts Ash, as his boots move away from me, "will learn, right now, the biggest rule of combat: never leave a brother behind!"

"Fuck you, Mack," hisses Lion as he pushes his body weight off the ground. "You didn't do nothin' special." He comes down again, and then up. "You," down-up, "will pay," down-up, "for this."

*

I groan as hot water loosens my muscles like fingers through tangled hair.

Squeezing my eyes shut, I imagine I am in the shower at home, or at Mandala, or anywhere else besides this drafty bathroom where five other guys stand naked and foamy beside me. I imagine I'm with Ray, instead of all these men. That this soapy water caresses down along the curves of her body and in between her legs, and perhaps she is close enough that I can reach out and touch ...

And then I stop and remind myself that I *am* in fact in a room full of showering men and, Jesus Christ, I can't be thinking about her wet, naked, slippery body right now.

"How'd you go today?"

"I survived," I say. Opening my eyes, I see a mud-caked Timothy turning on the faucet next to me.

His eyes drop and I pivot away, hoping he hadn't noticed my shrinking hard-on.

"What about you?" I ask.

He shakes his head. "It killed me. I don't know how I'm going to get through this!" Reaching for the soap, he rubs his face white.

"I just keep thinking of the person I love," I say. "I just keep thinking of Ray, waiting for me at home."

"Ray?" says Timothy.

"And my mom. And everyone. And I keep thinking of how upset they'll be with me if I *don't* get through this." I gargle and spit, and turn in his direction so the hot water-fingers knead and dig into my right shoulder. "So, I *have* to survive. Because if I don't ... maybe they won't either. And I wouldn't be able to live with that, even if I was dead."

Timothy smiles. "So, your parents ... they know about ... your relationship?"

"My mom is real supportive, and my dad ... well, it doesn't really matter what he thinks anymore. He died."

"I'm sorry."

"Me too," I say.

"You're lucky," says Timothy. "Not about your dad, I mean. I don't have anyone waiting for me at home."

"There has to be someone?" I say. "You're a good-looking guy."

Laughter like a braying donkey's echoes off the tiles as three guys whip each other with the ends of their towels. They run by, all limbs and cocks and drips of water.

Timothy watches them leave the room. "It's funny how some of the boys here act like they enjoy this place, you know?"

I shrug and turn my face back to the shower stream. "Maybe it's how they cope. Assimilation?"

"Maybe," he mutters, lifting his foot up to scratch a soapy fingernail over his toes.

When he peels away a small patch of skin, I gasp.

But he just smiles. "It's glue."

"Glue?"

"I read about this guy who got a 4F for having really bad foot fungus. So before I turned up for the examination, I poured superglue all over my feet."

I laugh. "Didn't work though, huh?"

"Nope. They'd seen it before. Swabbed me with turpentine. Washed a patch right off."

"Damn."

"Yeah. I tried everything. Well," he sniffs and looks away, "*almost* everything."

"Me too. I went to Canada. But they got me in the end."

"Listen," he says, "thanks for sticking up for me today."

"It was nothing. Way I figure it, we need to look out for each other. You and me, we're on the same side, right?" I wink at him.

His cheeks turn red under the hot water.

"Hey," I ask him, "what's your biggest fear?"

He laughs. "I need to pick just one?" Sighing, he shrugs. "I don't know; dying?"

"Nah, come on," I say. "That's the obvious answer. Especially in our situation!"

"Well, what's yours?"

I think for a moment. "Changing."

"Changing what?"

"Me. I'm worried I'll get home, and be so different to the person that left that no one will recognize me. They won't love me like they do now."

"Changing is the one thing I wish I *could* do!" he mumbles.

The bathroom door squeaks open and closed as more of the guys leave.

It is quiet in here now; Timothy and I have the whole head to ourselves.

I wonder if I should move away, so I'm not standing right beside him at this long wall of showerheads, but I don't want to offend him, and besides, it's nice to be able to chat to someone friendly.

"My biggest fear," he says, "is that my family will find out what I am."

I frown. "And what's that, man?"

"A coward," he whispers.

"The definition of a coward," I say, "is standing at the threshold of danger, and then turning and running away."

He smiles. "See, I thought that was the definition of smart!"

"You're here, man!" I say. "You're facing this, right now, with me!"

He nods.

"I'll make you a deal: I'll watch your back if you watch mine," I say. "And maybe, together," I shrug, "we can get through, we can survive, we can stay true to who we really are!"

"Stay true to ourselves?"

"Yeah," I say and hold out my hand.

Timothy reaches for me and his fingers enfold my wrist. He tugs my arm and, unbalanced, I stumble forward and crash my chest into his chest, my stomach into his stomach, and his eyes are level with my eyes, and his lips are soft on mine.

Christ!

At first I think it's just a horribly embarrassing and

awkward wipe-out on my part, and I go to step away. But then I feel his hand on my back. And his tongue on my top lip. And his ...

"Whoa!" I break away and hold my hands up. "I'm sorry!"

"Oh shit," he gasps. "I thought you wanted me to ... I thought you were ..."

I shake my head. "I have a *girlfriend*." And then my eyes fly wide as I realize what I said earlier. "*Ray*," I say, "is a *girl*. I'm not a ... a homo."

"Oh." His face flames.

"Are *you*?" I ask.

"No!" He shakes his head, droplets flying from him in an arc, as he turns off the water. Snatching his towel from the hook on the opposite wall, he wraps it around his waist and runs from me.

"Wait!"

But the door closes behind him with a whoosh as soft as a shocked breath.

"Shit." I run my hand down my face as I shut off the taps, and rub the water from my body with a towel. "Shit." I bite my lip. The one friend I make in this place, and I go and humiliate the poor guy!

Idiot.

And then, "Shit," I gasp, as the swish and gurgle of a flushing toilet smashes through the silence.

I freeze in the center of the room where the floor slopes down toward a drain. Trickles of water and soap slide over the tiles and through the grate and out into the big wide world, and I wish I could wash out on this tide and disappear.

"Well, well." Lion steps into view, thwacking a rolled-up newspaper against his palm. "All clean now, are we, Mack?"

I stare at him.

"So, uh ..." He looks toward the door. "We've got a cake boy among us, have we?"

"Just drop it, man."

"Who is it?" Lion snarls. "Who's the homo?"

Timothy's face flashbulbs in my mind: the fear in his eyes; the shame in his cheeks; the self-disgust in his heart.

I lift my chin and fix my unwavering gaze on Lion. My chest expands as I say the words: "What if it's me?"

Lion's nose wrinkles and he takes a step back, as if I might infect him. "I knew there was something off about you, dude. I knew it!"

Still dripping, I cinch my towel at the waist and push past him. "Grow up, Lion."

"Why don't you make me, fag!" He swings a fat, meaty paw at the back of my head, which knocks me sideways.

I crash onto the sparkling white tile as Lion swaggers out of the room and I am left alone with his echoing laughter hovering above my head.

chapter thirty-one

ray

Japhy sleeps beside me on the bed, peaceful, beautiful, here. I touch his cheek. I touch his lips. I kiss his nose, then his forehead, then his mouth. And he wakes up and he is naked, and I am naked too, and his hands send tingles of pleasure up my spine as he caresses my back.

I draw my mouth away from his and put my lips to his left ear. "Don't be a hero," I whisper. Then I get up and walk away, leaving a trail of red footprints behind me. I beckon.

He rises from the bed and chases me, calls me back, tells me not to go. But he can't catch up.

"Watch your step!" I call to him.

He frowns at me. And then he slips and falls to the ground with a *knock, knock, knock!*

I bolted into a sitting position in bed, gasping, and sweating, as the bedroom door opened and Nora stuck her head in.

"Sorry to wake you, honey, but there are some people here to see you."

"People?" I rubbed my face. "What people?"

"You want me to show them in?"

Had my parents finally come for me? Well, screw them.

I was not leaving this room. I was almost eighteen and they couldn't make me!

I drew my knees to my chest and locked my hands together. But when Leaf blew through my doorway, I sucked in a breath and huffed it out again in a huge grin and threw my arms out wide. Had he always been so big? So tall? So all-encompassing?

"What are you ... Why are you ..." I stammered and swallowed and tried again. "You're here!"

He held me, wrapped me up in cleansing heat, and for just a moment – safe in his arms and his smell – nothing was wrong with the world.

"How you doin'?" he muttered into my hair. "You okay?"

I shook my head. Hell, no. But telling the truth wasn't any easier than lying.

He pressed me into his chest as if trying to absorb my sobs into the unbreakable facets of his own heart. "No, of course you're not okay. What a stupid thing to say. I'm sorry."

The mattress sank again and I looked up through a veil of tears. Poppy's cheeks were sunken and her complexion pasty. Dark shadows rimmed her eyes – once beautiful, once full-of-life – which now glazed over with sadness. Her pupils were pinpricks so small they hardly existed at all. Her hair hung in limp, oily tresses of dull orange and she smelled like sweat and bleach and hopelessness.

She nursed a bunch of flowers in the crook of her arm like a newborn. With a shrug and crinkling of cellophane, she shoved them at me and wouldn't meet my eyes.

Or was I the one who wouldn't meet hers?

*

That night, as I lay in bed arguing with sleep, a fingernail tap-tapped against my bedroom door.

"Japhy?" I whispered.

"Ray?" said the silhouette in my doorway.

"Oh." I leaned back. "Leaf." I rubbed my eyes. "Come in."

"You sleeping?" he asked.

"Yeah, right." Pulling the blankets up to my chest, I shuffled over to make room beside me. "What's up?"

Sighing, he slid under the covers, the skin of his thighs warming my own. "It's Poppy." He ran a hand through his fuzzy hair. "She kind of kicked me out of the guest room. I'll sleep in the van tonight, but I'm not tired yet, and I thought you might be awake still."

I yawned. "I haven't slept since he left."

"Figured." He smiled. "You look like you need some cheering up."

"I do," I said. "Make me laugh."

"Why do people always do that? It's always, 'Hey, I heard you're funny; make me laugh!' or 'Hey, I heard you're sexy; get me off!'"

Something warmed in my chest but there was no laughter.

"Nothing?" He lifted an eyebrow. "Okay then. Why did Sally fall off the swing?" he asked.

"I don't know. Why *did* Sally fall off the swing?"

"Because she had no arms!"

"That was terrible."

"Okay, how about this one. Knock, knock!"

I sighed. "Who's there?"

"Definitely not Sally."

The laugh bubbled up from some forgotten place in my chest, cracking through the crust that had formed over my heart and spreading warmth like honey in my veins.

I wanted to tell him, thank you: thank you for coming here; thank you for being my friend; thank you for bringing some light back into my world. But I said nothing. I just smiled and leaned my head on his shoulder and hoped that I could somehow repay the favor.

"So, what's the deal with Poppy?" I asked. "She looks ..."

"Terrible?" He sighed. "I know. It's the smack."

"Smack!" I gasped. "She's doing *heroin*?"

Leaf squeezed the bridge of his nose and nodded. "She says it's for the pain. She went through the supply of morphine we got from the hospital and then Needles hooked her up with this shit, and she's been loaded for weeks. I can't get her to stop."

"Are *you* ...?"

"Hell, no!" said Leaf. "I'm not that stupid. Pot is one thing. Acid, sure. I tried sniffing coke once; didn't like it, the ice cubes got stuck in my nose. But, hey, I'm not an idiot; I'm not a heroin addict."

"Did she bring it with her ... here?"

Leaf didn't speak.

"Is she shooting up in the house?"

"In the van." His voice was soft.

"Jesus Christ, Leaf. Nora will have a fit if she finds out."

"She *won't* find out, will she?"

"She's not stupid. If she sees Poppy hazing around the place, all stoned, I'm sure she'll put it together. I can't believe this," I said. "God, I thought she was smarter than that."

"Before you criticize someone," Leaf sighed, "you should walk a mile in their shoes."

I guess Poppy has been through a lot, I thought, but still ... heroin?

"That way," Leaf continued, "when you *do* criticize them, you'll be a mile away and you'll have their shoes!" He laughed weakly at his own joke, but then ran a hand down his face. His cheeks were haggard. His eyes so very tired. "I don't know what to do, Ray. I'm losing her."

"I'm sure you're overreacting," I said.

He shook his head. "Tonight, I just tried to give her a hug, and she pushed me away. She told me I didn't want *her*, just her *bits*. She told me," and he laughed, "that I should come and see *you* for that instead."

"Me?" I frowned. "But we're not, you know ..."

"I know." He looked away. "That's what I mean, though. She's not herself. She would never have spoken to me like this before. She used to be all about freedom and love and being kind to everyone. Now ..."

I sighed.

"I don't think she loves me anymore, Ray."

"Oh, of course she does! I saw the way she used to look at you; you can't just switch something like that off. Trust me."

He shrugged. "She doesn't laugh. I used to be able make her laugh all the time. Now ... nothing. I miss that sound. So damn much."

"She's just ... healing. But we'll fix her." I took his hand. "We'll fix her. It's only been a few weeks."

He looked me right in the eyes. "It's been twenty-nine days."

"Yeah," I said. "Just give her time. Everything will be okay. It will all work out, for all of us! You'll see."

"I hope you're right." Stretching back on the bed, Leaf held his arm out at a right angle. An invitation. "Not even the Amish joke worked on her tonight."

"What's the Amish joke?" I asked, settling back against him.

"Knock, knock," he said.

I smiled. "Who's there?"

"Amish."

"Amish who?"

"Aww," he said. "Amish you, too."

I shook my head. "Terrible."

With my head on his chest, I closed my eyes and felt his body just exist beneath mine. Heard the rise and fall of his inflating and deflating lung tissue. Felt the muscle of his heart as it gently squeezed and released. Felt the numbness in my soul as it spread through my body until, in this beautiful, quiet moment, I was no longer in any pain. None at all.

I took a breath and inhaled him, and the comforting hand of sleep smoothed down my eyelids. My head swam, buzzy with nothingness for the first time since Japhy was arrested, for the first time, actually, since he'd received that damned draft letter.

"Leaf ..." I slurred as I sank blissfully into myself. "I need you ..." But I was too tired to finish my full sentence: I need you *to stay.*

I felt his lips press into my hair, heard his own whispered

words hanging in the air above us like smoke rising from glowing embers. "I need you, too."

chapter thirty-two

japhy

We line up at mess hall like a trail of ants, all jostling and bottlenecking at the doorway. I snatch a tray of food and hurry down the center aisle to find somewhere to sit; we only have six minutes to clean our plates. All the available tables suddenly have trays slid across them and I hear the mumbled words, "Seat's taken!" or "Can't sit here."

Timothy looks up at me as I approach the space beside him, and I smile, relieved to see at least one friendly face. But he shakes his head. Just two quick movements that almost aren't there at all. And then he looks away.

Fair enough, I think, he's still embarrassed about the shower.

I hadn't had a chance to get him alone and clear the air yet. Not that I really know what the hell to say to someone like him, anyway. I'd never spoken to a homosexual before.

The last table on the left is empty and I let my tray clatter down. I fall onto the seat and open my silver can of – what I *think* is – franks and beans, but really, who the hell would know?

"Anyone want to trade?" I ask, looking around at the boys closest to my table. They refuse to meet my eyes. One by one, they smirk at each other, and then lower their heads back to their own silver cans, digging out the meat with their forks.

"What's the matter, Mack?" Lion leans back on his chair. "I thought you *liked* franks."

Laughter rises around me like a tide, and when it subsides, I am left frothy and cold in its wake.

"What a fag!" someone whispers.

"He makes me sick!"

"He shouldn't be allowed to eat with us."

On the same table as Lion, Timothy's fork freezes half way to his mouth and begins to shake as his whole body rattles from the words muttered around him. Even though the words are aimed at me, Timothy is caught in the crossfire and his body jolts, wounded, with every razor-sharp syllable.

From my tray, I lift up the tin of franks, stab one with my fork, and bring it to my lips. "Mmmm," I say. I close my eyes, and I bite down on the disgusting nub of animal flesh, and I wait for it.

The laughter swells around me again.

"He admitted it!"

"Can you believe that?"

"He *does* like franks!"

"And he's *proud* of it!"

Watching Timothy out of the corner of my eye, I wait for him to nod at me, a thank you for keeping his secret.

But he presses his lips together, sighs, and dips his head.

Outside, a whistle blows and chairs scrape backwards. Bodies stand. Empty trays are stacked. I spit the hunk of meat on to my tray and shovel as many peaches as I can into my mouth as my platoon leaves me behind.

*

"Why are you doing this?" Timothy whispers from the corner of his mouth. He sits on the edge of my bed, shining the toe of his boot with a rag. He doesn't look up as he speaks. "Why are you taking the heat for me? Lion has told everyone that you are ..." he lowers his voice, "... *gay*. I mean, not that *I* am ... but ..."

"Because," I smile at him, "that's what friends do."

He scoffs. "You don't want to be *my* friend."

"Sure I do, man."

"All I'm saying," he says, "is that you didn't *have* to do that. You didn't have to lie."

"Well," I say and I stare at him, "neither did you."

His hands stop for a second, and then they continue polishing.

"Why didn't you just tell the Induction Board?" I whisper.

His lips press tight, and the rag moves so quickly now I expect smoke to rise from his fingers.

"Why didn't you tell them?" I ask again.

"Because," he looks up, "there's *nothing* to tell."

"But," I sit on his bed and the springs cry out in pain. "You would have got 4F!" I say. "You don't have to be here."

He laughs. Shakes his head. Keeps shining that damn shoe. "Just drop it, Japhy, please? It's no big deal."

"Yes," I say, "it *is*!" and I rip the rag from his hand.

"Hey!" Timothy snatches for it, but I hold it out of reach.

"You don't have to be here," I hiss. "You don't have to go to Nam!"

"I said, drop it, all right!" Timothy shoves me with the heels of his hands and I fall backwards, landing on the floor, hard.

My head slams into the metal edge of the next bunk.

Timothy glares down. "You don't know anything!" he breathes. "Just stay the fuck away from me, Mack!"

The room falls silent around us, and then a wolf-whistle rises like steam, and laughter bubbles up around it.

Snatching his rag, Timothy says, loudly, "Stay away from me, you fag!" and he flinches at his own word before he turns and stomps off to where Lion and the others are all pointing and making kissing sounds at me.

*

"How do you know who is your *friend* and who is your *enemy*?" Sergeant Ash stalks our line.

We all stare straight ahead as he passes, as he stops, as he stares us directly in the face, as he dares us to stare back.

"What's your name, soldier?" he asks the short, overweight boy beside me.

"Robins, sir."

"Private Robins, who do *you* trust at this very moment?"

"My country, sir."

"Your country?" Ash smiles and head-butts the boy in the face.

The sound of crumpling cartilage thickens the air like tension. Robins doubles over; blood drips through his fingers as he covers his nose.

"The correct answer," says Ash, moving along the line again, "is *no one*! You trust *no one* because, at this moment, none of these assholes will keep you alive in a warzone!" Coming back to Robins again, Ash bends forward to scream into the boy's bleeding face. "Stand up straight, Private, or you, and every single one of these shitheads, will run the length of this oval until your nose stops bleeding!"

Robins, shaking and pale, uncurls himself. Blood bubbles at his lips as he exhales. His eyes are bleary with tears.

"Private Robins?"

"Yes, sir!"

"Who do you trust at this moment?"

Robins pauses. Takes a breath. Steels himself. "No one, sir."

"No one? No one!" Ash punches Robins in the gut.

The poor kids drops to his knees, coughing.

Ash bends over him. "The correct answer is *your country*! Now stand the fuck up!"

Again, Robins stands. His jaw clenches and his hands fist at his sides. His chest rises and falls rapidly.

"Private Robins?"

"Yes, sir!"

Ash's lips peel back from his teeth. "Who do you trust at this moment?"

Robins swallows, licking blood off his trembling lower lip. "I don't know, sir!" His voice is thin, faltering, breaking apart.

"You don't know?" Ash steps forward. "YOU DON'T KNOW!"

Robins tenses, but he does not move away.

"You are one hundred percent God damned right!" The drill sergeant nods. "At this moment, you don't know *who* you can trust. You don't know which of these boys are capable of killing someone in order to save your pathetic life. Over the coming weeks, every man in this line will be forced to prove that he can be trusted to keep you alive. By the end of your time here, each and every one of you will know exactly who you can trust, and who you can't. And those who can't be trusted will not come home from this war!" He lowers his voice. "The Viet Nam War is unlike any war our country has fought before. It is a guerilla war. There are no rules anymore and there is not just *one* enemy. You will be hunted by the uniformed soldiers of the North Vietnamese Army. But you will also be hunted by the invisible guerilla fighters, the Viet Cong, who are civilians living in South Viet Nam, running businesses, raising families, secretly sympathetic to the beliefs of the Communist North. During the day, these people will smile and thank you for protecting them, and at night they will sneak up behind you and slit your throat before returning home to their sleeping children. In the jungles, they will strike and then vanish like ghosts. They will use tunnels and caves to appear out of nowhere. They will watch you from a distance, predict your moves, and lay booby traps to injure or kill. They could be frail grandmothers, hungry children, pregnant women. They could come up to you for assistance with a grenade hidden in their clothing. During this war, you may very well kill a grandmother, or a hungry child, or a pregnant woman. But you may also kill someone who was planning on killing *you* first. So, I'll ask again," he continues, "how do you know who is your friend and who is your enemy?" He stops and looks at us, one by one. "The answer is: you *don't*."

My stomach clenches into a fist.

"You kill first," he says softly. "You kill first, and then you just fucking pray that you won't go to hell for it."

chapter thirty-three

ray

Night was no longer the hardest part of my day; it was the time for which I yearned. When the sky turned black, and the house grew silent, I rolled up my sleeve and slapped my fingers against the crook of my arm. My hungry vein swelled with need and waited to be pricked. As Leaf slid like a needle inside my bed, blissful sleep slid inside my skin as silent and intoxicating as a secret.

I imagined myself standing in a circle and speaking loudly, proudly: "Hello, my name is Ray, and I am an addict!"

Night after night, I waited. My toes tingling with anticipation. My fingertips itching to feel his heat. My heart aching for its dose of pain relief that numbed like nothing else. I waited as the house grew silent with sleep. I waited as the night grew blacker with camouflage. I waited as, on the other side of this thin bedroom wall, he waited as well.

And then, the creak of a floorboard. The whisper of flattening carpet fibers. The inhaled breath of a warm palm against a cold doorknob.

Lifting the blankets beside me like an invitation, I closed my eyes and felt his body encircle me: legs ran the length of each other; arms tangled like tightly woven rope that would never fray. And his breath burned the nape of my neck as my skin and muscle and bone and soul all melted together in a beautiful soup of painlessness.

"Goodnight, Japhy," I whispered, already sinking into sleep.

"Goodnight, Lauren, my lovely," he murmured as he drifted away as well.

Before I even opened my eyes in the morning, I knew Leaf was gone. Not because the bed was empty, but because cold angst stretched out beside me where, hours earlier, that other warm body had been. The body that had allowed me to fall so gracefully and easily into a deep and peaceful, dreamless sleep every single night.

This morning, desperate to put some distance between myself and my horribly chilly sheets, I threw the covers off and jumped up, wondering if Leaf was up yet, or if he was still in bed with Poppy, pretending he'd been beside her all night long.

Would he be holding her now, while she slept, while she couldn't push him away? Or would he, like me, be distancing himself from the iciness of his linen?

I was surprised to find Poppy already up, sitting out on the porch swing, staring at the gray sky. Especially before noon. She usually slept all morning, made a brief appearance in the afternoon, probably got high in the van, and then – if she didn't crash out there – she pinballed her way back down the hall and into the guest room.

But here she was, aglow with a morning sun. Her orange hair pulled back in a tight ponytail emphasized how much weight she'd lost in her face. Beside her in a glass ashtray smoldered a cigarette; at first glance it appeared whole and untouched by fire, but on closer inspection the cigarette was just a stick of ash – fragile and held together by nothing but the will to be held together. With the slightest nudge, the entire thing would crumble into a pile of dust.

"Hey," I said.

"Hey." She didn't look at me. She never did anymore.

I tried not to stare at her arms, tried not to search for needle marks, tried instead to imagine she was the innocent young girl she appeared to be in her Mickey Mouse pajamas, and her face puffed with sleep. But I couldn't help wondering: was she jonesing for a hit right now, or was she already higher than the clouds she stared at?

The image of this beautiful, naïve creature crouching over a spoon, and a zippo, and a syringe haunted me.

Jesus.

"Poppy?"

"Hmm?" She looked across at me then, and I saw her eyes. Her pupils just pinpricks.

Damn.

I sighed as my image of this sweet little girl, smiling soberly and innocently on Japhy's front porch, crumbled. As fragile as the girl herself.

"Is there anything I can do for you?" I asked.

"Sure," she said, and coughed out a small laugh. "You can give me back my baby. You can hunt down those National Guard bastards and shoot every one of them in the stomach. You can go back in time and *not* tell me to march in that fucking protest."

"I'm sorry," I whispered.

"Whatever." She sniffed and looked back up at the sky. "It would have been a girl," she said. "Did Leaf tell you that?"

"No."

"Sylvia." Poppy cradled the name on her tongue. "We named her Sylvia. They gave us her death certificate, but not her birth certificate. How can you be officially dead if you never officially existed in the first place? I don't even know what they did with her body."

"I'm sorry," I said again, wishing I could offer her something more than this flimsy, pointless, five-letter word.

"Not only have I lost that little baby, but I have also lost all the other children that I was supposed to have in the future. The doctor said it would be very unlikely for me to conceive again."

I held my hands out, as if passing her a gift. "If I could, I would change everything. Believe me, I *would*!"

She rolled her eyes at me. "Talk to me when you are willing to give me your unborn child."

I flinched back as if struck, but then sighed and sat next to her. The swing creaked under the weight of my guilt. "Do you want to talk about *that* day? It may help."

"I just want to forget it ever happened." Her voice was as thin as a prayer.

"But," I shook my head, "it *did* happen. It's a part of your past; part of who you are now, and who you will become."

"No! I don't want it in me!" She scrabbled a hand at her chest, as if trying to grab hold of her heart and rip it out. "I don't want it to shape who I am. I don't want to give it the power! The satisfaction!"

"I know how you feel ..."

"Bullshit! You don't know how this feels! To go to sleep every night and relive the horror. To wake up every morning and, for one blissful second, thank God it was all a horrible nightmare. And then be crushed by the weight of truth as you *remember* and suffer that loss all over again! My life has been forever changed by this!"

"I was there too!" I said. "I wasn't shot, but I saw people get shot. I saw people die. I had blood on my hands that I can never wash away. Never. And you know what? I don't *want* to! I want to be able to hold up my palms and let others see those stains, to tell them about the injustice of that day so that maybe it never happens again. And so that maybe those people who died will never be forgotten. You may want to pretend that day never happened, and those poor kids were never killed." One by one, I counted off the names I'd read in the newspaper and committed to memory, holding my fingers, one, two, three, four, straight up like soldiers standing tall. "Jeffrey Miller, William Schroeder, Sandra Scheuer, and *Allison* ..." I paused to gather more strength because the death of Allison still stole my breath. "Allison Krause," I whispered, "and even your little Sylvia and all of the other future babies and grandbabies who will never be conceived because their parents were killed that day." My hands fisted in my lap. "You may want to forget they died, Lauren, but I sure as shit will never forget that they *lived*."

"Don't call me *Lauren*!" Poppy launched herself off the seat, knocking the ashtray onto the wooden boards of the veranda. Ash puffed up into the air and blew away on the soft morning breeze. "Lauren is *dead*. She died on that football field. And she is not coming back. If you and Leaf can't deal with that, then you can both go fuck yourselves! Or go fuck each other for all I care. Just don't fuck with me."

Then she turned and disappeared as quickly as the cigarette ash that blew away at my feet.

*

"This is *so* stupid," I said to Nora, as we pulled up in the parking area of the doctor's clinic. "I'm not sick; I'm just *stressed*."

"Yeah, well ..." She shrugged. "That's what I used to say, too. I'm not sick; I'm just *tired*. It's not a lump; it's just a bruise."

"So, because you have cancer – cancer that you are *not* getting treatment for, might I add – I now have to go through the embarrassment of a doctor telling me that no, I'm not sick, I'm just *stressed?*"

"Yes." Nora nodded. "You've thrown up at least once a day since Andy left."

"Because I'm upset!" I said. "I'm not dying!" My cheeks burned when I realized what I'd said. "Sorry."

"Please," she said. "For me?" She blinked at me with Japhy's eyes and I felt my resolve crumble.

I sighed. "Fine."

"Great! Now, get in there, before I grab your hand and pull you in myself."

"Ugh," I rolled my eyes. "Yes, *Mom!*"

And she smiled. She smiled so big. Her cheeks puffed out and her gums flashed pink and her eyes shone bright with almost-tears.

"This is so God damn unnecessary," I mumbled as I opened the car door and looked up at the brick building, inside which waited a medical professional who may or may not be about to tell me something was dreadfully wrong with me.

What if something *was* wrong with me?

I mean, Nora was stressed, and grief-stricken, and suffering from *cancer*, and she had at least kept food in her stomach for the last two weeks!

What if Japhy survived all he was about to endure – all the guns, all the bombs, all the death – only to return home to find me wasted away and sickly? Or already gone? Wouldn't that just be our luck?

I turned back to this woman who had placed a gentle palm on my forehead, and clucked a tongue at my barely touched plates of food, and pulled the covers up to my chin every evening as she said goodnight. I turned back to this woman who had opened her home and her heart to me. I turned back to her and I whispered, "Will you come in with me?"

She held my hand as we crossed the lawn. She squeezed it gently in the waiting room when my name was called out. She gripped it tight when a vampiric nurse jabbed a needle into my arm and stole my blood. She ran the taps loudly in the bathroom when I had to pee into a tiny cup but didn't need to go. And she rubbed my shoulders reassuringly when we were ushered out and told to return in a week for the results.

Staring out the window of a café, I watched life flash by me in blurs of shiny cars, and dirty sneakers, and great wide smiles. All of these people, I thought, have entire lives to live, to suffer through, to lose. How many of them appreciate the preciousness of it all?

A soft clinking brought my attention back as Nora placed two mugs on the table between us and sat with a heavy sigh. Her blond hair, held off her face with a purple kerchief, hung long and loose over her shoulders, freed from the high buns and hairspray prisons in which she had always confined her locks. Her face was clean and make-up free and no longer caked with the cosmetic need to look beautiful for a husband. And she wore belled jeans and a paisley shirt; all her floral, knee-length dresses had been donated to Goodwill because the woman who had worn those fifties-style dresses, and the bright red lipstick, and the beehive hair, had been Nora the Wife.

But this vibrant, shining being before me right now was no longer Nora the Wife; she was Nora the Widow, and she gave no hint of the black sadness swirling in a great cloud around her heart, like the very cancer that flourished in the tissues over it.

She slid a cup toward me and said, "I know you wanted coffee, but I thought this would be better for you right now. It's chamomile tea. It's calming."

"Herbal tea?" I raised an eyebrow and then my cup. "When did you become such a *hippie*?"

She shrugged a shoulder. "If you can't beat 'em, right?"

"How do you do it?" I asked, taking a sip and feeling the heat of the tea fill my stomach and spread outward in a wave.

"How do I do what?" she asked.

"How do you ... survive?"

She sighed and looked out the window at the well-washed cars, and the well-worn sneakers, and the wide smiles of life. "Who says I am?"

"Look at you!" I said. "You're glowing. Even after everything that has happened, and everything that is still happening, and everything that might be about to happen ... you *glow*. You're bright."

"Heather," she said, turning her brown, Japhy-like eyes to me – eyes that were suddenly wet and overflowing with truth – "brightness is only visible in the darkness. I may look like I am glowing, honey," she said, gripping my hand, "but it is only because our world is so dim right now that any light makes us squint in the glare of it. Sometimes I look at you, Heather – I *squint* at you – and I think exactly the same thing: she is glowing, she is bright. She is surviving."

"Who says I am?" I whispered.

And Nora nodded. "Exactly."

*

In the doctor's waiting room seven long days later, Nora stood when my name was called.

"No, it's okay," I said.

"You sure?"

I nodded.

"All right," she said and sat. "I'll be right here."

"I know." I smiled. "Thank you."

I walked to the consulting room, and as the doctor closed the door behind me, I saw Nora narrow her eyes at me, squint at me, and nod.

"Right. Heather!" Dr. Smyth clapped his wrinkled hands and pointed to the green vinyl chair in which I had sat a week ago. He lowered himself onto a matching chair behind his oak desk and opened up a manila folder that he peered at over the top of his glasses for what must have been an hour. I looked at the wall clock and watched the seconds tick around it so slowly I began to wonder if I wasn't confusing the second-hand with the minute-hand, and I chewed my bottom lip, and I crossed my right leg over my left, then I folded my hands in my lap, then I crossed my left leg over my right, then I pulled my hair back off my face and held it in a ponytail, then I let it fall back down over my shoulders, and I cleared my throat and thought: Why is my mouth so dry? I looked around his office: Why is there no water in here? I pulled my hair off my face again and thought: Why the shit is he taking so damn long?

"All right." He took off his glasses and laid them down on the open folder, then interlaced his fingers and placed his hands on the folder as well. "It seems we have worked out what is wrong with you."

Oh for Pete's sake! In the time it took for him to tell me he had worked out what was wrong with me, he could've already told me what was wrong with me!

I smiled and said, "Okay."

He placed his glasses on the end of his nose again, so he could peer uselessly over them. Then he took his time choosing one of the ten exactly-the-same-pens from the penholder on his desk. He wrote something down in the folder – or started to, but the pen wouldn't work properly, so he scribbled it around in circles for a minute and then sighed and reached for a second pen, which worked just fine.

"Heather, your tests are absolutely perfect." Again he placed his glasses down, followed by his clasped hands.

"Really?" I let out a long breath. "So there's *nothing* wrong with me?"

"You are perfectly healthy," he said.

"Oh thank God!"

"And so," he said, "is the baby growing in your uterus."

"Excuse me, what?" I said. "Did you say, *baby*?"

"I did." He smiled like he was giving me good news. "Congratulations."

"But ... but I *can't* be; I'm on The Pill!" That had been one positive of having a mother who paid absolutely no attention to you.

"The Pill is not one hundred percent foolproof, Heather. And obviously," he laughed, "not in your case."

Don't laugh; this isn't funny! I thought, wanting to throw something at this stupid little man who was single-handedly ruining my whole life.

"No." I shook my head. "No! I *cannot* be ... you know. It's impossible."

"Trust me on this, Heather; after all, I *am* the doctor here. You are pregnant." He snapped my folder closed. "Your urine and blood tests both came back positive. If your last menstruation is anything to go by, you are about eight weeks along."

Eight weeks?

My bedroom flashed bright in my mind. Japhy's face. The crumpled draft notice wet with tears. My little girl nightgown rising up my thighs.

Oh shit.

I was going to have a ...

Christ.

But I thought you couldn't get pregnant the first time? And then I thought of the times after that and I wanted to be sick. And then I thought, but I'm not ready to be a mother; I am too young; there are so many things I want to do before I am tied down to a child and all that responsibility.

"I ... I can't ..." Tears burned my eyes as I wrapped my arms around my middle, around the place where my own little tumor grew bigger with every second.

"Okay, it's okay." He came around his desk and sat beside me. "You do have some options. Adoption is ..."

"No!" I gasped. "No. I just want this to go away. Now. Please! Can you help me? Can you get rid of it?"

He peered his owl eyes at me, blinking quickly. "Gin and a hot bath," he said.

I looked up at him and raised my eyebrows. "What?"

"There's debate on how much gin to drink, and how hot the bath water needs to be, but my advice for both is: as much as you can handle."

"Gin and a hot bath?" I repeated.

"Failing that," he whispered and leaned forward, "there's always the knitting needle."

I gasped. "You're not serious?"

His eyes trapped me in a spider web stare. "I could ask *you* the same question, Heather." He pressed his lips into a thin line. "*Think* about what this means. Really think about what you have in there. And talk to the father first. Talk to Andy."

The father?

Oh, God.

The father!

I shook my head; no, Japhy has enough to worry about. I can at least spare him this added complication, and make sure that everything is as close to normal for him when he comes home.

"You need to take responsibility for your actions," he said. "And now, more than ever, you need to think about someone other than yourself, because, Miss Wren, you *are* pregnant, you *are* going to have a baby, and you will no longer be the most important person in your life."

Was he calling me selfish? I gritted my teeth.

"I already learned that lesson, sir. Why else do you think I'd be considering this?"

He blinked at me again and then he sighed and scribbled something on a yellow jotter. "If you do feel like you have no other choice but to terminate this child – because it is a *child*

– please don't do anything stupid. I have a friend at a women's clinic in Birmingham who owes me a favor. He can help you." He slid the paper across the table to me. "Tell him I sent you."

The writing was small and scratchy and I could barely read a word of it. Birmingham? I thought. How was I supposed to get into the city on my own?

I scrunched the yellow note, held it tight in my palm as if it were a little bird of hope that might escape if I loosened my fingers even the tiniest bit.

This would be my secret.

Another black stain on my soul that Japhy – or anyone – would never see.

Another reason that I would go straight to hell.

Because, unlike the last time I killed a child, this death would be premeditated. And wasn't that the exact specification for murder?

As I stepped through the door into the waiting room, Nora click-clacked two knitting needles in her lap. She flicked her eyes up at me and then jabbed the needle through the ball of yarn in her lap. It slid in easily, poking garishly out the other side.

"Well?" She stood. "What did he say?"

I couldn't stop staring at that needle – long, thin, pointed – and I pressed a hand over my stomach in an involuntary surge of protection. Surprised, I lowered my arm to my side.

"Well?" Nora asked again.

"Everything is fine." The lie slipped through my teeth as easily as that knitting needle slipped through wool. "Like I said, it's just stress." I liked the way the lie released me. As if saying it out loud somehow made it feel true. "It's nothing," I said, smiling as the lie wrapped me up in a kind of freedom, a kind of promise, a kind of truth that – if I said it enough – maybe I could force into being real. The heat of it throbbed inside me. Pulsed. Surged deliciously. "Everything," I said again, sighing with delight, "is fine."

chapter thirty-four

japhy

"There are two types of soldiers: the quick and the dead. What are *you*?"

"Quick!"

"What are *they*?"

"Dead!"

"What are *you*?"

"Quick!"

"What are *they*?"

"Dead!"

"Imagine a VC soldier has just appeared right in your face! He is so close you can see the sweat on his upper lip, smell the fish on his breath, hear the low rumble of his black heart as it beats in time with yours, and in the next five seconds either yours or his will stop beating. This man will kill you unless you kill him first. You will *not* hesitate in destroying this man with your bare hands. You cannot hesitate because *you* are the quick, and *they* are the dead. What are you?"

"Quick!"

"What are they?"

"Dead!"

"Hand-to-hand combat," yells Ash, "can be more terrifying for a soldier than anything else this war may show you. It takes the enemy from being a faceless bad guy and introduces you to a person just like yourself. It becomes real. It becomes personal. The soldier standing to your left is a VC. Take him down! NOW!"

There is a slight shuffling as, all along the line, we glance left, nervously and unsure, at the person beside us.

On my left, Private Robins looks away from me at whoever is on his other side.

And then my face is in the dirt, a body presses my chest to the ground and a thick forearm ropes around my neck. I scrabble my fingers at skin, trying to loosen the chokehold, but the muscles are bunched so tight my fingers slide right off.

I flip over onto my back and Lion straddles my chest. His full weight crushes down on my lungs and I can't breathe. He holds my wrists together in one huge paw above my head and slams a fist into my face over and over again.

"Private Mack!" Ash screams into my ear. "You are fucking dead! How does it feel?"

Gasping for air, and wincing in pain, I feel Lion's bulk lift from me. I roll onto my knees, coughing and wheezing and spitting blood into the dirt.

"Get up!" screams Ash. "Fall in!"

What's the point if I'm already dead? I wonder. But I grit my teeth and force my legs to hold me up in the line, and I squint out of my good eye at the drill sergeant.

"Private Leon," Ash nods at Lion, "is the only one – out of all you – who is currently still alive! That's one soldier out of fifty. And that is fucking pathetic. He is quick and you are all fucking dead! That is not fucking good enough! Go again!"

There are grunts, and gasps, and guttural screams as each boy lands on the ground and tries to attack the person beside him, rather than fighting off the one who is simultaneously attacking him.

It is a mess. A full-on scrum. A war zone.

Feet kick out at random bodies. Hands cover faces and then scratch out and claw someone else's skin. I drive an elbow into someone's chest as my chin scrapes along the ground.

In the distance, underneath the ringing in my ears, I hear

a slow clapping sound. Slowly, our fists stop falling and we all raise our heads.

Ash stares at us. A grin slashes his dark face with a line of white.

And he claps.

Very.

Slowly.

"Fall in!"

There are groans and hisses of breath as we all stand at attention again.

"Duty!" Ash screams. "Your duty as a soldier of the United States of America is not to act as an individual soldier in this company, but to be a *working cog*. You are no longer a single entity. You are part of something greater than yourself. You move in unison with your fellow soldiers. You are a team. If each of you tries to do your own thing in this war, you will be personally responsible for the deaths of every man who stands beside you right now." He stops and looks at each of us and then screams: "Be a team! Go again!"

Forty-nine pairs of eyes suddenly turn to me.

"Get the fag!"

I go down beneath the weight of my entire company.

I am crushed by their fear of the unknown.

I am beaten by their fists of prejudice.

I curl into a ball, shielding myself with the cloak of my own innocence.

But then I remember that this is *war*.

Here, I am the enemy.

And here, the word *innocence* does not exist.

chapter thirty-five

ray

Innocent. The word was a spider on my tongue, tickling and biting through the cold, web-thin lining to my fear.

Could I really go through with this? Could I kill an innocent baby?

Correction, I thought. Could I kill *another* innocent baby?

Maybe it was the kindest choice. I mean, it would be better off dead than unwanted. No one wanted to be unwanted by their parents; I knew that better than anyone. So, I am doing the right thing, I told myself as I lay awake next to a sleeping Leaf. So, I am doing the right thing, and I don't *need* to discuss this with Japhy. And it's not like the baby is even alive yet, right? It's just basically the same as all the unfertilized eggs that die off in my fallopian tubes every month. The same as all the gazillion sperm that die off in my cervix every time Japhy and I have sex. No difference, really. It's just that this particular egg and this particular sperm happened to meet up first along the way.

That's all.

I sighed, and rolled over.

Abortion.

It was another word. Just another insignificant, eight-letter word, just like *innocent*. No big deal.

Abortion.

Nope, no big deal.

Just a small procedure and it would all be over. That egg and that sperm would die off like they were meant to have done anyway, and I could go back to my Japhy, back to my college degree. I could have a career, and a life. A life that would otherwise be forever chained down by responsibility.

Responsibility. Now there was a word that was by no means insignificant. There was a word I didn't want in my vocabulary. And I knew that Japhy sure didn't.

What was it he'd said to me that horrible day at the jail? *Us? Have a baby? Jeez, that's the last the thing we need right now!*

I sighed and closed my eyes. Yes, I am doing the right thing.

Rolling over, I hugged the rough, scratchy material of the blanket up to my chin and imagined myself meeting Japhy at the airport in a year's time. His eyes search the crowd, and widen when they find me. The handsome smile stills, and then fades altogether. His eyes narrow and his lips snarl up at one corner. He strides forward, stabbing a finger at the bundle in my arms.

"What the fuck is that?" he yells. "I've just come home from war, Ray! From *war*! And instead of offering me comfort and peace, you hand me a baby? Jeez! That's the last thing we need right now!" He throws his little army hat on the floor of the terminal and glares at me. "I thought you knew me, Ray. I thought you knew me so well. But I was wrong. I was so damn wrong." He straightens up. "You want a baby?" he says. "You got one. I hope you two have a nice life together!" And then he walks away.

"No!" I call out to him. "Japhy?"

He turns.

I place the baby on a row of empty seats, and I run to where Japhy waits for me. He smiles and opens his arms, and I leap. "It's you," I say, as I kiss him. "It's just you and me."

"Just you and me?" He weeps. "You promise?"

"I promise."

And as he lifts me up and carries me away, I see Poppy and Leaf step up to the row of seats where the bundle of blankets starts to wriggle and cry. Poppy gathers the blankets in her arms, and dips her face to kiss what lies inside. "Hi, baby," she whispers. "You came back to me!"

"Ray?" Leaf calls to me across the room.

But I turn away from him and press my face into the scratchy material of Japhy's uniform.

"Ray, wake up!" Leaf says.

Japhy's arms jostle me.

"Ray?"

And then I blink and Japhy is gone, and Leaf stared down at me with his hand on my shoulder.

"You okay?" he asked.

"Huh?"

"You were crying in your sleep?"

I wiped my hands across my wet cheeks. "Oh."

"Bad dream?"

I thought about the solidness of Japhy's arms around me, and the look of motherly happiness in Poppy's sober eyes. "No," I sighed, "it was wonderful." I smiled and settled back against Leaf's warmth.

Reaching for his arm, I pressed his palm against the skin below my navel so that, in a way, he now held the child that grew inside me. He held it in his hand like a secret gift.

Again, I imagined all of us – Leaf, Poppy, the baby, and me – standing together at the airport, waiting for Japhy to come home. This time, though, I was not the one holding the bundle of blankets, and when I looked over at Poppy, her mouth formed two wonderful words: "Thank you."

*

The edges of the bedroom window glowed as golden as a gift when I woke to an empty bed the next morning. I scrunched my eyes closed and tried to force myself back into the arms of sleep. But with Leaf gone, with cold absence beside me, and with my decision tugging at my arm like an impatient child, I muttered, "Okay, okay!", tip-toed down the hall to the guest room, and cracked the door.

"Hey, guys?" I whispered.

"What the ...?" Poppy rolled over and buried her face beneath her pillow. "What time is it?"

"Ray?" Leaf squinted at me with bloodshot eyes. "Everything okay?"

"Yes!" I sat on the end of their bed. "Everything is great. Better than great, actually!" I grinned, unsure of exactly how or where to start.

"What?" he laughed.

"How much do you love me?"

He frowned and glanced quickly at Poppy. "Uh ..."

"Because I've worked out how to get our lives back on track, and how to help Poppy get clean, and ..."

"What?" Poppy lifted the pillow from her face. "Leaf, what have you been telling her?"

"Nothing!" He glared at me.

"You see," I continued, "I thought I was just tired and ill from all the stress, but nope! I found out from the doctor yesterday that I'm pregnant ..."

"What?" Poppy gasped and shook her head. "No."

"But it's great, because I'm not ready to be a mother, and neither is Japhy. To be a *father*, I mean, not a mother. And that's why I've decided – I'm sure he'll agree with me on this – to let you two ..." I paused and looked from Poppy to Leaf and back to Poppy, "... adopt our baby!"

Poppy's mouth fell open.

"How far along are you?" Leaf asked, his eyes wide.

"Eight weeks," I said. "We'll have to go back to Mandala, at least during the pregnancy – I think it would be better if Nora didn't know anything about this – and of course, Poppy, this gives you an excuse to get yourself sober, and back to your old self again before it's born."

"I don't believe this," Poppy muttered.

I grinned. "You're welcome!"

"Eight weeks?" Poppy glared at Leaf and then narrowed her eyes into two black slits. "Are you fucking high?"

"Of course not!" I said. "I'm pregnant."

"No, seriously. Are you high? Because this is crazy!"

"I know!" I beamed at her. "I don't know why I didn't think of this first. Luckily, I didn't go ahead with the abortion ..."

"Abortion?" Leaf sat forward. "You were going to get rid of it without even speaking to Japhy? Or ..." he paused, "... to *me*?"

"You?" I smiled. "Thanks for wanting to support me, but it's not your baby. Not *yet*, anyway!" I laughed. "But, no, the doctor said conception happened at the end of April, and that was before that night we ... you know ... *met*."

"Ray ..." Leaf ran a hand down his face.

"And I was planning to go to the Women's Clinic and have it taken care of, but then I realized ..." I slapped a hand against my forehead. "Poppy and Leaf! Of course!"

"Ray!" Poppy stared at me, and why wasn't she smiling? "Eight weeks pregnant doesn't mean the baby was conceived *eight weeks* ago."

"Of course it does!"

"It means," said Poppy, rolling her eyes, "it's been eight weeks since your last monthly visit, you idiot. Conception happened *six* weeks ago, which would make it around the time that you and Leaf ... you know ... *met*!"

"This baby could be yours?" I whispered to Leaf.

Nodding, Leaf looked down at his hands.

Poppy blew out a long breath.

And me? Well, I felt a smile curl itself around my whole body. "That's even *better*, right? If it's Leaf's baby, biologically, then it's only you, Poppy, who will have to adopt it."

Poppy huffed a laugh and shook her head. "Unbelievable."

"I told you the other day, remember, that if I could change everything, I would. Well, here you go. This is my chance to make everything right again."

"Get out," she whispered.

"What? Why?" I said. "Aren't you excited? You're going to be a mother! Just like you were supposed to be!"

"Get the fuck out!" She shoved me.

I fell backwards off the bed and my back thumped onto the carpet, knocking the breath out of me.

"Hey! Hey!" Leaf helped me up off the floor and held his arms in front of me like a shield.

"Oh, yeah, that's right! Quick, protect the pregnant girl!"

"Lauren ..." he said.

Poppy slapped his face; the sound cracked the air like a whip.

"Don't *Lauren* me!" she snarled. "Don't you dare." And then she leaned around him to glare at me. "I've seen how close you've been getting with my husband. You two must think I'm so stupid!"

"Lovely, it's not like that," said Leaf, rubbing the blooming handprint on his cheek.

She narrowed her eyes at him. "I know you fuck her every night after you think I'm asleep."

"We don't ..." I started to say, but Leaf held up a hand to silence me.

"So?" he hissed at her. "What am I supposed to do? *You* don't want to touch me!"

Poppy shook her head and turned her icy eyes back to me. "You're just a pity fuck! You know that, don't you?" she said. "You think he would willingly have sex with a freak like you and actually *enjoy* it!"

"Don't talk to her like that!"

"Fuck you, Leaf! Why can't you be on my side for once? Why can't you just agree with me?"

"Because then we'd both be wrong!"

"You can't tell me what to do; you're not my father!"

"No, I'm not! I'm your *husband*, remember? I love you."

"Love me?" She laughed. "Bullshit. You said we weren't going to stay in Alabama in case Sanderson catches up with us. But we're still here! We've been here for weeks. He could turn up any day and I'll be dragged back home to that fucking convent and we'll be separated." Her eyes widened. "Or maybe that's what you want? Me out of the picture, so you two can get on with your perfect lives, and have your perfect baby together." She stepped around us toward the bedroom door. "Fuck you both."

Leaf grabbed her by the arm. "Wait!"

"Let me go!" She tried to pull away from him, but he dug his fingers into the flesh of her biceps. "Ouch! You're hurting me, you asshole!"

"What has happened to you?" he whispered.

"I was shot," she said through clenched teeth. "In the stomach. And my baby died. Remember that, dear? I know *Ray* does. Right, Ray?" She turned to me. "Of course you remember," she hissed. "You were the one that talked me into marching in that stupid rally. So yeah, okay, maybe I have been taking some *stuff* to help deal with the pain, and the hurt, and the grief, but so what? It's just morphine, really. And that can't be *too* bad if the hospital sent me home with it in the first place."

Leaf slid his hand to interlock his fingers with hers. "We're just worried about you, that's all. We love you. We want you to get better."

"You make me sick sometimes." She slapped his hand away. "Get better? I lost my *child*! It's not as easy as just *getting better*!"

"She was my child too," whispered Leaf.

"Why don't you act like it, then?" Poppy shouted. "Why don't you grieve for her, like I do? Why don't you act like your whole world was taken away in that one moment? Why don't you care?"

"I *do* care! Jesus Christ, Poppy, how can you say that to me? I think about her – about Sylvia – every minute of every day. And if a minute does go by that I don't think of her, I feel guilty and terrified that I'm going to let her slip away. I wish I could take the coward's way out and stick a needle in my arm and pretend that the world is not continuing to turn without her in it, but I can't do that! I can't, because if I disappear into myself, like you have, then there will be no one left to look after *you* – the only other thing that I love in this world. Please, Poppy ... Lauren ..." He took her small, shaking hand is his big, steady ones. "Come back to me. I want my wife back. I want our future back. Just because we lost Sylvia, doesn't mean we have to lose everything else."

"I am not a coward." She pulled her hand away again.

"Sorry, maybe coward is the wrong word." He narrowed his eyes at her. "I meant junkie."

She gasped.

"You are a fucking heroin junkie, and I can't watch it anymore. I can't watch you slowly kill yourself, kill everything we ever hoped for and dreamed about together." Leaf slipped his wedding ring off his finger and thrust it at her.

"What ..." Poppy's eyes were as round as the ring she stared at. Her chin trembled and her words shook. "What are you doing? Don't!"

"Choose," said Leaf. "Me and forever. Or you and oblivion."

"You're giving me an ultimatum?"

"You gave me one first."

"This is crazy!" Poppy shook her head. "I don't use that much anyway; only enough to keep me straight, really. It's not like I'm getting so high I can't function. And it's just for the pain. Just for the next couple of weeks, and then I'll stop, okay? She pressed the ring back into his palm and curled his fingers around it. "Okay?"

But Leaf opened his hand and the ring fell at his feet.

Dropping to her knees, Poppy snatched for the rolling band of gold. It slipped between her fingers and wobbled toward the shadows beneath the bed, a glimmer of light disappearing into the darkness.

"You quit *now*," said Leaf. "Today. Or get out of my life now. Today."

Poppy stared up at him. Tears fell from her chin and puddled in the fold of her nightgown.

"So, what's your decision?" asked Leaf.

"I ... I ... need some time ..." she said.

"No, you don't." Leaf shook his head. "If I'm not your first and immediate choice, which, obviously, I am not – then I refuse to become your second choice. It's over, Lauren. We are over."

Wrapped in the fragile shawl of a sob, Poppy stumbled through the bedroom door.

Seconds later, we heard footsteps on the front porch, the

thunk of the van door slamming closed, the engine revving, tires squealing, and then nothing but the solid presence of her absence.

"Whoa." I let out my breath in a whoosh of shock. "Did you mean what you just said?" I asked.

"Of course not." Leaf ran a hand down his face. "I'm just trying to scare her straight; nothing else has worked; I don't know what else to do."

"We should go after her!"

He shook his head. "She's just driving off her steam. Trust me, this is how she handles shit. If you follow her, you'll make it ten times worse. She needs time to process, to get centered, to calm down. I just hope this works. Now," Leaf said, hugging me against him, "did *you* mean what *you* said?"

I looked into his deep, chocolate eyes. They were still as warm and friendly as always, but now they were tinted with something else. Hope, perhaps? I remember the first time I met this wonderful man, the first time I looked into these eyes, and I remembered the instant feeling of safety I'd felt in his presence.

It was the feeling every child should have when looking into the eyes of their father.

"Yes," I said, and I moved his hand from my shoulder to my stomach. "I meant every single word."

chapter thirty-six

japhy

It is two fifteen in the morning, and Lion slumps against the doorframe.

"Wake me up if Ass comes by," he says, and within minutes a soft snore whistles from his nose.

Good, I think. If he gets caught sleeping like this during our Fireguard Duty shift, he'll be in all kinds of shit.

I smile, and try to summon the Drill Sergeant with my thoughts.

Of course, I'll get in all the same kinds of shit, since it's my job to keep him alert and alive; I am his Battle Buddy, after all.

Battle Buddy. What a fucking joke.

Right now, I'd happily spend the entire night doing push-ups and star jumps until the sun rises, as long as this shit-for-brains suffers right alongside me. And the rest of the platoon included.

What a bunch of assholes.

They can all go straight to hell.

Again, I see the sniggers on the faces around me in the mess hall: the way Lion leaned back in his chair and crossed his arms proudly; the way Timothy just ducked his head, and kept on eating his disgusting food, while I took the blows that should have been falling down on him; the way he joined them in the corner of the barracks later to wolf-whistle and make comments about unrequited love.

Fuckers.

I sit back against the wall and fight to keep my eyes open. The lids weigh down with all the heaviness of this place, and I can't hold them up any longer. They drop; darkness wraps me in its warm, non-judgmental arms. I want to sink down and stay there forever.

My muscles are so sore. My brain so exhausted. My bones so brittle.

Sleep calls me like a siren's song with its promise of temporary escape. And the added attraction of entire-platoon punishment is just gravy. I could sleep *and* get revenge on all those jerkwads in one go!

Yesterday, when Ash had read out my name alongside Lion's, pairing us up as Battle Buddies, Lion had groaned. Behind him, suppressed laughter crackled in the air like static; it made the hair on the back of my neck rise.

"Tonight we will begin the nightly shifts of Fireguard Duty," Ash had said. "It will be your responsibility to make sure these barracks don't burn down. Make sure everyone is in their bunk. And, most importantly, make sure all you homos aren't butt-fucking each other!"

Stares had burned and blistered the back of my head, and the electric current of bottled-up laughter rolled like a storm around me again. Once Ash left the barracks, some of the guys whistled and thumped Lion on the back.

"Lucky man!" I heard someone say.

"Hey, Lion," someone else called out. "Just close your eyes when he sucks your cock; a mouth is a mouth, right?"

More laughter.

I wondered if Timothy had joined in on the fun.

At the memory of this, heat burns away all desire for sleep, like fire clearing away cobwebs.

I open my eyes. Lion's mouth purses in slumber. And then he frowns, his whole face contracts, and tears leak from the corners of his eyes.

"No ..." he mumbles, twitching his hands. "Stop ... please

... *hurts* ... Daddy!" he gasps and sits up. "Don't!" His eyes are wide and he stares at me. "Don't let it happen again!" he whispers. "Please, Daddy? You're supposed to *protect* me!"

"Lion?" I sit forward. "You okay, man?"

His eyes close again. "Don't let it happen again, please?" And then, as the nightmare ends, his face smooths out like a fresh sheet.

I kick his foot. "Hey, jerk!"

"What? Huh?" He sits up, blinks at me, and looks around. "Is it Ass?"

"You were dreaming," I say. "And talking in your sleep."

"You didn't have to wake me up for that. Damn."

"Problems at home?" I ask.

"No." He crosses his arms and settles back against the door.

"Is that why you enlisted?" I ask. "To get out?"

"You're crazy," he says. But he looks away from me. "Just shut up, homo."

I shrug, but as I lean into the wall, I feel empathy press back, as cold and hard as the wood against my spine.

No one, not even assholes like Lion, should have to live in a home where fear is as much a member of the family as the mother and father. Perhaps this is why he is such a prick; he is just continuing the cycle of bullying he learned from his dad.

Standing up, I push away from the cold wall, but the chill of compassion stays with me, seeping into my bones until I shiver from it. I rub my hands over my arms, trying to thaw it out of me; I don't want to feel sorry for this cheese-weasel.

Lion lifts his knees to his chest, wrapping his arms about his legs. His forehead rests on his forearms and he curls into a ball like a child who tries to shrink so the person looking for him will walk straight by.

Lapping the barracks, on the lookout for Ash, I let Lion sleep, even though my tired legs can barely hold me up.

At four o'clock, I nudge him awake and we stagger back inside. My eyes are itchy and desperate for sleep. Even though I'll only get one hour of shut-eye before that damned bugle will sound at five and I'll have to get up anyway, I long to finally let my eyelids fall closed.

Timothy is starfished across his mattress.

"Hey, Murdoch." I shake his shoulder. "Wake up. It's your shift."

Timothy groans and hits my hand away.

"Careful, Sleeping Beauty," Lion whispers to Timothy, from the other side of my bunk. "Mack might try and kiss you awake!"

At that, Timothy sits up and rubs the drool off his chin.

I crawl under my covers, where the shushing of onrushing sleep grows loud in my ears, and I think I hear the soft whisper of Timothy's words: "I'm sorry, Japhy." But perhaps it is just the sighing of my bones creaking under the weight of a crushing secret that isn't mine to share.

*

"For those of you who have women waiting for you at home," calls Ash, "forget them!" He spins on a heel and walks back. "For those of you who *want* a woman, here she is!"

Black, sleek, cold, and the ugliest thing I have ever seen, my M-16 rifle gleams up at me like the shiny body of a black widow spider.

They lie on tables in front of each one of us.

Ash lets his fingers drift over his gun adoringly.

"This beautiful body stretched out in front of you is now your wife!" Ash says. "She is a lightweight, gas-operated, air-cooled, magazine-fed, shoulder-firing spouse! You will love her. You will respect her. You will fucking fantasize about her when you whack off in your cots at night! IS THAT CLEAR?"

"YES, SIR!" we all scream back.

"HANDS ON!" calls Ash.

To my left, Lion slides a finger inside the hand guard, stroking the trigger gently.

To my right, Timothy places his hands on the barrel. His fingers explore the smoothness of the cold steel from base to tip and back again.

"This is a semi-automatic rifle!" yells Ash. "It is not a *gun*.

Show it your respect! You would not refer to your mother as a *whore*, and you will not refer to this rifle as a *gun*."

I lift my arm from the safety of my side and hover it above the metallic body. Is it *new*? I wonder. Straight from the factory? Or has it been shipped back from Nam?

Has this gun protected?

Has this gun killed?

Will this gun kill in the future?

My hand shakes as I try to lower it, to press my fingers against the cool steel, but I just can't close the distance. There is a solid pillow of memory between metal and skin that I cannot push through.

I breathe in. The air against my throat sounds like the words: *All right, Guard ...*

And every heartbeat is the *crack-crack* of shots.

And every blink is the image of a student falling to the grass.

Yet every throb in my gut is also the undeniable surge of *power* that I know holding a weapon will produce.

"What the fuck is your problem, Mack?" Ash is in my face. The heat of his breath burns my eyes. "I said, hands on!"

"Yes, sir," I say, but I still can't touch the disgusting thing in front of me. I ball my fist and drop my arm back against my hip.

Sergeant Ash places his palms flat on either side of the rifle and leans forward so his nose almost touches mine. "Put your fucking hand on your fucking rifle, Private, or I will force it so far up your fucking ass that you'll have to pull it out of your fucking mouth!"

Lion snorts. "You'd probably like that, wouldn't you, Mack?"

Ash snatches the gun off the bench with both hands and slams it into my chest. The air gasps from my lungs with the cold, bruising force of the steel frame against my sternum. I stumble backwards and fall.

The weight of the M-16 pins me to ground like a rapist, and a shadow rises over me as black as despair. I close my eyes and wait for it all to be over.

How am I going to get through this year if I can't even *touch* a gun? Fuck.

The tips of my fingers tingle as they brush against the weight on top of me. I want to reach, want to curl my hands around the cold, black steel, to caress it, to grip it tightly and never let go.

Yet, at the same time, the very idea of touching this horrible thing makes me want to be sick.

It's just a piece of metal, I tell myself. Just sculpture. Just art.

Just get up. Just get through this. Just survive.

A hand touches my shoulder. "Come on, Japhy." And I feel the weight lifting from my aching ribs.

Slitting open my eyes, I see Timothy crouching, smiling, and offering me a hand.

"You can do this," he says, nodding. "Do it for Ray, remember?"

Yes, I think. Do it for Ray.

I grip Timothy's hand and stand tall.

For Ray.

Cradling the gun in my arms – my fingers singing – I imagine I am not holding the metal frame of a machine that takes life, but, instead, the body of the one who will save my life every time.

I imagine I am holding Ray.

Which makes it easier to admit that this rifle feels fucking amazing in my arms.

My chest swells. My head clears.

"Today is a lesson in love-making, boys!" Ash yells. "You will learn how to seduce your new lover, strip her naked, clean her out nice and good ... and then put her pieces back together so she's better than she was before. You will learn to do this quickly, you will learn to do this often, because a clean rifle is a maintained rifle, and a maintained rifle will not jam. A jammed rifle will get you killed."

Ash stands behind the table in front of us, looking down at his M-16. "Lock the bolt to the rear, push the rear disassembly pin, push the front disassembly pin." His hands blend into the black metal, become part of the gun itself, and the gun becomes a part of him, and I feel a hot surge of jealousy at seeing the ease with which this rifle submits. "Separate the upper and lower receivers. Remove the handgrips. Pull the charging handle. The bolt carrier group will drop out. Remove the firing pin. Remove the retaining pin. Remove the buffer assembly. Open the butt-stock."

It's hypnotic and beautiful. A perfectly choreographed dance.

And then he steps back and the gun is suddenly in a hundred thousand pieces.

"You have three minutes." Ash grins. "Go!"

I stare at him. And then I turn and stare at Timothy. Heads pivot on shoulders all along the line.

"I said, go!" Ash screams. "Or do I have to make you assholes drop?"

"No, Drill Sergeant!"

Tentatively, I run my fingers along the barrel, trying to remember what Ash had done to transfer such a solid and powerful object into nothing but individual pieces.

"Two minutes!" he screams.

My hands shake as I lift the rifle and turn it over as if there will be a big red arrow on the other side that says, *press here, idiot*. But the other side is just as structurally indelible, and apparently seamless, as the first side was.

"One minute!"

I hear a chink somewhere to my right, as someone manages to pull some piece off some other piece, and everyone turns toward the sound to get a clue of what they are supposed to do.

"Ten seconds!"

Shit.

"Three! Two! One! *Drop!*"

I hit the dirt, and begin to count off my push-ups in time with the whole company.

How the hell are we supposed to break into pieces something so strong and apparently unbreakable? Something held together with so much might that it resists change, resists division of itself in any way?

My shoulders ache. My chest burns. My palms sting against

the gravel as I push up and lower myself, push up and lower myself, and I wonder how long I can remain here, mentally intact, structurally indelible, and apparently seamless.

"It appears that I am being made a fool of!" Ash walks up and down the line. "It appears that someone high up in command thinks it's funny to assign me this worthless company of dickheads. They plan to watch me fail at improving you assholes from the lowlife scum you already are! But I have news for them! I will *not* fail! I will turn every God damn one of you scrotums into a soldier this country will be proud of. And then *I* will be the one who is fucking laughing at *them*!"

I picture the rifle laid out on Ash's table. I watch again as it is magically reduced to pieces of itself, stripped down and rendered harmless, before it will be rebuilt in just the right way to give it the ability and the power to kill.

Again, I see his hands blurring with ease over the gun, and I realize, it's easy for Ash – and other Drill Sergeants just like him – to break apart something so apparently strong and infallible; after all, the United States Army does this every single day.

chapter thirty-seven

ray

By lunchtime, Poppy had not returned.

We called Mandala, but no one had heard from her. Leaf phoned her best friend in Virginia, who hadn't heard anything from Lauren since she'd left with Leaf, months ago. He called her older sister in San Francisco, but, again, no trace.

Dinnertime came and went, and the sun set, and the stars pricked the heavens with diamond light, and the moon rose round and full as optimism, and Poppy had still not come home.

"Where *is* she?" Leaf leaned against the porch railing and stared up at the moon and the stars as if searching their mirrored depths for the whereabouts of his wife. "Should have gone straight after her," he muttered. "Shouldn't have let her leave in that state."

I sat on the porch swing, my feet crossed at the ankles back-and-forthing like a pendulum ticking off the passing seconds. "What about her parents?" I suggested.

"Trust me," Leaf laughed. "That's the last place she would go."

"Maybe that's exactly why she *would* go there." I shrugged. "Because you think she won't."

He shook his head. "You don't understand."

"Try me." I stood from the seat and crossed the distance between us, taking his hand and squeezing. "What were you two running away from? What happened that was so bad you feel you can't tell me?"

"It doesn't matter," he said.

"It does to me!" I dropped his hand. "I'm your friend, and it hurts that you feel you can't trust me with this big secret. What are you hiding?"

"Ray ..."

"My *real* name is Heather Wren! What's yours, Leaf?"

He pressed his lips together and turned away, staring up at the moon again.

"I offered to give you my *baby*, and you can't even give me your name?"

"It's complicated," he muttered.

"Is it in Swahili or something?" I said, crossing my arms. "Hard to pronounce?"

He didn't answer, just kept his damn liar eyes fixed on that damn moon.

"Okay, fine!" I pushed away from the railing and headed to the front door. "If Poppy isn't back in an hour, I'm calling the police."

"No!" Leaf spun around and held his hand out to me as if trying to fend off a blow. "You can't do that."

"Yes, actually, I can. What if she is hurt somewhere? What if she went off to buy some more drugs and found some dirty junkie and she needs our help and we do nothing because you have some big fucking secret that is more important to you than the safety of your wife?"

Leaf sighed. His shoulders drooped. He turned to me. "My name is Gabriel."

"Gabriel." I felt the weight of this new name on my tongue. The first syllable was round and long ... *Gabe* ... and the rest flowed from it in two quick sounds ... *Ree-elle*. Staring at the face of my friend, whose name I now knew, I smiled and cocked my head to the side. "You don't look like a Gabriel."

For the first time that day, he laughed (Heh! Heh!). "My friends call me Gabe."

"Okay, Gabe." I sat once again on the porch swing, and patted the space beside me. "What's your story?"

He sighed. His legs folded him onto the seat. "When I first met Lauren, she was ..." Leaf's eyes clouded, "so innocent."

I tensed beside him, and leaned forward so I could catch every word.

"She was with her friend, the kind of girl that every male eye in the room is drawn to, you know: blond hair, short skirt, high boots, pouty lips. Completely gorgeous. But," he said, and smiled, "it was the girl beside her that I couldn't look away from. Lauren stood off to the side, in the shadow, as if to give her friend the spotlight. But I'll tell you something: standing amid those shadows, Lauren glowed!

"When I first introduced myself to her, she refused to look at me. She talked into my chest, and wouldn't meet my eyes." He laughed. "God, that drove me crazy! I never wanted anything more, in that moment, than to be able to look into her eyes. No matter what I did, or said, she just wouldn't lift her head up another inch. At the end of the night, when she said goodbye, she took a breath, closed her eyes for a second, and then she blinked them open and fixed her gaze on me. Man ..." he sighed. "What a fucking rush. You know sometimes when you see something so awesome that it's hard to breathe?"

I nodded, thinking of Japhy holding out his draft letter to me.

"I fell in love with that girl right then and there. But of course, she didn't feel the same. And it was the hardest thing in the world to hold back from. I just wanted to touch a hand to her cheek, to feel her fingers entwined with mine, to tell her that I wanted her; but I couldn't. She was like a scared little rabbit. If I moved too fast she'd scamper away and I'd never see her again. I had to move so slowly ..." Leaf shot to his feet and squinted as headlights fell across the porch, and we were both blinded.

"Lauren?" He ran to the steps, holding his hand over his eyes to try and see through the brightness.

A taxicab grumbled at us. Blared its horn. I could see a man in the driver's seat and I narrowed my eyes, trying to make out the shape of another head in the dim light of the car's interior, but the passenger seat and the back seat were both empty.

Placing my hand on the small of Leaf's back, I felt him quiver. "It's not her," I whispered.

And he nodded.

Behind me, the screen door screeched open.

I turned to see Nora stepping out toward us. Her hair, parted in the center, fell straight down on either side of her face, curtaining her eyes for a second. She wore a pair of blue bell-bottoms and a psychedelic orange dashiki. Behind her, she dragged a suitcase.

"Nora?" I frowned.

"Hi." She grinned at me. "And bye."

"You're leaving?"

"I wanted to tell you earlier, but I was afraid you'd talk me out of it!"

"Where are you going?"

"Phoenix."

"Arizona?"

She nodded.

"Why?" I gasped.

"There's a program there for people like me."

"Crazy people?"

She laughed. "Survivor people."

"How long will you be gone?"

"Depends how long it takes," she said.

"How long *what* takes?"

"To become free."

"Free?"

She smiled. "Free. Could be two weeks, could be twelve months. Who knows?"

I looked at Leaf, who glanced from Nora to her suitcase, as if he couldn't quite put the pieces together.

"Unless," said Nora, "there is some reason that I should stay? But I figured you didn't really need me here; you have Leaf and Poppy to keep you company, and of course I want you all to stay *here* at the house, just in case ..." She stopped and pressed her lips together, but I heard the words she tried to squash. I heard them as clearly as if she had leaned into my ear and shouted: *in case a telegram arrives.*

"Twelve months?" I said. Then I glanced down at my waist. Soon it would be ballooning with Nora's (maybe) grandchild, which I planned to keep a secret and give to Poppy, and pretend I'd never been pregnant in the first place. Maybe Nora had just handed me a get-out-of-pregnancy-free card. By the time she came home, the baby would be born and cradled in its new mother's arms. "Will you be coming back to visit or anything?"

"Oh, sweetheart." Nora put her arm out and wrapped me in a warm hug. She smelled like carrots. "I'll miss you, too. I can take leave whenever I want, but they recommend full-time commitment to the program. So if – for whatever reason ..." Again she squashed her words, and again I heard them shouted in my head anyway. "... if I need to come home, I can. But I have to do this. I have to get well."

"Can I get hold of you if ..." This time, I was the one to bite down on words. "If I need you?"

"I've left all the information on the kitchen counter," said Nora. "I've also left an envelope of money to cover the expenses of the house: bills and all that stuff. Plus whatever you'll need for day-to-day living."

"Nora ..." I shook my head. "I can't take your money."

But she simply waved a hand at me. "Don't be so uptight, Heather. It's not a hand-out; it's a *job*. I need a caretaker for the house until I get back."

"Can you afford this?" I asked her, looking toward the waiting car.

She smiled sadly. "Michael had life insurance."

The door to the taxi opened and the driver stepped out. "You ready, Missus?"

Nora nodded to him, kissed me on the top of my head, kissed Leaf on his cheek, and then danced a quick-step down the stairs. "When Poppy wakes up, tell her I said goodbye, won't you?"

"We will." Leaf's voice cracked slightly under the weight of his lie.

Pausing beside the open passenger door, Nora took a long breath and frowned up at the house where she had lived with her husband and son, where she and her family had created a lifetime of memories. I recognized that look, that confusion: how can something remain so unchanged on the outside when on the inside everything is completely upside-down? Then she closed her eyes, and slid into the front seat, and didn't look at the house again.

"Airport, please." Nora's words drifted through the open window, and as the taxi pulled away, she held her hand out with two fingers spread wide.

Headlights swept over us in an arc and then cold, lonely night fell on us again.

I leaned into Leaf's side and wrapped my arm tightly around the waist of the only person I had left to hold on to. The only person that still remained to hold on to me.

chapter thirty-eight

japhy

I can barely see through the fog of gas that swirls around me, and I clasp desperately to my mask, making sure it stays properly sealed around my face like the sucker of a giant squid.

I pull in short gasps of clean air through the mask, but no matter how many breaths I take, I'm suffocating. My head is light and there are white flashes at the edges of my vision.

Beside me, Timothy is something from my nightmares, with those giant, circular goggles and double snout. Just like the National Guard. Just like the monsters that stalk my dreams.

The faint taste and smell of the peppery gas – even through the protective mask – slingshots me backwards in time, and I am there again, at Kent State, on that God-forsaken football field, where stones and insults and canisters of tear gas fly back and forth between the students and their slayers.

I close my eyes and shake my head and keep myself focused on *now*.

I am safe here.

Safe.

The army would not put me in a situation that may damage one of their precious soldiers. Not before I am damaged by the war, at least. They need me to get through this first. So therefore, I am safe here.

And then Ash is in front of me, with his hand on my shoulder, and it is my turn.

I freeze.

My palms sweat and my heart hammers and my stomach churns, but I raise my arm, take a deep breath, close my eyes tight, and rip the gas mask from my face.

The microscopic particles of CS squirm beneath my eyelids and into my nostrils and throat and lungs and I drown in my own saltiness. Tears. Snot. Sweat.

"State your name and social security number, private!" Ash screams. Safe behind his own mask, his voice is far away.

"Andrew Michael Mack." I try to get it all out in one breath, but as I recite my social security numbers, stumbling over the vowels and consonants, my lungs empty themselves and I can't help it; I inhale fire. My nose and throat fill with sludge. I lean forward, coughing and spitting. Snot streams from me in ropes.

Ash grabs my helmet from my head, shoves it against my chest, and screams something I can't understand.

I fumble with the helmet and the gas mask, and both clatter to the floor.

Shit!

I drop to my knees and scrabble. Blind. My lungs burn and wheeze with every single breath.

And I need my stupid mask. And I need to get out. And I need fresh air. And screw this, I'm leaving!

I crawl toward the exit, but Ash pulls me to my feet and slams me against the wall of the gas chamber. I gasp another breath of fire and I want to scream.

"Put your mask on, private, or you will stay in here for a full hour!"

"Let me out!" I scream. "Let me out, I can't breathe!"

"I said recite the Soldier's Creed!" he yells.

But I cough and shake my head. "I can't remember it!"

"Well, remember!" He turns and faces the ten others in here with me, standing, squinting, coughing, with their backs straight and faces exposed. "Private Mack has forgotten the Creed. Remind him!"

As I drop again, and squint through my tears, and slap my hands against the floor and walls in a desperate search for my mask, they splutter as one and their voices echo and bounce around me: "I am an American Soldier. I am a member of the United States Army – a protector of the greatest nation on earth!"

My lunch curdles in my stomach and I cough on the mucous that chokes me as the words of the creed are shouted and swirl around me in the haze.

"As a soldier, I realize that I am a member of a time-honored profession – that I am doing my share to keep alive the principles of freedom for which my country stands!"

A hand squeezes my shoulder and someone squats down in front of me. My helmet and mask are pressed into my hands, and then the figure stands and continues to recite the Creed: "I will use every means I have, even beyond the line of duty, to restrain my army comrades from actions disgraceful to themselves and to the uniform!"

Through the blurry clouds of gas and my acidic tears, I can't tell who has helped me. Maybe that is why whoever it is *did* help me: because here, in this gas chamber, he is invisible. No one else can see exactly who helped the faggot.

In here, as in battle, we are all alike. Skin color doesn't matter, religion doesn't matter, sexual preference doesn't matter; in the end, we all bleed the same.

Staggering upright, I fit my helmet on, then slide the mask over my face and press the release. The next breath I take is magic. It doesn't burn anymore. Although the mucous still streams, and I have to sniff and swallow to clear my sinuses, every breath is cool and smooth again.

"Private Mack," screams Ash. "Recite the rest of the Creed!"

I steady my breathing, calm myself, and focus before pulling off the mask again. "I am proud of my country and its flag," I say. "I will try to make the people of this nation proud of the service I represent, for I am an American Soldier."

"Remember that." Ash nods as I replace my mask again. "If you lose your shit on the battleground, you may lose your life! Your equipment is your friend."

Brightness fills the room. Sweet, glorious liberation. And we all file toward the door at the end of the chamber like ghosts gliding toward heaven.

Once I'm out in the sunshine, I rip the mask off and spit, and open my eyes to the cool breeze until the tears stop falling.

"Don't think this makes us friends."

I turn at the sound of the voice behind me. "*You* helped me?" I frown up at Lion. "Why?"

"I just wanted to get the hell out of there, that's all."

I shrug and raise my palms. "Thanks anyway, man."

"Don't mention it," he says. "And I mean that."

Clouds of tear gas seep beneath the chamber's door, like souls slipping out through the cracks of hell, as Lion walks through it and vanishes.

chapter thirty-nine

ray

As I drove the empty moonlit streets, I glanced over at Leaf in the passenger seat. Lights slid across his face every few seconds, striping him in clean white and black lines like the uniform of a convict. He stared straight ahead. He didn't even blink. His jaw clenched and released. And I didn't know what the hell to say. We'd been searching for two whole hours, but Poppy, and the van, had disappeared from our lives.

By the time Leaf and I pulled into Nora's driveway, he had folded in on himself like a desiccated leaf that curls its edges inward, trying to protect itself even as it catches on fire.

"You win." His voice crackled and snapped as his eyes met mine in the darkness. "Call the police." As he followed me up the path, his head drooped, his feet dragged, like a man shuffling to his own execution.

Inside, he slumped on the sofa, staring at the blind cyclopsian eye of the television while I spoke to Officer Mulroney, while I gave a description of Lauren and the van, and while I listened to this officer explain that, although they will keep an eye out for her, they will not begin an official search until she has been missing for a full twenty-four hours.

"But that's not until tomorrow morning," I said, and thought to myself: it could be too late by then.

"That's correct, ma'am," said the policeman, before disconnecting the call.

I slumped onto a kitchen chair, prepared to sit there and wait for the sun to rise like hope in the sky.

It was close to midnight when three banging blows rattled the front door on its hinges, or perhaps the door rattled with the force of the life-altering punch that waited on the other side of the threshold.

Had I known who stood on the welcome mat, and had I known the news that I was about to hear, I could have covered my ears with my hands and crawled beneath my bed and waited for this knocker to go away and leave me alone. Then, perhaps, I could have continued living in this life where hope still illuminated my world, and where news like this had absolutely no place.

Leaf rose from the sofa and stared at the entrance hall as if he too contemplated running and hiding beneath his covers, and I stood from the table, where I'd been gazing blindly at the pamphlet Nora had left on the counter: *The Phoenix Cancer Healing Center.*

"Maybe it's Poppy?" I whispered. "She may not feel comfortable just letting herself in after what happened this morning."

But it was not Poppy.

And as I drove to the Liberation County Hospital, following the demon-red eyes of the police car's tail lights, I kept wondering if it would have made a difference if I'd ignored Leaf and called the police sooner.

The parking lot of the hospital was practically empty. I found a space near the entrance, and turned off the engine. The silence that filled the car pressed down on my chest and I couldn't breathe from the pressure.

Beside me, Leaf didn't move. He just stared out the front window and bit down on nothing.

"Come on," I whispered.

He jumped, and closed his eyes. Then he nodded and I saw him crumple at his fire-blackened edges even more.

Officer Mulroney waited for us in the foyer. He nodded

and offered us a quick smile as the glass doors parted and we stepped toward him.

Shaking Leaf's hand, the officer whispered, "Thanks for coming down at this hour. She's just down here. Please, follow me."

After riding the elevator, we walked slowly along a bright but deserted corridor. Fluorescent lights blared like suns above our heads, and at the end of the hall, one light flickered on and off every few seconds. As I approached this final light, which buzzed each time it blazed on and fell silent whenever it blinked out, I thought about the human soul: did it go out quickly, just like a light? Or did it hold on, flickering with indecision? Off or on? Leave or stay? Die or live?

I wondered if Poppy had been given this choice, or had that decision been taken out of her hands?

The officer pushed open a door, then stepped back to let us pass.

I always imagined a morgue to be cold. But it was surprisingly warm in that room. Maybe because it housed the body of someone who had burned so brightly that now, even after her soul was gone, her shell remained hot and heated the air. Her life heated this room the same way guilt charred my insides and blackened my soul.

"Phil." The officer nodded to a man sitting at a desk, chewing a pencil.

The man, Phil, had thinning black hair brushed back across his bald spot and glued in strands over his pink scalp. His eyes flicked up to the officer and then dropped back to the crossword puzzle. "Oh, hey, Derek," he said. "What's a six-letter word for hope?"

Lauren, I thought.

Officer Mulroney cleared his throat. "I have the identifiers for our Miss Jane Doe."

"Oh, sure thing." Phil stood up and gave us that same exact pity-filled smile that the police officer had given us before. "Right this way, please, folks."

A ring of keys jangled in Phil's fist as he unlocked a plain white door beside his chair.

I held my breath, terrified, as we followed him inside.

Two feet poked out from beneath a white sheet. They looked so unbelievably small that for a second I hoped that maybe this was the unclaimed corpse of a child, and not my beautiful dead friend.

Not my Poppy. Not my Lauren. Not my baby's mother.

She lay beneath a shroud like a bad Halloween ghost. Breath rattled in Leaf's throat as he hiccoughed beside me, and I reached for his hand. He squeezed my fingers, crushed my bones together until they began to throb – but that was okay. That was pain I could handle. Physical pain. It was nothing compared to the deep ache in my heart.

The officer stood on the other side of the stretcher. As he reached for the sheet, I silently prayed to any deity listening that the face I was about to look upon would not be Lauren's. I begged time to stop right then, to freeze in this moment where I could live in the belief that maybe Lauren was still out in the world somewhere, on her way back to us right now, and that we would laugh about this misunderstanding later while raising a glass to the poor dead Jane Doe who still lay unclaimed in the Liberation County Morgue.

Muscles bunched in the officer's hand. His fingers tightened into a fist as a corner of the white material was trapped inside his folded palm. And then his arm bent at the elbow and lifted the sheet.

A lock of fiery orange hair slipped out, and Leaf turned away from it, closing his eyes.

Oh, Lauren. I drew in a sharp breath as I took in your face. Your eyelids and lips are a pale, robin's egg blue and look just as fragile. Like you are made of porcelain. Like you are some kind of fairy tale heroine. Like you have been cursed and need true love to save you. Only your true love is so broken-hearted over this cursed transformation that he cannot bear to *look* upon you, let alone kiss you and break the spell, thus dooming you to this unfortunate eternity. To this unfortunate death.

"Do you recognize this woman?" the officer asked.

"My wife," said Leaf. When he tried to speak the word

wife, his voice shattered down the center, and sobs spilled out through the cracks.

"What was her name?" the officer asked me, flipping open his notepad.

"Lauren," I said.

"Family name?"

I said nothing, because I didn't know what her real name had been.

"Lauren Marie Johnson," whispered Leaf.

"Thank you, sir." The policeman wrote her name down. "Do you know her parents' names?"

Leaf clenched his jaw. "No."

"Do you know of any other relatives we can contact?"

He shook his head and clenched his jaw again. "She had no other family. Besides us."

I swallowed. "What happened ...?"

"We can't be certain until the autopsy is carried out," said the officer.

I pictured a gleaming scalpel running the length of Lauren's pale torso, a thin ribbon of red unspooling in its wake. Beside me, Leaf stiffened.

"But she was found in the lake," he continued. "All her clothes were left neatly folded in the van, so we assume she went for a swim."

"No!" Leaf shook his head. "She wouldn't ... she hated ..." But then he bit down on his words and swallowed them.

"Mr. Johnson," the officer said slowly, "could your wife swim?"

Leaf looked at his shoes. One lace was untied and left a wet stripe across the floor. "Of course she could," he muttered.

The officer bowed his head and gave us that pitying fucking smile again. "I am so sorry. I'll give you both a few minutes with her if you like," he said, backing toward the door, where Phil and his bad comb-over waited, his head bowed too. "I understand this is a very difficult time, and the last thing I'm sure you want to do right now is to relive the details, but I will have to ask you both some questions."

I nodded.

"Right now?" asked Leaf.

The officer tipped his head and smiled. "I guess it can wait until the morning. Why don't you both go home and try and get some sleep. I know that probably sounds crazy, and sleep is probably the last thing you feel you need right now, but trust me, it will help."

Leaf closed his eyes for a second. "Thank you."

"You can both be reached at the same address from tonight?"

We nodded.

"All right. I'll be in touch tomorrow," the officer said, and closed the door behind Phil and himself, leaving Leaf and me alone with the ghosts of our own guilt.

"What am I supposed to do now?" Leaf gasped for air in between sobs, and smoothed the hair off Lauren's forehead. "What am I supposed to do for the rest of my life, huh? Jesus, Lauren, Jesus Christ, why did you leave me? What am I supposed to do now?" He leaned down and whispered in her ear. "Knock, knock." He paused. As if listening to her response of who's there. "Amish," he said, hovering above her, and then in order to keep his lips from trembling, he kissed her.

As he pressed his mouth to hers, I held my breath and waited for her to gasp, for her skin to bloom soft and pink again, for the curse to be broken by true love's kiss. But she remained pale porcelain. She remained forever broken.

Leaf's knees buckled and he caught himself on the side of the metal stretcher, the movement rocking Lauren's head from side to side as if she were trying to shake off death. "I think I need some air," he said.

I grabbed hold of his arm to steady him on his feet.

"Just give me a minute alone?" he said. "Please?"

"Sure."

And then he turned to me and wrapped his whole self around my tiny frame. Arms. Hands. Chest. Heart. Grief. Everything. "Oh, Ray, thank you so much for everything you and Japhy did for us. Thank you so, so much." Then he paused, and whispered: "I am so sorry." Then he kissed my forehead and jogged from the room before I could even respond, and the swinging doors gave a quick *clap-clap* as if applauding his exit.

He was sorry? Wasn't I supposed to be the one who says that to him?

I stared at the door, frowning, telling myself to stay put even though my gut wanted to follow Leaf, to chase him down the hall and clamp my hand around his hand and not let it go.

But that was just silly. So what if he'd had a strange note to his voice just then? So what if his hug had lingered a few seconds longer than they normally did? As if he were savoring it. As if he didn't plan on doing it again. As if he were saying goodbye.

I shook my head. No. Leaf wouldn't do that to me. He wouldn't leave me now. Not now. He wouldn't leave me to deal with all this on my own.

Turning back to the stretcher, I stepped closer and reached for Lauren's hand.

It was as hard and cold as dried cement.

"Ugh!" Snatching my hand away, I wiped it on my jeans. She was completely gone. Even her softness no longer existed in this world. This was no longer my friend, my sister, the mother for my child. This was just a corpse.

Pinching the edge of the sheet between two fingers, careful not to touch any part of that stony body, I draped it back over the dead face.

"Goodbye, Lauren," I whispered, looking up at the ceiling fan. "And I hope, wherever you are, that you can forgive me. I am so sorry. I love you. Goodbye."

As I left her behind me and walked back along the corridor beneath that damn flickering light, I let my hand brush against the wall, just in case I grew lightheaded again, and just to make sure that the world around me, which was suddenly surreal and inside-out and nightmarish, didn't pop like a soap bubble and leave me floating in a black vacuum. With nothing to keep me anchored, I would rise up and away into the atmosphere where the oxygen would grow too thin to breathe.

I coughed and walked faster toward the doors of the hospital, through which, I knew, my only anchor waited.

As the hospital doors opened on to the night, I heard that strange note in Leaf's voice again. That strange way his words sounded: thin, stretched, guilty.

Outside, the darkness pressed against me like a force through which I could not move. I leaned against the wall. I ran my hand over the solid, rough brick at my back. I stared, disbelieving, at Nora's little red station wagon, empty, in the parking lot.

As my eyes filled with tears and spilled over my cold cheeks, I wrapped my arms across my chest and hugged myself as tightly as I could. Because now there would be nobody to do that for me. There would be no one to hold me. No one to tell me that everything would be okay. No one ...

A small part of me had known that Leaf would not be waiting at the car. Still, the tangibleness of his absence crushed my already bruised and broken heart. At a time when all we had in the whole world was each other, I was completely alone in this tragedy.

Lifting my chin, I stepped off the curb and crossed the short distance to the car, where I slid gratefully into the warmth of the cabin.

With a sob, I started the engine, and waited until my blinding tears began to slow.

The sound of knuckles rapping the driver's window made me jump. I cried out when I saw Leaf squinting at me through the glass.

He opened the door and smiled down at me. "Move over. You're in no state to drive."

I sighed and shuffled across and, once Leaf was behind the wheel, reached out and clamped my hand around his hand and held on to it and did not let it go.

When Leaf pulled the car back into Nora's driveway, I stared up at the sturdy house that was illuminated in the headlights.

"Come on," he whispered. "You need to get some sleep."

"I can't." I shook my head. "It just feels wrong to do something as normal as *sleeping*, when the entire universe has veered into abnormality."

He nodded. "I know. But your body needs to rest. It is building a whole new little human in there, remember?"

Yes, I thought. And wasn't that just a punch in Lauren's face. Life goes on, and all that bullshit. But I *was* exhausted, and the idea of being able to shut down for a few hours sounded blissful to me.

"Hey." He placed a hand gently on my stomach. "Don't forget who matters now. This little seed is the most important thing in the whole world. More important than death. More important than friendship. More important than anything you think may be bringing you down. Will you remember that?"

"Sure."

"I mean it," he said. "Promise me you'll put this little one first, no matter what might happen."

"All right, I promise."

"No matter what!" he said again.

He stared at me so hard I had to look away. "No matter what," I repeated.

"Thank you," he muttered, and then Leaf was at my side, scooping me into his arms and carrying me up the porch steps.

"Thanks for being here," I whispered. "For taking care of me."

His arms tightened around me, but he didn't speak.

In the bedroom, he pulled off my shoes, and I crawled, still dressed, under the covers and waited for his warmth to stretch out beside me. At least I still had that. At least I still had that one constant.

As my eyelids drooped closed, I saw Lauren's face, all cold and hard and blue around the edges, and I throbbed with pain. I needed to see her alive again, warm and soft and pink, to replace that horrible memory of the empty body on the morgue table. I wanted to remember the Lauren who was full of life and energy and heat. I wanted Leaf to finish the story he had started telling me on the porch. I wanted to see her transform from the scared little rabbit girl he'd first met into the beautiful butterfly I had known. I wanted to experience love through his memories. I wanted to keep Lauren alive inside me. I wanted every detail, from the moment she had made eye contact with

Leaf to the moment she had pulled the van over to pick up a bruised draft resister and his girlfriend.

But I couldn't ask that of him. Not now. It would be too cruel to make him relive all they had shared together, all the moments that had tumbled, one after the other, inexorably toward this very moment in which Lauren Marie Johnson no longer existed.

There would be time for all of that, though.

There would be plenty of time.

Rolling into Leaf's chest, I breathed in his scent until I was numb and pain-free. "I love you, Japhy," I murmured.

"I love you too, Lauren, my lovely." His lips were soft and warm on my forehead. "I love you so much."

Solid arms wrapped around me, and I nuzzled into them, letting his heat wrap me up like a blanket. Unconsciousness tugged at my seams and Japhy's face, frayed at the edges, was now inches from mine.

"I missed you so much, Japhy," I said.

"I'm going to miss you so much, Lauren."

When he kissed me, I curled my fingers in his hair and pulled him closer. He unbuttoned my shirt and I unraveled from him just long enough to shrug out of my clothes, and when I reached for him again, my fingertips brushed skin, and my legs wrapped and knotted him against me.

With my eyes closed tight, I mumbled his name into the warmth of his neck: "Japhy, Japhy, Japhy."

And as he moved inside me, filling me with love and contentment and wholeness, he whispered my name too, even though the syllables didn't quite match up.

The orgasm unstitched me and, exhausted, I fell away into unconsciousness, into a million different threads of myself, while somewhere, far off in the distance, I heard the heart-wrenching sobs of two people crying in each other's arms.

*

It was still dark when I woke. Maybe hours later. Maybe only minutes. I stretched my hand out over the smooth sheet, searching for the warmth of Japhy's body, aching to tell him about the nightmare I'd been having. Beside me, the bed was cold, and I realized with a sickening throb in my stomach that Japhy had been taken from me and that Leaf was the one whom my fingers sought.

Yawning, I rose up on an elbow and rubbed the heel of my hand into my eye. Leaf must have snuck back to his room, back to Lauren, I thought, to be there for her when she wakes.

So I remained there – in that precious moment where the brain isn't fully awake yet, where nightmares only exist behind the solid walls of sleep – comfortable in my own ignorance for ten seconds or so.

Nine, eight, seven.

And then ...

Six, five, four.

... It happened ...

Three, two.

Wham!

I sat up and doubled over, gasping as the previous day kicked me in the gut and the chest and the head simultaneously (*Wham! Wham! Wham!*) and I remembered everything. Every single horrible thing.

"Leaf?" I half-called and half-sobbed as I slipped from the bed and staggered down the dark hall to his and Lauren's bedroom, expecting to see him with his face pressed into her pillow, inhaling her before the scent faded away as easily as her soul.

My fingers flapped against the wall, searching for the light switch.

I squinted against the brightness, dazzled, and then I blinked, and blinked again, trying to force my eyes to see something different than this empty room.

Empty, not just of Leaf, but also of his and Lauren's possessions.

"Leaf!" I ran to the living room, to the dining room, to the front door, lights blinding me as I ran.

And finally I found him.

A small part of him, at least. Just one word, scribbled in his messy hand on a yellow note stuck to the front door.
SORRY.

chapter forty

japhy

Like a baby bird with his wings outstretched toward his first liberating leap, I stand 50 feet above the earth; the toes of my boots perch over the edge of this wooden wall with its drop straight down and nothing to break my fall. A warm breeze touches my cheeks and I smile.

Tying a thin, black rope around my waist and through my legs to form the only thing that will keep me from plummeting to the ground, I cinch it tight and tug the knots as I reach for the safety rope.

Beside me, Ash says, "One wrong knot, and you are dead!"

I nod. I think I'm okay.

It could be worse.

I look over at Lion. Oh, it could be so much worse.

Standing straight as a steel rod, but as fragile as a fractured egg, Lion's face will crack apart at any second. His eyes squinch tight as if the very act of seeing how far off the ground he is will shatter the platform on which he stands, and he'll drop down down down.

"Private Leon!" Standing at the edge of the wall, Sergeant Ash holds out the clip of Lion's safety rope. "Step forward."

Lion flinches. His grip tightens on the railing at his back.

A thin whimper slips through his pressed lips, which start to shake.

"Private Leon, step forward!"

There is the tiniest flick of his head, back and forth. And then his mouth cracks – a spiderweb fracture – and out streams the liquid whisper of: "Fuckfuckfuckfuck …"

For the last month in this awful place, this bigot has threatened me, bullied me, single-handedly turned the whole company against me. He has even forced me to dislike myself for feeling sorry for him. But because I don't want to become that person, because I can't afford to lose my soul within the muddy grounds of this Basic Training facility, because I choose to stay true to myself – even if that means helping someone who will never return that favor – I step back from the edge and place a hand on his shoulder.

"It's okay, man," I whisper. "Yes, this is scary, but you know it's all just a mind trick, right? They are trying to push you right to the edge of yourself, to that place where you've never been before, and they want to you cross that boundary to prove to yourself that you have no boundaries. Because once we leave here, and we go to Nam, they can't afford for us to have any boundaries left."

Lion shrugs. "Get the fuck off me." His eyes close even tighter.

"You are strong!" I hiss at him. "You can do this. Just imagine there is someone waiting at the bottom who *doesn't* believe in you. Someone who has spent years beating you down. Someone who never expected you to fight back. Now is your chance," I whisper. "Prove him wrong. Show your father you are stronger than he is!"

Lion's eyes rip open. "Don't you dare talk about my dad!" He lets go of the railing and shoves me away.

"Fine, then." I shrug. "Be a coward. Just like him."

"I am not a coward! I was the only one in my house with any damn balls. I used to go to bed with black eyes, and cigarette burns, and even bruises from a God damn frying pan, but I never, *never*, became the weak one."

"Until now, you mean?" I reach down, unclip my safety

harness and snap the belay around his harness instead, and he's so good and mad at what I've said that he doesn't even notice I've anchored him.

Lion blinks as if my words have blinded him for a moment. And then he shoves my shoulder again. "Oh yeah?" he says. "Yeah? Come on then, tough guy, if you're so fearless ..."

I step away from his hands and the solidity beneath my boot vanishes.

I go down on my side. My gut hits the edge of the wall and the air is sucked out of me by all the sharp intakes and gasps and cries below.

Fifty feet below.

And I am about to plummet.

Yes, I tied my square knot, and my overhand knot, and my half hitch knot perfectly. Yes, my hip rappel seat is positioned perfectly between my legs. And yes, my rappel rope is the perfect length and is secured at the bottom with a spotter, so I can't fall to my death, as Ash has already made clear.

But these things will only save a person whose rappel rope is connected to his rappel seat. And mine is currently connected to Lion's.

"Fuckfuckfuckfuck!" I mutter.

The metallic chink of a closing steel belay replaces the booming of my heart and I look across at Lion, who has repelled down the wall far enough to attach the second safety rope on my harness, to which Ash is holding tightly above.

"You all right, Mack?" Lion asks.

"Yeah," I mutter. "Thanks."

Leaning back in the seat, with my feet pushing me out from the wall, I thread the rope through my harness and grip it in both fists.

Then in one, two, three, Lion and I push off the wall and swing out like twin pendulums, bouncing off the wall another two times before our feet land squarely and securely on the dirt below.

Lion grins as he unclips the belay.

"Hey!" I smile at him. "Don't think this makes us friends or anything!"

He turns to me, pauses, and then dips his head in a small nod.

*

I lie on my bunk and stare at the ceiling and listen to the rustling of paper as every other person in this room tears open envelopes, and unfolds letters, and presses pieces of paper against their faces to try and smell home.

Her scent is still perfectly encased in my memory: dirt, and sex, and patchouli. I don't need to hold a flimsy piece of paper against my skin, imagining that sheet of paper is her fingertips and those written words are really whispers. No, I don't need that poor substitute for Ray in order to have her with me.

A month has passed in this place. In that eternity, surely "home" has crumbled away into dust and all that remains are broken buildings and sun-bleached skeletons.

And yet, only a microsecond has passed in this place. In that single ticking of time, surely "home" has barely even had a chance to notice my absence at all.

I am glad I told Ray not to write me. I am glad I am not, right at this moment, staining her glorious penwork with my tears. I am glad I remain unaware of all she is going through. And I am so fucking grateful she remains unaware of what I am going through.

Rolling over in my cot, I pull the covers up over my head, blacking out all the glowing faces and gleaming eyes and hands sharing letters with other hands.

Because I don't care.

Because I don't want a letter anyhow.

Burying myself away, I press my face into the pillow and let it absorb the hot, wet salt that threatens to drown me.

chapter forty-one

ray

Alone.

I was all alone. But surely not for long. He would be back. He hadn't really left for good.

I rolled over in bed. Crumpled up beside me was the note that Leaf had stuck to the front door.

Snatching it, I peeled it open and smoothed it flat on the mattress, hoping that because I'd been half-asleep when I first read it, perhaps it would say something different now when viewed in the brightness of clarity. But no. It was still there. The last thing he had left me, printed in shaky capital letters: SORRY.

That was all.

Just that one word. Just five simple letters.

Sorry for what?

I didn't believe Leaf would just disappear like that. Yeah, okay, I had suspected he might run at the hospital, but when he had proved me wrong, I'd felt guilty for even *thinking* that he would leave! Of course he wouldn't do that, I'd thought on the drive home. I'd told myself: Leaf is my friend, he cares about me, about the baby; he's not going anywhere. And, with those thoughts heavy and warm in my chest, I had slept. Only to wake up in this nightmare.

What on earth was he running from?
What did he do that was so bad?
Had he accidentally killed someone?
Had he *purposely* killed someone?
Had he purposely killed *multiple* someones?

I tried to imagine Leaf with blood on his hands and a thrilled gleam in his eyes, but I just kept seeing those gentle hands holding me as I cried and those warm eyes gleaming with nothing but honest friendliness.

I knew the size of that man's heart – at least I *thought* I did. He wasn't a serial killer.

So *what*, then?

And then I snatched up the note again and looked at the word he had left me: SORRY. My heart pounded and my stomach ached with a sudden, paralyzing throb of fear. What if he was apologizing, not because he had killed in the past ... but because he was about to kill in the future? What if he was so broken that the only way he'd be whole again was to reunite with the other half of himself? To be with Lauren again?

No, I thought. Leaf wouldn't kill himself. He wouldn't do that. Would he?

I curled in bed, blinking at the ceiling until the sun finally yawned and stretched and beamed a new day into brightness, and I waited to hear the front door open and close, and Leaf's footsteps in the hall.

Because he would be back soon.

I knew it.

Birds chirruped. Car engines rumbled. Paperboys threw rolled up newspapers onto front porches. Wives kissed husbands goodbye.

Hearts continued to beat. Lungs continued to breathe. Lives continued to be lived.

Life just fucking went *on* while I lay in bed. While my spiritual husband trained to survive a war in the Vietnamese jungle, while my friend turned to stone in a morgue drawer, and while my touchstone vanished into the night, life went on. And I finally admitted to myself that Leaf was not coming back and so, thanks to that gutless asshole, I was now completely alone.

Actually, no, I wasn't alone, was I? Not really.

I placed my hand on the flat skin below my belly button.

I was not alone. I had a tiny human seed to keep me company. For a little while at least.

"Hey," I whispered. "How you going in there? Nice and snug and warm, I bet. With no idea of the horrors that are waiting for you out here. Life is hard, baby. It's so hard. I almost wish that you didn't have to come into this horrible world. I wish I could somehow protect you from all the sadness, and the evil, and the pain. But I can't." My eyes stung and I blinked up at the roof. "I can't because it doesn't matter what you do, or how hard you try, or how far you run. It doesn't matter how much you love. It will never be enough." Tears tickled my cheeks and dripped onto my pillow. "There will always be people you think you can trust, but when you need them the most, he'll leave you. He'll sneak away like a fucking coward. And after everything we have been through, the son-of-a-bitch won't even say goodbye! Just 'sorry', which is bullshit because if he was truly sorry then he wouldn't have left in the first place!"

Sitting up, I grabbed my tear-damp pillow and hugged it against my aching chest. Buried my face into its softness and sobbed. Tried to wash out the feelings of betrayal and shock. But I could still smell Leaf deep in the fibers of the fabric. With a guttural roar that tore at my throat, I fisted my hand and smacked the pillow as hard as I could once, twice, three times, four, grunting and screaming with the effort, before throwing it across the room, where it thunked into the wall and then slumped on the floor, misshapen and sad-looking.

"Well, fuck you, Leaf, or Gabriel, or whatever the fuck your name is!" I wiped my hand across my cheeks. "Fuck you! Don't you ever come back here. I don't need you. *We* don't need you."

The phone rang, a shrill scream, and my heart raced.

I threw off the covers, ran through the bedroom door, and skidded to a stop at the small phone table before the third ring.

Snatching the receiver off the cradle, I brought it up to my ear, pressed it there, and waited for his deep, sweet voice to answer me. "Leaf?" I gasped.

"Heather? It's Nora. I hope I didn't wake you? It's almost six here, so that makes it about eight for you, doesn't it?"

"Oh, Nora." My fingers slackened around the handset and I dropped onto the chair. "No, I was awake."

"I just wanted to let you know I arrived here safe and sound."

"That's great."

"I think this is exactly what I've needed. I feel so much better already. This place is so amazing, you should see it! I have my own room with a balcony overlooking a gorgeous ..."

I stared at my feet. Why wasn't Leaf the one calling to let me know he was all right? He didn't have to tell me where he was, or even why he had left, or even to apologize for deserting me and acting like a complete asshole. Just that he was okay. That's all I wanted. That's all I deserved. Didn't I deserve that much? Wasn't that the respectable, honorable, considerate thing to do for a friend? Jeez, I mean it wasn't that much to ask, really, was it?

But what did I care anyway? I didn't! Leaf could go and jump. So what if he didn't call me? So what if I never heard from him again! Good riddance to him.

"Heather?" said Nora.

"Sorry?"

"I asked how things are going there."

"Oh." I cleared my throat and gripped the receiver tightly. "Everything's just fine here."

"Good. Well, I'd better go. I start my first meditation class in ten minutes."

"Great," I said.

"Call me if you need anything, won't you?" said Nora.

"Yes."

"All right then, tell Leaf and Poppy I said hello."

"I will."

After Nora hung up, I kept the handset pressed against my ear so hard it hurt. "Poppy is dead," I choked out the words in a whisper. "And Leaf ran away. And I'm pregnant. And I have no one to help me through this."

"*If you would like to make a call,*" said a tinny, operator's voice, "*please hang up and dial again. If you would like to make a call ...*"

I dropped the phone, wrapped my arms around my knees, and cried.

Until the familiar sound of Leaf's van pulling into the driveway snapped my head up.

I held my breath and listened. The engine idled, low and comforting like a cat's purr. The sound of that van was etched into my memory. It was definitely him! He had come back.

Oh, thank God. I knew he would.

My bare feet clapped the kitchen tiles like welcome applause.

Leaf was here. Leaf was home.

He hadn't lied to me. Not really. He'd said he'd needed some time alone, and that's exactly what he had done, and what's wrong with that? I mean, the poor man had just lost the other half of himself; surely he was entitled to take as much time as he needed. And, yeah, okay, maybe he could've told me he was skipping out, and maybe he could've told me when he'd be back, but that didn't matter now because he *was* back.

All I cared about was that my friend was here again and I couldn't wait to wrap my arms around him and press my face into his chest and hear that big heart of his pounding away, and feel that sense of relief that I only got from him.

Everything would be all right now.

I wrenched open the front door just as Officer Mulroney lifted his hand to knock, and I reeled backwards, startled.

"Good morning, Miss Wren," he said, gazing down at my rumpled clothes and bare feet, "I hope I didn't wake you."

I frowned, and then leaned around him to look out at the empty porch. Nora's car was gone; Leaf's van shone in the morning light parked in the exact place we had left her car.

Jangling a set of keys in the space between us, Officer Mulroney smiled. "I brought Mr. Johnson's van back."

Mr. Johnson's van.

Which had been seized by police yesterday.

And which Leaf had obviously *not* been driving back into my life.

Of course.

I swallowed and nodded and reached for the keys.

The son-of-a-bitch really was gone.

Just like everyone else.

And the jerkhead had stolen Nora's car.

No, I told myself, *borrowed*. The jerkhead had *borrowed* Nora's car.

That, in itself, was proof that he would be back. Not that I cared anyway.

"Would you mind if I come in and ask you some questions about what occurred yesterday?" asked the officer.

"Not at all." I stepped back to let him pass, and then followed him to sit at the dining table.

"Can you please state your full name for the record?" Officer Mulroney slid a notepad from his pocket and placed a tape recorder between us.

"Heather Wren," I said. "No middle name."

"Plain and simple, huh?" he smiled.

"That's what my mother always told me."

He smiled for a second, but then frowned, serious again. "When was the last time you saw Mrs. Johnson?"

I wrinkled my nose. Mrs. Johnson? It sounded so formal.

"*Lauren*," I said, emphasizing her name, "left the house yesterday morning around ... seven, I'd guess."

"And you mentioned that she had been quite distressed at this time."

I nodded. "Leaf and I had confronted her about ..." I sighed. "You have to understand, she'd just been through some real heavy stuff, so she'd started to ... experiment ..." I shook my head and looked down at the table. "Shit," I muttered. "We told her to get clean or get out of our lives." When I looked up, Officer Mulroney was busy scribbling. "But we didn't mean it! We didn't think she'd actually do it! We just wanted to scare some God damn sense into her!"

"So, Lauren had been using substances?"

"Yes, sir."

"What substances?"

"Heroin."

"Anything else?"

"She hadn't been exactly upfront about it. I only knew because Leaf let it slip."

"Do you believe Mrs. Johnson could have taken her own life?"

I shook my head and opened my mouth to say, No, no way in hell, she would never do that! But the words wouldn't come. They just grew larger in my throat, choking me.

The officer leaned forward and scribbled in his book. "So, this man you call *Leaf* was her husband? The man you were with last night? Mr. Johnson?"

I nodded and wrinkled my nose again: Mr. Johnson. Leaf. Gabriel. Criminal. Car thief. Stranger. Traitor. Call him what you want.

The officer pointed to the tape recorder.

"Yes, sir," I said, "Mr. Johnson is her husband."

"I assume his real name is not Leaf."

"That's correct."

"What is his real name?"

I looked down at the table again. "I don't know."

"He is your friend, isn't he?"

My friend? His question draped over my shoulders like a wet blanket. The weight of it sagged me.

"Yes," I said. "He is my friend."

"Then surely you must know his name." The officer tipped his head to the side and studied me.

Does he know I am lying? Is it an offence to lie to a police officer? Shit, I just lied to a God damn police officer! What the hell am I doing? Just tell him the truth: Leaf's name is Gabriel. And he is wanted. At least I *assume* he is wanted. Just tell him; it's not like I owe anything to Leaf now. It's not like he deserves protection. He ran out on me!

Shit.

Raising my head, I met the officer's eyes. "I'm sorry, sir, we only ever used our nicknames. I never knew his real name. It was never important."

"Do you know who owns the van Lauren was driving?"

I shrugged.

Does Officer Mulroney know the truth, and has he been testing me, and does he know I'm lying? If they run the plates, surely they will find out who Leaf is and what he has done. Wouldn't they have done that already? Wouldn't that be one of the first things they'd do?

Unless Leaf swapped the plates. Or unless the van itself is stolen. He is obviously quite adept at taking other people's cars. Oh shit, Leaf, what the hell did you do?

"Where were you yesterday?" he asked.

"Leaf and I were both here all day," I said. "We didn't want to leave in case Lauren came home. Although we did go out looking for her around six. I called you after we got home, when we hadn't been able to find her."

"Can anyone verify this?"

Yes, I thought, Nora could verify that we were here until six. But in order for her to do that, she would have to be questioned in relation to Lauren's death, which would mean she would *know* about Lauren's death, which would mean she'd be on the very next flight to be by my side, instead of getting this crazy but maybe beneficial treatment. And if Nora's cancer progressed because she walked away from this insane coffee-enema therapy, I would never forgive myself ...

"No," I said. "Leaf and I were the only ones home."

"All right, Miss Wren, I understand this is a hard time for you, and for your friend. Is he available, by the way? I need to ask him some questions as well."

"No," I said. "He's not here."

"When will he be back?"

You tell me, I thought.

For a second, I felt the pang of fear in my gut again and wondered if I should tell Officer Mulroney about Leaf's letter and the possibility of it being a suicide note, but then I shrugged because he would never do that, and said, "He'll be back soon."

The officer handed me a small card with his name and a telephone number on it. "Please give me a call when Mr. Johnson returns, or if there is anything," he paused, "you think I should know."

"Right." I nodded. "Great. Thanks."

He stared at me. "By the way, we matched your friend's identity to that of a missing girl from New Jersey. Her real name was Lauren Marie O'Connell. There is apparently no such person as *Mrs. Lauren Marie Johnson*."

He continued to stare.

His gaze itched up my spine, and I wriggled in my seat.

How was I supposed to respond to that? I just shrugged again, and said, "Oh."

"At this stage, it appears there are no suspicious circumstances. Lauren's blood contained traces of opiates and we have a witness stating that your friend was indeed alone at the lake. We therefore believe this was a suicide and will not be investigating further."

Again, my words grew thick in my throat but I managed to squeeze them out. "She drowned herself?"

"According to her parents, she couldn't swim." The officer sighed. "I'm very sorry."

I couldn't breathe. Horror and sadness swirled, liquid, around me, pouring into my nose and mouth to pool inside my lungs and drag me under.

We'd told her to go. We'd told her we didn't want *to watch her* kill herself. So she'd gone someplace else to do it.

I stood, too quickly, and my chair fell backwards, and the room swayed beneath my feet, and Officer Mulroney grabbed my arm.

"Hey, whoa, take it easy," he said. "You all right?"

Closing my eyes so I wouldn't have to lie to his face again, I said, "Yes, thank you, I'm just fine."

chapter forty-two

japhy

A hand grenade weighs approximately sixteen ounces. That's a stick of butter, five bucks in nickels, or two human hearts held together in the palm of your hand.

However, unlike the warmth that constantly fills you when you are lucky enough to have another's heart, a grenade raises gooseflesh on your skin, it chills you to the bone, and it freezes you in place.

It is like holding on to a smooth lemon. A lemon that has the power to explode and turn you into smoke right along with it.

Copying the sergeant, who holds his own grenade level with his chest, I slip my index finger through the metal ring of the safety pin while squeezing the lever down tight.

"Pull out your pin!" yells Sergeant Ash.

No one moves.

"Pull!" The sergeant yells again. "Pull, you bunch of cowardly turds!"

One by one, all along the line, I hear the twang of metal pins sliding free. Yanking my arm, I feel the terrifying, yet slightly satisfying, *give* of the metal.

"Hold that lever down, boys!" The sergeant smiles. "Once you let go of that lever, and it springs open, it will activate the firing pin, which strikes the primer, and you will then have about four or five seconds before you become a twitching stain on the grass."

The muscles in my hand ache. I squeeze harder. The grenade slides in my sweaty grip.

"Which of you pussies is the weakest, I wonder?" Ash walks up and back, his eyes dance as he watches hands trembling on levers. "Hmm? Who is going to throw that deadly explosive away from them first? Who here is the biggest chicken?"

My fingers loosen but I grit my teeth and force them tight again.

And then, to my left, I hear a guttural, gurgling groan. Lion screams, "God damn it!" as his arm windmills in a circle and his grenade flies in an arc into the distance where it lands, waits, and then gives out a quiet and pathetic *pfft*. A small spiral of smoke curls up from the detonated test grenade.

"Ah, Private Leon," says Ash. "Congratulations. You will now be the first to throw a live grenade. Let's hope you don't blow your hand off."

The sergeant throws his own test grenade, and we all copy him, relieved to finally let the muscles in our hands rest. We fling our grenades over our heads, the way we'd been shown – overhand with a straight elbow – and watch the thin lines of smoke rise up one by one.

Sergeant Ash walks to a wooden crate and takes out the real thing. It looks exactly the same as the test one, but it looks completely different. Because this grenade could kill us all in a single heartbeat.

"This," says the sergeant, "is an M26A1 fragmentation hand grenade. It has a blast radius of forty-nine feet, which might not sound like much, but trust me, boys, if you trip over one of these babies in those jungles, then running that short forty-nine-foot distance will feel like a million miles, I can promise you that. When it blows, its case will shatter and those razor-sharp metal shards will fly through the air in every direction, so y'all better be sure as shit that when your grenade goes off, you – and, more importantly, *me* – are nowhere near it. You may have seen movies where the hero throws himself over a grenade to save his buddies? Don't do that! You will die. And, most likely, so will all of us! Just run! Run like stink, you hear me? However, if any of you do get hard over the thought of suicide and sacrifice, then throw yourself over your buddy, instead of the grenade. Maybe you'll get lucky in those last precious seconds. And speaking of lucky," he smiles, "Private Leon?"

"Yes, Drill Sergeant," says Lion.

"Here you are, soldier."

Lion takes the grenade, holding it in both hands, moving slowly. He jumps when Ash yells, "Everyone in position!"

The rest us of crouch down behind a wall of sandbags that stretches across the field like a giant, beige arm.

"Now," Ash talks softly. "Easy. Squeeze the lever in. That's the way. Pull the pin. Release the jungle clip. Good. Breathe, soldier, breathe, you're doing fine. Now, when you are ready, throw."

I kneel up and watch Lion pull his arm backwards and then, like a catapult, he fires.

His arm rotates.

He lets go too early.

The grenade rises into the air.

Straight up.

It hangs for a second, and I don't see it fall.

The sergeant is screaming for us all to climb over the wall now, get to the other side of those bags now, get down, get down, hands over your heads, and then ...

Boom!

I've never heard anything like that sound in my life. Not in my whole life. It is a thousand thunderclaps all at once. It is the true sound of shock. It splits me into pieces, and for a second I honestly think I've been blown apart. As I lie there in fragments, with nothing but noise existing around me, I think about how that massive explosion was born from a single object that is equal in weight to two human hearts. And then I think of Ray. I think of her heart beside mine. And I wonder how earth-shakingly devastating our individual explosions would be if my heart was never allowed to beat beside hers again.

chapter forty-three

ray

Boom! Boom! Boom!

The front door rattled on its hinges as the noise rushed down the hallway to shake sleep from my bones. When my eyes flew open, I expected to see Lauren's swollen, waterlogged face – which had just been haunting my dreams – leaning down over my bed, her red hair dripping onto my pillow. But the room was empty and I didn't know if that was worse.

Boom! Boom!

I threw the blankets off and staggered to my feet, moving across the room slowly, as if wading through a lake.

As I passed the bathroom, I saw a flash of red in the mirror. Like the snap of flame-red hair rippling under water. It was there, and then it wasn't. I gasped. My heart raced. I gripped the doorframe to steady myself, but when I looked again, all I saw was my own ghost-pale reflection.

Boom! Boom! Boom!

A small squeal rushed from my lungs and I covered my mouth with my hand.

I shook my head. I am just tired, I thought. And emotional. And stressed. And hormonal. That's all.

I am *not* delusional, I told myself, as I continued to swim through the house toward the front porch where the door practically bulged beneath the fists that pounded it from the other side.

Crossing the kitchen, I passed the glass of the stove door, and saw Lauren's bright green-blue eyes glaring at me. She winked, and I screamed, and the door boomed again.

Breathing fast, I stared at the reflective surface, but Lauren was gone.

"Shit," I muttered, and rested my head on the kitchen counter. "I'm sorry," I sobbed. "Lauren, if you can hear me, I am so sorry!" A wave of sadness and tears crashed down on me, pinning me there as, once again, the front door bruised the knuckles of the person who desperately wanted to speak to me. Raking my fingers down my face, I tried, but failed to claw out the images of Lauren holding a flame-blackened spoon in one hand and a syringe in the other, while behind her rose the shadowy form of a dark angel – black wings unfurling, arms reaching, fingers clawing for her skin.

I took a breath and called out, "I'm coming!" and finally the door stilled.

Who the hell did this person think they were, anyhow? Didn't they know what I had just been through? That I was mourning the death of my friend? That I didn't need this shit today, of all days, when I had to somehow find out the details of Lauren's funeral, and somehow get there, and then somehow get through seeing that young body, that wasted life, be lowered into the cold earth.

I wondered where her body was. Was it being transported back to the town from which she'd given everything to escape? Where, now dead, unable to fight, unable to run, Lauren would be dragged back into her own hell.

Hell.

And then I wondered where her soul was.

But then, did I really want to know the answer to that?

I yanked the door open. The words, "Jesus Christ! What is your problem!" surged to escape my throat, but when I saw who stood there, I snapped my lips closed, trapping the words inside my body, where everything started to tremble.

"Where is he!" Lauren pushed by me, through the door. "Where is that black son-of-a-demon!"

I stared at the flame-orange hair that streamed out behind her. I stared at the aquamarine eyes that glinted with faceted anger. And I stared at the body, which I had seen, cold and dead, on a slab, but was now warm and very much alive, and standing in Nora's living room.

Is this real? I thought. Or another delusion? A ghost?

Maybe Lauren didn't know she was dead. Maybe she was just continuing the argument she had walked out on. Maybe she didn't remember getting loaded and wading into that lake and leaving her body tangled among the reeds.

Lauren crossed her arms and narrowed her eyes at me. Her words snaked from thin, angry lips. "I suppose you are Heather, are you? Officer Mulroney said you were the last person to see my daughter alive."

"Darlene, you can't just storm into these people's home!"

At this new voice, I whirled back toward the door to see a man with graying temples and dark, sunken eyes. His skin was so pallid it blended seamlessly with the gray in his hair as if he'd been bleached of all color.

"These *people* took our daughter away from us." She said the word *people* as if referring to me and Leaf as *humans* was difficult and untrue. "I will treat them in any way I damn well please!"

I saw now that her hair was streaked with silver, her mouth was bracketed with wrinkles, and her body was plumper than Lauren's had been.

"You're her mother?" I whispered.

Her lips pressed thin. "I *was*."

As Lauren's father crossed the room to take his wife's hand, I wrapped my arms around my suddenly hollow chest. "I am so sorry for your loss, ma'am, sir."

She laughed then, and it was the most evil, chilling laughter I've ever heard in my life. "Not as sorry as we are. Now, where is Gabriel Williams?"

"Williams?" I frowned. "You mean Gabriel Johnson."

"Just because he told you something, dear, doesn't mean it was true. Where is he?"

I shrugged. "I don't know."

"I just had to identify my daughter's body. I just had to watch it be loaded into the back of a funeral home van! So, you tell me: where is he?"

"Your guess is as good mine."

"Ah, the spineless snake has just scurried away again, has he?"

Snakes don't scurry, I thought, frowning at this horribly rude woman. "He's in shock, ma'am," I said. "He just needs some time ..."

"Oh, that man needs some *time*, all right. Behind bars!"

"Listen," I said, holding out my hands, "I understand that you are very upset, and you have every right to be, but placing blame where it doesn't belong is not going to help anyone. What happened to your daughter was a tragedy, yes, but it was no one's fault."

She looked at me then, for a long moment, until my skin prickled beneath her stare, until a smile curled at the very edge of her mouth. "He never told you, did he?"

I said nothing.

"That's why you're defending him, isn't it?" She spoke slowly. Her words unfolded syllable by syllable. Her smile widened. "Would you like to know what he's been hiding, Heather? Would you like to know the truth about your so-called friend?"

Truth was truly a wicked temptress. At this woman's words, I felt my stomach throb with dread, my chest constrict around my hammering heart, my hands shake as they grasped for answers that I wasn't sure I really wanted, after all. What if I learned things that I could never look past, never forgive? But at the same time curiosity tingled through me like electricity. My mind whirled with satisfaction that now, finally now, I was about to discover Leaf's great, big, dirty secret. The secret he had refused to tell me. The secret he thought I didn't deserve to know, or perhaps couldn't be trusted with. The secret that had perhaps driven Lauren into the cold black lake.

However, whether or not I *wanted* to know about Leaf's past was irrelevant. There was nothing I could do to stop it; this woman had filled up her lungs with air, and was about to blow truth through my world like a storm.

I tensed my muscles and prepared to be buffeted by her tempest.

"A year ago," she said, "that horrible man raped my fifteen-year-old daughter, and then kidnapped her, drugged her to keep her from escaping, and has now, finally, killed her."

At first I laughed. Then I shook my head and frowned. Then I stiffened with sudden questions, unsure which to ask first. "She was *fifteen?*"

"She was just a baby," said her father. "Our baby. Just a little girl."

"Until *he* came along," said her mother. "He stalked her for weeks. Followed her everywhere in that sleazy van of his and kept begging her to go out on a date with him. Well, my poor daughter was terrified, obviously. She refused to leave the house by herself in case he was around, which he always was, watching from somewhere. She told him to leave her alone, that she was not interested in him, that he was far too old, but he wouldn't give up. We even called the police but they could do nothing because technically he'd done nothing wrong. Well, next thing, my daughter was pregnant with his spawn, and then she just ... vanished! He snatched her when he found out she was getting rid of it. He kidnapped my daughter to make sure his demon seed could enter this world unharmed."

No, I wanted to say. Ridiculous, I wanted to scoff. But when I opened my mouth, the words of disbelief would not come.

"And now my daughter is dead, and he is on the run."

I shook my head and finally managed to form words. "Gabriel did *not* kill her ... I was with him all day! He didn't do it."

"Maybe not directly," she said.

"I don't think you understand," I said. "Lauren loved him! And he loved her! Very much. They were happy!"

"I'm sure that's what he wanted it to look like from the outside. But my daughter was terrified of him."

"They were *married*," I said.

"Were they?" She raised her eyebrows. "Because I don't remember signing any permission forms, and I don't believe any states in this country will allow a minor to marry without parental consent."

"But ..." I frowned and shook my head. "No ..."

"Did he tell you what he does for a living?" Lauren's mother asked. "He is an *actor*, Heather. An actor. And he has worked his magic on you too, it seems."

"I don't believe this," I muttered.

"That man stole my child. He stole her innocence. And now he has stolen her life. She was a prisoner at his side all this time, too scared to run from him in case he found her again ..."

"That's not true," I whispered. But, in my memory, I heard Leaf mumbling to Lauren at the kitchen table that night at Utopia: *Don't you ever leave me, lovely! I'll never let you go!* I saw the way she'd giggled, and at the time I'd thought it was sweet, that she'd been coy; but what if she hadn't been shy at all, but nervous? What if she hadn't been in love with him, but in fear of him? What was it she'd said to me that next morning? *You know, the first time I met Leaf, I was absolutely terrified of him ... I couldn't get away even if I wanted to!*

"My daughter finally escaped from that man in the only manner she thought she could, to the only place where he wouldn't be able to follow her: Heaven."

Again I shook my head, dazed.

"Don't worry, love," she continued, and pulled a tissue from the depths of her handbag.

It wasn't until she thrust it at me that I realized tears streamed down my face.

"Don't worry," she crooned again. "They'll catch him, don't you worry about that. I guess you're just lucky that he *has* fled; you may have been his next victim, the next vessel to carry his vile offspring."

My hands dropped over my abdomen, covering it like a shield, and the woman's knife-sharp eyes followed. Her mouth opened and she made the sign of the cross over her body.

"It's too late," she whispered. "You are pregnant, too!"

I didn't tell her I was *not* pregnant. I didn't tell her it was *not* Leaf's. I just fell into a million pieces.

It was too much. All of it. I curled in on myself and sobbed, and then I felt her arms, surprisingly warm, bundle me up and start to sway me back and forth. She shushed gently in my ear. I wanted to shove her away in case she had more poisonous lies, I didn't want her touching me in case her very skin could contaminate, but in that small moment everything dropped away and I was just a girl and she was just a grown-up. I was allowing her to be a loving mother again, and she was allowing me to be a beloved daughter. So I let her comfort me, and I let myself drown in her warm, parental embrace.

*

After Lauren's parents drove away, I lay on my bed – the bed I had shared with Leaf – and stared up at the ceiling, letting the weight of words fall down on me.

Fifteen. Kidnapped. Raped.

Those words pressed down on my skin, which fought against absorption. They pushed my body down into the soft mattress until I was completely entombed by consonants and vowels that I did not want touching me.

Too scared to run ... terrified of him ... finally escaped in the only manner she could.

And as each projected word faded on the backs of my eyelids, it was replaced by a full-color image of Leaf smiling, of Lauren kissing him, of the matching gold bands on their fingers.

They had been in love. I knew this. Anyone who'd seen them together would have known this. But then, his words ...

Don't you ever leave me, lovely ... I'll never let you go ...

I saw again the way Leaf recoiled when I mentioned calling the police. I saw the way his eyes flared when Officer Mulroney said he'd need to question him. I saw the small yellow note he had left stuck on the front door: SORRY.

Sorry for what, Leaf? For bailing on me? Or for kidnapping

a fifteen-year-old girl? Or for tricking her into believing she loved you? Or for letting her think her only way out was suicide?

God. Oh God. I shook my head. Stop it! I couldn't think like this; I knew the truth; I knew what really happened.

Didn't I?

Placing a hand over my stomach, I curled my body into a protective ball as sleep clamped over my mouth and nose like an open hand. I gave in to it. I didn't fight. I let myself be taken because it was so much easier that way.

"Ray?" Leaf's voice is soft in my ear.

I sit up, and cry out, and scrabble away from him to the foot of the bed. "Don't take my baby!" I scream at him.

But Leaf just smiles and lets out that warm laugh of his: Heh! Heh! And then he stands up and his dark skin melts away into the blackness and he is no longer there. His sudden absence cuts me and I feel wetness warm on my cheeks.

"No," I whimper. "Come back!"

Reaching out a hand to where he stood only seconds before, I gasp as my palm cups his invisible face. The solid heat of his cheek beats against my hand like a pulsing heart, and I hold on to it.

"I'm still here," he whispers. "You can't see me, but I'm still right here with you."

As he speaks, his voice changes; it becomes higher, it becomes softer, and it becomes Lauren.

"I'm still right here with you," she says, and she steps forward out of the darkness. Her skin glows and lights up the entire room, which is suddenly filled with people who glow just as brightly as she does. And then the crowd of people part down the center as a man strolls forward with his arms stretched out to the sides. He wears a brown suede jacket with fringe that dangles and sways with each step. Dark hair touches his shoulders, and half his face is hidden by facial hair. His bright eyes are hazel-green and gentle and glorious.

"You?" I frown at him.

"Me," he says.

He glows more brilliantly than any of the souls in the room, and when he smiles at me I feel its warmth penetrate deep into my heart, and all my sadness dissolves, just like it always does whenever I listen to him sing.

"Are you ... *God?*" I ask.

James Lee Stanley lifts a shoulder and lets it fall again, and then he turns to Lauren and they both hold hands, take a breath, and open their mouths wide in song.

"*Hesitating in a waiting room. Every flight is over all too soon.*"

Their acapella harmonies roll and tumble over each other like lovers, naked, without the satiny covers of musical accompaniment.

"*And every eye can see the life that each is living. Isn't each blossom on the vine only for giving? Only for giving? Flowers for the living. Flowers for the living.*"

The living, I think as I gaze around the room. I scan eyes, and mouths, and bodies, but I can't see his among these faces of the dead.

"*Standing all night in the morning line just to trace the face this one last time.*"

My heart speeds up as I turn away from Lauren and James, and I push my way past elbows and shoulders and chests. Each new set of eyes has my breath freezing in my throat one second and releasing in relief the next, and then I sob and move forward again to the next face and the next set of eyes and the next prayer that they will not be familiar ones while behind me, Lauren and James keep singing.

"*And all the room is filled with flowers from the living. Isn't each blossom on the vine only for giving? Only for giving?*"

Their words follow me and fill me with fear, until ...

"*Flowers for the living. Flowers for the living. Flowers for the living.*"

... Until I woke covered in sweat and tears. Sunlight glowed through my curtains and lit the whole room. I sat up, gasping for air, squinting into the natural brightness that was now, in reality, empty. As the edges of the dream began to fray and the clarity of all those faces fell away like cobwebs, I couldn't remember exactly whose face I had been searching so desperately for.

All I knew was: today Lauren's body would be farewelled.

Another goodbye I didn't want to hear.

By the front door, I stood and reached for the keys. The metal was cold as a corpse in my palm. When Lauren had snatched up these very same keys just days ago and run from the house, had she known she would never return? Had she planned her death even as she slid the key into the ignition?

In the driveway, Leaf's Kombi sulked as I jogged toward it. Did it miss its owners as much as I did? Or was it glad that the suffering was over now?

Christ, don't think like that!

I didn't want to take the van. I never wanted to sit in it again for the rest of my life! But, sighing, I climbed behind the wheel and forced myself to face forward, to not look back into the space where Lauren had spent her last hours. Where she had thought about the ultimatum we had given her. Where she had cooked up, and hammered in, and stripped naked, and said goodbye to this world.

I twisted the key in the ignition, because now it was time for me to say my own goodbyes.

Lauren's parents had given me the details of when and where the funeral would be held, in Meadows, New Jersey, but that sheet of paper was in a neat little ball in my trash.

I parked the van outside *Bouquets*, the local florist, and felt the green energy rise up around my feet as I stepped over the threshold and a little bell tinkled above my head.

"Heather?" said the wrinkled woman at the counter, her spectacles, which hung on a chain against her massive bust, bounced with every syllable. "Heather Wren, is that you?"

"Yes, Mrs. Daws, how are you?"

"I'm well, dear. Gosh, I don't think I've seen you in here for years. How is your mother?"

"Oh, she's just fine."

"Good. Well, is there something I can help you with this morning?"

"Yes," I said, walking over to the side of the store where a field of colorful petals swayed in pots. I remembered standing in this exact spot with my mother, years ago, helping her to choose the varieties of flowers we'd planted together in the garden. We'd been so close back then. Back before I'd ruined our lives.

And now, here I stood again. With yet another ruined life under my belt.

"Those ones are particularly lovely this season, aren't they?" said Mrs. Daws, fingering the petals of the plant I had chosen.

She took the pot from me and I followed her to the counter where the familiar *ka-ching* of her antique cash register had me balancing on a tight-rope between the past and the present.

As I handed over the money, I glanced down at the front page of the local paper she'd been reading when I walked in, and my whole body stilled beneath Lauren's penetrating stare.

A smile was frozen on Lauren's face, which was chubby-cheeked and glowing with health – the way she had been when I'd first met her. The corners of her eyes crinkled in laughter. A shiny blue ribbon held back her flaming ringlets, which tumbled down over her left shoulder and blue school dress. Her face looked so warm, so friendly, so carefree, it was almost garish in contrast to the words written in bold lettering above: *Kidnapped Schoolgirl Found Dead In Liberation Lake*.

"Oh, yes." Mrs. Daws clucked her tongue. "Terrible, isn't it?"

I couldn't look away. My eyes kept flicking between the photo and the words as if trying to connect the two, as if my mind just could not comprehend why Lauren's photograph would be printed in relation to such a horrible statement.

"And to think this all happened right here, in our own backyard." She shook her head. "Just terrible. I feel so sorry for her poor parents."

Yeah, her poor parents, I thought.

Parents who, I realized, had not once asked me about Lauren's baby, their grandchild, the last biological link they had to their daughter.

Parents who, I realized, never once referred to Lauren by her name. It had been just their daughter, their child, a possession that had been stolen from them.

I remembered Lauren's expression now as she yelled at Leaf on that last day: *I could be dragged back to that fucking convent ...* And I remembered the coldness in her mother's face.

"Wait ..." Mrs. Daws gaped at me now. "The penny's just dropped. Mrs. MacDonald mentioned something about you yesterday, but I didn't connect. Oh, Heather, I'm so sorry. You knew her, didn't you?" She tapped a fingernail against Schoolgirl Lauren's flat, papery cheek. "You knew this Lauren O'Connell?"

"No. I didn't know Lauren O'Connell." I picked up my pot and walked out of the store. Crossing the parking area to the van, I unlocked the door and smiled as I placed the poppy plant on the passenger seat. "But I *did* know Lauren *Johnson*."

With my indicator flashing left, I waited for the traffic to thin so I could pull out. I thought of the hearse that may, right at that moment, be shuffling Lauren's body slowly toward the cemetery. I imagined the coffin and, within it, the body of a schoolgirl whom I had never met, and therefore didn't need to farewell in person at a memorial service.

She was not my Lauren. My Lauren wouldn't be there, in the town she hated, with those people she had run from.

Pulling out into the traffic, I drove the van to where *my* Lauren waited, where her memory was very much alive.

Liberation Lake was breathtaking at this time of day. The early sun dyed the smooth water gold. Butterflies floated by like petals on a breeze. Amid lotus flowers, a family of ducks skated across the water; the ripples from their madly paddling feet sent widening circles across the otherwise glasslike surface. It was so beautiful here, and I was pleased this was the last image my friend would have seen.

Some people believe that your final thought will lead you to your next life. As I stared around me at all this peace and tranquility and beauty, I hoped to God that theory was true.

Kneeling, I stabbed until the earth's wound was large enough for me to fill with new life. I lowered the flower's hair-thin roots and their ball of dirt into the hole I'd made, before pressing soil back over the top gently as if tucking blankets around a newborn, and then I watered the poppy plant in with my tears.

"Bye, Poppy," I said. "Bye, Lauren. I'll keep you with me always, I promise. Every flower I see for the rest of my life will make me think of you. I will keep you alive." Touching my finger to the soft cheek of the flower, I started to sing. "*Standing all night in the morning line just to trace the face this one last time. And all the room is filled with flowers from the living. Isn't each blossom on the vine only for giving? Only for giving? Flowers for the living ...*"

Of the two flowers I'd planted, one was not yet open; its stem was bent double under the weight of its own pregnant bloom. The second poppy was open wide; blood-red petals as thin and fragile as paper bobbed in the breeze, waving back and forward like a hand saying hello.

Or goodbye.

july

Love means never having to say you're sorry.

~ Erich Segal, Love Story

chapter forty-four

japhy

Every night, as I drop into sleep, I go back to that very first moment when she spoke to me, and I say a silent thank you to Jack Kerouac. He was, after all, the man who introduced me to Ray. Of course, she hadn't been Ray then. She'd been Heather, and I'd been Andy, and Jack Kerouac had been dead for five months, but there we were, all three of us, standing together on the threshold of our linked futures.

It was March, the end of spring break, and I was waiting for the bus that would take me away from the claustrophobic boundaries of Liberation, Alabama, and back to University. Classes started the next day. Across from the station was *Hyland's Books*, a book store and café, so while I waited, I'd wandered in there, planning on getting something to read during the three-hour bus ride to Mobile.

I'd stood at the shelves, in front of the K's, and reached for the cover with the jolly gold Buddha wearing John Lennon sunglasses and a marijuana cigarette smoldering between his serene lips.

But when I reached out for that book, a small hand had shot out and snatched it off the shelf.

"Oh!" she'd said. "I'm sorry, did you want this book too?"

I looked down then, and she was there. She was right there in front of me. "No. I mean, yes, but no, you take it, Heather."

Her face had bloomed. "How do you know my name?"

"I used to go to your school," I said. "I graduated last year. I'm ..."

"Andy Mack." She nodded.

I smiled. "How do you know my name?"

"I used to go to your school, too, you know." She winked, and something in my chest stuttered.

"So, you're in college now?" she asked.

"Yeah. South Alabama. It's pretty neat."

"You're so lucky. I can't wait to get out of here. I've applied to Berkeley."

"Berkeley?" I raised my eyebrows.

"Yep." She held up the book. "Thought I'd do a little research."

When she tipped her head to the side, I felt the solid floor beneath me tilt as well, as if my whole world was lopsided by her smile.

"Say," she said, "would you like to, maybe, go get a soda or something?"

I looked down at my watch. "No, I can't."

"Oh," she said. "That's okay."

"It's not that I don't want to," I said, "but my bus ..."

"It's fine," she said. "I'm pretty busy today, anyway. Here." She pushed the book into my chest and backed away. "You take it easy, Andy Mack."

And as fast as she had appeared, she was gone, and I wanted to go after her but my bus would be here in less than ten minutes, and if I missed any more classes I could be in danger of flunking out and getting drafted, so instead of running after her, I bought the book, and sat out the front of the bus station, cracking open the first page and hearing the voice of Ray Smith for the very first time ...

Hopping a freight out of Los Angeles at high noon one day in late September 1955 I got on a gondola and lay down with my duffel bag under my head and my knees crossed and contemplated the clouds as we rolled north to Santa Barbara.

When the brakes of my bus hissed through the words on the page, I looked up. The door swung open. A few passengers lined up, showed the driver their tickets, and boarded. As I watched them make their way down the aisles and choose their seats and sit and stare blankly out the windows, I wondered where they were going. I wondered *why* they were going. I wondered who they were going to. Going from.

"You coming or what, sonny?" called the driver.

I sat there. Gripping the book. And trying to get Heather's face out of my mind. Heather. Heather Wren. Heather freaking Wren had asked me to go for a soda and I had said no! What was wrong with me?

This was her.

This was the girl.

The girl who'd fascinated me ever since I'd seen her lead the debate team to victory arguing *for* capital punishment while wearing a t-shirt that read: *Kill capital punishment*.

The girl who liked Kerouac, and applied to Berkeley, and had just asked me out, and to whom I'd just said no.

No?

Shit.

I shook my head at the bus driver and the doors shushed closed with me on the wrong side of the glass. Or maybe the right side. Standing, I grabbed my bag and walked inside the bus station. I mean, I couldn't go home: my folks would lynch me. So I'd stayed in there all night, stretched across a row of seats with my duffel bag under my head and my knees crossed, contemplating the lives of these two characters, Ray and Japhy, flipping through page after page of Kerouac's tale until, after the sun rose the next morning, I read the final line, closed the cover, and then walked across town to the high school.

And, oh, the look on her face when she'd seen me walking through the corridor toward the senior lockers – the way her eyes had widened just a fraction, the way she'd hitched in a quick breath, the way she'd frowned and a tiny vertical wrinkle had appeared between her brows. Oh, that wrinkle.

No words for how it made me feel.

Just, *oh*.

I knew I was in trouble. I knew this was her. This was the girl.

So, that's what I replay in my mind, night after night, in the hopes that I will fall asleep and dream up a whole new ending for us.

Maybe an ending in which I don't drop out of school, don't come back to Liberation to wait for Heather to graduate, don't assume that my college deferment will keep me safe from Uncle Sam's great pointing finger, don't receive my induction letter two weeks later, and don't watch in astonishment as this girl gives up her whole world to remain in mine.

Maybe an ending in which I could be trying to fall asleep right now in the Berkeley dorm, while somewhere else in that same building she would be trying to fall asleep too, and that, if I wanted, I could simply sneak through the halls and knock on her door.

An ending in which she'd be here, she'd be right here with me, instead of just in my dreams, unreachable, untouchable, and as insubstantial as a ghost.

chapter forty-five

ray

The daily paper was spread like a sheet across the kitchen counter. Leaning against the bench, I drank coffee and flipped pages and saw Japhy's face in every photograph. With every new page I wanted to look away, but with every new page I needed to make sure those faces were not really his. And then, near the back of the newspaper, buried amid the boring stories that no one cares about, I froze. My eyes snatched the black text from the white background and rearranged the jumbled letters into shocked understanding, and I crumpled, boneless, onto the stool.

F.B.I. Find Guardsmen Guilty Over K.S.U. Shooting

A story printed in the Akron Beacon Journal this week explains that a special Justice Department summary of the F.B.I's investigation into the shooting at Kent State University on Monday May 4, which resulted in the death of four students and the wounding of nine, may provide guidelines for possible prosecution of the Guardsmen under federal law.

Until now, the Ohio National Guard have maintained that firing loaded weapons into a group of unarmed students was warranted as a result of self-defense, that a sniper had opened fire upon them, and that the supply of tear gas had run low, allowing the crowd to charge the surrounded Guardsmen, who would have been otherwise killed by the rioting mob.

The new investigation has concluded, however, that there was no sniper, that the Guardsmen had not been surrounded, that the rock throwing had not been widespread nor as dangerous as previously claimed, and that the shooting was "not proper and not in order."

The summary states that "photographs and television film show that only very few students were located between the Guard and the commons." It states that, of the nine students wounded, the closest was about 20 yards away, and those killed were 90 yards, 100 yards, and 130 yards away, respectively.

The report continues to refute the previous stories of the Guard by noting that "although many claim they were hit with rocks at some time during the confrontation, only one Guardsman was injured seriously enough to require any kind of medical treatment. He admits his injury was received some 10 to 15 minutes before the fatal volley was fired. His arm, which was badly bruised, was put in a sling and he was given medication for pain. One Guardsman specifically states that the quantity of rock throwing was not as great just prior to the shooting as it had been before."

It has also been concluded that there was no sniper. "No weapon was observed in the hands of any person other than a Guardsman, with the sole exception of Terry Norman. Norman, a freelance photographer, was with the Guardsmen most of the time during the confrontation. A few students observed his weapon and claim that he fired at students just prior to the time the Guardsmen fired. Norman claims that he did not pull his weapon until after the shooting was over, and then only when he was attacked by four or five students. His gun was checked by a Kent State University Policeman and another law enforcement officer shortly after the shooting. They state that his weapon had not been recently fired."

The F.B.I. now believes that the Guardsmen's claim of their lives being endangered is false. One of the Guardsmen has admitted that "his life was not in danger and that he fired indiscriminately into the crowd. He further stated that the Guardsmen had gotten together after the shooting and decided to fabricate the story that they were in danger of serious bodily harm or death from the students."

As I read, tears plopped onto the newsprint, smudging these wonderful words into spreading circles, but I wiped my eyes clear and stared down, reading the article over again and again, afraid that the truth – finally this truth – would disappear as quickly as my evaporating tears of happiness.

*

The weeks had been passing in a blur of wonderful lies.

Every night at six on the dot, the telephone rang, and I answered it instantly, having already sat down on the hallway chair to pick at my fingernails and wait and watch the clock count down until the moment I would be able to speak, once again, to a real, living, breathing person.

"Hi, Nora!" I'd say, once I'd snatched the phone off its cradle. "Tell me everything you did today."

And she would laugh, and sigh, and recount to me every boring detail of her day-to-day recovery and I would nod, and say "Oooh", and relish every God damn second.

"I got new test results back today, and the tumor has definitely shrunk!"

"Oh, that is wonderful," I'd say.

And then she'd ask: "How are things with you?"

"Oh, you know," I'd say, before launching into whatever story I had spent my day carefully scripting out. Such as: "Lauren got a job delivering flowers for Mrs. Daws at *Bouquets*. She is really getting herself together now, been sober for weeks; you'd barely even recognize her." Or: "Lauren and I were in the supermarket this morning and we overheard a farmer talking about how some of his hens are getting old and only laying an egg every *other* day. He was about to go home and make them into his dinner! We convinced this guy to sell them to us for a dollar! Can you believe it? We've named them all: Shelly, Henrietta, Yolko Ono, Pecker, and Mother Clucker. Blame Leaf for those last two! So, anyway, while Lauren and I drove out to pick them up, Leaf stayed here and built a chicken coop for them out the back – I hope you don't mind – so when you come home you can have fresh eggs ... Are you allowed to eat eggs anymore? Oh, no, that's right: no animal protein! Shoot!"

We wouldn't talk about Japhy. We wouldn't talk about the war. We wouldn't talk about how many mothers had lost their sons this week.

And after about fifteen minutes, Nora would wind the conversation up, despite my efforts to keep her on the line just that little bit longer, and she would say goodnight and I would be left with nothing but a telephone handset and the silence that otherwise filled my days.

As the weeks passed, my stomach rounded, and soon a little bump appeared above the waistband of my jeans and I could no longer get the button through its hole; I left it open and held my pants up with one of Japhy's belts. I spent hours standing in front of Nora's full-length mirror, staring at my profile, watching myself grow just the tiniest bit every day, and talking out loud to the little seed inside me. Because, after all, it was the only someone I had to talk to.

According to Dr. Smyth, I was now 13 weeks along, my baby was the size of a peach, and had even developed its own unique set of fingerprints.

Every day I patted my stomach and felt a warmth settle over my shoulders like a blanket. Love, perhaps? Resolve? Fear?

I wondered who this baby would resemble, and a chilling thrill would rush through my bones.

And every day I missed Leaf. God, I missed him so bad.

I began telling myself that if the baby kicked seven times before lunch, that Leaf would come home. That if I refrained from eating chocolate, that Leaf would come home. That if I forgave him, Leaf would come home.

And that if he came home, so too would all my answers.

But every night, I went to bed alone.

And every night, as I lay there, I would take out my notebook and write a letter to the one I missed more than anything else ...

Dear Japhy,

I really struggled today. After every horrible thing I've been through this year, I am shocked to discover that loneliness is the hardest and most painful thing to endure. It's worse than guilt, and fear, and betrayal. Because – if you die Over There – loneliness is the one thing that will never change for me. I will be lonely for the rest of my life.

Actually, that's not really true, because now, no matter what happens, I will never be alone again. I can't believe I had even considered giving up our baby! Must have been the crazy hormones. The thought of losing this child ... God, I can't even finish that sentence. Our baby is the only thing that makes me smile these days. I wish you could see this miracle unfolding like I can. I wish you could place your hand on my belly and feel the soft movements from inside me. I wish you could feel this amazing amount of love that grows bigger every day. It is an absolute wonderment.

But it is a wonderment that I do not deserve to experience.

After all, I have killed a child before. And killers do not deserve to feel this happy.

I wish I knew what to do. Do I tell you about our child? Do I surprise you with the most beautiful gift on your arrival home?

Fuck.

Fuck. Fuck. Fuck.

Oh, please, Japhy, tell me what to do!

Yours, always,

Ray.

Tearing out the piece of paper from the notepad, I'd fold it perfectly in half, and then perfectly in half again, before ripping it into a hundred thousand pieces and throwing them all into the trash.

And then I would fall asleep with my hand gripping a different letter. One that bore the seal of the United States Army. One that stated Private Andrew Michael Mack requested the presence of Mrs. Nora Mack and Miss Heather Wren to join in celebrating his achievements in completing Basic Combat Training. Picnic lunches or buffet meals would be provided for Family Day at noon on Friday July 24. And on Saturday July 25 at 10:00am we could witness the acceptance of

Private Andrew Michael Mack into the Armed Forces of the United States of America.

The creases on the paper were so thin from all the unfolding and refolding. Each time I read those words they became muddier in my head. I imagined Japhy in full army dress, and I imagined flinging myself against him and holding on, and I imagined the creases of confusion on his forehead, as sharp as the folds of the letter in my fist, as he wondered why my body would no longer press flush against his, the way it used to. I imagined him looking down at this bump of life that would forever come between us and seeing his face twist. I imagined myself – hands protecting my stomach – being forced away from him by an invisible and expanding bubble, inside which was one word: *Choose.*

But then maybe it would give him something to come home to? Something to hope for? A baby. A family. A life.

Or would it make him act even more reckless Over There?

As the days sped by, and the date I'd circled on the calendar – July 24 – crept closer, I imagined more bubbles of words. Sometimes they sucked me forward and into Japhy's embrace, sometimes they pushed me farther and farther away from him.

Happiness.
Family.
Yes.
Risk.
Loss.
Heartache.
Choose. Choose. Choose.

I unfolded the invitation one last time.

"What do we do, baby?" I whispered. "Should we go and see your daddy on Friday?"

As if in answer, I felt the baby move; a rolling, swooping sensation like hitting the middle of a rollercoaster. Like wonderful excitement. Like dread.

As if in answer, I felt the baby move; but I had absolutely no clue what it was trying to tell me.

chapter forty-six

japhy

Today, I am awake before the dreaded bugle call. Today, I can't stop smiling. Today, I am nervous as all hell.

My heart speeds up and my stomach rolls like an angry ocean and I can't keep still, so I shower and dress and just wait, wait, wait for it all to begin.

In this place, time isn't measured in seconds. Here, time moves differently. Whole days blink by, and weeks are but a few thumps of my beating heart, and in two great breaths, it is all over. I press my lips together to keep this day, this moment, from whooshing away from me. I press my lips to keep today trapped in my lungs for as long as I can. I press my lips and wait for the moment when I can press them against hers.

I have survived eight whole weeks in this place. I have survived eight whole weeks without Ray – a hell far more intense than all the early mornings, and the exhausting physical training, and the humiliating stripping of my soul.

Tomorrow I will graduate from Basic Combat Training and become a fully-fledged soldier of the United States Army. Tomorrow I will learn my Military Occupational Specialty and what the odds will be of returning home from this war.

But tomorrow is another lifetime away.

Today, however? Well, fucking A. Today is Family Day!

Today I will see *her*. Finally, finally, *finally* I will be able to hold her again.

We are lined up on the parade field while Ash lectures us on the protocols of the day, but I'm not really listening. What other rules do I need besides Ray, Ray, Ray?

1. Hold her.
2. Smell her.
3. Kiss her.
4. Ingrain her inside my skin so deep it will easily sustain me during the next eight weeks of A.I.T. and then twelve months of Nam.

They are the only rules that matter.

She is the only one that matters.

And maybe that is exactly why today is potentially so bad for me. I have been strengthening my resolve over the past eight weeks in order to prepare myself for such a long absence. I've sweated and bled and built a protective wall around the soft center of my heart, and what if all those bricks crumble away at the first glimpse of her face? What if she leaves me as useless and pathetic as a baby bird and I have to go into a war zone weakened and weeping?

I did not want to receive her letters, and it's for that very same reason I do not want to see her today. I don't think I can really bear it. Because seeing her again also means having to let her go.

But ... I also don't give a fuck about what is best for me right now.

I'm sick of being strong. I'm sick of being a brave fucking soldier. I just want to cling to her leg like a child and cry and scream and beat my fists on the grass, and not care who watches.

When the crowd of grinning teeth approaches, I twist, head swiveling, searching for Ray's long, brown hair and wide, green eyes; for the tightly woven crown of my mother's golden bun. I search for my family. For the ones whose existence I long to be a part of again – even if only for today. Even if only for a few hours. I need this reminder of who I am. Of who I *really* am. Rather than who I am becoming.

A whip of brunette hair glints in the sunlight and my throat clenches. I squint through the glare, but she isn't her.

Glancing down at my jacket – the gleaming gold buttons, the emblem on my chest – I touch a hand to the back of my neck where she used to run her fingers through the curls that are no longer there.

Will Ray even recognize me? Will she take one look at me, dressed like a United States soldier, like a hawk, like a traitor, and back away with a shaking head and two fingers raised in a hippie salute?

Or will she rush forward in a burst of pride, because *this* is the kind of man she wanted all along: brave, strong, powerful?

To my right, a hand waves in the air and a tall, blond woman calls out, "Andrew!"

My stomach rolls.

I swallow, my mouth suddenly dry.

But the voice is not my mother's, and I watch as her arms enfold a son who is not me.

Where are they already? A fully stocked picnic basket waits on the end of my bed, and I have a Leave Pass until twenty-one-hundred hours. There is an eternity of heartbeats between then and now, and I don't want to waste any more of them.

I wipe my palms against my thighs and straighten my cap.

To my left, Timothy shakes the hand of a man that could be his father, kisses the cheek of a woman that could be his mother, and then drops to a knee and hugs a boy that could be his brother. They are all grinning and wiping at proud tears for this brave man who is really too afraid to show them his true self.

Through the waves of laughter and sobs, Lion strides across the field to where a lone woman stands with pursed lips and a straight spine. She is thin and wispy. Birdlike. He bends to kiss her, and she pats him on the back ever so gently as if afraid her touch will shatter him into pieces.

I have a sudden image of this poor, brittle woman cowering in the shadow of a tall, faceless man; he stands over her with a raised fist before a courageous son steps between them to absorb the blows intended for his mother. How awful that must have been for them both.

For a brief moment, I wonder where Lion's father is, but then I look at his tiny mother and I'm glad that son-of-a-bitch hasn't shown up today to injure such a special moment, to bruise this proud day for them.

After that night on Fire Guard Duty and the day on the repel tower, I hadn't mentioned Lion's home life again. Some people have visible bruises on their souls that don't heal when the physical bruises do; those marks, as purple-black as violated trust, still bloom like ink over the smiles they paste and the strength with which they shield themselves.

I wonder if Lion feels guilty for leaving his mother unprotected?

I wonder if his mother feels betrayed that her son has left her vulnerable?

The woman holds back tears as she straightens Lion's uniform. He is an official protector now. A protector of the entire country, rather than of just her. Lion straightens his back, and lifts his chin.

And all the while, my heart continues to beat away all these wasted seconds as the crowd around me thins out. One by one, the faces suddenly illuminate with recognition – eyes brim and cheeks flush – and they each bee-line toward the son or boyfriend or friend they have come to visit. Slowly the straight lines of men beside me break away, and soon I am the only one left at attention.

There are no more girlfriends, or mothers, or friends searching for me.

I release the air from my lungs in a whoosh and I pray for this day to be over in one great breath, or a few thumps of my beating heart, or the single blink of a tear-filled eye.

*

The wicker picnic basket at the end of my bed mocks me. The

shining tip of the sparkling grape juice bottle, and the swollen, pink strawberries, and the crusty baguette that stands erect and excited by the possibility of a blissful reunion.

Snatching up the basket, I drop it outside the barracks door where the sweet juice will grow warm, the strawberries will dry up, and the bread will go stale.

Then I sit on my cot and lean forward as the room spins around me. With my head in my hands, I breathe in, and I breathe out, and I attempt to steady the world again.

"Why?" I whisper. "Why didn't they come?"

"It can be hard for some families."

At the sound of this voice, I jump to my feet and wrench my hand to my forehead in salute.

He chuckles, softly. "At ease, Mack."

Lowering my hand, I stare as Drill Sergeant Ash walks toward me with a smile. "Do you mind?" He gestures to my bed and sits before I can nod my approval. "I was watching you earlier; your family didn't show."

I shake my head.

"Don't take it personal. This can be very confronting. Especially for those who may be," he pauses and raises his eyebrows, "against our country's direction."

I open my mouth, but he holds up a huge hand, waving me silent.

"I read your file, Mack. I know you tried to evade Induction. I know you don't want to be here. A lot of boys don't." He leans forward. "And if I were you, I wouldn't either."

"What?"

"When I was your age, I couldn't wait to turn eighteen to enlist and fulfill my duty to this country. I was hungry for it. There was nothing and there was nobody could have stopped me. I loved it then and I love it now. I love the way it makes me feel. I love the way others treat me because of these simple shapes on my arms. I love being a part of something greater than myself. Being in the army is the best thing I have ever done." Then he leans forward. "But *you?*" he says, cocking his head. "Well, you're not me. And no amount of training can make that so. Even though you tried to avoid everything that

I believe in, everything that I love, I still respect you because there was nothing and there was nobody could have stopped you from trying to do what you felt was right for *you*. So you and me? Well, we ain't really too different in that regard. When I joined, it was through my own choice." He leans back and shakes his head. "And choice is something that has been taken away from you – away from a lot of boys these days. It is something that I do not agree with. But it is not my job to agree; my job is to take a civilian and give him the tools to stay alive in a war zone. Because by doing that – in the long run, at least – I hope I'm giving you back your ability to choose."

Sighing, Ash removes his wide-brimmed hat and places it between us on my bed. "My family didn't come to see my graduation neither, so I know how you are feeling right now." He smiles at me in the same way my father smiled at Bill O'Malley, the neighbor's kid, who returned from Nam with only one leg. "You're a real hero." The same words spoken to Bill O'Malley. And then he shakes my hand and slaps me on the back. Just like with Bill O'Malley. "I'm proud of you, son," he says. "And I hope you are proud of yourself, too."

"I am," I mutter. And then I say it again, louder. Because, hell yes, I *am* proud! I am *damn* proud. And so what if the Japhy from two months ago would never have felt proud to wear this uniform? So what if that Japhy would have looked away from these dog tags at my neck in embarrassment? So what if my priorities have changed just a little? It doesn't mean I am breaking the promise I made to myself to not let this experience change me; it just means that sometimes change isn't such a bad thing.

And it isn't.

Right?

Ash stands, twirls his hat between the palms of his hands, and then flips it onto his head. He raises his fingers to his forehead and waits for me to do the same before turning on the heel of his gleaming boots and marching out of the empty barracks.

I blink and slowly lower my hand as the salute he gave

me reflects off every clean surface, as crisp and sharp as satisfaction.

*

Mailey's Tavern is located down a narrow alley, behind the bowling lanes. The fact that this place has no problems serving alcohol to minors from the army base is not the only reason for its popularity with the guys on Leave: it happens to sit directly beneath a brothel – which also has no problems serving minors from the army base.

With my hands shoved deep in my pockets, I turn down the shadowed walkway and spot, beside an overflowing dumpster, the bright green tavern door.

As I open it, I wrinkle my nose at the stench of the place. Sweat. Stale beer. And is that piss? The smell gives me a headache and I'm not even inside yet.

Taking my last hit of clean air, I step forward and let the heavy door thud closed, blocking out almost all natural light.

A white-bearded man behind the bar looks over at me and I freeze in his icy stare.

"Get the hell out!" I imagine him sneering at me. "You ain't twenty-one!" I expect him to crash the glass he is drying down onto the greasy wooden bar and start shooing at me with his towel. But he just sniffs and returns his gaze to the rag and glass in his hands.

Slowly my vision adjusts to the dimness. Apart from one other man slouching at the bar, the place is empty, which isn't really surprising considering the time of day.

I walk by a jukebox and I stop at it briefly, but there is no James Lee Stanley in its menu, so really, what the hell is the point, and I keep moving toward the bar and the keeper with his glasses and this other man – who I now realize is wearing the same clothes as I am: the greens of a United States soldier.

Lion's shoulders hunch forward as if two great wings are tucked and hidden beneath his shirt. Before him, two rows of perfectly spaced shot glasses line up like tiny army men.

Golden liquid gleams like ungranted wishes at the bottom of each one.

"Hey, man." I lean against the bar beside him. "Thought you'd be out with your mom."

His left shoulder rises, falls in a shrug. He swoops up a glass off the shiny wooden bar and grimaces as the whisky fills his mouth and his throat and his belly.

"She decided to go home," he says, and when he turns to me, I gasp.

The right side of his face is red and swollen. His eyebrow bulges blue.

"Jesus."

"Nope," Lion says. "Wasn't Him."

"So your dad was here too, huh?"

"My *dad*?" Lion spits the word and then washes his mouth out with another shot of whisky. He coughs and gasps as the spirit ravages his throat. "You were right, you know? He *is* a fucking coward." Lifting his arm in the air, he calls out, "Can I get a round of shots for my friend, here?"

Friend? I think, and I feel a smile pulling and tugging at my seams. "Thanks, man," I say and drop onto a stool. "But, hey, at least they turned up for you today."

"They?" Lion asks.

"Yeah, *they*. Your mom and dad."

"What makes you think my dad would be here? I haven't seen him since he abandoned me thirteen years ago."

The bartender places six shots in front of me.

Lion arranges my glasses in two perfect rows of three, just like his. "I still remember the last thing he ever said to me. He said, 'Son, just hang tight, I'm going to come back for you. I promise. We'll both get out of here. Just hang tight,' he'd said. 'Just hang tight.' So I waited. I hung fucking tight. But he never bothered to come back. He just left me there." Shaking his head, Lion picks up another shot. "I was just a kid, and he left me there in that fucking house." Coughing down the whisky, his lips peel away from his teeth and he throws back his head to howl at the ceiling like a wolf crying at the moon.

"Wait." I frown at the fresh bruises on his skin. "So, if it wasn't your *father* who rearranged your face, then ...?"

Lion simply nods as images of his sweet, gentle mother come flying out at me from the shadows of my mind. I see the way she pats his back, softly, as if afraid she might break him; I see the way her eyes fill as she straightens his uniform, as if she knows he is no longer her vulnerable little boy; and I see again the way Lion had – for a fraction of a second – stiffened beneath her touch in both of those moments.

I lean backwards as the truth rocks the ground beneath me, and then I raise my glass high. "To the army," I say.

Lion smiles and raises his glass. "To freedom."

The sound of our clinking glasses hangs in the air, ringing clear and sweet like a bell.

"You know?" Lion drapes a heavy arm around my shoulder. "I'm sorry I gave you such a hard time about being a faggot," he says. "If you want to be a faggot, you just go right ahead and *be* a fucking faggot! You're a good guy, Mack, and if you want to suck dick, it's got nothing to do with me. Unless, you want to suck *my* dick – then I'd definitely have a problem with you!" His smile vanishes and he widens his bleary eyes. "You *don't* want to suck *my* dick, do you?"

"No!" I laugh. "Shit, no."

"Well, all right then!" He smiles and claps me on the back and then downs his final shot. Smacking his palm against the bar, once, twice, three times, he smiles at me and rasps, "Man, that's some smooth shit, huh?" Wincing, he touches a finger to the swollen tissue around his eye. "Hey, do you mind if I tell the boys that I got into a bar brawl?"

"Sure thing," I say. "As long as you say *I* beat the shit out of you!"

"Deal."

Lifting the first shot of whisky to my lips, I swallow it and my chest is a ball of flame and my throat blisters as I drink down the truth of Lion's shame, adding it to my slowly growing collection of army secrets.

*

"Infantry." Timothy stares up at me, pale faced, as I unbutton my shirt.

My fingertips are numb and feel too big to use, and I wonder how the hell I'd managed to hold on to those tiny, delicate shot glasses with hands that are suddenly so big and unmanageable. It takes three tries before I slip a button through its hole and then look down at Timothy and concentrate my drunk brain on whatever it is he is mumbling about. "What are you mumbling about?"

"Infantry," he says again, louder. "In-fan-tree!"

And those three syllables manage to sober me. My legs fold.

Oh Christ. What the hell have I gotten myself into? The one and only time I ever go against myself – go against every moral fiber of my being – and look where it lands me: staring deep into the glowing red eyes of a front line.

"Are you sure?"

He nods. "The M.O.S. list was put up on the bulletin board about an hour ago."

"But I applied for journalist," I say to Timothy. "You applied for photographer; how come we're in infantry?"

"*Everyone's* in infantry," he says. "Apparently the service needs of the army come first. Apparently there's some war going on somewhere at the moment, so we are all 11-Bravo. We can appeal, but ..."

"Great!" I stand up, but the rooms spins so I sit back down. "Let's go. Who do we see?"

"No." He shakes his head at me. "We'll have to extend our tour a further year or more."

"That's not fair!"

"Fair?" He shrugs. "Why would he start now?"

"*He?*"

"Sergeant Ass," says Timothy. "Who do you think assigned us all?"

I frown at him. Nothing makes sense.

"Ass," explains Timothy, "assigned everyone to infantry regardless of their choices."

Sergeant Ass?

I'd refused to use this nickname for the Drill Sergeant. I'd thought it was the guy's *job* to be a masochistic cheese-eater. I'd thought he was simply doing whatever he could to keep us alive, not because he was an asshole, but because he *wasn't*.

And after what he'd said to me earlier about trying to keep us all alive in order to restore our ability for choice ... well, was that just all a steaming pile of bullshit, then?

Because ... infantry? Fucking *infantry*?

Well, fuck you, you malicious asshole.

Just fuck you.

*

The next morning, with a snare drum *crump crump crump*, fifty pairs of feet all march in step, in perfect rhythm, like they belong to one entity. And maybe we are one entity now? All of us. Me, and Timothy, and Lion, and all these boys who now have the same goal of survival. All working as one, the way organs in a body work simultaneously to keep it alive.

On the parade field is a large white square of plastic chairs in which everyone else's family is seated, and I am the only one who does not break form and sneak a glance as we crump by them.

Actually, no, that's not true. Lion doesn't glance at the audience either.

Instead, we gaze up at the flag of our country. I press my white-gloved hand to my forehead in a salute, and I speak the vow of a soldier to this flapping rectangle of fabric, and I mean every God damned word of it because at least this flag is here to bear witness to my transformation from citizen to soldier.

At least this flag gives a fuck about me.

chapter forty-seven

ray

The phone rang, and as usual I was ready for her. "Hi, Nora."

"Well?" she asked. "How was Andy? How was the graduation?"

"It was great," I said. "He looked so handsome. We arrived early and got to spend a whole extra hour with him before the ceremony. It was hard for Lauren, though, being around all those uniforms again; it took almost that whole hour for her to stop shaking."

"Did you take any photographs? Can you send me some?"

"Yeah, sure," I said. "I took a whole bunch. I just need to finish off the roll and get the film developed and I'll post them right out."

"He wasn't too upset I couldn't be there, was he?" she asked. "You explained it all to him, didn't you?"

"Of course," I said. "He wants you to get well more than anyone. You know that."

"I know," she sighed. "I know. And you were right to talk me out of going. I'm doing so well here, why risk halting that progress?"

I nodded. "Exactly."

"Do you think he'd mind if I write him now?" Nora asked.

"*No!*" I said, stiffening in my chair. "No, don't do that! I asked and he said he still doesn't want letters from us."

There was a pause on the other end of the phone.

Did she believe me? Were my lies getting so thick now that Nora could hear the weight of them dragging down every syllable I spoke? And if she couldn't yet, how long would it be until she did recognize that heaviness for what it really was?

"I just feel so guilty ..." Nora gasped. "What if I gave up the last opportunity I will ever have to ..."

"*Stop!*" I closed my eyes against her words. "Don't say it. Don't even think that! You'll see him again. We both will."

"Yes," she whispered. "Yeah."

And I whispered "Yes" too, because all of a sudden I realized I'd made the worst mistake of my life.

But I'd had no choice. I looked down at my stomach. I couldn't have gone to visit him right now. Not like this. There was no way Japhy would accept it. He needed that jolt of love that only happens through physical connection, like when you feel your baby moving for the first time – either within the circle of your arms, or within the depths of your own body.

I loved this baby so much now, and I wanted it so badly, that I couldn't risk Japhy not accepting it. And he *wouldn't* want this baby, not while it was still locked away inside me; he needed to *meet* his child in order to fall.

Just like I had.

So, I'd had no choice but to keep this secret from him. This secret, and all the others.

Because if he knew that Nora had canceled the surgery ...

Because if he knew that Lauren had killed herself ...

Because if he knew that Leaf was who-knows-where, on the run from the law ...

Because if he knew I was alone ...

So, I'd had no choice.

Right?

I hung up from Nora and curled up in bed to write my nightly letter to Japhy, and I told myself again that I'd really had no choice but to keep these secrets from him.

And I was so good at lying now that I could even fool myself.

*

I walked every morning. I walked because Dr. Smyth said expectant mothers should keep their fitness levels up. That was all. No other reason. It had nothing at all to do with the fact that my chosen route took me right past my parents' house.

And each morning – as I hovered by the hedge that separated my parents' driveway from the house next door – I wondered if they were inside and if they were thinking about me right then.

Not that I cared if they were, anyway.

Every morning, at the same time, I huddled and waited for the mailman to come by. Every morning as he approached the mailbox, my mother flew through the front door and met him at the street. She snatched the letters from his hand, thanked him with a nod, and then flipped through the envelopes, one by one. Then she kind of drooped a little and shuffled back into the house, closing the door slowly behind her.

What is she waiting for? I wondered. Then I reminded myself, again, that I didn't care anyway. And I would push away from the hedge and run to the end of the street and vanish, like a memory, around the corner.

This morning, though, as I crouched by the hedge, uncaring, I froze, transfixed, as my mother and father walked out onto the front stoop. My mother paused, smiling down at the flowerbed while my father locked the front door, and then she took my father's proffered elbow, and together they walked down the flagstone path to the garage and rumbled the door up.

They spoke softly, but the words "bread ... telephone bill ... sunny ..." managed to reach my ears through the thick insulation of foliage between us.

Just an everyday, ordinary discussion. Groceries. Bills. Weather.

But then, what had I expected? A tearstained soliloquy about their beloved missing daughter?

Right.

As their car hummed off up the street, I sprinted around the hedge, along the driveway, and snatched up the key from its hiding place. Then I was inside the foyer with my back pressed against the front door.

What are you doing? I asked myself, and wished that I didn't already know the answer to that.

No matter how hard I willed myself to stop, and turn around, and run back to the safety of Nora's house, my feet kept shuffling me forward to where I would confront the worst part of my entire life. The place where the missing shreds of my soul hung like old curtains.

Because it was finally time.

Because if I was truly about to give birth to a child, then it was finally time.

Because if I wanted to be worthy of my child, then it was finally time.

The kitchen sparkled neatly, with everything in its place. No dirty whisky glasses crowded the sink. No refilled pill bottles lined up like soldiers on top of the refrigerator. My absence created none of the cracks that had earthquaked through this household in the wake of that *other* absence.

But then, I thought, as I crossed the dining room and the living room, it is just *me*. Why should *my* absence bring anything but pure joy to my parents?

Step by step, I climbed to the second story, my hand gripping the banister so tight it ached like a broken heart.

In the hallway, I stopped at the door that had drawn me back into this house in the first place. The room opposite my own. The room I was always forbidden to enter.

Touching the balloon of my stomach, I drew strength from its solidness and took a rattling breath. "Here we go."

My hand shook as I raised it to touch the small wooden letters that had been stuck there five years ago. Letters that I had helped my dad paint pink, and sprinkle with glitter, and stick on the door to surprise my mother when she arrived home from the hospital with my new baby sister.

The pink, glittery letters spelled out KATE.

A four-letter word that had not been spoken in this house for years.

Not out loud, anyway.

"Happy fifth birthday, Katie," I whispered.

I stood at the threshold of this room, which I had not entered since I was twelve and Kate had been asleep in her crib and I had killed her.

As I pushed the door, the hinges squawked like a screaming infant. Or maybe like the ghost of one.

In one corner was a pink bookcase lined with teddies and dolls and alphabet blocks that she'd never had a chance to play with. Opposite this was the rocking chair my mother had seen at a yard sale during the early weeks of her pregnancy; she'd made my father buy it on the spot, and we'd tied it on the roof of the car with a single rope and then held it steady through our open windows, and driven home at three miles an hour, laughing the whole way. Against the far wall was the change table, still stocked with fresh diapers and talcum powder. And in the center of the room, as hard to avoid as truth, was the crib, painted pure white like a dove's wing.

The room was spotlessly clean. My mother – who was the only one allowed in here – came in once a week to dust and vacuum and make sure that everything was just as Kate had left it that night. As if she was coming back.

Even the pink crocheted blanket was exactly as it had been left that night: scrunched into a wrinkled pile at the foot of the crib after my mother had screamed and wrenched it off her dead baby.

My heart pounded so hard it shook my whole body. My legs trembled and I had to lurch forward and steady myself on the side of the crib, and then I reeled away from it as the image of fingernails – so tiny and so blue – scratched out at my subconscious.

I sat down hard on the wooden rocking chair and worked

to steady my breathing as the room around me swayed forward and backwards and forward in time with the moving chair.

Breathe in. Breathe out. Breathe in ...

And then I heard the screams in my head. The screams that still kept sleep away from me sometimes. "She's not breathing! Oh Jesus, Jesus! She isn't breathing! Do something!"

My hands gripped the armrests and I closed my eyes. But that didn't help; out of the darkness strobed flashes of her tiny body, as floppy as a doll. My father carries her past the twelve-year-old me in the hallway. Red-faced, he runs with her, his keys jingling in his pocket. They jingle like reindeer bells on a sleigh. And that's when I start laughing. I just start fucking laughing. My baby sister is dead, and it's Christmas Eve, and it's all my fault, and I'm laughing like the horrific monster I've become.

Opening my eyes to the present again, I clapped a hand to my mouth as something warm and airy bubbled up my throat.

Not here, I thought. Not now, not in this room. Don't you dare laugh!

But it was a sob that rose up from the depths of my memories.

"Forgive me." I spoke these words to the empty room. I sent them out into the universe – not to Kate's spirit, or to my own conscience, or even to my parents – I said these words to my baby. To this child that I desperately wanted to keep in my life, to watch grow old, and to love with all my heart.

And I sobbed because I now had the answer I'd come into this room to find.

Standing at the crib once again, I lifted up the pink blanket that had not been touched in five years. As my tears plopped loudly onto the mattress, and as I tucked in the edges of the rug, and as I smoothed out all the wrinkles, my heart burned with the heat of my reached conclusion: in order to obtain redemption, there needed to be great sacrifice.

"Forgive me."

In the corner of the crib lay a rumpled brown teddy bear, the only toy that my five-month-old sister had ever had a chance to love. She used to suck on the round plastic ball of its nose. It calmed her when she cried. It soothed her when she couldn't sleep. And it had been gripped in her hand when they found her.

I thought about Nora, then, with her eyes all wild, muttering about karma as she buried all the food in the back garden. I thought about karma and balance and sacrifice as I snatched Kate's beloved teddy bear up with both hands, and pulled. Hard. The seams popped and the material ripped with the sound of a guttural scream. Stuffing spilled from a wide gash in the neck, and all around me pieces of down floated like snowflakes falling in my hair or on my shoulders or around my feet. Each single white feather landed as silently as absolution.

"Forgive me," I whispered again.

Hugging the ruined bear against my chest, I left Kate's door open wide and I ran from this house and this ghost that might finally leave me alone, because now I had the power to make everything right again.

I had taken away my mother's baby.

I had taken away Lauren's baby.

So now the only way to atone for these sins was to take away *my own* baby.

chapter forty-eight

japhy

"God damn it!" I punch the seat of the bus as we drive away from the Basic Training camp and head to Advanced Infantry Training at Fort Polk, Louisiana.

"They might as well just sign our death certificates now," says Timothy.

"Hey, man, don't talk like that. You are coming home, I promise you that."

He looks at me and raises his eyebrows. "You can't promise that."

"I promise," I say again.

"Whatever you say, soldier." And he turns his face to the window.

Soldier?

Me?

If that's what it takes, then hell, yes, I'm a soldier. I will march through anything. I will survive it all. And I will go home, and marry the best girl in the world, and start a family, and forget this whole part of my life ever happened.

I imagine the beautiful faces of the children that Ray and I will have one day.

Ray and I never really talked about the future. About where we'd live, and how many kids we'd have, and how soon we'd have them. We hadn't had the time. We'd discussed college, and maybe finding a halfway-house to share in California, but that's as far as we'd gone. Because we hadn't had the time. Uncle Sam rudely barged his way into our burgeoning relationship – which had only just gotten over the excitement of our first real make-out session – and pushed our intensity up to a hundred. We'd gone from teenage kids, holding hands and sharing milkshakes and blushing awkwardly at each other, to two consenting adults leaving wet stains on the bedroom carpet and fleeing the country and giving up everything for the other person.

Although, I think, that right there – that sacrifice – is the kind of vow you can't even get with marriage. What Ray gave up for me. For us. Encapsulated inside that sacrifice is the discussion we never had, because we hadn't had the time. But really, because of that sacrifice, we never *need* to have that discussion at all. It is all there, waiting in my future. Just waiting for me to reach it.

I can see a little girl with dark hair and blue eyes who smiles up at me with Ray's lopsided grin, and there is a little boy that frowns with Ray's adorable forehead wrinkle, and there is Ray leaning on a doorframe with her hand on her stomach that balloons once again with the greatest miracle in existence. I hear laughter and high-pitched voices calling out, "I love you, Daddy!", and I feel the solidness of my children's arms around my neck, and I love them more than anything already.

I love this future more than anything.

I love it even more than the possibility of seeing it all come true.

I wonder if I should finally write Ray. To tell her about my dreams, and about our future, and about our beautiful kids, because if I am really and truly honest with myself now, I may not get the chance to ever tell her in person.

"Can I have some of your paper, man?" I whisper to Timothy.

"Really?" He bends down and rifles through his bag. "I thought you didn't do letters."

I shrug as he hands me his notepad and a blue pen.

The nib hovers over the white paper, shaking in my fingers.

What am I supposed to say to her? *Dear Ray, I just want to you know – in case I die Over There – that I want us to have a family.* Christ. And then, what happens if I really *do* die? She will think about these words for the rest of her life, always wondering what we might have had, always grieving for the future that died along with me. I can't do that to her.

Handing the notepad back to Timothy, I say, "You're right, I guess I don't do letters."

Anyway, I think as I watch him settle back in his seat and scratch out his own words on the notepad, it's not like Ray needs to know, right now, that I want children as soon as possible.

I pull my cap low over my eyes and think about one of the guys in our company, Phillips: he just found out that he knocked his girlfriend up the night he left for Induction. Imagine that. Imagine stepping off the plane after the Nam tour is over and walking into your own instant family! Being able to make up for all this lost time.

I picture Ray grinning at me in the airport with a tiny bundle wrapped in her arms. I see myself rushing forward and lifting them both off the ground with the sheer force of my happiness.

Man, that would be the best thing to come home to. The best thing in the world.

chapter forty-nine

ray

The advertisement showed the silhouette of a stork; a child in a blanket dangles from its beak like a weight in a set of scales. It reminded me of the scales of justice. Although, there was no second scale in this picture to act as a counterbalance.

There was no right versus wrong.

Would it be this easy to have my weight of burden removed? Or would it be something I would end up carrying around with me for the rest of my life; a new burden of guilt simply replacing the old?

What if I made this horrible sacrifice in the search for my own inner freedom, to balance my karmic imbalance, only to find that it made no difference? What if I was still haunted by Kate's death, but on top of that heaped the guilt of giving up my own beloved child for nothing?

Gritting my teeth against tears that burned my eyes, I ripped the page out of the phone book and marched to Leaf's van with the crumpled sheet of paper in my fist.

When I reached the adoption center in Birmingham, I just sat there, in the parking lot, staring up at the simple gray stone building, inside which entire futures were changed. Destinies were taken off their current paths and repositioned in a whole new direction.

What direction would my baby be sent on? I wondered. And what path would it lead to?

It had been all fine to hand this baby over to Lauren and Leaf, because I would still be able to watch it grow. I would have remained a part of its life. Maybe been the godmother or at the very least, cool Aunt Ray.

I imagined handing over the wriggling bundle of blankets to a stranger who would then turn from me and disappear forever. Just disappear with my baby.

My baby.

I sighed, and as I emptied the air from my lungs, my body deflated and I crumpled forward.

But then the image of Kate's empty crib dotted with pieces of cotton wool and falling feathers flashed across my mind, and I forced myself to straighten in my seat.

This wouldn't be so bad. I wanted to go to university. Japhy didn't want a kid anyway, and Leaf was nowhere to be seen, so he didn't care either. It would be *wrong* to keep a child with parents like us: a father who didn't really want it and a murderess-mother who didn't deserve her baby's love.

Especially when there were so many worthy families desperate for a child to call their own.

Lifting my chin, I left the van and marched across the parking lot. Four steps led up to a set of mirrored doors. With each step I ascended, I watched my reflection grow taller in the glass, like a child growing into a woman. As my hand reached for the handle, my reflection reached for me and its hand took hold of mine.

Was it possible to miss something you'd never have?

Yes, I thought. God, yes. It was.

I squeezed the doorknob and imagined the solidity in my palm was a tiny hand as we took first wobbly steps together, or crossed a road, or entered a schoolyard for the very first time.

Clenching my fist, I pushed open the door and crossed the threshold.

To my left was a small waiting area. A woman sat reading a magazine.

Was she receiving the greatest gift? I thought. Or giving it up.

I looked away from her as she glanced at me; I didn't want to know the truths that were visible in her eyes.

Or perhaps I didn't want her to see mine.

"Can I help you?"

I jumped and turned to see a short, fat man with sauce on his tie, and I took a step backwards.

Well, what had I been expecting? Beautiful, willowy women floating around in white chiffon like fairy-fucking-godmothers?

"Miss?" said the man. "Can I help you?"

"Yes." I kept my eyes down and all their horrible truths diverted from him. "Can you tell me where the nearest gas station is?" I backed away, and without waiting for his response, I pushed open the mirrored doors and ran down the steps with my hands clasped around my stomach, fingers tightly together like the unbreakable links in a chain.

*

"Miss Wren!" Dr. Smyth beamed at me as he sat behind his desk. He flipped open my file, and his little black eyes sparkled as he read his notes. "So we are now approximately fourteen weeks along, yes? Good, good." He looked up. "How are you feeling? Still nauseous?"

I nodded. "I've felt nauseous for weeks, ever since Andy left for Basic Training."

"Hmmm. Well, that could be plain stress. We need to alleviate that. Are you a smoker?"

"I don't mind them every now and again, sure," I said.

"Buy yourself a pack on the way home."

"It's not bad for the baby?" I asked.

"Not at all," said Dr. Smyth. "In fact, I urge all my mother-to-be's to smoke during their pregnancies; it lowers stress levels, which," he raised a finger, "is especially important for someone like yourself. How *is* Andy doing anyway?"

"He's fine," I said. "I get letters from him all the time. Every day, actually. He's just fine."

"He's a smart boy, that one." The doctor winked at me. "He'll get through this and be home before you know it. Now," he stood and gestured to a bed in the corner of the room, "lie down on here and lift up your shirt."

The silver disc of his stethoscope was as cold as truth against my stomach, and I sucked in a breath.

"Sorry," Dr. Smyth muttered. He breathed heat onto it and then replaced it on my skin. After a moment, he plucked out the earpieces. "Heartbeat sounds perfect, Heather. Very strong."

"Thank you." I grinned, as if it were *my* heart that were perfect, and *my* heart that were strong. But of course, that was not the case.

At least not yet.

There was just too much crud around my heart these days: the build-up from years of guilt, plus the current lacing of lies that calcified a new layer every day. My heart beat slowly, muffled, as if the muscle was covered in dried mud. But soon, it would be washed clean again, cleansed by sacrifice.

Soon my heart would beat louder than a thunderstorm, and it would be filled with pride, and light, and peace. Because I was doing the right thing. I was doing a good thing. A selfless thing.

A heartbreaking thing.

"All right," said the doctor. "Shoes off, please, and step up here."

As I slipped off my sneakers and balanced myself on the scales, I wondered, could the weight of my burden be measured by modern technology? Or would the decision of my impending sacrifice – the knowledge that I would soon be giving up my entire world – balance everything else out?

I stared at the little white numbers and at the tiny arrow that flitted nervously across them, like a butterfly across a too-still lake.

"Lovely," the doctor said, writing my weight down in my file. "Couldn't be more perfect, really."

"Thank you," I said again.

"All righty. Well, I'll see you again next month, just to make sure everything continues on as it should. I'll be right there with you, the whole way, to make sure this little baby is as healthy and happy as possible. And just think: in about six short months you'll be holding him or her in your arms."

I nodded at him and smiled. I wanted to tell him I wouldn't be keeping the baby. I wanted to tell him it would be some other woman who would be holding it in her arms, and smiling down through her tears to welcome it into the world. I wanted to tell him about my baby sister. I wanted to tell him about Japhy's silence. I wanted to tell him about everything. But instead, I thanked him, and left his office clutching tight to the words he had said: "I'll be right there with you, the whole way."

With those words heavy as a sleeping cat in my lap, I drove home, back to my empty house, and for the first time in weeks I didn't feel alone.

*

The hedge beside my parents' house was dense and cold against my face – a welcome contrast to the hot morning sun that seared my exposed cheek.

I pressed myself against the leaves and held my breath and prayed I had not been seen.

As I'd drawn closer this morning, wishing for the house to be empty again so I could creep back into Kate's room and beg for another solution, I'd heard a sound that had dropped me to the ground. Now I huddled down and closed my eyes tight and begged my tears to stop clawing up my throat where they wanted to break free into a sob.

My mother faced away from me, bent forward on her knees in the garden bed. She wore a sun hat that was so ridiculously large that the shadow from its wide brim fell entirely over her substantial width. In her hand was a trowel, and as she stabbed and stabbed the dirt, the rhythmic *chink chink chink chink* wrapped around me like a pair of long-lost arms. It was the sound of my childhood. The sound of me working alongside her in that exact spot, planting daisies and roses and lilies, and all the while that *chink chink chink chink*, and me with my own silly hat and chubby child's hands covered in soil as I helped to tease out the roots.

"You need to space them out evenly," my mother had said, placing the flowers in their holes. "A flower needs room to grow, to spread its roots, otherwise it will feel stifled and it will shrivel."

How had I forgotten about that?

A flower needs room to grow, yes. But if you give it too much room and too little attention, its branches will grow wild and out of control.

Another memory rose up in my mind like a new flower breaking through the dirt. She is standing in the frame of my doorway, upside-down because I'm laying on my bed with my head hanging backwards off the mattress. I must be fourteen? Two years after I killed Kate. She raises a small pot in the air like a question. I flap my hand at her, like she is a fly, and turn my attention back to the telephone cradled against my shoulder and the nail polish I'm applying to my toes. Her face droops, and she gives a forced smile before leaving the only child she has left.

What if that had been her white flag? What if she had been offering me forgiveness and I had refused?

I swallowed and stepped around the driveway hedge, but then I hesitated. The memory of the day Japhy and I left came back with the same force as the slap my mother had given me, her words stinging again just as much as my cheek had: "If you leave me too, Heather Wren, don't bother coming back," she'd screamed. "If you leave, you'll be dead to me!"

Japhy had draped a warm arm around my shoulder and whispered that I didn't have to go with him. But as my mother's words left welts on me, I knew that I couldn't stay here any longer anyway.

Now, with no loving arm to shield me, I took a shaking breath and stepped forward.

"Momma?"

The trowel stabbed the dirt once more as she turned.

"Heather?" She stood. Her face drooped. Her lips curled in a forced a smile. "Oh, my girl. Oh thank goodness!"

She held out her arms to me and I ran into them as tears clawed their way free and sobs came and came and came.

"Hey," she whispered in my ear. "Shhh. You're home now. Everything is going to be all right."

"No!" I cried, my voice muffled by her shoulder. "It's not!" And then I opened my mouth and the words just tumbled out one after the next with no breaths or pauses or punctuation just words words words and I thought that they would never stop.

I told her about the Kent State shootings and the Canadian commune and Japhy's arrest and induction and how fucking much I missed him.

Through my memories, I introduced her to Leaf and Lauren, and I watched her face crumple in pain as I described seeing Lauren's corpse and finding Leaf's goodbye note stuck coldly to the front door.

"And this?" she asked me, once my tears had dried, and my sobs had silenced. She placed a hand on my belly and smiled. "My baby is having a baby?"

"No." My face twisted into a knot. "I'm putting it up for adoption."

Stepping back, her eyes wide, she pressed her hand to her cheek as if I'd slapped her face. "Are you sure?"

"Yes."

Her eyes flickered back and forth, searching my face. "Why?"

"Because." I looked away from her and I filled to the brim with tears again. "I'm not ready."

"I understand," she said. "You want to be prepared. You want to have your life all set up so that when your child does come along you can give it everything it could ever want. I know you, sweetheart; you want to travel, and go to college." She smiled then, and shook her head. "Having a child will educate you far more than any college degree. It will give you far more joy than any travel experience you can dream of. It is something you can *never* be prepared for. And no matter what you do for that child's best interests, you will feel like it wasn't good enough. You will feel like you have failed her."

"Exactly," I said, clutching on to her as my legs weakened. "That's why I have no choice."

"Heather, this is a big decision."

I bit my bottom lip. "I know."

"And it is one that nobody should have to make all on their own." She wrapped her arm around my shoulder. "Everything is going to be all right now."

Those words. Oh, those words!

Instantly, my shoulders relaxed and a heaviness – approximately equal to that of a newborn child – lifted from my bones.

"Momma?" I gripped her hand. "Will you help me do this?"

"Oh, darling," she laughed quickly. "That is a question a child never need ask its mother." And then she handed me a small potted plant, raising it in the air like a question. Or perhaps like a white flag.

Taking the plant in my hand, I knelt in the dirt beside my mother, shaded by her ridiculous hat. She picked up the trowel, smiled at me, and stabbed the tiny shovel into the dirt, breaking through the hard, dry ground: *chink chink chink chink.*

"When are you due?"

"January twenty-fourth," I said.

"And the father?"

I hesitated. "In the army, I told you that."

She stopped and looked at me; a half-smile pulled at her face. "But what about the *other* one?"

I sighed, and then I just shrugged, because really, what else could I say? And she shrugged too, and we both continued to dig.

"Do they know?" she asked.

"Leaf knows I'm pregnant, and that I planned on giving it up. Japhy knows nothing; that's the way he wants things while he is Over There. But I know he doesn't want kids just yet; we talked about it once."

"I wasn't talking about the pregnancy, darling."

I frowned at her.

"I mean," she said, "does Leaf ... *know*?"

"Know what?" I asked. "Anyway, what does it matter? He ran off and left me to deal with all of this by myself! He left me alone with a baby that might be his. He lied to me about who he really is; God knows what else he has kept secret. I can't trust him. So I don't even *care* where he is, or how he is coping, or if he *never* comes back!"

"If you really believe that, Heather, why are you crying?"

"Because!" I wiped at the tears that traced my cheeks and betrayed my words. "I'm angry."

"But *why*?" she said. "Like you said: What does it matter?"

"It matters because I thought he was my friend!" I snatched the trowel from her hand and stabbed the garden bed. "It matters because I need him!" *Stab, stab.* "Because it's so hard to wake up alone and remember that he isn't here." *Stab, stab.* "Because I feel halved without him. And because ..." The trowel dropped from my fingers and I covered my face with my hands. "Because ..."

"Because you are in love with him," whispered my mother.

Her words settled like seeds in the dirt around me and, watered by my tears, they broke free and stretched up to the sky like sunflowers turning their faces toward the blinding brightness of truth.

Taking a breath, I lowered my hands and met my mother's eyes, and then I tested those words on my own tongue. "Because," I spoke slowly, "because I am in love with Leaf."

Oh shit, I thought. Oh holy fucking shit.

No.

You meet someone, you fall in love with that someone, you marry that someone, and you live happily with that someone for the rest of your life. That's the way I'd always thought of love.

Never in that philosophy was there ever a *second* someone to whom my whole heart would belong. The math just didn't quite work.

Or, at least, it shouldn't. Yet, somehow, it totally did.

Being in love with two people at once was a lot easier than I thought it would be.

The difficult part was not the concept of broken monogamy, or betrayal of trust, or anything like that. The difficult part for me was being in love with someone I *hated*.

I hated Leaf for leaving in the middle of the night.

I hated Leaf for not saying goodbye.

I hated Leaf for lying and keeping secrets.

But most of all I hated Leaf because I still loved him in spite of all the reasons that I shouldn't.

Love makes you realize the possibility of a higher being: fate, destiny, karma, God. Because there are certain things in your life over which you have no control. And if *you* don't control them, then something else must.

So, when had it all changed? I wondered. When had my feelings shifted up a notch from friendship to *this*?

I remembered the very first time I'd seen him, and the way my eyes had met his, and I'd thought, Oh, yes! This is my soul mate. I recognized something within him that had clicked within me. Not in a romantic way, but with that same sense of safe *familiarity* you feel when you return after an absence to the place where you know you belong.

I remembered the moment when he'd blown through the bedroom door at Nora's and my heart had stuttered just that little bit and I knew I would no longer be alone. Had that been the moment? That little skip of my heart which hadn't really slowed down since.

I hadn't really thought about why he'd had that effect on me; I hadn't cared at the time. All I knew was that in his arms I no longer ached everywhere. Had he been eclipsing my sorrow for Japhy with affection for himself?

I remembered the last night he'd held me, and the tender way we'd made love, each using the other as a substitute. Or so I'd thought then. I'd covered his face with a Japhy mask, and he'd covered my face with Lauren's, but with a jolt I saw in my memory the pink skin of that Japhy mask curl up at the edges, dislodge, and fall to the floor. I saw myself turn away from it, not bothering to reach down and replace it, but instead to continue on with Leaf unmasked, and myself unprotected.

Had that been the moment, then? Had I fallen in love with Leaf, and with his unyielding presence, at the very moment when he'd been planning to leave me?

chapter fifty

japhy

"Welcome to your new hell! I am your training officer, Drill Sergeant Slate, and I am the man who will be saving your lives, so y'all had better listen to every single, motherfucking word that I say. Is that clear, you maggot-filled scrotum sacks?"

"Yes, sir!"

Here we go again, I sigh, as I watch this new drill sergeant walk the line and scream and puff his chest out in the exact same way that the old drill sergeant had.

I am so sick of this bullshit. Why do they all have to screech at us like this? Why do they have to make the last few weeks we will spend on home soil such negative ones, especially when – for some of us – they will be the last weeks spent, *ever*, on home soil.

Yeah, okay, I get that they need to make sure we are disciplined and strong-willed and all that crap, I can dig it ... but seriously ... they are sending us all away to Nam to risk our lives for them. Couldn't they just treat us with a little fucking respect? A little fucking niceness? Was that really so fucking hard? Sheesh!

"Are you listening to me, Private?"

I blink into the swollen, red face of this new asshole and I shrug. "No, sir."

"Well, maybe I am not talking loud enough for you, son!" He leans forward and shouts right into my ear. "Is that better?"

I wince and say nothing.

"Get down on this fucking ground and give me fifty!"

I don't move.

"Now!"

Still I don't move.

"What the fuck are you waiting for? A written invitation?"

"No, sir," I say. "But a simple *please* wouldn't kill you, would it?"

He punches me, smiles as I drop backwards into the mud, and says in a sneer, "Please."

"Thank you," I whisper and start to lift and drop my body, counting off each push-up in a loud, strong voice.

*

I curl my fingers around the bamboo bars of this cage I've been locked in for six whole hours now and, shivering, stare out at the stars.

I am a Prisoner of War.

I have been captured by VC, stripped down to my shorts and thrown into this tiny cell where I can almost reach from one side to the other if I stretch out my arms. The floor, and therefore my bed, is the earth, cold and hard and unforgiving beneath my bones. In one corner is a bucket I can piss and shit in. Next to that is an empty rice bowl that will be filled only once during these 24 hours, and a metal cup that is still half-full of water, which I've been rationing in case I get no more. For the last hour or so, I've been staring at that cup, telling myself to hold off just another minute, just one more, just one. And for the last hour or so, my dry mouth has begged for mercy.

When I hear movement, I stand and squint into the darkness, barely recognizing Phillips and Jenson as they swim out of the night. They wear black pajamas and conical bamboo hats – the uniform of both the innocent Vietnamese farmers, and the invisible enemy: the guerilla Viet Cong.

From behind us somewhere, I know Drill Sergeant Slate watches, wearing his own army greens and hideous smile – the uniform of both the United States Army and *my* invisible enemy: Uncle Sam.

Jenson and Phillips do not speak to me. They grunt and indicate I am to turn around and place my wrists backwards through the bars. When I do, they tie my hands together with twine so I am tethered to the bamboo wall.

The door swings wide and they stand in front of me.

"What is your name, rank, and serial number?" Jensen shouts at me.

We have been given only a few rules to survive being captured:

1. Don't tell. They will use any information given in any way they can. In the past they sent a bogus K.I.A. telegram to a soldier's wife because he gave out his address, so therefore, no matter what, don't fucking tell.
2. Don't die. If they didn't kill you to start with, chances are they won't kill you now, so hang in there, get through one day at a time until you are rescued.

And that is basically Survival 101 for the Prisoner of War. Don't tell and don't die. Simple.

"What is your name, rank, and serial number!" Jensen shouts again, and he slaps my cheek hard.

It startles me and I suck in a breath. My face burns in the cool night air, but I keep my head down and I don't tell.

Phillips bends down and picks up my empty bowl and cup. As if in answer, my stomach lets out a long grumble.

"You hungry?" he sneers. "Thirsty?"

I shake my head.

"There will be no food or drink for you until you answer our question."

Still I say nothing.

And then he unzips his pants and takes a God damn piss in my God damn cup. Placing it back down on the ground, neatly so he doesn't spill a precious drop, he stands and smiles. "Enjoy. If you want seconds, let me know."

Laughing, they leave my cell, lock the door, untie my hands, and melt backwards into the night.

Sitting down again, I stare at my cup. My tongue is as dry as paper and keeps sticking to my teeth. My lips feel hard and cracked. My throat burns and I can't think of anything besides quenching the flames of dehydration.

That son-of-a-bitch, I think. He'll keep. Soon it'll be my turn to play VC to his prisoner.

Thoughts about how I can pay the bastard back actually take my mind off the pain of dehydration for a while.

Revenge is one reason wars exist.

I don't want to become like that, I don't want to change, but, Jesus H. Christ, the effortlessness at which my brain just switched, the naturalness of progression from anger to sworn vengeance, and worse, my ignorance that any shift had even occurred ... well, shit.

I have just experienced my biggest fear.

I have just experienced my biggest weakness.

And it turns out they are both the same thing.

Maybe my enemy is not Uncle Sam at all. It is not the Viet Cong. It is me.

I am the one holding a gun to the temple of my true self.

I am the one shouting into the face of that innocent and moral me.

I am the one bullying that me to join the side of the enemy, where it is okay to get angry, and get even, and get another man's blood on your palms.

Damn.

I hug my knees to my chest.

I curl my fingers around the bars of this flesh-and-bone cage I've been locked in for nineteen years and, shivering, stare out at the world.

I am a Prisoner of War.

august

There's blood in the streets, it's up to my ankles.
Blood in the streets, it's up to my knee.
Blood in the streets, in the town of Chicago.
Blood on the rise, it's following me.

~ Jim Morrison, Peace Frog

chapter fifty-one

ray

My mother grinned at me as I answered the front door. "I had a serious discussion with your father last night."

"Hello to you, too," I said, yawning and stepping back to let her inside.

Kissing my cheek, she placed her palm on my stomach as she passed, stooping over and whispering, "Good morning in there, little one!"

"So, what's up?" I flicked a switch on the coffee percolator and leaned against the counter, listening to it hiss and gurgle.

"You shouldn't be drinking that horrid stuff in your condition," she said as she lit a cigarette and offered one to me.

I shook my head, thinking about Dr. Smyth's recommendation. "Coffee is the only thing I can keep down in the morning."

"Ah." My mother nodded. "Yes, I remember: I had the worst sickness when I was pregnant with you. It lasted *all* day long, and *all* pregnancy long! None of this *morning* stuff." She smiled then. "Must have been a sign."

"Of what? That I was going to make you feel sick every day? Thanks a lot, Mom!"

"No." She shook her head. "The things that we work

hardest to obtain," she said, "are the things that we end up loving the most."

Pretending to prepare the coffee, I turned away to hide the tears that rose up in me.

"So, as I was saying before," she said, "I spoke to your father last night about this baby of yours." She stepped forward and whispered, "Your father and I will adopt this baby."

Her words came at me like dust motes. They floated and hovered in my peripheral vision, but every time I tried to focus on them directly, they vanished, blended back into the darkness.

I shook my head. "I don't understand."

"Your father and I can raise this child. Raise it like our own. Give it the life we always envisioned giving to you. And to ... your sister."

I closed my eyes, and I saw my baby in my mother's arms. I saw a brightness in her face that hadn't glowed there for five years. I saw once again the brightness that I had taken away from her.

An eye for an eye.

A baby for a baby.

This was the alternate solution I had been seeking.

The best solution for everyone.

Something bloomed in my heart. Relief, perhaps?

Taking a breath, I blew out my answer. "No."

My mother frowned. "Just think about ..."

"No!" Walking to the front door, I held it open wide. "You need to leave."

"Heather, please." She didn't move. "You asked me to help you do this. You *asked* me!"

"I meant," I said, "to help give it away."

"But why? Why give it to a complete stranger? That's not the right choice, darling."

"Well," I said, "then it's a good thing it's not *your* choice to make. It's my choice and it's what I need to do."

"Why do you *need* to?" she asked. "Why give away the most beautiful gift you'll ever receive?"

I still couldn't look at her; I stared down at my fingernails, which were short and bitten down to their quicks. "Because," I whispered, "of Kate."

"Kate?" she gasped. The name came out as thin as air. "What does ... Kate ... have to do with this?"

I shrugged. "An eye for an eye."

"Oh, sweetheart, no!"

As her arms wrapped around me, warm and solid, I realized that I was sobbing.

"Shh." She rubbed a hand in gentle circles on my back. "What happened to Kate was not your fault." Her words cloaked me like silk (*not your fault, not your fault*) but their slippery folds wouldn't stay put; they kept sliding off me and pooling on the floor. "It wasn't your fault."

"But I *heard* you!" I gulped. "I heard you tell Daddy that you shouldn't have left her with me."

"You heard that?" She winced. "Yes. I did say that. And I still believe that."

I stepped away from her, wounded.

She came at me. Grabbed my shoulders, and spun me to face her. "But not because I blame *you*, Heather. Because I blame *myself*. I'm her mother, and I should have been there for her, every single night. Just like I should have been there for *you*. Just like I am trying to be now. If you'll let me. If you'll forgive me."

"Forgive *you*?"

Her words just wouldn't make sense in my head. Because of me, Kate was dead. I should have checked on her more often. I should have sat in the room with her the entire night, making sure that blanket rose and fell with every single God damn breath. Instead, I sat in the living room and talked on the phone to a girlfriend for hours and ignored my little sister who wasn't crying or anything so surely she was fine. But she hadn't been fine. And if I'd checked on her sooner, maybe I could have saved her life.

"I know it was you," she said, her voice low. "In her room the other day. The blanket? The teddy bear? And you know what?" She laughed. She actually *laughed*. "It was exactly what I needed. I'd been holding on so tightly to the daughter I'd lost that I let the one I still *had* slip right through my hands. I'm so sorry, Heather. Let me help you."

"No," I whispered. "Please, leave."

My mother stared at me, her mouth slightly open, her cheeks slightly pink, her eyes slightly wet, and she didn't move.

"Now!" I screamed.

She flinched. "All right." As she stepped by me and out onto the porch, she kissed my cheek again.

I slammed the door and ran down the hallway to the bathroom. Staring into my eyes, I tried to peer down into the depths at the loose, flapping shreds of the damaged soul within.

She said it wasn't my fault.

And I so wanted to believe that.

But if that were true, why did I still feel torn up on the inside. And if that were true, how torn up must *her* soul feel?

I knew the devastating effect that losing a child could have over a mother; Jesus Christ, I'd seen it firsthand. Lauren hadn't survived it. And my mother ...

One month after we covered my little sister with soil, I came home from school to find my mother unconscious in her bed. The side of her chin was streaked with vomit. On the bedside table was a water glass, an empty bottle of Nembutal, and a note.

To what remains of my beautiful family,

It will always be a parent's job to take care of her child, so I need to leave and do my job! I need to take care of Kate. Please don't hate me for this, and please remember that I love you both so very much. I know that you will take care of each other.

With steady hands and dry eyes, I'd placed that note back on her nightstand and backed away. I'd left her there. I'd left her, just like she was leaving me. Upstairs in my bedroom, with my mother dying directly beneath my floorboards, I'd put on my headphones, and cranked my stereo, and drowned out the sound of my soul shredding again.

So now, what if she adopted my baby, and for a while that

brightness, that *life*, returned to her eyes until, once again, devastation struck? What if, next time, my father doesn't come home early to find her unconscious and covered in sick?

After five years, I had my momma back. And I would not risk losing her again.

*

The wonderful thing about music was the power it had to transport you through time. Whatever was happening in the present moment was completely replaced by another moment that lived in your reality for as long as the magical song continued to play.

I sat on the floor of Japhy's room with my legs splayed around the turntable, watching the needle dip and bump over the grooves of the forty-five. I sat there beside the ghost of my past – beside a younger Andy – watching him smile at me through the fog of this music that transcended time itself.

The track ended and Andy vanished and the present time took his place. I scrabbled for the arm of the record player, returning the needle again to the beginning of the song I had been listening to, over and over, all morning long. The song that was pulling me backwards into the past, the song that had wooed me on that day when both Andy Mack and James Lee Stanley were new and shiny with possibility and I had felt myself falling in love with these two men at once.

I sighed as the intro began and I was sucked away from this hot August day, back to a colder month that was so much hotter ...

"It's a far out feeling," says Andy, "knowing you're about to change someone's life forever. Are you ready?"

I inhale the heat and excitement in his words, and feel it spread through my chest and my stomach. "I'm ready," I say.

And he drops the needle with a sigh.

The music floats over me with an upbeat happiness, like calliope music. I feel my youth, bubbly and bright, and time stretches out to encompass all the wonders that I could ever dream about for myself. Right now, anything is possible.

"*Wait for the summertime,*" sings James. "*Only in the summertime will you be free with me.*"

Andy closes his eyes and nods his head, a smile wide on his face.

"*Wait for the summertime. Only in the summertime will you be free with me. Be free with me.*"

I stare at those lips and I wonder ...

"*Be free with me to wander hand in hand.*"

I wonder what it would be like to kiss him.

For him to kiss me.

To feel his soft palms cradle my face as his breath becomes my breath.

"*Be free with me to love you if I can ... and I can.*"

He opens his eyes and I inhale sharply and look away, shocked at the thrill surging through my blood at something as simple as another person's gaze.

"What do you think?" he asks.

"I think you were right," I whisper. "You have changed my life."

"*Wait for the summertime. Only in the summertime will you be free with me.*"

"Can't you just feel the August heat on your skin?" he asks, eyes closed again. "And school's over. And it's just us; it's our time, you know?"

"*Wait for the summertime. Only in the summertime will you be free with me.*"

Our time? I think. Ours? His and mine? Far out.

"*We stayed out on the beach 'til it was almost dark. We bought a toy balloon and lost it in the park.*"

I'm staring again. Imagining what my summer will be like this year now that my world is completely different and anything is possible.

"*Wait for the summertime. Only in the summertime will you be free with me.*"

This time, when he opens his eyes and catches me staring, I don't hide it. I don't care. Because he wants to be free with me.

"Be free with me while summer breezes blow."

He leans forward then and brushes a hair off my cheek.

"Be free with me to go where no one knows that we're alone ..."

I close my eyes.

"... We're all alone, we're all alone ..."

As I wait my skin sings.

"I can't wait for the summertime. I can't wait for the summertime ..."

And then I feel a chill as he moves away, clears his throat, and does not kiss me. Maybe I'd been wrong about him? Maybe I'd been right to doubt that Andy Mack wanted me? Maybe he'd somehow seen into my soul, and therefore did I really blame him for backing away?

"I should be getting home." My words are raspy and raw.

"Of course," he says, helping me to my feet. "Let me walk you out."

I don't look at him as we leave the bedroom, or cross through the house, or step out onto the front porch.

"Well," I say, "I'll catch you."

"Heather?"

I pause, but I still don't look at him. I can't afford to; I can still leave this place with that song buoyant in my head, with my dreams still intact, with the feeling that maybe Andy Mack could still be interested in someone like me. But if I look at him now, I know I will see truth there. And truth is not always a good thing.

"Heather." His fingers wrap my wrist and he jerks my arm, spinning me around and off my feet.

Unbalanced, I fall against his chest.

"I'll catch you," he whispers as his soft palms cradle my face and his breath becomes my breath.

My first kiss had been one of the most amazing moments of my life. Reliving it now, though, was absolute torture. Because here I sat, in Japhy's room, and I could finally feel that August heat on my skin, just like he'd said, and school was over, just like he'd said. But it was not *us*. It was not *our* time. It was just *me*.

All alone.

"... *We're all alone, we're all alone* ..."

As the song ended, I gently lifted the arm and returned it again to the beginning of the track I had been listening to, over and over, all morning long. The song that had wooed me on that day, when both Andy Mack and James Lee Stanley were new and shiny with possibility and I had felt myself falling in love with these two men at once.

The music started, and I smiled through my tears as Andy grins at me. "Are you ready?"

september

Freedom's just another word for nothin' left to lose.

~ Kris Kristofferson, *Me and Bobby McGee*
(recorded by Janis Joplin)

chapter fifty-two

japhy

On the back of an army jeep, we ride in silence through the base until we are no longer in America.

A lush rainforest rises up on either side of the muddy road, forming a canopy above our heads in every shade of green you can imagine. Sprinklers hiss to life and it rains down on us. Water trickles inside the plastic ponchos we wear, down our backs, like the icy, teasing finger of Death himself. As the rain falls onto the hot earth, steam rises like souls, and makes the air hot and wet and hard to breathe.

In the distance, on a great wooden sign, I read the words: *Tiger Land – Birthplace of the Combat Infantrymen of Viet Nam. Fight Win Engage and Destroy.*

I sigh as I pass it, imagining an invisible border across which I have just been shoved. From which I may not return. Because this is the edge of the world. And here, there be monsters.

*

Once again, I am stripped bare and rebuilt from the bones out. The me who was, is no longer.

I stand, holding a broom, sweeping the floor of the small

grass hut in which I live with my husband. The roof leaks, and drops of water pool on the floor. In the corner is a crib, a small box, where my infant child sleeps. I smile over at her and then stare out the doorway, through the gray sheets of rain, waiting for the first glimpse of my husband, who will be returning at any moment from his day in the rice fields. At least, I hope he will be returning today. I try to sweep away my fear as easily as I sweep away the mud from my door. Fear is a constant in this new world, a daily companion, a terrible shadow that haunts me right up until that moment when my family is all together and I know we are safe for another day. But that moment of fearlessness always seems to be just out of reach; no matter how hard I sweep, the mud just keeps returning.

Then suddenly I see him. My husband, Timothy, striding purposely toward me with a smile as warm as the sun. And I feel something hitch in my chest. He has survived another day in this land.

I step out from the shadow of my doorway to greet him.

"Hello, wife," Timothy grins.

"Oh shut up, husband," I say. "Or you can cook your own dinner!"

We both laugh easily, and inside that sound, there is no war.

And then, movement. In all directions. A great wave of green surges around us like the ocean and we are swept backwards on its tide.

Eight US soldiers point rifles in our faces and scream.

"Where are the VC sympathizers?"

"We know this village is hiding them!"

"Are you VC? Are you VC?"

But of course, my husband and I don't speak English, so we simply shake our heads at them and chant, "No speak, No speak!"

Our neighbors are driven from their huts and rush into the street beside us, saying, "No speak, No speak!"

"Maybe this will help you learn some English, then!" One of the soldiers screams. His eyes bulge from his face in elation as he turns around to the doorway of my home. Producing a silver lighter he touches the small yellow flame to the roof of my hut and in a single second it is engulfed in rolling fire.

"No!" I step forward. "My baby! My baby!"

But he holds me by the arms, and makes me watch the roof collapse down around my sleeping child. Some of the other soldiers meet my gaze, but then they look away, as if they can spare themselves any horror, any guilt, any responsibility by not hearing my words or seeing my face.

"Why would you do that?" I scream at them, in perfect English.

Sergeant Slate steps forward, frowning. "Private Mack, you're not supposed to speak English, remember? You're just a Vietnamese village woman!"

"Yes, sir," I say. "Exactly! So why are we burning her house down and killing her child?"

"Because," he says, "maybe you *aren't* really just a Vietnamese village woman."

And I don't know if it is tears or rain that wet my cheeks anymore.

And I don't know why we are fighting this war anymore.

And I just don't know anymore.

chapter fifty-three

ray

"You don't have to do this, you know." Although Momma said these words aloud, calmly, beneath them I heard the words she really wanted to scream: *Please, don't do this!*

During the last few weeks, I heard that silent plea a whole lot. I heard it every time she gazed at my stomach and sighed when she thought I wasn't looking. I heard it with each swish of a page on my baby album when she insisted I sit with her and pore over every photograph. And I heard it when I took her hand and asked if she'd like to feel a kick, and she had simply shaken her head and pulled her hand from my grasp.

But after those silently screamed words, *please, don't do this,* I also heard: *But you are my daughter, and I will support you and love you no matter what.*

We sat in the car park in front of that gray building with the stork on the side, waiting for two o'clock, when I would have an interview with a social worker who would take on my case and remove this baby from my world.

I took my mother's hand and she squeezed it.

"You don't have to do this," she whispered again. *Please, don't do this!*

"Yes, I do," I answered. *I'm so sorry that I can't explain, but I really have no choice.*

My social worker's name was Sheridan. Unlike the old, fat man I'd seen in here previously, Sheridan was young, and wore dangling, star-shaped earrings and a white chiffon dress; the only things missing were a set of glittery wings and a magic wand. She was the perfect mediator to whom I had imagined handing my child. She would place my baby in the most perfect family in existence: a loving and beautiful mother who has always wanted a child of her own, and who will therefore shower this baby with love; a handsome and wealthy father who will teach the child about strength and the importance of family; a golden retriever named Happy who will sleep at the child's feet and meet it at school every afternoon; maybe even a younger sister that my child could protect. I saw the blurred faces of these two future siblings, their arms around each other's shoulders.

Behind Sheridan's desk, her wall was papered with thank you cards and Polaroids of smiling mothers and handsome fathers – just like the ones I had imagined – with their arms wrapped lovingly around tiny pink newborns with squashy, wrinkled faces.

This woman created families. Just like God.

"So." Sheridan looked up from her notes and steepled her fingers together beneath her chin. "Can you tell me about the baby's father?"

Within me, I felt my child move. Japhy's child. Leaf's child. It rolled like the throb of dread in my gut.

"His name is Andy," I said, and I saw my mother frown. "He is the gentlest, kindest, most generous man in the whole world. He'd make the perfect father." I bit my bottom lip. Why had I said that?

"But you don't feel he would be supportive if you kept the baby?" Sheridan asked.

"Of course he would!"

"So he *agrees* with this decision to adopt the child out?"

"He doesn't exactly *disagree*," I said.

Momma leaned forward. "He doesn't *know*."

"Oh," said Sheridan. "I see." She scribbled something in my file.

"He's going to Nam!" I said. "I just want everything to be the same for him once he gets home."

"Heather, it's all right." Sheridan smiled and held up a hand to silence me. "Adoption is a difficult choice for a pregnant woman to make. *You* are the one that keeps this baby alive. *You* are the one who gets sick, and gets fat, and gives birth. It is inside *you*, and is soothed by *your* warmth and *your* voice and *your* heartbeat. Right now, it is a piece of *you*. Therefore the choice to adopt is not the father's." She paused and looked at Momma. "Nor is it the grandmother's decision to make. It is," she said, turning back to me, "yours, and yours only."

Momma stared at me with her God damn pleading eyes, *please, don't do this*. I closed my eyes so I wouldn't have to see her face, and instead I imagined a nameless woman, and her pleading eyes, *thank you so much for making me a mommy*, but then I had to turn away from her too, because all of a sudden I saw the only eyes that really mattered in all of this. They were bright sky blue eyes, not caramel like Japhy's, or chocolate like Leaf's, but they terrified me and they gazed up at me with so much love. They gazed up at me exactly the way Kate used to.

I lifted my chin, and over Sheridan's shoulder I caught my reflection in the glass door of her office. I could see my eyes now. And I blinked away from the bright pain in them.

Sheridan smiled and patted my hand. "I understand," she said. "You should be very proud of yourself. This is the most selfless thing you will ever do in your whole life. In somebody's world, Heather, you are about to become a hero!"

I clutched at those words before they dissolved into nothing, and I repeated them over and over again.

In somebody's world, I was about to become a hero.

I only hoped that *someone* turned out to be my baby.

*

That night, I sat at the kitchen table reading over the paperwork Sheridan had given me. The colorful brochures showed photographs of smiling families, and every time I saw them I touched my stomach and I smiled. I was about to become a hero. Me. After everything that had happened, all the pain and sadness and death I had caused, I was about to become a hero.

My slate would be wiped clean.

My guilt assuaged.

But most importantly, Japhy will return safely and our lives will continue on as planned.

I read the legal document three times, and then I sat and I stared at the last page, with its yellow highlighted box in which I was supposed to sign my name.

Once the simple letters were scribbled in the exact order that formed my signature, I would be a hero, and everything would be all right.

The pen shook in my hands, and with a deep sigh, I pressed down. I felt the microscopic particles of paper give under the weight of what I wrote as I formed words on a blank notepad.

Dear Japhy

I know you said not to write. And I've tried, really I have. But this is pretty heavy stuff and you need to know what is going down.

Actually, if I'm going to be honest, I'm not writing just because you need to know; I'm writing because I need to know that you will forgive me for all of the following:

1. *I am pregnant.*
2. *I don't know if the baby is yours.*
3. *I'm placing the baby up for adoption.*
4. *Lauren died and Leaf has vanished off the face of the planet.*
5. *I think I'm in love with Leaf.*
6. *When I was 12, I let my baby sister die.*
7. *I also did the same thing to my mother.*
8. *I love you.*
9. *I hope you still love me.*
10. *I don't deserve you.*

Yours always – no matter what you do,
Ray.

When I finished, I folded the letter perfectly in the center, and then in the center again, before sealing the addressed envelope and carrying it outside to the mailbox, where I dropped it and heard it thud dully against the tin; the same sound my anxiety made as it hit the lining of my gut.

It was done. In the morning, the postman would take that innocent little white envelope and start it on its journey of truth. Its journey into Japhy's hands. I imagined those familiar fingertips shaking as he ripped open the seal and slid the letter out. I imagined his beautiful brown eyes flitting left and right across my words. And I imagined his smile shrinking.

I may be about to become a hero in someone's world by completing their little family, but I was not an idiot. Yes, this child was growing inside my body, and yes, this was my decision to make, but I could *not* make it alone, just as I did not make the child alone in the first place.

I may have made up my own mind, but I couldn't make up Japhy's for him. Even though I knew he would agree with me, and this was the best road to take, I couldn't risk giving away a child that he may actually want.

I couldn't do that to him.

Then I really *would* be a monster.

Raising the small, red flag on the mailbox, I turned and dragged my feet back into the house, where I looked down at the adoption paperwork, snatched up the pen once again, and hesitated.

Japhy had made the choice to leave me.

Leaf had made the choice to leave me.

So, fuck it, wasn't it my turn now?

I scrawled my name in the little highlighted box on the very last page of the document and then howled as I threw the pen across the room.

chapter fifty-four

japhy

"Mail's here!" Someone calls out, and Timothy leaps off the top bunk beside mine. He scampers to the other side of the room with everyone else.

"What you get today?" I ask when he returns and stops at the foot of my bed. I ask only to be polite because, in all honesty, I'm more focused on chewing down my thumbnail than hearing the details of his home life. Because hearing about how his family are continuing on with their normal daily lives while we are stuck in here being trained to kill and die makes the fact that we are stuck in here being trained to kill and die all the more hard to take. Out there, somewhere, his mother is baking an apple pie as if nothing more important matters. Out there, somewhere, his father is polishing the chrome on the bumper of his car as if nothing more important matters. Out there, somewhere, his little brother is inching his hand beneath the shirt of a girl he is sweet on as if nothing more important matters.

As if *we* do not matter.

And I am so happy that Ray isn't as selfish as them. That she doesn't feel the need to inform me of every tiny detail I'm missing out on at home. I am so happy that she understands me and honors that one request. I am so happy to know that nothing more important matters.

"Nothing for me today," he smiles. "This one's for you."

"Me?" I sit up. "Are you sure?"

He hands me the small white envelope and I recognize the flowing, loopy lettering on the front: the way the tail of her Y's curl into a perfect spiral; the way she uses a capital R instead of lower case; the way small hearts dot her I's.

"Yep." He grins. "It's from your girl."

"His *girl?*" Lion frowns and leans close to me: "Does she know about ..." He wiggles his eyebrows. "You know?" Then he lowers his voice even further. "She know you don't *like* girls?"

I ignore him and stare at the envelope in my hand.

Even though the letter is thin, probably only one page, the paper is too heavy in my fingers and I drop its weight onto the bed; I simply don't have the strength to hold it up any longer.

Is something wrong? I wonder, staring hard at the white paper. Or worse, is nothing at all wrong?

"The trick is," says Lion, leaning his lanky frame against the metal ladder of our bunk, "you have to *open* the envelope! Doesn't matter how fiercely you stare at it, it won't do it on its own."

"Yeah," I mumble. "Right."

"Here, let me." Lion stoops and reaches for Ray's letter.

"No!" I shout and snatch it from his fingers.

"Jeez," he says, taking a step back. "I wasn't going to steal it or nothing, man."

Timothy and Lion shrug at each other as the barracks door opens and shuts with a sharp *snap*.

I slide Ray's letter into my pocket as we all scramble to line up and stand at attention.

"Fall in." The sergeant's voice is soft. Gentle. Like a swaddling baby's blanket.

In his hand is a black clipboard and, with a quick flick of his wrist, he ticks off our names one by one as he calls them out.

"The base is on alert," says Sergeant Slate. "This you already know. What you don't know is you have been alerted for overseas movement and even though it's a little premature, you have three minutes to get your web gear, your duffle bags, your pistol belts, your helmets, your balls, and get onto the waiting hanger. It's war time, boys! Let's move it out."

Huh?

I stand there, frowning.

What did he just say?

All along the room, the other guys scurry about, packing their stuff into their bags, trying to keep their breathing steady.

"Japhy," Lion mumbles and sniffs.

Is he crying?

"Japhy!" he hisses. "Get your shit, man!"

I turn to him. "What?"

"It's time!"

"Time? Time for what?"

Placing a steady hand on my shoulder, Lion meets my stare with a watery gaze. "It's time to go."

"Oh." I nod, and turn, and pack, and salute, and march out, left right left, toward the black gaping mouth of the plane. Up and in I stomp, into the belly of this beast, and I sit against a wall, and I wait, because it is time.

It is time to go.

I close my eyes and I bring Ray's face forward. The edges are blurry now. Her color faded. What was the exact shade of her eyes again? How far down her back did her hair reach? Exactly how deep was that crevice above her top lip?

Shit. I'm not ready to go yet. I need to see her one last time, because I can't take this crappy faded image of her with me as sustenance for a whole fucking year! Why had I told her not to write? Why hadn't I brought a photo? Why the fuck had I left in the first place? I could have made it back to Mandala. I could have been in bed with her right now, just looking at her. Just looking. That would be enough. God, that would be enough for the rest of my life if I could just get out of here and get back there.

Somewhere in the distance, Drill Sergeant Slate booms and echoes, "... So remember your training and you will return home carrying the body bags, not rotting inside them!" His voice becomes soft and sad. "Make me proud, boys, and don't get your stupid asses killed ..." and then he fades out beneath the roar of the engine, and then the roar of the engine fades out beneath the roar of my heart. And in my pocket, Ray's unopened letter throbs against my chest like a second beating heart, a backup, a spare just in case my own gives out.

*

We land at an airport in California, where we file out of the army plane and into a bustling hub of travelers crisscrossing from one side to the other with their heavy suitcases dragging along behind them.

As we all sit on a row of blue velour seats in the waiting lounge, I notice a woman not much older than Ray standing at the great window overlooking the runway. In one hand she holds a sign with the words *Welcome Home Daddy*, and in the other she holds a little boy in a sailor outfit. The baby bangs his chubby hand against the glass and gives out a beautiful, high-pitched giggle.

"He's cute," I say, standing beside her.

"Thanks," she says. "My husband is coming home from Viet Nam today. It'll be the first time he's ever seen this little one."

"He hasn't seen pictures?"

The woman shakes her head. "He didn't want them. He said it'd be too hard to see his son and not be able to hold him."

"I can understand that."

"You heading out?" she asks.

"Yeah."

"Scared?"

"Shitless!" I expect her to laugh at this, and then touch my arm and tell me I'll be fine and not to worry and I'll be home before I know it.

But instead she nods and says, "Good. You should be. Fear may be the only thing that keeps you alive."

Just then, there is a squeal of rubber. Smoke puffs from

under the wheels as the plane hits tarmac and wobbles like a toddler.

"Oh!" The woman jostles the child in her arm. "I almost can't stand this! Waiting these last few minutes is almost worse than the whole year!"

The plane finally stops and the stairs are wheeled out and the door rises like a waving hand, and soon another door at the side of the waiting room opens and people begin filing through.

A crowd of gathering family members surges forward and swallows the returning soldiers, one by one, in a sea of arms and lips and tears.

"Oh." The woman's hand flutters at her mouth like a butterfly. "He is so thin! And his *eyes* ..."

I watch the woman with her baby as she gulps, breathes, and bursts forward, running at a tall man who has stopped just inside the open doorway.

What must this man be feeling? He is about to see his son for the very first time, and his wife after a whole year, and he is home from that damn war and it is all over for him.

Relief? Joy? Excitement?

That's how I would react if Ray met me here, in one year's time, with our child in her arms.

But not this man.

There is fear in his eyes. And shame. And he jumps when a door slams somewhere in the lounge.

His wife is at his side now, her face pressed into his shoulder. His son is in his arms, dog tags clutched in fat baby fingers.

But this man is looking at me. I wonder what he sees. A soldier? A survivor? A man who will not be broken?

He shakes his head and closes his eyes and turns his face away.

I turn my face away too, suddenly afraid that I am not witnessing this haunted and broken man's present, but instead my future in which I am alive on the outside, but inside I am hollowed out and brittle.

*

"Peanuts?"

"Excuse me?" I frown up at a gorgeous brunette leaning over my seat. Her tits are right in my face, and she smiles at me with perfect white teeth and blue eyes the size of my palm.

I marched onto this commercial plane alongside businessmen in brown suits with matching leather briefcases, and retired couples in Hawaiian holiday shirts, while being greeted at the gate by beautiful stewardesses with perfect makeup and mini-dresses.

I looked around me as we were all seated – army greens beside Hawaiian shirts beside business suits – and I wondered if these other travelers gave any thought to going home. Or did they just take going home for granted?

Us, on the other hand …

She holds up a paper bag of peanuts and shakes it so they rattle. "Would you like some peanuts, sir?"

Seriously? I am heading into a war zone, and she is offering me peanuts?

But I sigh and I take them. Who knows when I'm going to get the luxury of peanuts again.

"Thank you," I say.

She nods. "Thank you, soldier."

I am not a soldier, I think, as I watch her shimmy in her tight dress back to the cart in the middle of the aisle.

A soldier? Ha. A soldier is brave. A soldier can look into the eye of another human that is trying to end them and still pull the trigger. A soldier is a martyr. A soldier is someone they write songs about, and build monuments to, and leave flowers for.

I rip open the bag of peanuts and place one on my tongue.

A soldier is a gambler.

I suck off the salt and grind the nut into a paste between my teeth.

I've never won a game of chance in my life.

Crunching down on a second nut, I rest my head against the seat and chuckle to myself. Oh man, I am so fucked!

"Don't worry."

The hot whisper burns my cheek, and I open my eyes to the stewardess again.

"There's more of you coming home than you think," she continues. "We'll bring you home, too."

She smiles at me, and I desperately want to believe her but she won't look me in the eye.

"I know," I say, and I smile: a lie just as good as hers.

"Would your friend like some peanuts?" She points to Timothy beside me, who is lost in the clouds.

"Hey." I nudge him and he turns from the window. "Peanuts, man?"

"Um. No. Thank you." He smiles and turns back to the clouds.

"What about a drink?" the stewardess asks him. "Can I get you ... something *wet*?"

"Tim?" I nudge his arm. A smile curls the corner of my mouth and it feels so wrong but so wonderful. So normal.

"What?" Tim says.

"The lovely lady here is offering you a drink." I grin. "Or *something*."

"No, nothing for me." He glances up at the woman. "Thank you, anyway."

"Oh, well, then ..." She doesn't look away from him. "If there is *anything* at all I can offer you ... this is a long flight ... just let me know if you need my services, soldier." Winking, she moves away.

"You know," I say, leaning in to whisper to Timothy. "I think she likes you."

He shrugs.

"Have you ever been with a chick?" I ask.

He shakes his head.

"So how do you *know* ... you know?"

He turns to me, his cheeks crimson. "How do I know what? That I like cock? Is that what you mean? Jesus, Japhy!"

"Well," I shrug. "I guess so, yeah. Sorry, man, I don't mean any disrespect; I'm just curious is all. How do you know?"

"How do *you* know," he hisses, "that you *don't*?"

"Okay," I mutter. "But what if you're not really gay?" Turning to watch the stewardess bend over a row of seats, the hem of her dress riding up to reveal the round curve of her ass, I point. "What if you just haven't acquired a taste yet?"

"You don't always have to eat something to know it's not suited to your palate."

"Fair enough." I shake a handful of peanuts into my palm and hold them out to him. "Nuts?"

A wide smile brightens his face and he laughs until tears stream down his face. He laughs genuinely, and deeply. He laughs like that – I wonder – perhaps for the last time.

And as I watch him laugh like that, my own smile shrinks back to nothing as quickly as a gunshot.

*

I plant my feet on foreign ground for the first time. Our overnight flight has skipped today and we are now safely locked in tomorrow, so not only am I no longer in the same country as Ray, I am not even in the same *day*. Her today is my yesterday, and my today is her tomorrow.

We march single file across the airstrip into five or six waiting choppers. Their rotors spin faster and faster with a whir that grows louder with each second. It stirs up a foul stench that presses against us like prostitute lips on our exposed skin, like fingers scrabbling beneath our clothes.

"Ugh, what is that smell?" Timothy holds his hand over his nose and mouth. "Is it rotting fish? Mixed with ... shit, and something else ..."

"Gasoline," says Lion. "They use it to burn off the excrement." He crosses his arms as he hurries by. "So fucking disgusting!"

Strapped into our choppers, we rise up into the air together like a flock of giant, ugly birds, with feathers oiled in death and fear, thick and viscous like honey and I can't breathe.

Below me, turquoise rivers weave through deep green mountains and lush rainforest. Vietnamese farmers with their black pants rolled up to their knees plough rice paddies alongside gentle water buffalo, while little children play and laugh.

But bodies float in those weaving turquoise rivers. Soldiers try to kill each other in those deep green mountains and lush rainforests. The paddy fields are pockmarked with craters. And thin wisps of black smoke rise from a village where those farmers and their children probably live. Or lived. And they do not even look up as we fly low over their heads in our noisy choppers.

We approach our base, and the ground slowly lifts up to meet us, until we all tumble out. Within seconds, the loud chopping of the rotor blades folds back into the cloudy sky like origami: one sound becomes another metamorphosed.

Bombs. Explosions. A regular *boom-boom! Boom-boom!*

The earth rumbles through the soles of my boots like I'm standing on the chest of a monster whose heart throbs beneath me.

Boom-boom! Boom-boom!

And it is hot! Jesus Christ, it is hot here. Surely I have just been thrown into the yawning mouth of hell itself, and its fetid breath blisters my skin with every exhalation.

"Privates Mack, Murdoch, and Nelson: you three are sleeping in billet one-fourteen."

As I duck my head through the tent and my eyes adjust from the blearingly bright sunshine outside, I see four cots, one in each corner. All empty except one, and I try not to think about why these beds are empty, nor about when they will be empty again. A man looks up from a magazine as we all stumble in. A cigarette dangles from his bottom lip. It just hangs there, defying gravity.

"Hey," he says. "I heard I had new roomies. How you guys doing? The name's Solomon." He unfurls his legs, which are folded beneath him, and stands, holding a hand out toward Timothy, who hesitates but then nods and says his name.

Without speaking, Lion pushes by me, kicks his bag under his chosen cot and unfolds the sheets and blanket at the foot of his bed, snapping the creases from the linen and making his bed like his life depended on it.

"I'm Andy, but call me Japhy. How you doing?" I say when I am offered Solomon's firm, friendly handshake.

Solomon turns to Lion. "How you doing, brother?"

"Christ," he mumbles, shoving a stained pillow into its clean case. "I ain't your fucking brother."

Shrugging, Solomon turns back to Timothy and me. "So you are the latest F.N.G's."

"F.N.G's?" said Timothy.

"Fucking New Guys." The cigarette in his mouth jumps up and down with every syllable. "Sure as shit hope you three don't snore. The last guys were like dang car engines revving all night long. Boy, am I glad their tours have finished." He laughs a high-pitched boyish giggle that doesn't seem right as a chaser to his deep voice.

So, the previous owners of our beds weren't killed or wounded in action.

Damn, what's happened to all my optimism? Maybe I *have* been broken down after all? Maybe I *have* changed?

Lion huffs out of the tent then, shouldering past Solomon.

"Well, he seems like a friendly lad!" says Solomon, laughing his girlish giggle again.

"He's not so bad," I say. "He'll come around, don't worry."

"What, me?" Solomon places his hand over his heart. "Worry? Shit, no! Hell, I understand what its like arriving in this shithole. That cat just wants to go home, like all of us." Solomon sits down on his bed and looks at me. "So, what's your bag, man?"

"My bag?" I shrug. "I don't know, man. My chick, I guess. My whole future is wrapped up in her."

"You got an old lady, huh? She pretty?"

I smile. "She's beautiful. When I get home, we're gonna get married, officially, and start a family."

"American dream." Solomon nods and looks over at Timothy. "What about you man? You got a chick?"

"Uh, no." Timothy sits beside Solomon. "Who needs 'em, right?"

"Hmm, I is sensing heartbreak, my friend." Solomon slaps a hand on Timothy's back. "Did some gorgeous young thang break your heart?"

"Something like that," I mumble.

"It's nothing," Timothy says. "What about you?" he asks Solomon. "Do you have a girlfriend?"

"What, you mean, just *one*?" Solomon laughs again. "How traditional."

"How long have you been here, man?" I ask him.

He puffs out his chest. "One hundred and twelve days."

This guy has been here for eight months. Eight whole months, and look at him: totally relaxed and well-adjusted, as if this is home.

Maybe it won't be so bad here. Maybe there isn't that much to stress over after all.

Solomon reaches his hand beneath his cot. "Here." He smiles as he hands us each a beer. "To new friends."

"To not getting our balls shot off," says Timothy.

"To freedom," I say, popping the cap and bringing the bottle to my lips.

And oh, sweet motherfucker of God! The beer is warm, but I tell you this, man, it is the *best* beer I've had in my life. The bubbles hit my tongue and burst against the back of my throat and I'm as light as the air that escapes from them. My shoulders droop as if my marionette army strings have finally been severed.

"So, how bad is it here?" I ask Solomon. "Really?"

"How bad?" Solomon lets his head fall to the side. "Bad," he says. "It's hot, and uncomfortable, and tiring. You're constantly hungry, and thirsty, and needing to piss. There are men with guns hiding in the shadows waiting to jump out at you." He shakes his head and takes a long swallow. "But then, you get called out into the jungles for a holiday and get to leave this shithole camp behind for a whole month!"

Striding over to my cot, he clinks his bottle against mine. "It's no big deal, you just wait and see. I know how you feel. When I first arrived, I was like you guys – I guess we all are – I hoped the year would pass with no conflict, no action, and

I could go home. But then the days passed, and the weeks passed, and the months passed, and I just got honest-to-shit *bored!*"

"I'll take boredom over death, thank you very much," says Timothy.

"You say that now, but you just wait. I've been in a few heavy situations with gunfire and explosions all around, but they were never close enough to cause anything more than an accelerated heart rate. I just returned from another one-month holiday out there – out in the boonies – searching for Charlie, hearing him, knowing he is near, but never, ever, seeing him. Never. They're like ghosts, man." Solomon exhales his words in a cloud of smoke that drifts away like a spirit. "People think the second you get out there, you're gonna get your ass shot at, but it's not like that. It's boring! God damn it all to shit, is it boring! After six months of nothing, you need to see some action! You just wait." He nods. "You'll see."

"I'm with Tim," I say. "I'll take a dose of boring, thank you."

"Whatever, man." Solomon shrugs. "So what made you decide to join up?"

"I was drafted." I point my bottle at Timothy. "We both were."

Solomon swigs his beer. "Bummer."

"You *weren't* drafted?" I ask.

He shakes his head. "No, sir."

"You mean you *chose* to come here?" Timothy's brow creases.

"Damn straight. If they need me to die for my country, then I will, no hesitations."

"Asking you to die for your country is just a camouflaged way of asking you to kill for it." I take another sip. "Can you live with the fact that you are personally causing the deaths of other people exactly like yourself? People who have loved ones, and unfulfilled dreams, who've also been asked to die for their country."

"Yeah." Leaning back on the bed, Solomon crosses his feet at the ankles. "I love my country, man."

"You love your country, but does your country love you

back? Some states still have segregated drinking fountains, for shit's sake! And you're saying it's okay for a black man to be shipped off and killed for a state that refuses to view him equally with white folk?"

He smiles. "Okay, what about freedom, then? Ain't it better to fight and die for freedom than to live under oppression? Freedom ain't free, brother."

"Now, see?" I shake my head. "Material freedom might not be free, but personal freedom is. If you have personal freedom, then material freedom shouldn't be all that important. It doesn't matter what conditions you are living under, true freedom exists in one place and one place only." I touch my finger to his forehead. "The individual consciousness, man. The Establishment tries to brainwash us into thinking that freedom is something that can be taken away, and therefore we are willing to fight for it, to protect and keep it. To die for it."

"Tell me that when you're locked away in a P.O.W. camp somewhere, man." Solomon grins and raises his beer in the air. "I like you, Japhy. Your roof is leaking, but I dig you!" he says. Rolling off the bed, he kneels down and pulls out a small, thin promise of escape.

I smile. "Oh, hell yes!"

How long has it been since my veins flowed with intoxicating substances? Too damn long, anyhow.

He lights the joint and hands it to me with raised eyebrows. I take hold of it gently, as if it is the most precious thing in the whole world – pinched between my thumb and forefinger like Leaf showed me – and I hold it to my lips as softly as a kiss. I inhale and drink in the smoke.

God, yeah.

We all sit on Solomon's bunk, our backs against the canvas tent, drinking warm beer and passing the roach, and pretending that we are not really in Nam at all.

"I'm starving! Are you guys starving? I'm *starving*!" Solomon looks at his watch. "We best get over to the mess hall. First rule of survival in this place: get to mess first, otherwise all the powdered mash goes, and that's the only thing that's worth eating!"

I float behind him through the tent door and freeze. It is pitch black. It was bright daylight when I entered the tent maybe half an hour ago, but now, as fast as a closing eyelid, the world around me is as black as death.

"Does it always get dark so fast?" I ask.

"What?" Solomon pauses and looks up. "Yeah, I guess." He shrugs. "I barely notice it anymore."

Rubbing the chill from the back of my neck, I follow Solomon into this new, unknown world where things go from light to dark, good to bad, alive to dead in an instant.

chapter fifty-five

ray

So. All right. If I was going to get my life back on track – the same track it had been on before Japhy's shadow was violently ripped from beside mine where it belonged – I needed to finish high school. That way, when he returned home, we could both pack our bags and walk onto the campus of California University hand-in-hand, with all this shit behind us and only possibility ahead.

My study material arrived from the Alabama Department of Education, and I had only a month to prepare for my G.E.D. test. I laid it all out, end to end, in a line all the way across the living room floor. Atop the green shag carpet, the books looked like stepping stones across a lawn. Math, science, reading, writing, and social studies. I removed my shoes and socks and, one by one, book by book, subject by subject, I crossed the floor on this new pathway that would lead me from the place where I had been, to the place where I would end up. From past failure to future success. From bad to good.

When I stepped on the final book, I turned and looked down along the path beneath my bare feet.

I sighed, disappointed.

Standing at the end didn't feel any different than it had when standing at the beginning.

*

I chewed my fingernails and spat crescent moons onto the carpet as I stared, wide-eyed, at the footage on the news. Men, arms and legs loose as noodles, being carried by other men whose faces were streaked with mud and blood and tears, and Japhy was out there somewhere.

More men, and some women too, dressed in black pajamas, lay in the dirt like felled trees, and just as magnificent in their deaths, and Japhy was out there somewhere.

Men wearing green, firing into the distance, hoping to kill, turning to smile at the camera, and Japhy was out there somewhere.

Three and a half *thousand* Americans had been killed just this year, and Japhy was out there somewhere.

I launched off the sofa as if a grenade had blown me across the room, and clicked the television off, blinding it. The great black eye of the screen now held more horror in what I could not see. I replayed all those images in my head, only now it was Japhy's face everywhere: on the injured, on the dead, on the murderous.

Covering my face in my hands, I tried to catch the sobs that drained from me like blood.

*

An entire month had passed since I peered through the window to watch the postman take my letter from the mailbox and send it on its way to Japhy. An entire month and I still hadn't received an answer. I lay awake every night, every single night, wondering if it had gotten lost, or worse, if it hadn't.

I lay awake every night wishing I had never written it in the first place.

Although I hadn't received any confirmation, it had been over sixteen weeks since Japhy left on that bus, so he must have completed his training and would be somewhere Over There by now. Maybe my letter had arrived at his US army base just a day after he'd been shipped out, and it was right now in a giant bag of unsorted mail on its way to find him in South East Asia.

Maybe it had been delivered to *another* Andrew Mack by mistake? It was a common name, after all.

Or maybe the letter had indeed been received by its intended recipient. And maybe inside his silent non-reply I have received my answer. Maybe, in this lead-up to losing the baby that I love so much, I have also lost the only other person I ever wanted in my life?

And maybe that is exactly what I deserved.

Did Japhy hate me now? No, surely I would feel something like that. A change that magnificent would surely reach all the way around the earth and stab itself deep into my heart like a barb.

Surely Japhy of all people would understand exactly why I had to do this. He was the most forgiving person I knew. It was the first quality I recognized in him, and it was the whole reason I fell in love.

Or maybe he was simply leaving the decision up to me, because, Jesus Christ, he had enough to worry about! Why had I sent it? Why, why, why? It was the *one* thing he'd asked of me, and I hadn't been able to do it. No distractions, he'd said. And before that, no kids. He'd already answered the stupid question, and I'd known that! So why, oh, why had I written those words and sent them into his hands, in a war zone, when the one thing he should be concentrating on was *not getting killed*! Now it would be my fault if he got hurt Over There, because I'd been too damn selfish to honor the one request he'd given me.

*

I cracked the shell of an egg into a bowl of milk, sugar, and flour. As I stirred the ingredients together, I hummed the tune of *Happy Birthday*, and wondered if anyone would sing that to Japhy today. His nineteenth birthday.

I wondered if he would celebrate this day at all. The date

that had betrayed him. If he'd been born one day earlier, or one day later, he may never have been drafted in the first place.

The mixture smoothed out under the force of my spoon as I bashed away any lumps. I reached for the cocoa powder. And then I stopped.

Did Japhy *like* chocolate cake?

Maybe he preferred carrot? Or sponge?

Did he favor many palm-sized cupcakes over one large cake?

I didn't know. In fact, I didn't really know that much about him at all.

We'd only been on a few nervous dates, only started to hold hands and kiss each other goodnight before that letter had arrived and forced us to grow up in an instant.

What was his favorite color, his favorite word, his favorite memory?

Did he prefer The Monkees over The Beatles?

What was the name of his first pet?

Did he, like me, have a secret he never planned to reveal?

I set the spoon against the side of the bowl and sat on the stool.

There were so many things about him I didn't know. What if I never got a chance to find out because of *this* fucking day? Because of September fucking fourteen.

Grabbing the bowl, I dropped it into the sink and turned on the faucet, washing the cake batter down the drain.

Happy birthday?

I wondered if that would ever be true for Japhy, or me, again.

*

I blinked down in shock at the front page of the newspaper that had thunked onto the front porch this morning. The words in the headline must have been some kind of mistake. A misprint, perhaps? Or were my sudden tears distorting the letters and rearranging them into this horrid lie?

Because gods were not supposed to die.

Gods were supposed to live on forever.

Gods were supposed to teach all of us mortals the meaning of life.

Gods were supposed to prove to us that miracles really did exist.

And yet ...

Jimi Hendrix was dead.

Jimi Hendrix was dead.

Jimi Hendrix was *dead*.

Taken out by something as simple as beer and prescription sleeping pills. It was so ... human.

I began to cry. I cried for all the future music that would never come. I cried for all the beauty that had now sluiced from this world. And I cried because if a god like Jimi Hendrix could be killed as easily as any mortal, then what the hell kind of chance did Japhy have?

october

When the power of love overcomes the love of power,
the world will know peace.

~ Jimi Hendrix

chapter fifty-six

japhy

The envelope is fat beneath my fingers and growing heavier with every second.

Really? I am here, in Viet-Fucking-Nam, risking my life, risking my sanity, risking everything ... and *this* is what I get for it? Fuck that.

I stuff the envelope under my pillow where I no longer have to see the thin writing on the front that spells out my name, rank, and serial number. I squeeze my eyelids shut. Clench my jaw. Fist my hands. But I can't block it out. Truth drapes over me like an unwanted lover.

In the distance, I still hear the crumping of mortar attacks and the peppering chatter of rifle fire, but it's not like it was when I first arrived here, three weeks ago. Now it's soft at the edges. It has faded away into the muffling folds of everyday life; still there, yes, always there, yes, but now only if I concentrate. Like hearing a ticking clock only when you listen for it. Almost as if the war is happening someplace else. In some other country. Someplace far away. Not just outside the perimeter of this army base.

Here we have hot showers, warm meals, cold beer, and strong pot. Clean clothes, comfortable beds, and a feeling of safety. During the day, there are games of volleyball, blaring radios and a portable television set. At night we watch movies and play card games and miss home. It is more like a holiday resort than a military base in the middle of arguing communists.

Only when casualties come screaming in are we reminded of how close we are to it all. Are we reminded that this is, in fact, hell. Are we reminded that, at any moment, those bleeding, moaning bodies could be ours.

My platoon will be heading to the jungles in a week. Just seven days and I will be in a beautiful rainforest searching out the enemy and shooting to kill. Flushing them out of their hiding places and calling in air support to bomb the shit out of them.

Just seven days and I could have blood on my hands.

Just seven days and I could be dead.

But I can't think about that right now, because next week doesn't exist for me. Not anymore. Not since receiving the news that has totally floored me. The news that means my life will change, will never be the same again.

"You all right, Japhy?" Solomon frowns down at me as I sit on my bed and stare.

I nod. At least I think I nod.

Is this real? Is this really happening?

I open my mouth to ask him, to have someone else verify it, but my voice is just a strangled squeak in my throat.

"What's wrong with him?" asks Lion, as he saunters into the tent, pauses to look at me for a second, and throws a wet towel onto his bed.

"Not sure," says Solomon. "Maybe he was bitten by that scorpion."

"What?" Lion scrambles up onto his bed. "What scorpion? Where is it? Where did it go?"

"Dunno, I think I saw it run under your bunk."

"Shit!" He leaps from his bed to the next, keeping his feet moving up and down the whole time.

"Calm down, white boy," laughs Solomon. "I didn't see no scorpion."

Wiping a hand down his face, Lion mumbles, "Fuck you."

But as he jumps down and returns to his corner, folding his towel neatly and draping over the railing of his bed, there is the smallest curl of a smile on his lips.

Seeing this crack in Lion's tough shell finally breaks me out of my own shock. I bolt upright and grab hold of Solomon's arm.

"Is it true? Is it really true?"

Solomon throws his arms wide in exasperation. "Is *what* true?"

From off my bag, I unclip the button that Ray had made. The small, round, blue circle of hope. *James Lee Stanley for President!* And I clip it to my shirt, right over my heart.

Then I close my eyes, try to squash the image of that horrible envelope under my pillow, and whisper the name of God, and I keep whispering it all week long until I am standing just feet away from him. *Him.* With his blue jeans tucked into brown cowboy boots, and his fringed suede jacket draped over the back of the chair, and his full, dark beard, and piercing hazel-green eyes which are looking right at me.

Him.

With his scratched acoustic and his battered guitar case open as if he is a busker on a street corner playing only to me.

Him.

With that voice that penetrates my soul and stops time and makes everything that is wrong suddenly nonexistent.

James.

Lee.

Stanley.

And wait. Just fucking wait until I tell Ray!

Then he bows his head, prayer-like, and begins to speak. His voice is smooth and gentle. "Thank you for making the time to come out here today – I know y'all have far more exciting things to be doing ..."

A wave of laughter lifts me in its surge.

"You know," James clears his throat and continues, "the Chinese say that if you live long enough, everything will happen to you. Sounds like a sucky reason for sticking around, doesn't it? But I got to thinking about it because those Chinese people are *deep*. I mean, hell, they invented topiary. You know, that's where you plant a tree and your grandchild carves it into a bird. These guys are thinking *long*. Meanwhile, we're all thinking, hey, when am I going to get my next burger?"

Around me, I hear laughter and whistles.

"So I realized," says James, "that if we are going to live a long time – and I truly hope that all y'all here today will – and that if everything *is* going to happen to us, then, at some point, we are going to be the hero."

Around me I hear clapping and shouts of agreement.

"We are also going to be the goat," says James. "We're going to be the victim. We're going to be the perpetrator, the betrayer, and the betrayed."

Around me now, I hear nothing but silent contemplation.

"And so, if we're going to be all these things, each and every one of us, then maybe we should find it in our hearts to be a little more kind, a little more understanding, a little more patient with each other." And then his words melt into music as he starts picking at the strings of his guitar. *Bum da-da de-dum.* He slaps his palm against them, suddenly stilling their vibrations to give the song its heartbeat. *Crack!* And then again: *Bum da-da de-dum – crack! Bum da-da de-dum – crack!*

And when he sings, I feel his voice enter my body; I start to shake and rattle and hum.

"*It's so hot here, the wind forgets to blow. Only the heat waves move in the streets below.*"

Bum da-da de-dum – crack!

"*The days are long, wind gets lost at sea. And where it goes is a mystery. And it's dangerously hot in this country. Strangers listening on the phone, I think they're on to us! And people fall in love a lot because it's dangerous as hot on the lam.*

"*Down in the land of sugar cane waiting on a sight of rain. Mission confidential. See no, hear no, speak no, you know, silence is the order keeping three monkeys in your heart.*"

Bum da-da de-dum – crack! Bum da-da de-dum – crack!

"*It's so hot here, the black sand burns like coal. Choose between your body and your soul. Raindrops sizzle and pop on the dusty road. There's messages and secret codes. And there's beaucoup kinds of heat in this country. And they've got soldiers in the streets and urgent telegrams."*

I sway amid a sea of naked chests, sweat-shiny and tanned, as we all sit in the scalding sunshine and drink in the escapism that James gives us.

I shut my eyes against this land and shirtless soldiers.

War? What effing war?

With my eyes closed and the voice of God in my ears, I am not in a remote US army base hidden somewhere in Nam, but am instead sitting right beside Ray, and Leaf, and Poppy, at a music festival on United States soil, with flowers in our hair and freedom in our lungs. The war is over. The guns are down. And peace is just a way of life.

But with my eyes closed, I could just be listening to a live J.L.S. album. So, with a sigh, I lift my lids, and my imagined world of Ray and peace and safety bursts like a soap bubble. Because James is standing feet from me, throwing back his head and stamping his boot, and breathing the very same air that I am breathing, and I can't afford to not watch this taking place. Because, all too soon it'll be over and the world will spin back in place.

After almost an hour, James, red-faced and dripping sweat, salutes us and staggers off the stage into a waiting car, which speeds him away so fast I'm barely out of my chair.

Damn. I'd hoped that somehow I could have met him. Could have shaken his hand. Could have actually spoken words to him. Could have thanked him for shaping my life.

But perhaps it is better this way. What if he turned out to be a jerk and therefore stained every song that is a thread in the tapestry of my memories? But surely someone who writes lyrics like his, someone who sings with such presence, could be nothing less than a sincere and genuine soul?

Or a brilliant actor.

"So!" Solomon claps me on the shoulder. "It has recently been brought to my attention that our boy, Timothy, has never had his cabbage boiled!"

"Huh?" I frown at Timothy, who stares back at me, pale-faced with his lips pressed flat together.

"And," says Solomon, "seeing as we are all going into the battlefield tomorrow, we need to get this boy down to the riding academy! Introduce him to some loverly roundheels, maybe get him the scramble egg treatment from the torso-tossers?"

"What language are you speaking?"

But he just grins and grabs me and Timothy by the shirts tied around our waists, and pulls us along behind him.

"Get your bread, boys!" he says.

I shake my head and think of the envelope the base had given me last week. Fat with colored bills. Military Payment Certificates. For my life, the army was awarding me sixty-five dollars of Overseas Pay, thirty dollars of Combat Pay, and for my rank of E-3, Private First Class, a whopping two-hundred dollars. So, all in all, it turns out that my life is worth a total of two-hundred and ninety-five bucks a month for as long as I can stay alive.

"I don't want their dirty blood money."

"Well then, give it to me!" says Solomon. "The place we're going takes it as currency. Don't need to worry about getting it changed over into Vietnamese piasters. Saves a cock-load of time, brother. No pun intended!"

"Fine, yeah, take it, man." I snatch the fat envelope out from under my mattress and press it to Solomon's chest.

"Hey, whoa, I was just kidding, Japh. I'm not taking your bread!"

"Well, I don't want it."

"Tell you what." Solomon takes the envelope and slides it into his pocket. "Come with me, into town."

"No, I don't want to spend it. It makes me sick. They think they can just *buy* me? Pay me for my life?"

Solomon smiles and squeezes my shoulder. "Trust me." Then he leads me and Timothy back outside to a vehicle waiting with an impatient engine and two men. "Japhy, Tim," says Solomon as he leaps into the back seats, "meet Black Cat, your future R.T.O," he says, pointing to the skinny man at the wheel, who raises a hand, "and Bricks, the Point."

The one in the passenger seat winks. He is huge, and barely fits inside the jeep.

"These are the F.N.G's bunking with me," says Solomon.

"First time to this village?" asks Bricks, the bigger one.

"First time to *any* village," I say, climbing in between Timothy and Solomon. I smile at them nervously. "Is it really true about there being disguised VC everywhere?"

"Those bastards are all over the place," mutters Black Cat, who takes hold of something on a leather cord around his neck and presses it to his lips.

"Kissing that disgusting thing is gonna keep you safe, is it?" asks Bricks, grinning.

"What?" Black Cat tucks it back beneath his shirt and starts the engine. "It's my lucky rabbit's foot, and it's been lucky so far."

"Wasn't too lucky for the rabbit, was it?"

"Hey, if it stops me from getting killed out here," he shrugs, "then to heck with the darn rabbit!"

We salute a soldier at the compound gate, and then Black Cat accelerates. The jeep bumps along a dirt road and wind whips my face. The breeze is warm, though, and does nothing to cool me down.

"So where exactly are we going?" I yell over the rush of air.

On my left, Solomon says, "To paradise!"

In the front, Black Cat and Bricks grin.

And on my right, Timothy slumps in his seat and looks like he is about to be sick as we jolt and sway all the way into the town.

When we arrive, I follow Solomon into a bar with a dirt floor and bad lighting. The smell of sweat is everywhere, and as solid as a wall. I cover my face with the palm of my hand.

"What's so good about this place?" I ask Solomon. "Can't we find somewhere that has better ... everything?" The seats are sticky and I wipe my hands on my shirt as I sit, grimacing.

Solomon nods his head toward a raised platform at the end of the room. "Nowhere has better everything!"

A dozen young Vietnamese women stand there like mannequins. They are all wearing tight dresses, heavy makeup, and fake smiles. Something in my stomach clenches as I look into their wide eyes that don't meet mine; they keep their gazes slightly above our heads.

As I watch, a lanky man with a ponytail walks up to the stage and says something I can't understand. The second girl on the left nods, smiles, and pulls the straps down on her dress, exposing her breasts. The man shakes his head and points next to the girl on the far right. When she does the same thing, the man is still for a moment, then he nods and walks toward a doorway beside the stage, where a beaded curtain sways. He sweeps it aside and waits for the girl he chose. She bows to him as she passes beneath his arm, and his mouth draws up over his yellow teeth in what looks more like a gleeful snarl than a smile.

Looking back at the remaining women on the stage, I study their faces. They all seem barely older than Ray. Just kids, really. Just like us. Kids, who are forced to grow up way before they should because of this war.

I shake my head and I turn my eyes from their eyes because I can't bear to see the black emptiness where innocence should instead shine.

Timothy gapes around at everything, and then he jumps up and backs away. "I'll help Bricks with the drinks!"

"You know, man," I say to Solomon, "I don't think sex is the answer."

"Of course it isn't," he says.

I'm surprised at this, and I sigh and lean back in my chair, relieved.

"Sex is never the answer," he says. "Sex is the *question*, and the answer is *yes!*"

"Right," I mutter.

At the table beside us, a fat man with white hair runs his fingers down the bare back of a tiny, half-naked girl sitting across his lap with her legs crossed tightly at the knees. She giggles and wriggles away from his hand as it moves down to her hip. Sliding up the hem of her short dress to reveal her thighs, his fingers pry between them and he clenches her against himself, rocking her tightly, and whispering something in her ear. She lets out a startled, "Ooh!" and grimaces a smile as his lips nibble her neck, but then her eyes lock onto mine. She reminds me of Ahn, the waitress who served Ray and me forever-ago in that small-town diner, the woman with the friendly smile and the haunted pupils.

I want to step forward and punch this perverted old man. I want to take the girl's hand and tell her to leave, to run, and to not come back. But really, what can I do?

My cheeks flame as I drop my gaze. I turn my chair around so I don't have to look at her anymore, and instead I nod my head toward Black Cat's open shirt from where his lucky rabbit paw peeks out. "So, you really believe in all that stuff?"

"Well, yeah. Got to believe in something." He smiles. "Like this." He lifts a gold locket from around his neck. "It's my girlfriend's. She gave it to me before I left for the army. Got a four-leaf clover inside to protect me."

"Don't let this crazy guy talk you into any of his voodoo practices." Bricks clinks a handful of beers onto the table between us.

"I was only explaining to the new guy that you have to have something to believe in to keep you grounded out here." He turns back to me and asks, "So, do you?"

"Yeah, I do," I say, reaching for one of the glasses. "I believe in not letting this war break me."

Black Cat and Bricks smirk at each other.

"What?" I say. "You don't think I can?"

"Not saying that." Bricks takes a long swallow of his beer. "But I've never seen anyone leave this place the same person they was when they arrived."

"I'm happy to be the first, then," I say, and raise my glass to his before gulping down the entire thing. Foam slides down the sides of my empty glass, pooling at the bottom, white and frothy and defiant.

And then – even though all around me people's mouths continue moving in conversation and laughter, even though bodies continue swaying to music, even though the bass undertone of pounding hearts continues thrumming – sound stops. Out of the corner of my eye, the door opens. A man strides through. And nothing else exists anymore as my mouth dries up and I hold my breath and I wait for all of my happy memories to unravel.

He reaches the bar in three purposeful steps and leans forward. Through my new silence, his words reach me loud and clear. "Is Li here?" And his voice is perfectly familiar.

"Of course," says the man behind the bar. "She is with client."

He winces as if struck with a fist.

"You want someone else?" asks the barman, raising a hand toward the women on the stage.

"No!"

The barman takes a step backwards. "You wait, then?" he asks. "For Miss Li? You wait?"

"I'll wait." He slaps a wad of cash down onto the bar.

I want to sink down through the floor as all the buoyant respect I'd had for this person floods out of me, leaving me leaden and heavy.

Narrowing his eyes, he pulls out a stool and sits with his spine straight.

As if I'm locked inside a dream, I push up from the table and somehow my legs carry me across the room, where I hover and look down on the man I've idolized for years, but suddenly don't want anything to do with. I don't want anything to do with him, yet here I am, grinning like a damn cheese-weasel.

"Hiya, kid," says James.

Says James Lee Stanley.

Says James Lee Effing Stanley ... to *me*!

And I smile and I say nothing.

Like an idiot.

Because this is *him*. This is the voice of my life. And so what if he likes to enjoy the company of women, and so what if he needs to pay for that privilege, and so what if these girls obviously hate this profession and it is therefore, for them, no different to what happened to Ray in the backseat of that car. So what? This is James Lee Stanley, right? He can do whatever the crap he feels like. It's none of my business! And what could I do about it anyway?

"Join me for a beer?" James raises two fingers to the barman.

His hair is still wet from a shower, and he has changed out of the sweaty *James Lee Stanley Was 'Ere* shirt that he'd worn onstage earlier, replacing it with a blue Cookie Monster shirt.

As his friendly gaze shifts from me, it focuses on something over my shoulder; his eyes narrow and he shakes his head, almost imperceptibly. When I crane my neck to see what has caught his attention, I see the man from my neighboring table walking behind the giggling girl. He slaps a hand against the meat of her backside and laughs loudly as the beaded curtains part in the center and then tinkle back together again; her pale face and troubled eyes vanish into whatever rooms wait beyond.

The barman carries over two large glasses. "I put this on your tab, Mr. Stanley, yes?"

"Yes. Thank you, Duc," says James.

The bartender bows slightly and walks away.

"Can you believe it?" James mutters to me. "A hundred thousand sperm and *that guy* was the fastest." And then clinks his glass to mine. "Cheers."

I gaze at that glass. My glass. Bought for me by *him*. To drink with *him*. As if *he* is a mere person that I can just sit with, and talk to, and watch our lives intersect as if it is no big deal.

He watches me over the rim of his beer as I lift my own shaking drink to my lips, droplets spilling onto my boots.

"You were in the crowd today, weren't you?" he says. "Right at the front?"

I splutter, spitting foam over him. "You noticed me?"

"How could I not?" He smiles, dabbing at his shirt. "You were singing almost louder than I was!"

"I love you!" I say, and then press my lips together to keep my stupid words locked inside my head where they belong.

James smiles. "Thanks, but you're not my type."

"Could I get an autograph? You're my biggest fan!" I dip my hand into my pocket and thrust at him the only piece of paper I have on me: Ray's unopened letter, which I've kept in my pocket like a good luck charm ever since receiving it on that last day in America.

"Of course." Leaning over the counter, James takes a pen from his pocket and scrawls on the envelope, marking the place right beside the words that Ray herself had written. The two of them, side by side.

"Seriously, Mr. Stanley," I say when he hands back the envelope. I fold it again, and stuff it in my shirt pocket. "Your music ... the songs ... please understand ... such a big part ... and I can't believe ... I mean ... it's everything ... you are everything! You're like ... a god!"

"I'm just the same as you, man: a freelance human being." He shrugs a shoulder and thrusts his hand forward, gripping my sweaty hand and shaking it with strong, calloused fingers. "I'm just James. It's really nice to meet you ...?"

"Japhy," I whisper, staring down at my hand in his. "I'm Japhy."

"It's nice to meet you, Japhy."

"It's nice to meet you too, James Lee Stanley!"

He smiles. "How long have you been here?"

"About five minutes."

"I meant," he laughs, "in *Nam*."

"Oh, a month, I think, I don't know, I forget right now."

"A month? Ouch. Long way to go, then, huh?"

I nod. "Feels like forever already."

"It'll go fast," he says. "I felt the same when I started my tour."

"What?" I gape at him. "*You* were in the army?"

"Air Force."

"But you're so," I shrug, "anti-establishment!"

"And how you think I got that way? I was over here in sixty-eight. Thought I could save the world!" He shakes his head and takes a sip of his drink, sucking the froth from the hair on his top lip. "Unfortunately, I learned that I couldn't save everyone. It was a hard lesson. And, boy, did it change me!"

"It changed you?" I whisper.

"Yeah. This war changes people, Japhy. It will change you, too." He fixes his eyes on me. "No way to stop it. All you can do is ride it out, don't resist it, and when it's all over, make that change into a positive one."

"How?"

James's mouth turns in at the edges. His eyes cloud over. He stares into his drink. "Don't look away," he says.

"Away from what?"

"From whatever you believe is wrong. I know, *duh*! It should be intuitively obvious to a tree," he shrugs, "but I wish I'd had someone point out the obvious to me. So, just don't look away, Japhy." He meets my eyes again, and what I see there jolts through me. "If you look away, if you pretend the bad shit isn't happening, then you are letting it happen. And you are therefore the one responsible for it. You need to face this war head on. Look it in the God damn eyes, and do not back down. Because if you do, if you look the other way ..." He blinks and releases me as his eyes slide over to the women standing on the stage. "You may end up spending the rest of your life trying to make up for it."

"Mr. Stanley?" The barman hovers at the edge of our conversation and smiles apologetically at his interruption. "Miss Li is ready for you."

James closes his eyes and nods. His forehead creases and he pinches the bridge of his nose.

"Are you all right?" I ask, leaning forward.

He nods again but doesn't speak.

"Thanks for the drink," I say. "I'll let you get to your ... uh ... appointment."

James laughs then, a dry coughing laugh. "I don't come back here because they give cheap hand jobs, kid. I come back to stare this place down. I come back to try and make things right. I come back because, for one tiny second, I looked away."

And then he opens his eyes, which are clear again and cloud free. He stands, drinks the rest of his beer in one swallow, and then holds out his hand again. "You stay safe out there, all right?"

I stand soldier-straight, and nod. "I'll do my best."

"Do *better* than that."

"Yes, sir."

We smile at each other, and then he turns to walk away.

"Wait!" I say, unfastening the small, blue button on my shirt. I thrust it toward him. "Here."

James takes the button and his eyes sparkle as he reads the words: *James Lee Stanley for President!* He stares at it in silence, then his fingers close into a fist.

And then this man – a man who is just like me – claps me on the back like an old friend and walks away. Half-way across the room, he stops and turns. "Hey, Japhy?"

"Yeah?"

He smiles, raises his hand in the V of peace, and says, "I love you, too!" And then he vanishes through the swaying beaded curtain and is gone.

Background noise rolls back into my life as if nothing extraordinary ever took place.

I watch the colored beads swing and tangle; the strands wrap around each other like limbs, and then unwind again. And I am suddenly even madder at this fucking war. It has taken me away from my home, my country, my life, and my love. And now it has taken away my god! James Lee Stanley is no longer a deity to me; he has been demoted to a simple freelance human being. Just an ordinary guy.

But then, I wonder, in order for him to have come down from those heavens, in his world have I then been promoted up from complete nonexistence? Have I become *that guy* he shared a beer with in a Vietnamese whorehouse? Have I become *somebody* to someone who is everything to me? Because if so, then that, in its own right, is godlike.

Back at our table, Solomon bangs another drink down on the table in front of Timothy. "Sure you can!" he says. "Get some of this into you. Loosen up."

"No, really man. I want my first time to be special. Something I'll always remember." Timothy looks at me. Pleading.

I meet his gaze and I do not look away. "Leave him alone, Sol," I say. "He doesn't have to do this."

"But ... trust me," says Solomon. "You will always remember Li!"

"Li?" I say, looking toward the beaded curtain through which James disappeared.

"Yeah." Solomon grins. "She's like nothing you can even imagine!"

Black Cat nods. "He's right. I don't know from personal experience, but from what I've heard ... phew!"

"Timothy, trust me," says Solomon, "you'll be fine. Plus, you don't have to impress these girls, man, so there's no pressure."

I lean forward. "Sol, look at these women, will you! They're basically girls! It's not right."

"Japh, all the sheep look like lambs in this country. It must be all the rice they eat or something."

"But look at their faces. Do you think they enjoy having fat old men sweat and come all over them?"

"Yes!" Solomon nods. "Most of these women are providing for their families in the only way they can. They're proud of it. Are you going to deprive them of that honor?" Solomon gestures to the barman and the little man approaches the table and gives a quick bow.

Solomon bows back. "We'll have Li, please, my good man."

Again the barman bows, but he shakes his head. "I am so sorry, gentlemens, but Miss Li is not available for the rest of the week." He looks at me and frowns. "Your friend, Mr. Stanley, he so bad for my business! Always come. Always buy Miss Li for a whole week! Take her away from here. And the stupid man! The crazy man! He buys the fruit but won't taste the juice! And when she gets back again, she all rusty from lack of use!" The barman shakes his head and rests his hands on the table, staring right at me. "He stupid! He think he can give her money, but that will not bring back her husband, her child, her village! It does nothing but remind her of what she lost, does nothing but make her sad, does nothing but lose me business! Your friend," he shakes his head at me again. "Very bad for me."

I realize then that sometimes being human means that you can also be godlike. I stand up, not taking my eyes off this short, greasy man. "My friend," I say, "is a better human than you will ever be."

The barman's face reddens. "You get out!" He shoos at me with both his hands. "Go! Go! All of you, get out of here!"

Timothy shoots from his seat to stand beside me.

"But *we* didn't do nothing!" says Solomon, holding his palms out to show his innocence.

"You are friends with this one!" The barman points at me. "So you leave! You *all* leave!"

Raising my eyebrows at Solomon, Black Cat, and Bricks, I cross my arms and wait for their decision.

One by one, they sigh and their heads droop, but they push out their chairs and stand. As Bricks walks by me, he mutters, "One of you boys better like sucking dick!"

Beside me, Timothy chuckles, and I can't help grinning.

*

No one speaks. Not even Solomon, who arranges the items for his pack out on his bed. Although, I can feel the edges of his silence tingling with a different anticipation to mine, and Timothy's, and Lion's. The anticipation that hovers over the three of us F.N.G's is black like a pregnant storm cloud; Solomon's cloud, however, is white with bright flits of sunshine at the edges.

We have to be up and out of here by 0500 hours tomorrow. The sun that rises then will illuminate a whole new me. A different Japhy. Japhy the combat soldier.

I take a breath and stare down at all the equipment that covers my bed. Map. Compass. Flashlight. Bug repellent. Combat knife. Canteen. Kool-Aid. Flak jacket. C rations. Can opener. Poncho. Toothbrush. Canvas boots. Helmet. Helmet liner. Helmet camouflage cover. Flares. M-16 rifle. M-16 rifle ammunition. Cigarettes. Zippo. Notepad. Pen. Fear.

Gritting my teeth in concentration, I place everything into my pack, piece by piece like a jigsaw puzzle, until the seams are stretched to bursting, the way my own skin stretches taut across my anxiety.

Will this be it, then? Will tomorrow be the day that changes me for the rest of my life? Is today the last day that I will be me? Completely me? The me that Ray loves? Will tomorrow, or the next tomorrow, or the tomorrow after that, be the one that ends Ray's love and replaces the man she knows with a stranger that she will never understand?

One by one, Sol, Tim, and Lion place their packs at the feet of their cots and pull their covers up to their chins and stare up at the canvas ceiling. And one by one, Sol, Tim, and Lion's eyes close and their breathing steadies out, and I am left alone in this tent.

As I pull my shirt over my head, desperate to feel the kiss of air against my still-innocent skin, I feel something crumple in the pocket. I take out Ray's envelope.

Across the front, James's words scrawl in messy looping letters that I have to study for a while before I interpret what they say:

To my friend, Japhy,
don't look away.
Take care,
J.L.S.
PS: You owe me a beer.

Carefully, I slide the letter into the pocket of tomorrow's waiting shirt. If this can't protect me – this piece of paper that is imbued with both Ray and James – then no amulet, or shield, or lucky rabbit's foot ever could.

Don't look away, I think as I stare at my pack.

Don't look away …

And I sigh, and I swear under my breath as I realize what these words mean for me. They mean protection. They mean absolute assurance that tomorrow will not be the day that changes me. Because it will *not* be the things I witness that will forever alter my soul; it will be the choices I make when there is no time to think, no time to argue with myself about what is right and what is necessary.

Don't look away.

Could I shoot a man? Could I line him up in my sights, and squeeze my finger, and *end his life*?

Placing a hand on the barrel of my unloaded rifle, I feel its malicious chill seep into my skin.

Could I?

With the answer to that question coiling sickeningly in the pit of my stomach, I remove the ammunition belt from my pack, lift up my mattress, and tuck it away where I can no longer see it.

*

I hear the Hueys before I see them: *whomp, whomp, whomp*. The air throbs with the sound of two UH1-B choppers. They land and we surge forward, an unstoppable tide.

This is it. This is fucking it. Oh fuck, oh shit, oh holy fucking shit!

My hands lock onto the rail at the chopper's opening but my legs won't take me up that last step.

And as another pair of hands grab my wrists, and as I hear a voice say, "Come on, soldier!" and as I hold my breath and grit my teeth and heave myself forward, I think about the stash of rifle ammo tucked beneath my mattress, hidden there like a big fucking mistake.

But within seconds we are in the air, and then within seconds we are landing again, and I hardly have time to wonder if leaving my ammunition behind will be the biggest mistake of my life or the savior of my soul.

I press a hand against my chest and feel the thin envelope press back. Beneath it, my heart beats like a trapped animal, searching the bars of my rib cage for an escape.

The grass below us flattens and ripples in the downdraft of the rotor blades as we gush out of the Hueys like blood from a wound. The last of us barely touches his feet to the ground before the choppers rise, their tails lift, their noses dip, they speed away, and the silence closes in around us like a squeezing fist.

Bent double, we run in single file from this open clearing to the safety of trees and camouflage in case VC are right now tracking us from the sound of those fading rotors.

Because now, we are both the hunters and the hunted.

"Why are you grinning like that?" whispers Timothy in the sudden darkness of the trees.

"I'm not," I say.

"You look crazy, man!" And he pauses for a second, before he turns and follows the other boys through the shadows.

Had I been grinning? Surely not. Maybe I'd just been squinting my face against the onrush of air and dust from the choppers. Because I am *not* happy to be out here. That *would* be crazy.

I crash through the thick jungle seconds behind the broad back of Solomon, who turns to me and claps my back and whispers, "Hell, yeah! You ready for this, boy?"

And I have to admit that my heart is racing and my skin is tingling and I am ... excited.

I am *excited*?

Because I am in the jungle of South Viet Nam with a target on my back. Because I may be about to witness murder. Because I may be about to die myself, and I am getting such a rush from it all that a part me doesn't want to ever go back to the base. I want to stay out here and feel this amazing feeling of being absolutely *alive*!

Maybe I *am* crazy, like Timothy said. I'd have to be crazy to feel like this. After everything I did to avoid the draft. After After everything I did to get through Basic with my spirit intact. After holding tightly to everything I believe in. After refusing to load my own rifle just in case I end up forced to use it on someone. After all of that, I am actually *excited* to be out here.

But, as we space out fifteen feet from each other and as I feel my pulse kick itself up another notch and as my eyes widen and my grin stretches wider still, I am suddenly more terrified than ever.

I squint through the darkness of the dense jungle. I creep over tree trunks, through bamboo that towers over me, banana plants, and razor-sharp blades of elephant grass that slice twelve feet into the sky. Creepers and vines snake all over the ground, slithering out to grasp my ankle and pull me down.

And through my brain, on tip-toe, creeps the *bum da-da de-dum – crack* introduction of *Three Monkeys*. James's words sneak with me, carefully, quietly, and excitedly, through these shadows, through this jungle that I hate with all my heart, and yet am relishing with all my soul.

It's so hot here, the black sand burns like coal.

The vegetation is so thick that I can't see more than a few yards ahead, and keeping track of the person in front is hard.

Choose between your body and your soul.

Our greens blend in so well that you just rely on the movements in front of you, but really, that could be anything! A tree, a bird, the enemy ...

The enemy!

There is another surge in the center of my chest. It blooms there, hot and wonderful.

Raindrops sizzle and pop on the dusty road.

Inside this dense thicket of foliage, the air is much hotter and more humid than it was in the clearing.

There's messages and secret codes.

It is dangerously hot in this country. There is no breeze except for any disturbance of air the mosquitoes make as they hum around me in their constant clouds. Sweat runs down my face. Stings my eyes. Trickles down my back like ghostly fingertips. The ground under me is slippery with red-orange mud and decaying leaves and I slide and fall flat onto my chest, pushed down farther into the stinking mud by the weight of my pack, which bites into my shoulder blades and bruises my back.

"Come on, Battle Buddy." Lion kneels beside me and helps me to my feet, and then his face drains of color as he puts a finger to his lips and drops down onto one knee.

Through the trees ahead of me, Solomon is down on one knee too, his fist raised just like Lion's beside me. I copy them, passing the signal (*Get the fuck down, and shut the fuck up!*) all the way to the back of the line.

I press my flaccid rifle close to my chest. Then I squeeze my eyes tight. And with Ray's face in my mind, I let James come forward again to take me away from whatever danger I am in. His *bum da-da de-dum – crack* helps to drown out the whooshing of blood that pounds in my ears. And helps me ignore that damn burning of adrenaline that rushes through my veins with a thrill I can't deny.

And there's beaucoup kinds of heat in this country. And they've got soldiers in the streets and urgent telegrams.

Telegrams ...

I can't help imagining a faceless man in an official uniform standing on my front porch and handing Ray and my mother a telegram. Bowing his head. Telling them that he is very sorry for their loss. Telling them that I was taken out just minutes into my first search and destroy mission. Telling them that, if only I'd had ammunition in my rifle, then perhaps I would still be alive.

Solomon lowers his arm and turns back to us. "Booby trap ahead," he hisses. "Punji pit. Those sneaky fuckers!"

I blow out the breath that I'd trapped in my lungs.

They are here, somewhere.

They could be tracking us, right now. Silently paralleling our own single-file line. Predicting our path and laying more traps for us.

Lion shoots me a quick relieved smile as we space out again and continue on our merry way.

My hands are shaking now. I can no longer discern between my absolute exhilaration, or my white-hot fear. Maybe this is the moment after all.

The moment I lose myself to absolute insanity.

Damn.

I'd hoped to last longer than this.

chapter fifty-seven

ray

I stood at the center point of the living room, the dining area, and the kitchen, turning in a circle like the hands on a clock. The sofa cushions were all askew, the crochet rug balled on the floor, the carpet strewn with pieces of dropped food, the television set so dusty I could write my name across the glass – and in fact I had done just that a few days ago. The kitchen sink was piled high with every dirty dish in the house. A tower of old newspapers swayed like a drunk beside the front door. And there was an insistent stench of mold and rotten food in the air, which no amount of joss sticks would mask any longer.

I grabbed out the roll of garbage bags, filled one after another with trash, and lined them up outside the back door. I wiped and swept and mopped and vacuumed. I washed and dried the dishes, the mugs, the silverware.

Sweating but satisfied, I stood once again in the center point of the three rooms that now sparkled and gleamed. Clapping my hands together, I grinned. At least I could keep one aspect of my life in order. I may not be able to control fate, but at least I could control something.

And that was when the doorbell chimed and all sense of having control vanished.

It was a child. A boy of no more than thirteen. His small,

juvenile hand held out an official telegram from the war department. Such a little kid carrying something that weighed more than the earth itself. How was he able to hold it up with that flimsy, skinny arm of his?

I stared down at this piece of paper in his tiny fingers, and I didn't want to touch it. I wanted to slam the door. I wanted to plug my ears. I wanted to scream and block him out as he cleared his throat.

I wanted to run.

But I just stood on the porch. Frozen. Waiting.

How could this be happening already? Japhy couldn't have been Over There more than a month! But really, was this such a surprise? I pictured him, hunching down in the jungles, under fire, under attack. Maybe everyone else around him is dead, too, or maybe he is all alone. I see him gripping a rifle and staring at a VC soldier who charges him. I see him not firing that gun. I see him closing his eyes. I see him choosing death over murder.

God damn him.

No.

Japhy! God fucking damn you, you selfish God damn asshole! Didn't you realize I need you? Didn't you realize, in your selfless sacrifice, that you have killed me too? That in choosing not to murder a man who wants to kill you, that you have murdered me instead?

And then the little boy on my doorstep – this cherubic angel of death – began to read. "The money order paid you herewith is from P.F.C. Andrew Mack, to the sum of two-hundred and ninety-five American dollars. Please give the below transaction number at your branch to reclaim your currency."

"What?" I frowned.

"What?" he said.

I just pointed at the telegram.

And the boy smiled at me. "These are the good telegrams, Miss. These are the ones you want to receive!" He handed it to me, winked, and then stepped back. "Have a good day."

I stared down at the telegram, searching for the words

missing, or *killed*, but he was right, this was in fact a good telegram. This was the one I wanted to receive.

Not only was Japhy still alive, not only was he wiring me the money he receives from the army, he was also sending me his answer. Finally. His answer.

It was fine.

He was fine.

All was fine.

*

Ohio National Guardsmen Cleared In K.S.U. Shooting

A grand jury investigating the shooting at Kent State University indicted 25 students and faculty today with a total of 43 offenses, including second degree riot, inciting to riot, assault, and arson. The Ohio National Guardsmen, who were on campus when four students were shot to death and nine others wounded on Monday May 4, have been cleared from any prosecution for deaths and injuries.

This investigation was requested by Adjutant General Sylvestor Del Corso of the Ohio National Guard in response to an F.B.I. report that Del Corso says was not factual, and which stated that the Guardsmen could be held liable to criminal charges in the shootings.

Del Corso stated that the F.B.I. assertions "fail to include many facts which we provided. The conclusions are just unbelievable ... that there were no troops injured, that no stones were thrown, and that there was a question whether there even was a riot."

After being in session for 25 days and examining over 300 witnesses, the grand jury released their findings.

"We do not condone all of the activities of the National Guard," the report stated. "We find, however, that those members of the National Guard who were present on the hill adjacent to Taylor Hall (scene of the shooting) fired their weapons in the honest and sincere belief, and under circumstances which would have logically caused them to believe, that they would suffer serious bodily injury had they not done so. They are not, therefore, subject to criminal prosecution under the laws of this state for any death or injury resulting therefrom."

The jury report stated that incidents in the town of Kent on Friday May 1 and on the campus on May 2 and May 3 "constituted riot", and the gathering on the campus on May 4 was in violation of a directive issued by a university official and that the participants failed to disperse on orders.

"These orders," the report said, "caused a violent reaction and the gathering quickly degenerated into a riotous mob."

According to testimonies of students and Guardsmen, the report stated that 58 Guardsmen were injured by thrown objects during the demonstration. Although some rioters claim that only a few rocks were thrown, the testimony has established that 200 bricks were taken from a nearby construction site.

"The circumstances present at that time," the report said, "indicate that 74 men surrounded by several hundred hostile rioters were forced to retreat back up the hill under a constant barrage of rocks and other flying objects, accompanied by a constant flow of obscenities and chants such as "Kill! Kill! Kill!"

While the jury agrees "with the principle of law that words alone are never sufficient to justify the use of lethal force, the verbal abuse directed at the Guardsmen by the students during the period in question represented a level of obscenity and vulgarity which we have never before witnessed. The epithets directed at the Guardsmen and members of their families by male and female rioters alike would have been unbelievable had they not been confirmed by the testimony from every quarter and by audio tapes made available to the grand jury."

Any attempts to fix sole blame on Guardsmen, students, or other participants "would be inconceivable," the jury noted, thus blaming the Kent State administration with forming "an attitude of laxity, over-indulgence, and permissiveness with its students and faculty. All the conditions that led to the May tragedy still exist."

The report concluded "that the group of Guardsmen who were ordered to disperse the crowd on the commons were placed in an untenable and dangerous position."

Arrests of the indicted 25 students and faculty will begin directly.

Calmly, I folded the newspaper in half and smoothed it flat.

Taking a long breath, I slid my chair away from the table and stood. With my chin held high, I turned and walked through the kitchen, down the hallway, and into the bathroom, where I lifted the lid on the toilet seat, and vomited.

The bile burned my throat. Bitter and acidic as injustice.

chapter fifty-eight

japhy

We hump our damn heavy packs up hills, down ravines, and over fallen trees. We slash our way through walls of vines, and wade waist-deep through rivers. My boots slurp down into the slimy floor. The warm water curls around my legs and there is no cooling refreshment in the water at all.

There are, however, leeches.

One suctions on to my forearm. Black and shiny. I try to pull it off but, unable get a good grasp of its slimy body, my fingers slip, squeezing it. Blood spurts. And my stomach rolls.

"Sorry, buddy, dinner's over," I mutter. Lighting a cigarette, I hold it close to the leech – even though it's just a bloodsucking slug that wants nothing more than my blood, I still can't hurt it.

The leech drops.

As I run my fingers over the great red welt where its mouth had been, I again picture the ammunition under my bed, and I swallow the doubt that squirms cold and slimy in my throat.

At 1700 hours, we search out a clearing, a landing zone where a chopper can bring in more supplies, and we dig out foxholes and set up makeshift tents by stretching ponchos over bamboo poles.

The lieutenant radios our coordinates back to the

command post and soon we hear the familiar *whomp, whomp, whomp* of an approaching Huey.

Three colored flares burst off in a triangle around the clearing; red, blue, and white smoke billows and swirls. The Huey appears as malevolent as a giant wasp, and then lands as gracefully as a dragonfly.

"So, how are you finding your first hump?" Black Cat sits on the ground, his pack between his knees.

"Oh, this is an absolute gas, this is," I say as I sit down beside him.

He laughs, nods, and hands me a can of soda from the new supplies.

As the warm soda fizzes down my throat, and I exult in the familiar normality of a bubbly drink, my gaze drifts around the circle of the other boys I hadn't yet met.

My gaze drifts until it stops on a very familiar face.

"Who is that guy?" I whisper to Black Cat, not looking away from the one person I never wanted to see again.

"Which one?"

"The one sitting beside Lion. The one with the red hair."

"Who, Uncle Sam?" Cat says. "Only been here a couple months. He's still really green but thinks he's soldier-of-the-year or something."

Bricks, who sits on the other side of Black Cat, leans in. "He's an okay guy. He always gives me his meat in mess. Doesn't eat it himself. One of those vegies. Says eating meat is cruel! But I just says to him, 'Sam, if God didn't intend for us to eat animals, then why did he make them out of meat?'"

Sam's blue eyes flick over me, and I see a spark of recognition in their depths, but he won't place me; my hair is short now, and my arms and chest are broad, filled out with muscle. I look quite different than I did on that day his friends beat the shit out of me and tried to rape Ray.

Cat and Bricks are still speaking to me, but their words are just meaningless white noise now as I stand and, with clenched fists, walk calmly across the circle.

"You're one of the F.N.G's, aren't you?" he asks me in that lisping voice that causes my muscles to bunch.

I stare at him and breathe slowly through my nose, trying to push down on the rage that boils in every part of my body. For the first time, I truly regret leaving behind my bullets.

"The name's Sam." He stands and holds his hand out to me. "Good to have you on board, soldier."

When I don't respond, he lowers his arm.

"So ... how you liking your first mission?"

Still, I say nothing.

He creases his brow as he stares back, and then he lowers his voice. "I know you, don't I?"

I hear a gratifying crack of knuckles on bone as I swing my fist and he falls backwards.

Swiftly, Solomon appears between us. "Whoa, brother, be cool!" he says. "What the hell, Japhy?"

Sam picks himself up, massaging his jaw, and places a hand on Solomon's shoulder. "Sol, let him be; it's cool. He kind of owed me that one." Looking at me, he says, "Can we sit down, or would you like to hit me again?" His lisp more prominent now over a swelling lip.

I clench my fist, and Sam grimaces, waits, but does not shield himself.

"Japhy?" Solomon squeezes my shoulder but I shrug him off.

"We're fine, guys," says Sam. "Can you just give us a minute?"

Bricks shrugs and walks back to his seat beside Black Cat, but Solomon waits for me to look at him and nod, before he turns away.

When I finally sit, Sam leans in and whispers, "Listen, I want you to know how bad I feel about what I did." He winces and rubs his jaw. "Was your old lady okay?"

"What do you care?"

"That's what I'm trying to tell you. What we did to you two that day ... it haunts me. I've never done anything like that before; I was high on speed, so I wasn't in control of myself." He holds up his hands and says quickly, "Not that it's an excuse. It isn't. The other guys were always bragging to me about how many girls they'd balled. I know I'm not much of a looker, so I felt ... I don't know, like I had to prove to them I wasn't a loser. I hate myself for what I did, and I don't expect you to forgive me, or even believe me, but I just want you to know that I'm sorry. I'm a good guy, I really am. We all make mistakes, do things we regret, things we have to deal with, and live with, for the rest of our lives."

I shake my head at him and look away.

"I understand how you must feel, seeing me again like this, here of all places, and I understand if you can't forgive me, but can we put it behind us? At least while we're out here? We have to be on the same side, you know; we got to stick together to keep each other alive." He holds out his hand to me again. "So, what do you say?"

"Just stay the fuck away from me. You'll have more chance of staying alive that way." I stand and stomp back over to where Solomon and Timothy wait.

"What was that all about?" asks Solomon.

"Nothing." Anger bubbles my skin. Singes up through my limbs, into my torso, converging into one huge wave that flows into my brain. My head throbs. I can't believe what I've just heard and I am so angry I could spit.

But I am not angry at Sam.

I flex my aching knuckles and I think again of the crunch as my fist hit his jaw, but I do not feel the warm glow of satisfaction I'd expected.

This is the jerk who attacked Ray.

This is the monster whose face I once dreamed about putting through a window.

This is a human who shows utter remorse.

And I hate him for that.

But I hate myself more for wanting to forgive the son-of-a-bitch.

chapter fifty-nine

ray

Seeing the halls of my old high school silent and empty on Saturday morning was strange in contrast to my memories. My shoes clacked and echoed down this familiar corridor, inside which my heart had expanded like a balloon only months before. I stopped at my old locker and placed a hand on the cold blue metal, wondering whose life was now stored safely behind its combination lock.

This was where it had all started. Where *we* had started. On that morning in March when I'd looked up to see Andy Mack striding down the hallway with his eyes on only me.

"Hi, Heather," he'd said.

"Hi," I squeaked back, still shocked that he was here. "I thought you had to catch a bus."

He shrugged. "I missed it." And he thrust a copy of *The Dharma Bums* across the space between us. "Thought you might want to borrow this."

I frowned at him. "It's your book. You should read it first."

Pressing the book into my hands, he grinned and dipped his head. "I stayed up all night and finished it this morning so I'd have an excuse to see you today."

My cheeks burned at these words. Me? He'd wanted to see *me*?

"You want to do something later?"

"Sure," I said, still stunned.

"Do you like James Lee Stanley?" he asked.

"Uh," I stammered, taking the book from him. "I've never really listened to his stuff."

"Are you serious? Oh far out! Okay, I'll pick you up after school. Your life is about to change, Heather Wren!"

"Master Mack!"

We both turned to see Principal Flinders striding toward us.

"How nice of you to grace us with your presence, Andrew, but in case you forgot, you graduated last year and no longer attend this institution."

"Yes, sir," said Andy.

"Well?" the principal said. "Is there something you want?"

Andy flicked his eyes back to me. "Yes, sir," he'd said. "There definitely is."

"Miss Wren!"

I jumped out of my memories. Principal Flinders stood in the doorway to the library, his arms crossed.

"Hello, sir." I smiled.

"Are you all ready for today?" he asked, ushering me through the door.

"I hope so."

"I'm sure you'll do just fine. You were one of the top students in the year. I was very surprised to hear you had dropped out." He touched my shoulder and frowned. "How is Master Mack doing?"

"He is doing just fine, sir," I said. "He'll be coming home soon."

"I'm glad to hear it." Then he clapped his hands. "Right. Take a seat and let's get this exam started."

*

There was something so satisfying about scooping out the guts of a pumpkin with your bare hands. Maybe it was the way the feeling slingshot you instantly back into childhood, when you sat in the backyard squelching mud between your toes and not caring about the stains on your pants.

Seeds slipped and squished in my fingers and I splattered them down into the bowl beside me.

Across the table, Momma grinned at me as she lifted a paring knife and began to carve a face in her pumpkin.

"You always used to carve happy faces," she said. "Do you remember? Never scary or angry ones. They all had to have wide, grinning mouths. If your father or I made an unhappy lantern, you wouldn't let us light the candle."

I nodded. "There was already too much negativity in the world – why make more?"

"And now?" Momma pointed her knife toward my own pumpkin.

Its eyes narrowed beneath a furrowed brow, and its sharp-toothed mouth grimaced, wickedly.

"Well," I shrugged, "I've learned now that you can't have true happiness unless you have experienced sorrow." I bit my bottom lip. "Love will not be as powerful if you have never felt hate. Peace can't exist without war."

There was a knock at the door then. Three quick raps.

Momma gasped. "They're early! I haven't set out the bowls of candy yet!" And she rushed into the kitchen, opening and closing Nora's cupboards until she found a large bowl, her floppy brown donkey ears swinging as she moved.

Watching her, I stifled a laugh.

It had taken me all day to convince Momma to hire these costumes. She'd thought it was in terrible taste, didn't see the humor or the irony. But what was more perfect a character for me to portray today than the Virgin Mary, swollen with a child that would bring about salvation and peace?

Smoothing my hands over the soft blue material that draped me from head to toe and ballooned out over my stomach, I fixed a benevolent smile on my face and reached for the door.

During the last few months, I kept imagining scenarios in which there'd be a knock, and Leaf would be standing on the porch with his melted-chocolate eyes heavy with apology. Sometimes I would scream at him. Sometimes I'd slap his cheek. Sometimes I'd throw a glass of water in his face before slamming the door and listening to his slow, sad footsteps fade away and disappear again – this time forever.

I never imagined I'd throw my arms around his neck, or kiss him, or cry out his name in relief, or sob with happiness that he was alive. So when the door opened and I saw those warm eyes heavy with apology, and when I threw my arms about his neck and kissed him and cried out his name in relief, I recoiled from myself, disgusted.

Leaf held out a bunch of wilted daisies and smiled at me sheepishly, his head bowed. "Knock, knock."

I couldn't help it; I didn't want to answer him, but I just couldn't help it. Damn him. "Who's there?" I said, releasing his broad neck and wiping my eyes with the Holy Mother's dress.

"Iowa."

"Iowa who?"

"Iowa you a big apology."

"That's terrible," I said.

"Is this *him*, then?" Momma said.

I could feel her standing at my back like a wall.

"Yes, Momma, this is Leaf."

"You never mentioned he was a ... *negro*."

"I never thought it made a difference," I said.

She crossed her arms and raised her chin and her donkey ears bobbed up and down. "And what does he think he's doing here?" She spoke to me, even though she kept her eyes unblinkingly on his.

Leaf looked from me, to Momma, and back to me again. "Can we go somewhere to talk, Ray? Alone?"

Momma sidestepped in front of me. "She's not going anywhere with you!" Her arms were solid armor at her chest, and her spine was as straight as a sword. Even at her full height, the top of her head barely reached Leaf's shoulder, yet she towered over him.

"Momma." I touched her arm. "It's okay. Really."

"Is it?" She turned to me. "That's not what you said to me yesterday, and the day before that, and the day before that!"

"I know what I said. But I've waited so long for an explanation," I faced Leaf and met his eyes, "that I'm not turning it away now."

"Fine. But if he hurts you in *any* way ..." She turned back, her gaze locked fiercely on Leaf, "... not only will he have to deal with every God damn cop in the country, he'll have to deal with *me*."

"Yes, ma'am." Leaf nodded quickly. "I understand."

She lunged forward and snatched the flowers from his grip. "I'll put these pitiful things in water."

As I stepped out onto the front porch and closed the door behind us, Momma slid aside the curtain and watched us walk to the swing.

Leaf sat by my side, and I desperately wanted to reach out to him. To hold his hand. To feel his medicating warmth against me. But I slid away.

He nodded toward the house, where Momma kept watch. "Nice ass."

I could hear the smile in his words. The warm sound of it made me want to punch him, and yet a small part of me melted and pooled at his feet.

Damn him.

God fucking damn him!

"Is she going to keep staring at me like that the whole time?" he asked.

"Why?" I whispered.

"Because she is giving me the willies," he said, his smile louder this time.

"I mean," I said, "*why?*" I turned to face him then.

When his eyes met mine, he shrank back from whatever truth he saw there. "Ah, shit." He dropped his gaze and ran a hand over his hair. "I'm *sorry*, Ray."

"Four months?" I whispered. "Four God damned months! What sort of person does that?"

"I think I kind of had a breakdown or something. It started that night, in that ... *room* ... in that hospital. There were cracks.

In everything. Everywhere. Like reality was breaking apart and there was just blackness behind. Like everything was turning into nothing. Everything was splitting open, breaking apart. It started in the walls, and the floor, even in your face." He reached his fingers toward my cheek and stroked my skin.

And I let him. And I closed my eyes. And, oh God. His hand. His heat.

"I went outside to escape it," he continued, "but the cracks were outside, too, in the sky, and they grew bigger and wider and soon I knew they were going to swallow me. So I just ... I just *ran*."

"You liar," I said.

"What? No, I ..."

"Just stop the fucking lies already, *Mr. Williams*! Yeah, I know all about you and that beautiful love story of yours. Did you ever tell me anything that was true? Actually, no, don't answer that, because I won't believe you anyway."

He sighed. "Yes, my real name is Williams, not Johnson. We changed it to Johnson when we got married so they couldn't track us; they would have taken her away."

"You mean, they would have taken her *home*," I said. "The home you stole her from!"

"What?" He shook his head. "No, it was Lauren's idea for us to go. I was against it but she convinced me."

"She was a kid, Leaf! A fifteen-year-old *girl*!"

"Come on, Ray. On the inside, Lauren was older than all of us! No one could have forced her to do something she didn't want to."

We were both silent for a moment. I tried to stop the memory of the last time she'd been backed into a corner, and how well that had turned out.

"Shit." Leaf fisted his hands and then tucked them beneath his armpits. "I should have known better. I shouldn't have made her choose."

And as I looked into his broken face, I could suddenly see all those cracks he'd been describing. He was still falling to pieces right in front of me.

I reached out and touched his cheek. He leaned into it as a

sob jolted from him and absorbed into my palm. It burned my skin. My muscles and bones ached from it, but I didn't take my hand away.

"It's okay," I whispered. "Everything is going to be okay now."

He nodded once, and then he folded in the center, tipping sideways to rest his face on my stomach and wrap his arms around my waist.

My dress warmed with the dampness of his tears.

"Thank you, Ray," he said.

"For what?" I stroked his hair.

"Thank you," he said, "for giving me a reason to *be*." And he placed a hand on my stomach and watched it move from the force of the child within. "I promise you," he whispered, "I'm going to be everything you will ever need. I'm going to be there for you, always. I'm going to be your world."

I listened to his words with a lump in my throat. I listened to them, knowing he no longer spoke to me. And I listened to them, knowing that I was about to take away his very reason for living.

Across the street, a group of children wearing white sheets with eye-holes hurried along, while the Grim Reaper loped along behind them.

"Leaf," I said. "I'm putting this baby up for adoption."

Leaf formed the word slowly. "Adoption?" Speaking each syllable individually as if he were only just learning to speak. "Like, to a stranger?"

I nod.

"But ... but you don't need to: I'm here now."

"You're here now?" I spat the words. "Oh, well then, you're right! That changes *everything*, doesn't it?"

"Yes, it does!" he said. "I'm here. I came back here for you. For the baby. I mean, I'd always planned on coming back anyway, but I'm here now and you don't have to do this on your own, Ray. You don't have to give away our child."

"Our child?" I said. "No. This is not *our* child. This is *my* child. And it is therefore *my* decision."

"What about Japhy? Have you told him?"

"Yes, actually." I crossed my arms. "He is completely supportive of this decision."

"I don't believe that."

"Are you calling me a liar?" My voice rose. "That's rich, coming from you! All you've done since we met is lie to me."

"That's not true!"

"Isn't it, Gabriel Williams?"

He sighed. "Okay, maybe I didn't tell you my real name, but so what? It's just a name. It doesn't change who I am, or what we've been through together."

"It does, actually," I said. "It changes everything! Because you made me fall in love with someone that isn't even real!"

He jerked back as if I'd slapped him. "What did you say?" he whispered.

I sucked in a breath, hoping that the words I'd just spoken could be inhaled back inside me again. "I said it changes everything."

"You said you've fallen in love with me."

Shaking my head, I closed my eyes so I didn't have to see his face, so I didn't have to look into those eyes. Those God damn eyes. "I ... I ..."

"Ray?"

He placed his palm against my cheek and I stilled. I held my breath. And a heavy, unstoppable tear spilled from the corner of my eye at the beautiful warmth of his touch.

How I'd longed for this moment. To be able to feel him again. His skin on mine. That instant flood of numbness that dulled everything but the intensity of my affection. The betrayal was gone. The lies did not exist. And I was filled with love and need and peace.

"Ray?" he said again.

I felt the heat of his breath on my lips. "Yes," I whispered, an answer to my name, and to all the questions he didn't need to ask.

"I love Lauren," he said.

"I know," I said, gritting my teeth against a sob.

Of course he didn't love me. What the hell was I expecting? That he could just replace the love of his life with me? And is that what I wanted, anyway? To live always in the shadow of her ghost? To always be compared with what he *could've* had if Lauren were still alive?

I swallowed.

Yes. Yes, that was exactly what I wanted. I didn't care. I would be happy to live forever under the shroud of her death if it meant that Leaf would always be there. Would never leave me alone with my pain ever again. Because I needed him. While Japhy was away, I needed him. And even when Japhy comes home, I'll need him still.

And then he kissed me and I fell away into myself. I no longer had to hold it together, because Leaf would do that for me.

And then he kissed me and it meant more than just two people touching lips. More than two people being together simply because being alone was too difficult. It meant more than that. It *did*. It had to.

And then he kissed me and I didn't care if he didn't love me. This would do. This would do just fine.

"I'm going home, Heather!" The front door slammed, punctuating Momma's statement with an audible exclamation point. "Happy Halloween." She stomped across the front porch, her donkey's tail trailing behind. "Let me know if you need anything." But she didn't wait for me to respond.

Not that it mattered anyway, because right at that moment I didn't need anything else at all.

*

"You hate me now, don't you?" I whispered the words, half hoping he wouldn't hear me. Because if he didn't hear me, then he wouldn't answer me. And if he didn't answer me, then there was no chance of him breaking me into pieces.

I'd held back these words as we'd sat outside on the porch swing. I'd held them back when he kissed me. I'd held them back as we stood up and silently walked through the house, hand in hand, toward the bedroom. And I'd held them back as

I burst into tears and let him heal me from the inside out. But now, as I gazed at his serene face, as I lay there too relaxed to hold onto those words in a tight enough grip, they slipped out and tiptoed across my damp pillowcase.

On the bed beside me, Leaf's eyes opened and I wondered what he saw when he looked at me.

Did he see the person who was giving away his child? Not that this was *his* child, anyway; this was Japhy's baby.

Did he see the only one left who loved him? Or is that what I saw when I looked at *him*?

Did we cling to each other now because we were the only life rafts available? To stop ourselves from drowning?

"No," he said, and he brushed a strand of hair off my face. "I don't hate you. In fact, I think you are very brave. And I will support your decision, whatever you decide, even if I don't agree with it, even if it kills me."

"Why?"

He sighed. "Because I'll do anything, as long as it helps you to forgive me."

"And will you tell me the truth?" I asked. "About Lauren? About where you've been all this time?"

Something cracked behind his eyes and his lips pressed into a line as if he were tolerating a sudden surge of pain. But after a beat, he nodded. "I'll tell you everything," he said. "I owe you that. If nothing else, I owe you *that*. So, yes, I promise to tell you ... one day. As long as *you* promise not to hate *me*."

I nodded and smiled. One day. That was his promise to be around for a long time. A promise that he was not going anywhere again. A promise that he couldn't leave until he revealed everything to me. So, therefore, I would never ask.

He lifted himself up on one elbow. "Can I ask *you* something?"

"Of course," I said.

He opened his mouth. Closed it. Took a breath. And opened his mouth again. "What if you give away this baby, this piece of Japhy ... and then he never comes home?"

"What?" I sat up and edged away from him on the bed, as if those words would come true if I got too close to them.

"Why would you say that? Why even think that? Of course he is coming home! Jesus, Leaf!"

"I'm sorry." He held up his hands. "It's just that death happens, right? If it can come for Lauren, it can come for any of us! And pretending otherwise will not hide you from it. Will not protect you, or me, or *him*!"

I clambered out of the bed, shielding myself with the protective shroud of the Virgin Mary's dress, but his words kept shooting at me like bullets.

"What if you give up the only living piece of Japhy left in the world?"

"Japhy *is* coming home."

"Yeah." Leaf nodded. "Yeah." But I could see the doubt in his eyes and I suddenly hated him for that more than anything else in this whole world.

Because if there was doubt, then it meant there was possibility. And if there was possibility, then ...

No.

Backing away from Leaf and his unsure eyes, I ran to the bathroom and locked myself in.

The hot shower faucet squealed as I turned it on full, and steam breathed around me. I looked away from the mirror until it became opaque and blind; I looked away so I could not see the doubt that swirled in my own eyes.

But Leaf's haunting question remained: What if I gave up the only living piece of Japhy?

I pressed the heels of my hands against my eyes until yellow sparks flashed in my brain.

I have no choice, I thought. Everything happens for a reason. I fell pregnant with this child, at this time, for a reason! So, if I am going to save Japhy, if I am going to guarantee his return ... then ... then I must ...

I stepped under the hot water, scalding myself so I would not be able to hear my thoughts beneath the screams of my own weeping body.

*

That night, I waited until Leaf's breathing was long and slow against the back of my neck. Each exhalation warmed my skin, and chilled it again as he inhaled the very warmth he'd offered seconds before.

His arm draped heavy across my hip. I slowly slid out from beneath its weight, gently, carefully, so as not to wake him.

At the kitchen table, I sat with my head bent over a yellow notepad, my teeth biting on my bottom lip, and my pen scratching out words:

Dear Ray,

How are you feeling? You must be getting big now? I'm so sorry I'm not there to help you with all of this, but please take heart in the knowledge that we are making the right choice to adopt out this child. It is the right choice for everyone involved. You and I can still have the life we planned. The baby will have everything that we are unable to give it. And we will be granting the wish of two people who would otherwise never have the joy of a child in their lives. That's so huge. I hope you are as proud of this as I am. I hope you are as proud of yourself as I am!

Things over here are going well. It's pretty scary sometimes, but I just keep my head down, and think about you, and count down the days until we'll be together again. Because I will be coming home. I promise you that.

I hope Leaf is coping with things. Will you tell him I think about him often? I think about Lauren, too. She is in my thoughts a lot. When I am out there, I like to think her spirit is with me, watching over me, protecting me. I like to think of her as my guardian angel.

Please write again soon. At least in that small way I can be with you.

Yours, no matter what happens,
Japhy.

I folded this letter, this proof of Japhy's support, and ran my fingernail across the crease until it was as sharp as a razor. I slid it inside the same envelope that my invitation to Japhy's graduation had arrived in. On the front, my name and address was typed neatly, and in the corner was the seal of the United States Army. The stamp was dated months ago, so I rubbed my thumb across it, smudging the ink. Then I crept outside through the darkness, dropped the letter into the mailbox, and headed back into the house, back into the bedroom, and back beneath the heavy shield of Leaf's arm.

He snuffled and rolled over in his sleep. I pressed my face into the back of his neck, and drifted away into dreams, into a world of complete unreality where nothing was real, nothing was true; a place that felt as familiar to me these days as home.

november

I believe every American deeply believes in his heart that the proudest legacy the United States can leave ... is that our power was used to defend freedom, not to destroy it; to preserve the peace, not to break the peace.

~ President Richard Nixon, Address to the Nation

chapter sixty

japhy

The black Vietnamese night blinds us like a hand over our eyes. And then comes the rain. Drops as fat as fists. Slow at first, then they pound faster, heavier, until there is a solid wall of water that drowns out all sound, and I am deaf to any noise the enemy might make.

They could be sneaking up on us right now.

Bent double, we run to the leaky shelters of our hooches, and I am grateful for this sudden downpour; even if the storm does render us deaf and blind to any oncoming attacks, at least I don't have to look at Sam anymore tonight.

My hands ball into tight, painful fists.

Being around him every day makes me question myself more than anything else this war has thrown at me. After all those months of resisting being stripped down and rebuilt, after all those months of making sure this war will never change who I am, it took just one minute in the company of that man for all my resolve to shatter. Just one minute and I no longer wanted to be true to myself.

Screw that.

I want to place my fingers around his neck.

I want to load my rifle and fire it right into his face.

I want to tell Ray that I made this son-of-a-bitch pay for hurting and humiliating her.

I want to fuck him up for trying to fuck her.

Taking a breath, I force my fists to relax, and I force my thoughts to halt on Ray's face. I let her calm me. She is the only thing that saves me, day after day, night after night. She saves me. And in saving me, she saves *him*, too.

Because, even if I no longer want to stay true to myself, I need to stay true to her. She wouldn't want me to become that vengeful person taking pleasure from hurting someone else, even if he *does* deserve it.

So I force myself to focus on that.

And on not dying.

Every now and then the land lights up from a mortar blast somewhere off in the distance, and that short burst of brightness reveals *no* VC soldier creeps up to me with his rifle aimed at my head. For a few seconds, after the liquid blackness surges and froths around me again like a wave, I breathe a sigh of relief, laugh at my paranoia, and then wait as those unseen ghosts of war creep back into my imagination again.

I've manage to get through weeks of this frightening delusion by holding my breath and wishing the nights were over, only to sigh with regret at the rising sun and wish to be cloaked once again in pure darkness; in daylight I am easier to kill.

When the day does come, I strip off my clothes, take a bar of soap, and stand naked under the gray sky, letting the warm water wash away as much grime, sweat, and resentment as I can. I lift up clots of mud and scrub until my skin grows red, and the insect bites and thorn scratches sting and burn and cleanse me with pain.

With each passing day of this mission I feel an itchiness. A burning desire for something – anything – to happen. Just as Solomon predicted. And now, after three weeks out in this jungle, I am sick to death of everything: humping my sodden pack; searching for Charlie until night falls; making a clearing; receiving supplies and mail by chopper; breaking up fights between someone and someone; calming my own need to hurt

Sam in any way I can; trying to sleep while ignoring the slimy presence of fear skulking around us in darkness so complete. All that is visible are the images behind my own eyes. And those images are the worst things of all.

When our mission is finally over and we return to the base, I can't help staring around at everything in wonderment: pathways and dirt roads that are completely clear and I don't have to hack my way through a wall of razor-sharp reeds to get to wherever it is I am going; a bed with a mattress and blanket; a toilet with plenty of soft, white paper.

Heaven.

During mess, I run my hands over the solidity of the tabletop, as if being out in the jungle for a single month has reduced me to a wild man who has never seen a table in his life.

Black Cat drops heavily into the seat beside us and shoves a crumpled piece of paper in Solomon's face. "She left me!"

"Who?" I ask, leaning over Solomon's shoulder to read the letter.

"Lucy," Black Cat groans. "She dumped me. Said she couldn't handle the stress of worrying about me anymore. Because she loves me so much she is breaking up with me and finding someone else. 'If you love someone, set them free.' What does that even mean, for fuck's sake?"

"Well, that's just typical of women!" says Sam, leaning backwards from the next table. "We're over here risking our dicks for them, but they can't even be stuffed worrying about us. Forget her, Cat. She ain't worth it."

"Thanks, man," Black Cat says to him. "But that's the problem: she *is* worth it, you dig? I'd *die* for that girl."

"Well, don't!" Sam shakes his head. "If I have anything to do with it, none of us is dying for anyone!" His blue eyes fall on me for a second, but I shrug them off as I hear the ghost of his words in my memory (*I really am a nice guy*) and I want to smash him in his nice-guy face.

"Chin up, buddy," Sam says, and leans over his tray again.

"What do you got against that guy, Japhy?" whispers Black Cat, and I realize I must be wearing my hatred like a mask. "He's an all right guy."

"So I've heard," I mutter, wondering what they would think of Sam if they knew what he'd done. That would serve him right. Everybody's favourite F.N.G. being treated like the scumbag he is. I could tell them. I could tell them all. Right now. I could ruin him ...

I open my mouth and straighten my spine and stare at the back of his red nice-guy head. "Just forget it," I say and turn my eyes back to Black Cat. "I'm sorry about your chick."

Black Cat sighs and puts his head in his hands.

"Listen," says Solomon, patting Cat on the back, "if you plan on being all cut up over this, brother, can I have your bread?"

Black Cat smiles as he folds the letter and stuffs it into his pocket, and I glance down at my own pocket, where my own letter is neatly folded.

What if Ray had written to me for the same reason? What if she decided she was in love with Leaf instead of me, and wanted to set me free?

But of course, she would never do that to me. I know Ray. I know her heart. Her mind. Her soul. And I know that all of her belongs to me.

But, then ... what *does* that letter say? It must be something pretty darn important, otherwise why would she have ignored my wishes and written to me in the first place?

My fingers tingle with a need to feel the paper, to smooth out the wrinkles and folds, to touch what she had touched. My whole body itches to see her familiar handwriting and to press the paper to my face in case some trace of her scent lingers there, fading with each passing day.

"Just read it already!" says Timothy.

"Huh?"

"Your damn letter from Ray," he says. "You're thinking about it again, aren't you? I can tell! Just put yourself out of your misery."

"Yeah, and all of us!" mutters Lion.

Everybody leans forward as I reach my hand up to my pocket. Their eyes glint as my fingers dip inside. My heart races as I feel the sharp fold of the envelope within.

And my head rings with the words from James Lee Stanley: *don't look away.*

My hand stills.

Once I read what Ray so desperately wants me to know, what she thinks is too important to wait until I get home, then I will not be able to look away.

Instead of looking for people who want me dead, I will see the loops and swirls of her lettering. Instead of listening for a twig snapping beneath an enemy boot, I will hear her voice in my head as she reads out those words to me. Once I see what is in that letter, I will not be able to *un*see it, and I will therefore not be able to see anything else.

chapter sixty-one

ray

Some people think a lie is dark thing. Dirty. Bad.

Some people think that once you tell one lie, more will surely follow on its sinister heels.

But I think sometimes a lie is a necessary thing. It protects. Like a piece of sand in an oyster, your lie is covered with protective layers of excretions, is transformed from a single speck of dirt into a beautiful, lustrous pearl. A jewel. A wonder to behold. Even if it's really made up of shit.

My lies were not dark things. Not dirty. Not bad. My lies were necessary. My lies protected. And my lies shone.

Japhy supports my decision.

Afternoon light slanted through the kitchen window and hit the sink at a perfect angle to bounce straight up into my eyes. The brightness made me wince.

I turned away from the light and grabbed an onion from a bag on the counter.

I am doing what is best for me.

The fragile brown skin of the onion cracked beneath my fingers as I peeled away the protective layer; it shattered from my touch with the sound of dry leaves being crunched beneath a boot.

Adoption is the right thing to do.

The onion's second layer was rubbery and tinged the color of tanned skin. It had to go as well. Beneath that, I removed a greenish layer, crisp and thick, digging my nails into the flesh until it popped free and I could rip that away as well. I wanted the white flesh. The untainted. The pure. So I kept tearing away these blemished coverings.

Lauren's death was not my fault.

The same with the next layer, and the next. Faster and faster, I scrabbled at the meat of this onion, telling myself that this would be the last one, this would be the last one, this one, this one, this one!

Japhy will come home.

And then my hands were empty. The onion was gone. As if it had never existed. And all I had left to show it had been there in the first place were the tears that splattered the chopping board.

"Are you all right?"

I turned to see Leaf leaning against the kitchen counter. One leg crossed at the ankle, arms folded over his chest, head dipped to the side, and those warm eyes – those beautiful, trusting windows of him – fixed on my face.

"Yeah." I nodded, took out another onion, and started to strip away the layers. "Everything is fine."

"What time are they coming?"

"Six," I said. "You nervous?"

"As all hell," he said.

"Don't be," I said. "They'll love you."

"Are you insane? Your mother already hates me. And your father, well, he *has* to hate me on principle, unless he wants your mother to hate *him*!"

"Momma doesn't *hate* you," I said.

"She does."

"She hates what you did."

"Well then, we have something in common," Leaf said. "Maybe I can open the conversation with *that* little ice-breaker, huh? Or we could all bond over the fact that I support your choice to give away her first grandchild. That's always a sure bet to win over the in-laws."

I crunched through the onions with a knife, reducing them to pieces.

"I don't suppose I can convince you to reschedule, can I?" He stepped up behind me and pressed his lips against that spot below my ear.

Christ.

"No!" I shrugged him off me. "You have been wriggling your way out of this for weeks! Anyway, it's Thanksgiving! We can't reschedule Thanksgiving."

He sighed. "Fine. But only because it's so important to you."

The onions hissed as I threw them into the fry pan; they bubbled and spat in the hot oil, as if struggling to escape the heat. And as I stirred, something pulled taut as a knot in my chest. Leaf had just referred to my parents as *in-laws*. Sure, he had said it jokingly, and sure, I planned on marrying Japhy officially once he came home, but still ... what if ...

"I think you're burning those," Leaf said. Leaning over me, he gripped my hand, which held the spoon, and like a puppeteer he stirred the smoking onions around the pan. His chest pressed flush against my back and his chin gently brushed the top of my head as he maneuvered my arm around in circles.

I imagined him doing this, a nightly ritual, a husband with his wife. I imagined myself in his arms and felt that knot in my chest pull tight again. Then I imagined another woman, a different wife, laughing and happy and perfect in his arms. The knot ripped through me and I gasped from the shock of it.

"Are you okay?" he asked and placed a hand on my belly.

"Yes." I smiled and nodded and then shielded myself, as always, behind my biggest and most bullet-proof lie. "Yes, everything is fine."

And for a while that night, everything *was*.

"What exactly are we eating?" My father frowned down at his plate.

"Salt and pepper tofu, Daddy," I said. "It's delicious, and it's good for you."

"Where's the turkey?"

"The turkey is where it *should* be," I said. "Still alive and thankful to us, on this day of thanks, that we have decided to let him live."

"Here we go," he muttered. "Heather, if God wanted us all to be vegetarians, he wouldn't have made animals taste so good!"

Beside me, Leaf snorted into his drink. I shot him a nasty look and he cleared his throat and swallowed his mouthful.

"Did you know," I said, "that by the year two thousand and fifty there will not be enough food to sustain everyone? Did you know that we feed more crops to *livestock* than to humans? I mean, no wonder there are so many starving people! And there's this thing called Global Warming, Daddy; all the cow farts are ruining the environment!"

"And who says this exactly?" my father asked.

"Statistics don't lie," I replied.

"Did you know," Leaf said, "that forty-eight percent of all statistics are completely made up?"

My father hid a smile by bringing his fork to his nose and sniffing the food. Across the table, Momma nodded quickly at him, and he hesitated and then took a bite. His eyebrows rose in surprise.

"See?" I grinned. "Told you it's delicious."

"It's not bad, I guess," he said.

"Why did the tofu cross the road?" Leaf asked.

"Why?" asked my father.

"To prove he wasn't chicken."

My father chuckled. "Not bad. I tried a vegetarian diet once."

"Really, Daddy?" I said, surprised.

"Yeah," he said, "but I decided it was a missed steak!"

Leaf snorted into his drink again. "A vegetarian walked into a doctor's office with a carrot up one nostril, a stick of celery up the other, and mushrooms in each ear. The doctor looks at him and says, 'I don't think you're eating right.'"

My father slapped the table and let out an actual hoot of laughter – a sound I'd never heard him make before. "What do you call a cow with no legs?" His voice was stretched thin with the effort of holding back more laughter.

"What?" asked Leaf, grinning.

"Ground beef!"

"All right, children!" I said, rolling my eyes at them both.

Leaf and my father cleared their throats, smirked at each other, and then looked down at their plates.

"Where'd you learn to cook anyway, Heather?" asked my father.

"Actually," I said, ignoring the quick flash of guilt on my mother's face, "Leaf made it."

"Oh?"

"I'm glad you like it, sir," said Leaf. "And Mrs. Wren, I hope yours is all right?"

"It's fine, thank you." She sniffed. "Heather, I do wish you would change your mind and come home. You're in no condition to be alone here now that you're ..." she pointed to my stomach, "... getting on."

"That's why I'm not alone," I said. "Leaf is taking care of me."

Her eyes narrowed. "Is he now?"

"Yes, ma'am." Leaf nodded.

"And who took care of you last month while Mr. Perfect was off who-knows-where? In fact," she turned to Leaf, "where exactly *were* you, if you don't mind me asking?"

"Momma!" I hissed.

But Leaf smiled at me. "No, it's all right. It's a valid question."

"Well, you don't have to answer it," I said.

"Oh, let the man make his own decisions," said Momma. She smiled at Leaf, folded her arms, and waited.

Leaf stabbed a cube of tofu. "I was in prison," he said, and popped the food in his mouth, chewing slowly.

My fork clattered onto my plate and the crash of metal against ceramic made me jump.

Momma leaned forward. Her eyes shone. "Did you say, *prison?*"

"Yes, ma'am, I did. Will you pass the greens, please?"

"Heather, I think you should leave the table," said my father, whose eyes were locked on Leaf, as if he expected him to grab a knife and lunge at me. His voice was deep now, all traces of high-pitched mirth from only moments ago were gone. "I don't want you to hear what I'm about to say to this young man."

"Oh, Daddy, please, I am not a child. And Leaf is my friend, and this is our home – for now anyway – so you will treat us like the adults that we are."

"If the state *penitentiary* can treat them as adults, Henry," said Momma, "surely you can, too."

Leaf placed his fork on the table and looked at my mother. "You're loving this, aren't you, Mrs. Wren?"

She sat back in her seat, her hand on her heart, as if she'd been deeply offended by his words.

"You want to know what I did?" Leaf said. "Fine, I'll tell you."

"No!" I reached out to grab Leaf's hand, but he moved and all I clutched was empty air.

"I fell in love with the most wonderful woman in the world. We were going to have a baby. And we wanted to get married. But, unfortunately, she was a little bit younger than me and her parents wouldn't exactly give us their blessing."

As one, my parents turned and stared at me.

"He's not talking about *me*!" I said. "He's talking about Lauren."

"Oh," said Momma. "You mean, the young girl who killed herself?"

Leaf winced. "Yes."

"You don't have to do this," I whispered.

But Leaf just closed his eyes and sighed. "When Lauren died, it broke me. I tried to run away from anything else that might make me happy." He reached out then, and squeezed my hand. "Because if you have something that makes you happy, then you also have something to lose, and I couldn't handle losing again. I barely survived it the first time. So I ran from it. But then," he paused, "something happened to wake me up and I realized that I was *not* the most important thing in the world." Leaf looked at my father. "You see, my mother and I came to this country from Jamaica when I was ten. My father was American, and my mother had finally saved up enough money to come over to be with him. But when we arrived to move into this new life, we found another wife and another son had beaten us to it. He shooed us off his doorstep like we were strangers. He threw away his family. A father should never throw away his family, and I'd always vowed never to be like that man. So after I left here, I turned myself in. I was charged with committing statutory rape: Lauren had been some months shy of turning sixteen and, therefore, legally a minor. I was sentenced to three months in jail. Once my time was up and my slate had been wiped clean, I came straight back to Liberation, to be here for your daughter and this baby." Picking up his fork again, Leaf smiled. "Now, Mrs. Wren, will you pass the greens, please?"

There was silence around the table.

Momma opened her mouth, but a swift glare from my father made her close it again. My parents could have an entire conversation with just their body language and facial expressions. I hoped I would have a connection like that with my husband one day.

"Why are you here today?" Momma asked. Her tone had softened ever so slightly now. "It's Thanksgiving. Why aren't you with your family?"

Leaf looked at me and smiled. "I *am*."

"Your *mother*, I mean," she said. "Why aren't you with her?"

"She passed away a few years back. Like I said, I am with my family." Leaf stood and reached across the table.

"Here you are, son." My father picked up the collard greens and passed them to Leaf.

"Thank you, Mr. Wren."

"Call me Henry."

I ducked my head and glanced at Leaf, who winked at me, and I wondered what he meant by it.

"So, Leaf," Momma said, "after going through all of that in order to be a better father, how do you feel about my daughter's decision to give away this child?"

"Ma'am," Leaf swallowed, "I came back here in order to support your daughter. And I am going to do that, no matter what it might cost me."

Something bloomed warm in my chest.

"Well," said Momma, "that's very noble of you, but my daughter is pregnant. A pregnant girl needs her mother around, not some ..." She looked at Leaf and then at my father, who shook his head quickly. Momma forced her mouth closed.

"Momma, you *are* around," I said. "Around the corner. It's very convenient really."

"Heather," Momma sighed.

But I held up a hand. "Please. Don't. You know *why* I have to stay in this house. Please just let it go, all right?"

An image of that young boy with a telegram in his hand cracked through my mind like a shot and I folded forward with the force of it. I pressed my palms against my face, trying desperately to stem the flow of tears that surged up. They washed away all thoughts of a future with Leaf, all thoughts of a future with Japhy, and in the darkness that was left behind, I was unable to imagine a future with even myself present.

I felt Leaf's wide hand on my arm, and then Momma's arms wrapped me up, and I cried on her shoulder while she rocked me and shushed into my ear and said the words that always seemed to fix anything: "Everything is going to be okay, love. Everything is going to be okay."

As I gulped in air and wiped my tears on her shirt, I wondered if she was just as big a liar as I was.

chapter sixty-two

japhy

Here is what I am thankful for:
   Blankets that don't itch.
   Muscles that don't ache.
   Mattresses that are not so thin you can feel the bedsprings in your back.
   I'm thankful for a full night's sleep, and an enjoyable meal, and a relaxing afternoon.
   Boredom.
   Privacy.
   Sex! Man, I am so thankful for sex! The oblivion that it brings. The way it frees the imprisoned, and uplifts the sorrowful, and reawakens the dead. The scent of naked skin, the feel of naked skin, and the way that pores sliding over pores sing like nothing else can.
   I am thankful to Kerouac for writing *The Dharma Bums*, to *Hyland's Books* for only having one copy available on that day.
   I'd like to thank the parents of James Lee Stanley.
   I'd like to thank the person who first married chocolate and peanut butter.
   I'd like to thank that one person who never gets acknowledged.
   And I am thankful for just *her*.

I am thankful for everything she has done for me, and will do for me in the future.

I'm thankful for light and dark and every shade in between.

And I am thankful for this war – this fucking war that has ripped my world apart like a wound – because it has made me thankful for everything that this war is not.

chapter sixty-three

ray

On a quiet, tree-lined street on the outskirts of Montgomery, Jim and Katherine Henshaw lived in a beautiful two-story home with shutters on the windows, a tire swing in the front yard, and a golden retriever named Lucky.

Next door, children took turns falling backwards into a pile of raked autumn leaves. High squeals of laughter wrapped around my stomach like a ribbon.

This was a charming neighborhood.

I stepped out of the van and smiled over at the two people staring at me from their front doorway.

"Hello!" Katherine Henshaw stepped forward with her arms held out to me. "Welcome. I'm so glad you could come." She embraced me, pressing herself gently against my belly.

"I hope the drive was all right?" said Jim, who, like his wife, enclosed me in a warm hug.

These were the two pairs of arms that would rock my child to sleep, and shield my child from harm, and pick my child up whenever it fell. And they were arms that felt strong and well equipped to do so.

"The drive was fine, thank you," I said.

"Please," said Katherine. "Do come inside. I've just made some hot chocolate and a batch of biscuits."

Leaf walked around the front of the van and joined us on the path. "That sounds wonderful." He forced a smile at the two people who would be raising my baby. "Hello, sir, ma'am, I'm Gabriel. Pleased to meet you both," he lied as he held out his hand.

"Oh!" Jim blinked at Leaf. "I'm sorry. I didn't realize you'd be bringing a ... a *friend* along."

For a brief second, I didn't think Jim was going to take Leaf's hand. Both the Henshaws simply stared at it. But then I blinked and they were all smiling and shaking hands like old friends, and I must have imagined there'd been any hesitation in the first place.

Inside, the house smelled of chocolate and love, a scent that any child would surely be happy to grow up with. As I crossed the threshold, I folded my arms across my stomach.

Leaf, Jim, and I sat at the table while Katherine fluttered around the kitchen, setting steaming mugs and a tray of warm biscuits before us.

Without waiting for permission, I grabbed a biscuit as light as a cloud and ate the whole thing in one delicious mouthful. "Oh my God!" I muttered, and reached for another.

We talked about how the pregnancy had gone so far, and if I had any medical history they should know about.

"And ... the father?" asked Katherine, keeping her eyes on the spoon as she stirred her hot chocolate. "Does he have any medical issues?"

"None," I said. "At least not according to the Induction Board."

"And what is your heritage?" asked Jim. "Where are you parents from? Your grandparents?"

"I'm Irish."

"And ... the father?"

"You know," I looked at Leaf. "I don't know."

Jim and Katherine glanced at each other.

"I think he mentioned once that his grandfather had an accent," said Leaf. "German, maybe?"

They smiled.

German? I thought. How come Leaf knew that about Japhy, and I didn't?

"*I'm* from Germany," said Katherine. "Somewhere along the line."

"Sheridan said the baby is due at the end of January?" asked Jim.

"Yes." I nodded. "The twenty-fourth."

"An Aquarian baby." Katherine grinned. "We need an air sign in the house."

"We'd better get that nursery finished soon, then," said Jim, "if we only have two months left."

"Would you like to see it?" Katherine stood and held out her hand.

No, I thought. No, thank you. I would *not* like to see the perfect room in this perfect house where my baby will be living its perfect life.

But I stood, and smiled, and followed Katherine down a bright hall to the first doorway. "We can't decide on the wallpaper …" Her words trailed off as she stared at the far wall where five swatches of paper had been stuck.

Anger – or maybe it was envy, I couldn't tell the difference – swelled from the very soles of my feet and surged upward, at her words. At the frustration I'd heard in them. At the fact that the only thing poor Katherine Henshaw and her husband had to worry about was which fucking wallpaper to use.

"The birds," I said, my voice too thick for my throat. On the wall, below a string of doves in flight, white feathers dropped from their wings. Dropped, but would never hit the ground.

"Yeah," Katherine crossed her arms. "That's the one Jimmy wants."

After about two hours of friendly discussion, it was time to say goodbye to this home where, soon, my child would be saying hello.

The Henshaws, arm in arm, walked us out to the van. After Katherine had leaned in for another hug, she paused. "Would you mind?" Her hand hovered above my swollen belly.

Yes, I thought. Don't touch me. Don't touch my baby.

But I smiled, and lifted my shirt. "Go right ahead."

She placed her palms on the curve of my skin and her breath hitched, her eyes welled. "Thank you so much for coming," she muttered.

As we drove away, Katherine and Jim stood out on the sidewalk, waving until we were out of sight.

"I've had a nice day," said Leaf.

"Really?" I said. "Because you looked in pain the entire time."

"Oh, no, I didn't mean *today*," he said. "I was just remembering one time in the past when I'd had a nice day."

"Well, *I* had a nice day, today," I said, and turned to look out the window so he couldn't see my eyes.

"I guess they seem like good folks," said Leaf after a long silence. "A good choice."

"A good choice," I repeated, wishing that the decision to give up this child had, in fact, been *my* choice to make. But when it came right down to it, there had been no choice, no other alternative. This was the only way I could save us all.

We drove for a while with no other sound but the hum of the tires and the drum of our hearts.

"Leaf?"

"Hmm?"

"What happened to make you turn yourself in to the police?"

He looked at me, blinked, and then turned back to the road. "Well," he sighed. "After I left you, I drove back to Canada."

"To Mandala?"

He nodded.

"Why?"

Again, he sighed. Grimaced. "I'm not proud ..."

"What happened?"

"I beat the shit out of that fucking junkie," he whispered.

I remembered the way Needles had always hovered near Lauren, offering her his promise of bliss. "Good!"

"No." Leaf shook his head. "I shouldn't have lost control like that."

"So, that's why you turned yourself in? Because of Needles?"

"No." He cleared his throat. "I couldn't stop thinking, what if? What if we never went to Kent State that day? My life would be completely different. I'd be a daddy. Lauren would be a mommy." He gave a quiet laugh. "Lauren would be *alive* ... So, what if, what if, what if! But, what if will never change anything. All what ifs do is make you go slowly crazy. And maybe that's what happened. Because somehow I ended up finding one of those National Guardsmen. I ended up sleeping in Nora's car every night and watching him come and go from his house. I ended up taking a job as a pizza delivery guy to save money for ..." His lips sealed over like a tomb.

"For what?" I whispered.

He took a breath and blew it out in a long whoosh.

"Leaf?" I asked. "What were you saving the money for?"

"A gun."

"Oh, Jesus." I covered my mouth with my hand.

"I watched this guy for about a week. Every time I saw him smile, I thought of all the smiles he has taken away from me, I thought of the future that he killed with one tiny curl of his index finger, I thought about how he has gotten away with murder, and how easy it was. How easy it could be ..."

I stared at Leaf. Even though I saw his lips moving around these terrible words, I could not believe they were coming out of his mouth. Had he killed a man? Had he dealt out his own form of justice? And how did I feel about it if he had?

That last question was the one that scared me most of all ...

I leaned forward, eager to hear the end of this story, and hating the rush of merciless excitement that pulsed in my veins.

"But then," said Leaf, "I watched this man come home, and a young boy rushed out the door to hug his father around the waist. A wife leaned up against the door jam and smiled across the yard at her husband. And I realized that if I killed him, I would be no better than he was. I would injure these innocent people's lives, I would steal their smiles with one tiny curl of my index finger. And what gives me the right to do that? Certainly not anger or vengeance. Heck, that's what started all this shit in the first place, right? So I started the engine and drove to the first police station I saw, because," he sighed, "I was scared I would end up changing my mind."

*

"Will I get to see the baby after it's born?"

I jumped at the sound of Leaf's voice in the darkness. "I thought you were asleep!" I said, pressing my hand against my racing heart.

"Will I?" he said again.

I rolled onto my back beside him. "I don't know," I breathed. "I don't really know what happens ... afterward. I never asked. I assume they just ... take it away."

I couldn't see his face contort at those words, but he winced. It was in the way his breath hitched for a second, in the way his body braced itself, in the way the air between us suddenly thickened.

"Yeah," he muttered. "That's what happened before."

"Before?" As soon as I said the word, I realized exactly what he'd meant, and I wished I could snatch that question back.

"We never got to see Sylvia. Lauren was unconscious when they ..." He sniffed. "And I was in the waiting room. I thought that, you know, if this baby *is* mine, and if I could see what it looks like, then maybe I'll know what Sylvia might have looked like. Maybe they resemble each other, you know?"

"Oh, Leaf. I'm so sorry that happened to you. But this baby is *not* yours."

"You don't know that for sure, Ray!" He threw back the covers and towered over me. "You don't fucking know that, and it *could* be my child, and you are taking it away from me!"

"No!" I said.

"Yes! You are! Oh Lord, give me patience ... right *now*!" He paced through the dark, back and forth like a caged animal searching for a way to escape. "You made this decision about my child, and I don't even get a say? I don't even get a choice? That is not fair!"

"Leaf." I sat up and switched on the bedside lamp. "Please don't ..."

"Don't *what*, Ray?" His hands fisted at his sides. Forehead creased. Eyes wild. "Huh? Don't what? Don't *care*? Well, I'm sorry, but I do care! If this is my kid then I want to be in its life. I want it to have a daddy that loves it. I want to be there for this kid, because that's what fathers should do! Christ, I'm trying to be supportive here, I really am, but fuck it's hard. This is killing me. This is absolutely killing me."

"Listen." I pressed my hands together in front of my chest, a prayer. Then I reached out and clasped his palms, as if giving him an invisible gift. "I got my period the day after we ... the day we left Utopia. I should've told you earlier, and for that I am sorry, but I guess I was still mad at you for just running off, and I was still really hurt, so a part of me wanted to make you pay for that a little bit, which is a terrible thing to do and I'm *so* sorry! But the father of this baby is *Japhy*, one hundred percent. Not yours. And not anyone else's."

He held on to my hands and squeezed gently. "You're sure?"

I felt the pressure release me as it released him. Felt myself rise up through the tides of his relief. Felt my face break through the surface and I gasped in a mouthful of clean air. My lungs filled with light. I looked him straight in the eye and shook my head. "I'm sure this baby is definitely *Japhy's*."

december

*And in the end the love you take
is equal to the love you make.*

- Paul McCartney, *The End*

chapter sixty-four

japhy

My days at the base drag by like wet pant legs and then, just like that, I'm back in the jungles again. The intense boredom of it all. The intense excitement of it all. It pulls at my limbs and makes me heavy. The whole thing has become a huge game of Russian Roulette. I am now addicted to the thrill of jumping out of a Huey, sprinting for the cover of trees, hugging my rifle to my chest and picturing the rounds of ammo still tucked away beneath my mattress.

This time, when I press fate's barrel to my temple and pull the trigger, will I hear the hollow *click* of an empty chamber, or the skull-shattering *boom* of a bullet?

Will this be the mission on which I finally learn whether it was a mistake or a blessing to leave behind the ammo?

Will this mission be my last?

I sigh. Because I know it *will* be Solomon's last.

He is now only thirty days short. Just thirty days! He can practically smell the jet fuel that will carry him home. What will this place be like without his laughter? Even more boring than it is now!

Around us, the jungle is silent as death. In the distance throbs the popcorn staccato of chattering guns and mortars. But here, right here, it is peaceful and dreamlike. The sun is low in the sky, and light slants through the greenery like rods of gold.

Ahead of me, Bricks pauses, struggling to reach his canteen.

"Here, man." I unclip it for him and hand it over.

He nods and takes a drink. "Think we'll see anything today?"

"Who knows?" I shrug. "It's as quiet as always. We've had hardly any stops. Hopefully that's a good sign."

"Hmm." He forces a smile. "Can I tell you somethin', Japhy?"

"Of course, man, anything."

"You promise you won't laugh at me?"

I nod. "I swear."

Taking a deep breath, he looks down at his feet and whispers, "I'm really scared. I'm scared of dyin'." He pauses and keeps his head down. "I never told that to no one before, but for some reason I feel okay tellin' you. Somethin' about you ... I don't know what ..."

"That's nothing to be ashamed of," I say. "We're all scared. Every last one of us."

"But the other guys, they all look up to me."

"Yeah, you're the tallest guy here!"

"You know what I mean. Because of my size I'm supposed to be this fearless, bear-like warrior or somethin'." He turns his face away. "You afraid to die?"

"Nope," I say.

"Bullshit!" He hisses. "You tellin' me you don't care if you die?"

"Not caring about dying, and not fearing death, are two completely different things, Bricks. I don't fear death because it will happen no matter what I do, so why waste time worrying about it?"

He nods as a single tear leaves a white trail down his cheek, cleansing away the grime.

"Realizing that death might take you in the next minute forces you to appreciate every second of life," I say. "All we have is the *now*. Even right now, being stuck out here in the middle of a war, instead of dwelling on the fact that I might step on a rigged grenade in the next few minutes, I look around at the trees and the sky and appreciate how beautiful it all is. Yeah, I am still shit-scared, but not of death."

"Then what *are* you scared of?"

I shrug and look around. "Leaving her behind."

"I wish I could do that. I wish I could think like that," he says, shaking his head.

"Haven't you noticed," I say, "that out here, with the aura of death thick in the air, you are more aware of how *alive* you are?"

"I guess so."

"Well, there you go. Just hold on to that feeling, and there you go." I smile at him and he smiles back. A real smile this time. One that is not hidden behind a smokescreen of fear.

"It's that simple, huh?"

"Yup." I nod. "Meaning of life, brother. Meaning of life."

"You're saying the meaning of life is that we are all going to die?" Bricks raises an eyebrow.

And then the whole world explodes.

chapter sixty-five

ray

A stranger blinked at me from the large mirror on the back of my old bedroom door. Her cheeks were fatter than mine used to be, her skin now milky and smooth. Her eyes far more piercing than mine had ever been, and her hair glowed down to her back in rolling brown waves. She seemed taller than me somehow, as if all the growing up I'd been forced to do over the last six months had manifested itself through physical stature. She wore a black gown that fell straight and loose over her ballooning belly, the sleeves puffed from shoulder to wrist, and on her head sat a matching cap with a yellow tassel.

"Look at you," Momma murmured. From over my shoulder, she met the eyes of this unfamiliar me in the mirror. "Such a beautiful woman."

A woman? I thought as I scrutinized myself standing in a room with my old single bed, and stuffed toys, and posters of The Monkees and Peter Tork on the walls. Yes, I guess I was a woman, wasn't I? When had that happened?

"Did you know," Momma dabbed at her eyes with a balled Kleenex, "I always dreamed about helping you get ready for your graduation? And then when you left, when you quit school a month before your final exams, I thought you had not only taken away my dream, but all of yours, too. But now look.

You came back! You've made mistakes, yes, but you're doing your best to clean them up, honey, and I could not be prouder of the woman that you are today. I guess there are some lessons that no school education can ever teach you."

"Like you can always rely on your momma," I said, and hugged her tightly.

"Always." She nodded, wiping at her eyes. "No matter what. Now, let's go; you don't want to be late for your own graduation!"

"I don't think it will start without me, somehow."

As we walked out to the second-floor landing, Momma kissed me on the cheek, wished me luck, and hurried down the steps, muttering about having to get her camera.

I paused, alone, on the threshold of this moment: behind me, my childhood; ahead, well, who the hell knew what was waiting there?

As I placed a shaking hand on the banister to steady myself, classical music swelled from the floor below me. Beneath the strains of *Pomp and Circumstance Number One*, I could hear Momma sniffling and blowing her nose.

Step by careful step I descended, unable to see my feet beneath the great girth of my stomach. I gripped the rail, leaning backwards slightly to counterbalance my weight, and waddled to the beat of the graduation song.

Don't fall, I thought. Not now. What kind of omen would that be?

I reached the bottom step and grinned across the foyer at Leaf and Momma, who stood, clapping and whistling at me as I remained on the raised stage of the first stair.

The music faded, and all three of us placed our hands on our hearts as a different song began and we opened our mouths and sang the words: "*Oh, say, can you see by the dawn's early light ...*"

When the Anthem ended, my father left the stereo at corner of the room and joined Leaf and Momma in the entry hall. We all laughed our way through the *Pledge of Allegiance*, and then my father asked Momma and Leaf to please be seated as he stepped up on the stage beside me.

"I'd like to welcome you all here today to celebrate this graduating class of 1970."

In their white plastic chairs, Momma and Leaf clapped their hands politely, and I gave a curtsy.

"Growing up in this age is not an easy feat," said my father, "and it is something each and every one of these high school graduates will have to discover for themselves. As parents, the hardest thing to watch is your child stumbling over the very same obstacles we did when we were young. All we want to do is take them by the hand and say, 'Kid, I made this mistake so you don't have to. Let me help you down the easy road.' But the truth is, in life there is no easy road. A parent has to watch that child fall. A parent has to let that child fall. And a parent has to be there to help them stand up again, because that is *our* journey. That is our lesson. And so, I would like to thank my daughter, Heather Wren, for being such a wonderful teacher." He turned and winked at me. "And now, without further ado, I would like to introduce this year's Valedictorian, Miss Heather Wren."

He shook my hand, and stepped down, taking the empty plastic chair between my mother and Leaf. He took Momma's hand and kissed it, and then he turned to Leaf and smiled.

As I looked down at these three people – my mother, my father, my best friend – I didn't see the ones who were not here today. I saw only the ones who were. I didn't think about the past, or even the future, because really what was the point? The past had happened and couldn't be changed. The future was unstable and uncertain and unpredictable. All that mattered was this second. *This* second. *This* one.

"Thank you, Mr. Wren," I said. "You know, you're absolutely right. In this life, it doesn't seem to matter how many plans you make, how many guarantees you put in place, how many rules you follow. The only guarantee you can rely on is that there are no guarantees. The only plans that matter are the ones that you make up on the spot. And the only rule you need to live by is to roll with the punches. Because I was punched. Hard." I shook my head. "And it dazed me so much that I lost my way. But, I found a new way. And who's to say that the direction I'm heading in now is not the one I was meant to take all along? The point I'm trying to make is ..." I sighed, "... that I have absolutely no idea what I'm talking about. And maybe not knowing is somehow the only way to get where you need to be." I grinned down at them. "If you had asked me a few months ago if I was happy, I would have laughed in your face. I would have said, 'How the hell could I be happy after everything I have been through? After everything my friends have been through? After all the unhappiness I have seen?' But if you ask me that same question today, my answer is, 'Hell, yes, I am happy.' And as for all that bad stuff I went through before, I'm not bitter. I don't regret being a part of any of it. I *can't* regret it, because all that bad stuff made me into the happy person who stands on this platform, smiling down at all y'all, and knowing that, for the first time, everything is just right. Everything is fine."

They clapped and cheered and Momma cried some more and I bowed, and then my father approached a small table beside the step, on which lay a sheet of paper and a white, rolled-up tube tied with a red ribbon.

"Ladies and gentleman, I will now proudly present the high school graduates of this year's class with their diplomas." He cleared his throat and lifted the sheet of paper, reading the only name written there in his own neat script.

"Miss Heather Wren." He called out my name and I walked up to him and he handed me the roll of paper, which I knew was blank but didn't really care – my real diploma was being mailed out to me by the Alabama Department of Education and should arrive some time in the new year.

As he pinched the tassel on my cap between two fingers and moved it ceremoniously from the left side of my face to the right, a tear slipped down his cheek.

I took the fake diploma in my left hand, and grasped my father's right hand.

"Congratulations, princess," he whispered. "I'm so proud of you."

"Thank you, Daddy."

We both turned, posed with our hands twined together,

and smiled at Momma as she clicked and clicked and clicked her camera, immortalizing that moment of pride onto a piece of film.

In the future, I would gaze at this photograph for hours, studying the light in my eyes, the glow in my cheeks, the radiance in my whole being. I would stare at this picture and marvel about how fast one of those fucking life punches could snap out at you from nowhere and launch you once again onto a whole different pathway. I would cry over that image and wish that I could shout a warning through time to myself to raise her fists, protect her face, and prepare herself for the biggest blow yet.

chapter sixty-six

japhy

I flatten myself into the dirt. Contour to the earth's surface. Become invisible. Around me, voices both curse God and pray to Him, as the earth's heartbeat rattles against my bones.

Whiteness blinds me. Seconds later, whooshing hot air claws at my skin. My ears ring from the blast.

To my left, I hear the chatter of an AK-47 rifle.

"Get him!" someone screams.

And Bricks raises himself up on one elbow. Brings his M-16 up to his shoulder.

All is silent as his rifle fires beside my head, blowing away all sound, so I don't hear Bricks scream as he flips backwards and writhes in the dirt, which turns to mud as blood pools beneath him.

"Medic!" I scream as I pull myself across the ground and press my hands down hard on the wound in Bricks's right shoulder.

I don't hear the bullets that come for us, I just see the spray of dirt that fountains up around us and I flatten again, covering my head.

Flashes of light burst like suns from Solomon's rifle and the fountains of dirt around me stop and Solomon's mouth forms the words: "Taste that, fuckers!"

He crawls over to us as sound returns; my ears ring and his words are faint whispers beneath it.

"Ain't this a blast!" He grins at me.

"Bricks is hit!" I yell. "We have to get out of here!"

He widens his eyes. "You crazy?"

"Are *you* crazy?" I ask. "We're surrounded by angry men with rifles who want to fill us with bleeding holes, and you want to *stay*?"

"Damn straight! I been waiting for this, man! This is my moment!"

"You're going to get yourself killed!"

"Maybe, but it's all part of being a soldier."

The ringing fades even further and I can hear my voice clearly now. "You're *not* just a soldier, Solomon! You're *not* just a useless pawn that is being used by your country. You're my *friend*. You're a man who deserves to get out of this place alive. You're a person who has to go home and help his country by loving it instead of killing it!"

"You get out, Japhy. Get Bricks out. I'll see you back at the base!" He turns from me, jumps up into a crouch, and disappears through the scrub, as the medic crawls to us.

He replaces my hand on Bricks's chest. "Hey, man," he says, leaning into Bricks's ear. "You're going to be just fine, all right? It's just a flesh wound." He looks up at me and grimaces and I don't know if that means he is telling the truth or not.

"They've called for a Huey," he says to me, nodding back the way we came. "Help me carry this guy to the L.Z."

"I'm fine," says Bricks, groaning as he sits up. "I can walk."

And then I hear a second burst of machine fire. But the piercing noise is nothing compared to the scream that follows it.

I remember the promise I made to Timothy so many weeks ago during training. *You will be coming home.* And then the trees and the scrub blur by me.

"Japhy!" Bricks calls after me. But I ignore him and dive through the trees ahead, searching for my screaming friend.

I run blind. Bombs steal my vision and replace it with light so bright all I can see are stars, or thick smoke that falls like night. I try to follow the sound of voices, try to let the screaming pull me forward, but the needle in my perception compass just spins in useless circles. I can't tell from which direction anything comes. I take a few steps toward Timothy's voice, only to hear him again a second later behind me. So I whirl around and head back that way, only to whirl around again.

But I keep crawling through the mud and rotting leaves. Through the razor-sharp grass cutting up my face and hands. Through the smoke choking me with the stench of burned hair and skin. Through the rain of bullets and explosions. Following screams that issue from nowhere.

And then I land on a body.

It takes me a few seconds for my eyes to adjust and focus and register what I am looking at.

A lucky rabbit's foot. It is no longer fluffy and white. But bright scarlet.

It is twisted around on Black Cat's neck so it lays against his back.

"Cat?" I whisper his name as I roll him over.

Words fall from my mouth, pour out of me like water, dripping over and over onto Cat's ruined and bloody face: "Oh-Jesus-Christ-Oh-Jesus-Christ-Oh-Jesus-Christ..."

I roll away and vomit. Then I vomit again, and again.

My eyes sting with tears and smoke.

My hands shake.

My throat burns.

My stomach squeezes.

I want to crawl up into a little ball, hide away, and wait until it is safe to come out again. But Timothy is still out here somewhere. Screaming.

At least I hope he is still screaming.

Slipping the bloody rabbit's foot over Black Cat's head, I hang it around my neck and crawl away into the smoke and the unknown.

And then a hand grips tightly to my ankle. I flail around. A scream opens like a flower in my throat, blooming, expanding, blocking my airway.

When my smoke-drenched vision clears, I see Sam's face, inches from mine, all blue eyes and red hair and white skin – as close to me now as he would have been to Ray in the back seat of that car. I smell his bitter sweat and his foul breath and his rancid fear – an acidic mixture that Ray would have wrinkled her nose against too. And the fear that choked me silent only seconds ago boils over into rage that blisters my conscience raw.

I could do it. Right now. Right here. I could kill him with my bare hands. Squeeze his throat like he squeezed hers. I could end him. Right now. In the middle of this war. And no one would ever know.

No one, that is, but me.

Sam stares at me. Terror is painted across his face like a mask, transforming him into a completely unrecognizable person. But his eyes, however; his eyes shine out at me and they glimmer brilliantly with deep and honest concern.

"Japhy!" He grabs my shoulders. "Are you okay?"

"Yeah. You?"

Ignoring my question, he rises into a crouch. "You're going the wrong way."

"No, I'm not," I say, pulling away from him. "I have to find Timothy."

"Don't be an idiot; you'll get yourself killed!"

"I don't care."

"Well *I* do!" he screams. "You have to get out of this place, man! You have to get back home to your girl."

I bristle at the mention of Ray. "Don't you dare," I spit, "don't you dare talk about her, don't you even think about her, you fuck!"

He grabs my shoulders again and shakes me. "You have to make a life with her! A great one," he yells over the boom of a grenade.

In the warmth of his grasp, I feel myself wilting. I close my eyes for a second and when I open them again, I see him differently.

"You're right," I yell back.

His face floods with relief. "This way!"

But I pull loose, shaking my head. "No. I meant, you're right about being a good guy." And then I punch him. Full in the face. One great, solid, wonderful *crack* of bone on bone. "And fuck you for making me admit that!"

I leave him on the ground and I run. Stumbling again through the jungle, I call out Timothy's name, and then my foot catches on something and I fall. My chest hits the earth and the breath is knocked from me.

The mounting-dread drone of my beloved Hueys grow louder, closer. I'm blasted with sound and wind as they tornado directly over me. And then everything is white.

I think for a moment that perhaps I am seeing heaven. Beautiful and pure and magnificent. But then a blast of scorching air throws me backwards into a tree as an accompanying boom arrives seconds later. There is a second explosion off to my left and I curl into a ball, protecting my face from the skin-melting heat. I am as small and insignificant as a tiny feather, being blown around by the breath of a storm.

I curl tighter. Waiting to be taken. Waiting for it all to be over. Waiting for peace.

Until I hear it. It wraps around me like the protective arms of angels. Her voice. Cool against my burning skin.

"Run," she whispers. "*Get up and run back to me, you stupid son-of-a-bitch!*"

Ray's voice is so clear in my mind that I snap my head up, sure that she must be leaning right over me.

"*Now!*" she screams.

Staggering upright as another blast tries to blow me down, I stumble forward, tripping over the helmet that has fallen from my head, and I keep running.

"No!" Ray screams. "*Go back. Go back!*"

Smoke-blind, I wheel around and drop to my knees, feeling through the dead leaves and fallen branches until my fingers sweep across the tortoise-shell of my helmet. Jamming it back on my head, I crouch and move again. Reeds and branches whip my face. Heat and smoke lodge inside my chest, which blooms in pain with every breath. But I pump my legs so God damn fast, and I jump and swerve and run, I just fucking run, until the smoke thins, and the screams fade, and explosions muffle with the pillow of distance.

Until I stand alone, gasping and crying in a beautiful rainforest where the pure tranquility threatens to tear out my heart.

The golden light cleanses my soul. The birdsong fills my chest with awe. The shushing of leaves soothes and calms me like a mother's hush in my ear.

And not even the Viet Cong soldier lying on the ground in the middle of the clearing can steal this magical feeling of calmness from me.

chapter sixty-seven

ray

"So what would you like to do?" Leaf asked me as he started the ignition. "Your wish is my command. Dinner? Drive In?"

"That would be lovely," I said, pulling the cap from my head and combing my fingers through my hair, "but I'd really like to just go home and lie down. Put my fat feet up. Relax."

"You don't want to celebrate?"

I shook my head. "Maybe tomorrow."

"But tomorrow won't be the day of your graduation."

"Are you really arguing with a pregnant woman?" I yawned. "My feet are sore, my back aches, I'm getting those Braxton Hicks cramps again, and I'm *starving*! So if you don't take me home right now, Gabriel Williams, I'll *eat* you!"

He chuckled. "All right, fine. Home it is."

As we pulled into the driveway behind Nora's little red car, I had my head down as I fumbled in my bag for the keys, which is why I didn't see it right away.

"We should get out of here," Leaf murmured, his voice low.

"No!" I said. My fingers curled around the cool metal of the keys and I popped open the door and slid out.

"Ray!" Leaf called out. "Wait. Stop!"

"What is your problem?" I said, snapping my head around to face him. As I did so, I caught sight of something white flapping in my peripheral vision and I turned to look at the front of the house. "My God," I whispered.

The porch railing was covered in toilet paper that wound around the beams of wood like bandages on a mummified corpse.

But it wasn't until I had my foot on the bottom step that the stench hit me.

I gagged and pressed my hand to my face. "What the hell ..."

And then my stomach tightened in fury. Written on the front door in brown, smeared letters of shit were the words: *Go home Niger!*

Idiots couldn't even spell right!

"Get back in the car," said Leaf, as I marched up the steps of the porch. He ran after me and grabbed my wrist. "Ray, they might still be here!"

"Yeah?" I said. "Good!"

I ripped at the sheets of toilet paper that sheathed the rails, rolling them up into a great ball that I then threw down on the ground. Stomping across the front lawn, I unrolled the garden hose and turned the water on full, closing the distance between me and that filth in one cleansing arc. I didn't know what was more disgusting: the excrement, or the meaning of the word it spelled.

The force of the water battered against the door and slowly the message vanished as if it had never been there in the first place. But the thing about the human language is that even when it isn't being spoken, you can still hear it. Even though the wood was now clean, I could still see those words there, as clear as my own hatred.

I turned off the tap, and then I stood, bending with the heels of my palms in my back. I groaned as the aches in my body pushed their way to the highest level of importance in my head. Taking a few slow deep breaths, and trying to ignore the stitch in my belly, I looked around for Leaf.

He sat on the porch swing, staring at the door. His face was drawn. His clothes were damp where he'd been splashed with the hose's spray. He shivered in the chilly winter air.

"Leaf?" I climbed the steps and sat beside him. "You all right."

He shook his head. "I'm sorry."

"What for? You didn't do anything wrong!"

"I'm sorry you had to clean up my mess."

"It was not your mess."

But he shrugged. "Wasn't it?"

"No!" I took his face in both my hands and I made him look at me. "Fuck them," I whispered. For a second, Leaf's face morphed into Japhy's on the floor of my bedroom, with his hand clutching his draft notice, his eyes full of terror, and our only option to run. When I blinked, Leaf was Leaf again, with that same fear in his eyes. "Fuck them," I said again, because I wouldn't run from the bullies this time. The war, the frat boys, the National Guard, the Grim Reaper, the racist vandals – they could all just go and fuck off because I would not let them intimidate me anymore. And I wouldn't fight them anymore either. "Don't let them in," I whispered, placing my hand flat on Leaf's chest. "If you do, then they win."

"So I'm just supposed to, what?" he said. "Just go about my day as if nothing happened?"

I nodded to him. "Be stronger than they are. Rise above it. Rise above everything."

"You're so good to me," he said. "I don't deserve that."

"Everyone deserves that." I took his hand and squeezed, and then I fumbled with cold, numb fingers, at his buttons. "Now let's get you inside and out of that wet shirt before you catch pneumonia."

"Why, Miss Wren," he grinned at me. "I thought you said you were tired."

As I opened the front door, he wrapped an arm around my waist and pressed his face against the slope of my neck.

Teetering on that glorious line between laughter and excitement, I was so focused on the heat from Leaf's lips on my skin that I didn't notice the suitcase in the middle of the room. So drugged by the high of Leaf's touch that the figure of the person staring at us was too blurry for me to recognize.

But when I heard her speak my name, everything blinked into perfect, sober clarity.

"Heather?"

Nora's gaze left an icy trail on my body. It slid down my arm, which was roped with Leaf's, our fingers knotted together. The skin on my stomach prickled with chill as she frowned in confusion at the roundness pulsing beneath my dress. Her gaze flicked toward the front porch, where trails of white toilet paper still flapped, and her mouth closed and then she looked me right in the eyes and I could see a hundred million questions all rising and squirming to get to her tongue first. "Um ..." she said in a soft voice. "Where are the chickens?"

chapter sixty-eight

japhy

He wears black pajamas and sandals made from an old rubber tire. He is tiny, with toothpick limbs, and if we were to stand side by side, the top of his head would not reach my shoulder. Surely just a boy. Fourteen, maybe? His eyes are closed. His stubble-free face pale. His left arm wet with blood; two of his fingers are gone.

It isn't until this moment that I realize I am clinging to my unloaded rifle. My chest aches with the bruising force of my grip. But I let the strap fall from my shoulder and I drop the hollow M-16 to the ground. Because suddenly I long for something heavier to wrap my arms around. Something with the ability to protect me.

Stepping forward, I place my feet carefully so as not to make any noise. The soldier's chest rises and falls, rises and falls, beneath the weight of an AK-47 rifle, whose belly is surely full of bullets.

I dive. And as I pluck it off him, something shifts from under his shirt and glimmers in the sunlight: a small, gold Buddha on a thin plait of rope around his neck.

The soldier groans, and I jump away, gripping the cold metallic body in my hands. It throbs beneath my palms. It throbs with its own life force, powerful and mighty and divine.

It's been so long since I've held a loaded gun. So long since I felt that pull and surge of godliness that sings through my blood. As I gaze down at the enemy, my head starts to tingle with pride and longing and satisfaction. I've caught one of the bastards. And I will end him now. I will end him for my friends whose lives have just been ended by him.

My hands shake; I take a steadying breath and tighten my sweaty grip on the wavering barrel.

How many people has this lowlife injured? Killed?

How just will it be that the soldier's own bullet will pierce the very center of his forehead. Point blank, motherfucker.

His golden Buddha winks at me in the light, and I squint away from it.

Search and destroy. That is our mission. Kill the enemy. Shoot anything that moves.

But this boy isn't moving …

I take another breath and grit my teeth.

Want to shoot some Cong. That's what I'd said to Ray in the jail cell. *Want to shoot some Cong* …

My finger slides on the trigger.

The soldier groans again.

Closing my eyes, I see a flash of him in my mind, jolting once and then lying still after the bullet smashes through skull. Turning brain to mush. Destroying all memories of love and family and faith that were stored within. And I see myself jolt too, as the ghost of a mirroring bullet smashes through my own skull, boring deep and mincing up everything that made me, me.

I drop the gun beside my own and kneel at the boy's side. Shrugging off my pack, I take out a bandage from the first aid kit. He groans again, louder, as I wrap gauze tightly around his hand.

He frowns and his small Adam's apple bobs up and down, up and down, as he tries to swallow. I take out my canteen and splash his face, rinsing blood from a deep gash in his cheek.

His features contort in pain, and then his eyes open.

They focus on me and brighten in terror.

But I put a finger to my lips and then raise my hands in the air. "It's okay," I say. "I'm trying to help you."

When I dribble some water over his lips for him to drink, he cries out and shakes his head from side to side, dodging the thin stream.

"It's okay," I say again, and take a big swallow. "See? It's not poison."

When I hold it out again, he hesitates and then opens his mouth wide, drinking in big swallows while watching me over the canteen with confused and frightened eyes.

From my C-rations, I offer him some dry biscuits. He sits up, takes one in his good hand, nods, and begins to chew.

"Sorry, they're not very good," I say.

So, I think as we stare at each other, this is my enemy. This is the big, bad Charlie that we, Uncle Sam, want dead.

But to me he is not an enemy; he is just a kid who, like me, has been forced into war. Just a young boy with a half-blown-off hand, and eyes that still have a trace of innocence at the edges.

"Japhy, what the *fuck*?" Sam's face is red and crisscrossed with welts. His left eye is swollen where I punched him. The deep concern for my safety is gone from his eyes now. And I can't quite recognize what has replaced it.

The barrel of his M-16 points directly at the boy's head. "Don't feed him, for shit's sake! Just shoot him and let's get out of here; they're sending more choppers."

I stand. "He's my ... my prisoner."

"He's a fucking Gook. Just shoot him."

"Come on, Sam, look at him; he's just a kid," I say.

Sam's brow dips into a V of confusion. "So?"

"So ..." I shrug. "Can't we just let him go?"

"Let him go?" Sam shakes his head as if a small insect buzzes around his ears. "Whose side are you on, Japhy? This is war, and he is our enemy. We have orders, and if you go against them, you're a traitor to your country!"

Am I a traitor? I wonder. As an American soldier, I am supposed to take this boy prisoner and drag him back to the base. Either that or finish him off right here. Maybe even cut off an ear, or a finger to take home as a souvenir; I'd heard stories about men doing that. This is war, after all. Search and destroy. Kill anything that fucking moves.

But I am not a soldier; I am a human being, and what right do I have to take the freedom, or the life, from another human? If I kill him, then yes, I will be a traitor – a traitor to myself, and isn't that the worst kind there is?

"Timothy's dead," says Sam. "I found him out there. Screaming and crying in pain. All crispy. Tried to pick him up and carry him out, but he disintegrated in my hands. Burned up so badly, the meat just fell off his bones. You know what the last thing he saw was before he died? The flesh from his legs in my fucking hands." Sam opens his fist and shows me the red-black grime that stains his palms.

No.

Tim?

Jesus.

I'm sorry.

He clenches his hand again and points to the boy. "And this slope is one of the ones who did that to him."

My stomach rolls.

"Don't you want to make him pay?" says Sam. "Don't you want to make this little shit pay?"

This kid killed my friends. My friends killed *his* friends. His friends killed other US soldiers ... When does the cycle end?

"Just look away, then," says Sam. "Look away while I do it."

"No." I take a step forward, blocking the boy with my body.

Sam blinks at me and I see something shift inside him, like dunes in a desert, whirling and changing in the hot winds.

"Pick up your gun and blow his brains out," says Sam in a soft voice, "or I will blow *yours* out and then his anyway."

"No, you won't," I say, but then I recognize exactly what it is that swirls in his eyes. I take a step back.

Sam cocks his rifle and aims it at my head. "I am an American Soldier. I am a member of the United States Army – a protector of the greatest nation on earth," he says. "I will use every means I have, even beyond the line of duty, to restrain my army comrades from actions disgraceful to themselves and to the uniform."

With my eyes locked onto Sam's, I bend down and feel around for my rifle – my unloaded rifle – my bluff. The only thing I have that may protect me. The cold metal brushes my fingertips and I keep my eyes on Sam as I lift it to my shoulder.

My palms throb with its useless power.

In my peripheral vision, I see the boy look from me to Sam and back again, as he slowly gets to his feet.

I shuffle sideways again, shielding him.

"I will not murder this boy, Sam."

"This is *war*!" he screams. "There ain't no such thing as murder *here*!"

"That's not true; if you want him dead, you will have to kill me first."

"Christ, I don't have time for this shit!" And Sam pulls the trigger.

Time slows down when you are about to die.

I watch the bullet unload from Sam's rifle and float toward me through the air like a sleek, shining butterfly.

The crack of the bullet entering my brain is all around me like a solid force, like giant arms of sound cradling me, rocking me, tackling me to the floor. I hit the dirt as the sound of a second bullet splinters open my world, as I lie there, as I wait to fade away, as I listen to a scream rise around me like a siren.

Sorry kid, I think. I tried, but I failed you. Just like I failed Timothy. Just like I have failed Ray.

But at least I didn't fail myself.

The wailing of agony gets louder.

And instead of me fading out of this world, the world starts to fade back in around me. My forehead throbs with a sharp ache. When I lift a hand up to feel the sticky remains of my skull, my fingers smooth instead across a swelling lump at my hairline.

I sit up and sway as the ground moves under me like the deck of a rocking boat. As the waves of dizziness ebb, I see that the boy is gone.

Not gone, as in *dead*. His body is not sprawled in the grass with a bullet in his brain. He is just no longer there.

All that is left in this clearing is my M-16, my helmet – upside down and still rocking from the bullet that blew it off my head – and Sam, rolling from side to side, clasping a bleeding leg in his hands, and screeching in a high-pitched howl: "You shot me! You fucking shot me, you fuck!"

Heavy in my lap is the AK-47 rifle. Smoke – thin, silver, almost imperceptible – uncurls from the barrel like retribution.

I crawl to Sam.

His screams slice like a shaking scalpel through my stinging head.

"It's all right man, just shut up, will you? I'll go and get help. You're going to be okay."

Still gripping the AK-47, I stumble away from Sam in what I hope is the right direction, and I hear his voice fading through the trees: "You fucker! Can't believe you actually shot me! You fucker..."

I run and walk and run through the jungle. With every jolting footstep, my forehead throbs in pain. It spreads over the top of my scalp, and down my spine, and I just want to close my eyes, just want to sleep, to not feel the ache of being alive for a while. My stomach rolls on an ocean of betrayal, rocking me with the shock of how close I just came to becoming a corpse. If I hadn't heard Ray's voice ... If I hadn't gone back to search for my helmet ...

Angry voices to my left freeze me in place like a frightened rabbit.

I crouch down.

I crawl forward.

I am invisible.

The grass thins out and I almost stand and rush forward and cry out, oh thank God, but relief chokes my throat silent. My body stills with calmness. My muscles slacken, and I drop on my knees.

It's over now. Everything will be all right. Because I have found my friends.

Ahead of me, Solomon and Lion are bent forward in

discussion, their faces inches apart. A cigarette dangles from Solomon's lips, jumping with every syllable.

Lion's hands gesture wildly, flapping on the ends of his arms like frightened birds.

Suddenly, Solomon steps back. "Are you all right?" His cigarette shivers. His words rise up, white as ghosts.

Lion has his back to me, hunched over, and his head moves side to side: no, no, no, no. As I watch, his shoulders pull back. His head stops shaking.

Solomon's cigarette stands tall, straight as a soldier between his tightly pressed lips. His hands open, palms out, as he raises his arms up high. "Lion?" he says slowly. "Brother?"

"I ain't your fucking brother!"

Even as I stand, even as I scream for Solomon to get down, even as I tell myself that the gunfire is coming from somewhere off in the distance, Solomon jolts in a strange, jerking dance. Roses of blood bloom from his chest while the cigarette continues to smolder, undaunted, in the corner of his mouth. As blood seeps from between his lips and stains the white shaft red, Solomon drops to his knees, falls forward, and doesn't move again.

Lion spins as my warning scream fades away. His eyes flash at me, sharp as diamonds. His lips curl. "Hey there, Battle Buddy." And he swivels the barrel of the rifle toward me.

Again, I am running through elephant grass. Not feeling the lacerations from their sharp leaves and not caring how much noise I make and not hearing anything but Lion's laughter and thudding footsteps.

I tell my legs to move faster, faster, but they get heavier with every step and I can hear the crashing of the brush behind me, and the panting of Lion's breath. He is so close. So close. Surely he can just reach out an arm and grab hold of my shirt. Or, better still, just lift his fucking gun and blow me away. He wouldn't even have to aim. Just hold the trigger and cut me in half. End me in one flashing second of brightness.

And then the brightness is gone.

The solidness of earth beneath my feet disappears.

I fall, like Alice down the giant rabbit hole.

Dirt walls rise around me like a grave.

Crumpling at the bottom of this pit, I cry out in horror at the bloodied bamboo spear sticking out of my right thigh. Pain clutches me, takes away all shock, all breath, all everything.

And then a shadow falls over me, and Lion's silhouette blocks out the sun.

Through my agony, I see him grin down at me. His teeth so white in the grimy surround of his face. That face now twisted and strange and unfamiliar.

My shaking hands raise the AK-47 and aim it at the lip of the pit. The image of those bullets blooming in Solomon's chest superimposes over everything I see as if I'm looking through a stained-glass window of red flowers.

What the hell? I think. Just what the fucking hell?

Cat is dead.

Timothy is dead.

Solomon is dead.

Sam is a traitor.

Lion is a psychopath.

I squeeze the trigger gently.

Lion's finger squeezes, too; I see the creases, the whites of his knuckles. When had the breaking point occurred for him?

When had he snapped? When had he been pushed past the point of mindless drone into comfortable insanity?

What will my breaking point be?

Through the waves of burning agony, I steady my breathing, try to think clearly, try to savor these last moments before I am killed, or I am a killer.

Either way ... I'll be gone.

My helmet, lost somewhere in the jungle, will not shelter me this time.

Lion's finger tightens further.

His breath whistles through his nose in fast little toots.

What if I just shoot him in the leg? It worked with Sam. And fuck, fuck it really hurts!

But I'll still be stuck down here, pinned like a rabbit with its foot in a snare, while he is up there determined to finish me off. A leg wound won't stop him for long. My only chance is to shoot to kill.

"Lion," I whisper, "please, put down your gun."

He shakes his head.

"Please, buddy."

"I ain't your fucking buddy." His smile widens. "You should have protected me. You should have taken me with you! But you left me there, with her, when you knew what she was like! You knew what she would do to me!"

"Lion!" I breathe. "I am not your father."

"You're damn right," he says, his lips trembling around a sob.

"*Japhy!*" Ray whispers in my head. "*Live!*"

So I do what she says. I pull the trigger, and the rifle spits death in Lion's face, and I live.

I slump against the cold earth wall. The chill seeps from the dirt into my skin and I start to shiver and rattle. In my hands, the rifle laughs at me and I throw it to the other end of the pit where I don't have to touch it again.

Lion is dead.

He is dead, and I killed him.

My bullet passed right through his snarling face and he crumpled to the ground with a satisfying thud.

I am a killer.

And I'm sorry.

I am so God damn fucking sorry.

Because, Jesus Christ, no, it feels *good*.

It feels absolutely fucking wonderful.

And I am so sorry.

When Sam told me Timothy was dead, I had looked at that Viet Cong kid and thought, even if he had been Timothy's killer it still doesn't give me the power or the right to kill, for then I would be just as bad as he was.

But now, I have killed Lion, and I couldn't care less if that makes me as bad as him.

And I wonder, does the fact that I don't care make me even worse? Does my lack of remorse make my act of murder even more heinous?

On the dirt around me, glittering in a million tiny pieces, is my vow: *I will never let this war change me. I will not let this war win.*

Well congratulations, Viet Nam.

A curdled mixture of pain and fear unravel my sanity strand by strand. As my lingering threads of logic fray, I see beneath the tapestry of reality into a world of vibrant color and sound and painlessness. I can hear music. A guitar being plucked to the beat of a slowly tapping foot. I begin tapping my foot, too.

"*I've been talking about what I don't know.*"

Someone is singing.

"*And I can't seem to mention what must show.*"

Someone is with me in this pit.

"*That I'm feeling unsure and somehow insecure.*"

Someone as familiar as my old self.

"*I don't know where the old me has gone to.*"

But it can't be *him*, can it?

"*But I'm gone, and I'm gone with no trace.*"

No way.

"*Yes, I'm gone and I'm gone ...*"

How on earth can James Lee Stanley be here, sitting beside me? And *why* on earth would James Lee Stanley be here, sitting beside me?

"*... With no trace.*"

Who cares! Because he *is* sitting beside me, and I can see him, and I can hear him, and I am going to let him sing to me without interruption.

"*On the edge of eternity crying. In the sea I can see people lying. Now my feet start to slide like I'm in some riptide. But it's me that is pulling me under, and I'm gone and I'm gone with no trace.*"

He still wears the Cookie Monster shirt he wore in the bar.

"*And it's like I stand beside me as I hear me cry ...*"

James sings in double harmony now, in two voices that sound strangely like my own.

"'*Am I drowning? Could I save me?' Then all at once I hang suspended from the look in my eye. And I'm choking on the wine they gave me.*"

Man, I am tired. I am so tired.

James raises up a beer in salute.

"*Now the father, the son, and his most holy ghost, raise their glasses to me, so I offer a toast to this place where we dwell, be it heaven or hell. And to life everlasting? Well, I wonder,'cos I'm gone, and I'm gone with no trace. Yes I'm gone, and I'm gone ...*"

My eyelids droop and I don't fight them anymore.

"*... With no trace.*"

As I fall into the darkness of my mind, away from all the pain, away from Nam, away from this pit, and away from James Lee Stanley, I hear him speak to me. "Don't look away," he says. And I want to tell him that I didn't look away. That I took his advice. But it's too late, he is gone, and then so am I.

Gone with no trace ...

*

It must be hours later when I wake, because the square of visible sky is dark now. Stars blink and shimmer. The moon peers down at me. And so do three Viet Cong soldiers, all aiming their rifles right at my head. But I just sigh, and close my eyes.

Wow. This just doesn't seem to be my day.

"Chieu hoi!" A VC with a squashed-up face and graying hair yells at me. In training we learned this Vietnamese phrase for surrender.

"Yes." I nod. "Chieu hoi."

One soldier grunts down into the hole beside me, confiscating my rifle. He speaks in fast, chopped up words, and they all laugh and point at my leg. Then he turns. He grins. And he pushes down on my thigh with one hand.

I buck at the waist and scream and push him away. But my arms are weak, weightless, rag-like. They simply flop and slap against him, feebly, and he laughs again, louder, as he tightens his hold on my leg and grips the bamboo stake with his other hand.

"No!" I cry out, realizing what he is about to do.

The thin spear slides through the meat of my leg like a skewer through chicken.

Rippling circles of pain undulate from the hole and break over me in foamy waves, flooding every cell of my body with scorching heat.

"Fuck!" I draw the word out into a long groan like an *Ohm* mantra. "Fuuuuuck!"

As the VC lifts me under the armpits, the edges of my vision pulse white, and blood freight-trains through the tunnel of my ears. *Whoosh!*

I sway, and lean against him as I grit my teeth and fight to remain conscious.

He speaks again – a high-pitched bark – and rips my dog tags off me in one quick tug. The back of my neck burns as the chain bites into my skin before it snaps. He throws my ID tags up to one of the waiting soldiers, who whoops as he jingles it in his palm, before kneeling down to make sure Lion's poor faceless and unrecognizable body is truly dead.

Teeth flash in my face as the soldier in the pit snatches Black Cat's lucky rabbit's foot from my neck. Then he dips his dirty little fingers into my pocket and steals away my heart. I try to back away but there is nowhere to go. Ray's letter catches a beam of moonlight; I see the little squiggle of a heart before the fucking cunt throws her precious words at his feet and grinds them into the dirt with his heel.

"No!" I pull away from him and try to bend down and snatch the letter back, but he just laughs and kicks me in the thigh.

Everything around me blasts with the bright threat of unconsciousness. I sag against the muddy wall and I sob great heaving sobs, as I watch, helpless, while the only piece of *her* I have is swallowed by the darkness of this land.

A long, wailing note streams from me, as thick and raw as pure vulnerability.

I don't fight them when they lift me out of the pit. I don't fight when they thread twine between my wrists in a figure-eight and pull it so tight my fingers pulsate. I don't fight when they jam the blood-covered bamboo stake behind my elbows, pulling my hands against my stomach so the twine cuts my skin. I don't fight when they loop a rope around my neck and lead me away like a dog.

I don't fight them, because these soldiers can do nothing worse to me than what I've already done to myself.

chapter sixty-nine

ray

"What in God's name are you doing, Heather?" Nora's eyes flicked in a triangle from my face, to where my hand plaited with Leaf's, to my protruding stomach, and back to my face again. It made me dizzy. "Andy loves you! How would he feel if he knew about ... *this*?"

I dropped Leaf's hand as if it burned me. "Andy *does* know about this!"

"I don't believe that."

"Are you calling me a liar?" I crossed my arms, while beside me Leaf buttoned his open shirt.

"If you are saying my son would approve of you holding hands with another man, then yes, Heather, I am calling you a liar! Or completely delusional."

"I can prove Andy doesn't care!" I said. "I have letters."

"And what about Poppy?" said Nora. "You can't tell me she approves of this? Where is she, anyway?"

Leaf's head snapped around to stare at me, but I couldn't face the question I knew burned bright in his eyes.

"What's the problem, anyway?" I said to Nora. "You act like love is a bad thing?"

"Love?" She narrowed her eyes. "You two are in *love*?"

My stomach clenched. Probably shouldn't have said that. "You wouldn't understand."

"No, *you* don't understand!" She cut me off. "You young people today, you have no idea what love is about."

I took a step toward her. "Actually, we know *exactly* what it's about. In fact, we know more about it than your generation ever will, because you are too close-minded."

"Close-minded!" She spat out a laugh. "Well, if loving one man with all my heart for twenty-two years makes me close-minded, then yes, I guess I am close-minded. I assume that poor Poppy is as close-minded as I am, huh? Is that why she isn't here? Did she leave when you two decided you were *in love?*"

"Ray?" Leaf said softly.

Another pang of dread gripped me around the middle and I hissed in a sharp breath.

"That poor girl," whispered Nora. "How could you do that to her? After everything else she's been through."

"You didn't tell her?" hissed Leaf.

I clutched at my stomach, grimacing slightly.

"Do I need to ask who the father of *that* is?" Nora pointed a shaking hand at my stomach, which seemed to recoil painfully from her outstretched finger.

"It doesn't matter," I said.

"Oh, no, of course it doesn't matter! You are absolutely right, Heather. Why should a child know who its biological father is? I suppose you all plan to raise it together, do you? All *four* of you, just one, big, happy family?"

"We don't plan on raising it at all," I said, lifting my chin. "I'm putting it up for adoption!"

That shut her up. That one shut her right the hell up.

And while her mouth was clamped shut, I used the cover of her silence as a chance to turn and run from the devastating questions that would be coming from both of them any second now. Firing at me as quick and deadly as bullets.

If I ran fast enough, if I ran far enough, the net of lies I had woven would not be able to trap me.

I heard footsteps behind me, but I didn't care anymore.

I heard unanswered questions clawing at throats, but I didn't care anymore.

"Ray!" Leaf was right behind me, but I didn't care anymore; I didn't care what they would think when they learned my truths. I didn't care about any of it.

Because I was suddenly doubled over on the porch. On the very spot where Japhy had first kissed me. Where Michael Mack had collapsed. Where I had confessed my love to Leaf. Where vandals had smeared shit. And now, where a widening circle of amniotic fluid spread around me and pooled hot inside my shoes.

I didn't have the strength to keep going anymore. Lies had fueled me these last few months, and had propeled me with the inertia, with the momentum I'd need to get me through what was coming. But now, with truth surging warm and wet down my legs, all that previous thrust sputtered and stopped dead. I couldn't remember how to move at my own speed without those burning lies driving me forward.

I *want* to give up my child.

Adoption *is* the right thing to do.

Everything will be *fine*.

Those lies were empty now. Because what had previously been just words would now have to become actions. Actions I would have to perform. Somehow.

I saw myself in a hospital bed with a bundle of blankets in my arms. Soon, two tiny pink fists will wave from within the folds of fabric. Sheridan will step forward, her arms outstretched toward my baby, and my own arms will straighten, lift the small weight of the child away from my chest and into her hands ... Where did that kind of strength come from?

I sagged backwards against the doorframe, too weak to stand, and I felt Leaf's arms wrap tightly and securely around my waist.

"Whoa!" he gasped. "It's all right, I've got you. Everything will be fine."

"Jesus," Nora said. "Well, if that really is my grandchild, you are not giving birth to it on my vandalized front porch."

Leaf lifted me up, and I curled against his chest like a child, closed my eyes, and began to whimper, "I can't do this, I can't do this ..."

"Yes, you can," he said. "Remember what you just told me. You are strong. Rise above it. Rise above everything."

By the time we arrived at the hospital, the contractions were coming fast and strong. I didn't cry out against them. I didn't wish for the pain to stop. Instead, I clutched on to every single agonizing cramp; I held on to each one as tightly as it held me. Because as long as those pains kept ripping through me, it meant that I still had my child. It meant that, for these last few precious moments – however wonderfully excruciating they may be – it meant my baby hadn't yet been taken away, and was still mine.

"You're doing great," Leaf said as he carried me through the hospital foyer and into an elevator. "Just breathe through the pain. It will all be over soon."

I sobbed into his chest as the aching in my heart swelled through my body, eclipsing even that of the crippling contractions.

As the elevator doors opened onto the labor ward, he said the words again. Words that were supposed to calm me. "It will all be over soon."

A nurse with shiny brown hair pinned at the nape of her neck in a perfect figure-eight rolled a wheelchair forward. "Heather Wren?" she said. "Your mother-in-law telephoned to let us know you were coming. We're all ready for you."

Leaf lowered me into the seat of the chair, but I scrabbled at his shirt, "No!"

The nurse peeled my hands away from him. "I'm sorry, sweetheart," she said, "but no one is allowed in the birthing room." She turned the chair and Leaf was simply gone from my view. Taken away in a single second of changing perspective.

I tried to swivel in the seat, to get one last glimpse of him, but we rounded a corner and I saw nothing behind me but a blank wall. Nothing but emptiness.

The nurse pushed me into a room with a bed in the center, upon which she and a second nurse lifted me. They were both shushing me, and patting my head, and telling me that everything was going to be fine, but Christ, didn't they know that was the biggest, fattest fucking lie of all?

"Here, sweetheart," said the nurse with the shiny hair. She rolled up my sleeve, slapped the skin inside my elbow, and slid a hypodermic into the vein that pulsed, hungrily. "Everything will be fine," she said again.

As she turned away from me, I realized that the knot of her hair, the figure-eight, lay on its side like the symbol for infinity. I stared at this intricate braid that went on and on forever. It became smaller and smaller, grew farther and farther away, as I sank down through my own body, through the bed, through the floor, and away into a place where there was just nothing at all. A nothing that went on for infinity.

Inside the warm, floaty depths of Twilight Sleep – a blissful cocktail of morphine and scopolamine – a mother is protected from the pain and stress of childbirth, and knows nothing about being shaved, about being sliced, about having her baby pulled from its warm cavity with forceps.

But I saw it happen. I swear to God, I did. I saw the moment my daughter rose up over the horizon of my belly like the most beautiful sun that ever transformed the darkness. Her skin was slick with blood and mucous, but I could see its paleness. Its definite Japhyness. Its definite *un*Leafness. I saw her, so small in their hands, as they cut the cord and lifted her away from the heat of my body. I saw them take my baby away. I saw them take Japhy's baby away. And in that moment I knew I had made the biggest mistake of my life.

I tried to call out, but I could not.
I tried to reach out, but I could not.
I tried to take it all back, but I could not.

I was sucked back again into the depths of twilight, where I was helpless, where the night blinded me, where there was no more sun to transform the darkness. And perhaps there never would be again.

chapter seventy

japhy

I don't recall getting here. Just being here. And being here, and being here still. For how long, though? Fuck knows. Time stops in this place. But isn't that what they say about the afterlife? About hell? That time does not exist in the spirit world?

Here, the soft sound of a grown man weeping seeps like chill through the thick cement walls.

Here, the concrete floor is as cold as a dead body beneath me. It makes my bones ache. But aching is good. Aching means I am still alive.

Here, the air smells of rotten food, sweaty bodies, and human shit.

My prison cell is small, cozy. I have a tiny, barred window high in the discolored wall. I have a comfortable concrete slab for a bed. A warm and welcoming rusty iron door. Home sweet fucking home.

I pull myself up to look out through the bars. It is daylight. The sky is a wonderful powder blue. Lazy clouds drift past as mockingly insouciant as freedom itself. Closing my eyes, I try to remember the cold softness of blades of grass on my bare feet, or the soothing kiss of wind on my cheeks, or the hot body of sunshine pressing seductively against me. I try to remember, but there is just ... nothing. Just these cold walls and the icy angst that emanates from them. Or maybe the chill is not coming from *outside* my body at all?

As my arms give out and I drop from the window in a heap of dirty clothes and useless flesh and raped soul, I stare down at my swollen leg, which throbs like hammer blows.

How much blood have I lost? I wonder.

How much blood can you lose before your soul drains out as well?

Grunting with effort, I rip both sleeves off my shirt; I roll one into a ball and press it down against the black hole in my thigh, and then I grit my teeth and count one, two, and on three I cinch the other sleeve tight around the wound and let out a searing, hot scream.

Tears wet my cheeks as I slump back onto the cold cell floor, gasping. I focus on the pain in my leg, delicious and all-consuming. It ravages my body and my mind like a lover. It takes me where my thoughts can not follow: a place where, for at least a little while, my own guilt can't reach me and I can writhe in the pleasure of that burning freedom. The only freedom I will probably ever know for the rest of my life.

Beads of sweat tickle my skin as they slide over me, one after the other, constantly, and I lie there, floating in the lake of my own saltiness. Burning with fever. I feel tiny little soldiers, wearing tiny little uniforms, carrying tiny little rifles, skulking through the tunnels of my veins, flushing out the enemy, the infection, that wants to kill me. Because surely, without medical reinforcement, my tiny little army will be overrun, and wiped out.

I don't move when the heavy door slides open. I don't have the strength to even open my eyes. And I don't really want to, anyway.

But when I hear it clang shut again, I force my neck to turn on its stiff hinge, force my eyelids to rise, and force my vision to clear.

By the door is a bowl and a cup.

A gurgle rises out of my throat, a strangled prayer of thanks, and I roll over and try to crawl.

My arms barely lift me. My good leg flops, useless. And my

breath can't come fast enough to sustain me for longer than a few minutes before I have to lie down, face to the concrete, and just breathe.

Minutes pass. Or maybe hours pass. Or maybe my whole lifetime has passed by the time I reach that stupid bowl and that stupid cup, which have become the only two reasons for living now.

Freedom? No, thank you.

Painkillers? Nope.

Ray? Ray who?

My brain, my thoughts, my everything is now a mute servant to the physical needs of my body, which does not want to give up just yet, thank you very much. All it wants is food and drink.

I grasp the cup first, bringing it slowly to my lips. My hands shake and I almost start to cry as I watch precious drops of water spill over the lip and fall in slow motion to the cell floor. But, oh, the wetness on my lips, my tongue, my throat ... well, that must be what heaven feels like. It coats me from the inside out, and seeps deep, flooding me with God, Himself.

Two mouthfuls and the cup is empty, but my body is saturated again. Blessed.

The bowl is full of cold rice. I grab the sticky grain by the handful and shove it into my mouth, hardly bothering to chew. Just grab and swallow.

And then, with a full stomach and a blissful mind, I lie back down and let the fever take hold again.

This isn't so bad, I think, as I fall away from myself. I can survive this with my eyes closed.

*

I am kicked awake. The squashy-faced Vietnamese man leans over me. He startles when I flinch, and we both jolt away from each other.

"Get up!" he hisses and shuffles over to wait at the open door.

Once I stand, he ties my hands with that fucking twine again, and jabs me in the back with the barrel of his rifle, pushing me through the door, and steering me down a corridor of closed doorways, and then into another concrete room.

On one wall, hanging like dead snakes, are leather whips in all different lengths and thicknesses. Like the deadly reptiles they bring to mind, they instill fear. What could they do to me? What have they already done to others?

And even worse than the whips are the four meat hooks, glinting silver, above my head like shiny crescent moons.

I look away from them, focusing instead on the floor to try and steady my rapid breathing and racing pulse, until I notice the concrete is splattered in dried blood.

"Please," I say, turning to the man who brought me here. I press my hands together in front of me and bow to him. "Chieu hoi." I repeat the words for surrender, hoping it is still imbued with the power to keep me alive. "Chieu hoi? Mercy? Please don't hurt me!"

His lips stretch thin and he unties my smarting wrists.

"Thank you!" I say, bowing again. "Thank you."

But then a second man appears behind him, and they each take one of my hands and tie me to the wall. My arms are outstretched to the sides, my legs are not strong enough to hold me, and I wilt there, Jesus-like, waiting to be crucified.

"What is your name, rank, and serial number?" the second man asks.

I stare at him for a second, taken aback by his almost-perfect English.

He steps forward and punches me in the ribs. "It is in your best interest to answer me, Yankee."

Yankee? I think, and I would have laughed if I'd had the breath.

"What is your name, rank, and serial number?"

I shake my head, trying to remember, but everything is blank. "I don't know."

He punches me again. "If you answer me with truth, then you will be taken out of solitary confinement."

"Andrew Mack," I gasp.

"What is your rank?" he asks. "Are you a Lieutenant?"

"No," I shake my head. "I'm no one."

And the man smiles. Keeping his eyes on mine, he takes out a knife and slices away my clothes with the finesse of a butcher. "What was your mission?" He lights a cigarette and blows the smoke in my face.

"Search and destroy," I whisper, staring at the knife.

"How many of my men did you kill?"

I blink and meet his gaze then. "None."

He chuckles. "You lie. You had one of our weapons."

"It's the truth," I say. "There was a North Vietnamese soldier, a young boy, I found him, injured. I helped him. I saved his life!"

The man draws deep on the cigarette, which glows like a demon's eye. "You are a liar." And then he touches the smoldering end to my nipple. "What were your orders?" he yells over my screams.

"I don't know!" I gasp through a pain-clenched jaw. "To flush out the enemy?"

"The enemy?" He steps closer and I can smell the sadism on his breath. "This is not *your* country," he says, and he laughs as he grinds the cigarette into the shriveled tip of my penis. "*You* are the enemy here, Yankee, not me! Take him down!"

I can no longer see through the tears of agony that blur my vision; my blistered dick hurts worse than my impaled leg, and I would gladly throw myself onto another punji stick rather than suffer this horrific burning.

My ropes are loosened and I drop to my knees, cupping myself. But touch makes the sting so much worse.

The two men force me to sit with my legs out straight and my ankles bound with more twine so I can't kick.

"No!" I cry out, like a desperate child. "Please?"

But they don't care. They don't stop. They don't help. Behind my back, they tighten a pair of wooden cuffs on my wrists with a ratchet until my bones almost fuse together to form one single limb. My fingers throb and swell up like bananas.

One of the men laughs as he pushes my head down

between my knees, ties a rope to the cuffs, and then yanks it upwards, pulling my hands right up over my head.

Just before I pass out, I hear a strange, musical popping as my shoulders slip out of their sockets, and those men just keep right on laughing.

*

The world is dim and unfamiliar. Cold. The floor beneath me shimmers and falls away. The real world cracks apart and vanishes beneath the agony that surges over me like a vicious and angry wave. It pounds. Pins me down. And I can not breathe. Or see. Or think.

Salt fills my mouth as tears drown me. I can't cry out or scream, for no sound exists to convey this level of pain. I just lie there, silent, while my body cries instead.

From the waist up I fizz and sizzle like too-hot oil in a pan and I can't tell what causes it.

From the waist down, my right thigh singes and blisters in the heat of its own oozing infection.

And in the center, my crotch crackles amid its own flames.

Kill me, I want to scream. But I forget how to form words.

So, I just lie there and pray for Death to hear my silent plea.

But when the answer comes, it is not Death that brings a salve of enlightenment. It is an angel.

"*Keep fighting, God damn you!*" hisses Ray.

And I sob at the beauty of her voice.

"*Your shoulders are just dislocated,*" she says. "*That's all.*"

That's all? I think. That's fucking all? Jesus Christ, Ray!

"Yes," she says, and suddenly I see an image of Solomon with bullets ripping apart his life; I imagine Timothy lying still as time on the jungle floor; I see Lion's face splitting apart and I hear Ray again. "*That's all.*"

That's all. Just dislocated. I just need to pop them back in. That's all.

So I clench my jaw, and I force consciousness to stick with

me as I use my one good leg to stand and limp over to the cell wall. Before I can hesitate, I throw my shoulder against it.

I bounce off and my legs fold and I land on the floor, where I listen to someone screaming and screaming and screaming.

"*Get up!*" Ray shouts over the noise.

But I can't even shake my head at her words; it hurts too much. "I'm sorry," I gasp. "I'm sorry."

Her hands are warm on my chest, and then they move to my leg and I flinch away as her fingers inspect my wound.

"Sit up!" she whispers in my ear, but her voice has changed; it is deeper now, her words clipped and quiet. "Let me help."

The thin threads holding me to consciousness snap and twang as hands loop around my chest and lift me into a sitting position. And I hear those screams of pain again.

The weight of the entire earth presses down on my left shoulder as my useless, floppy arm is lifted and twisted, and – sudden bliss – the agony flows away like a retreating tide. The same thing happens with my other shoulder, and as relief surges forward, I hear the scrape of my cell door closing.

Wiping my face, I blink around, but no one is here. In the corner, only a bowl and a cup watch me. I crawl to them gingerly, and lift the water to my lips.

But as I swallow and take the cup away, I see something gold glimmer at the bottom. I drain the water, and then let the object slide into my palm.

A small gold Buddha on a thin plait of rope.

Laughter echoes around the cell. It comes back at me and wraps around me like the arms of a lost friend. And I know I am no longer alone.

Time continues to tick forward, second by long second, and I survive.

The sun rises. The sun falls. And I survive.

My wounds heal.

I survive.

And I wait.

Because *he* will come back for me. I know he will come back for me.

I hide the Buddha necklace in a crack in the wall, I run my

fingers along it, proving to myself that I didn't imagine finding this gift in the bottom of my cup. Proving to myself that he will return. Proving to myself that he was here, that he helped to heal my shoulders, and that surely he will come back for me.

Soon.

He will come.

The boy whose life I saved out there in the jungle. The enemy soldier whom I should have killed, but instead shielded from a bullet with my own body. The one person who will therefore surely rescue me from this hell.

He owes me.

But then, what if he already *has* paid me back? He slipped my dislocated shoulders back into their swollen sockets, and then left that necklace for me to find. What if that was it? Debt paid? Thank you for your custom!

Or what if it wasn't even him? I mean, I never saw this person. What if it was just the camp doctor who goes around popping shoulders back in place so they can be dislocated again next time? What if I'm just grasping on to this delusion of being rescued because the truth is just too heavy to bear? Because, in reality, no one is going to rescue me, and I will remain in this cell until the end of the war, or until I die, whichever comes first.

The bolt on my cell door slides in its barrel and the sudden noise rings through the air, chiming with a whole new note, trembling and vibrating like a rusty tuning fork that never expected to be struck again. It is the sound of pure hope. And I sit up as the door scrapes open.

The boy steps forward and we stare at each other. Light floods into the room, silhouetting his small frame in a golden halo.

I stand and take a limping step toward him, pressing my hands together and bowing to him. "Thank you."

"No!" He shakes his head quickly. "You don't speak!" And then he lifts up a loop of twine and knots it, tight, around my wrists. "You come with me."

The twine cuts into my skin and I frown down at my hands. "It's too tight," I say, "it's hurting me."

The boy grins at me then, and his face ages into that of an enemy soldier. "This pain is nothing."

"Wait," I whisper. "Please, help me!"

"You want help?" he snarls. "Answer the questions correctly!"

No. I shake my head as he tugs on the twine and I stumble after him through the doorway, where a second soldier steps forward and jabs his rifle in my back. No, this is not how it's supposed to happen. Maybe he doesn't recognize me? Maybe he doesn't remember what I did for him?

"Please," I say. "Don't you know me? I saved you. I helped you. Please tell them. Tell them!"

But then again, I think, as I remember that flash of glee I'd just seen in his eyes, maybe he just doesn't give a fuck? He *is* the enemy, after all.

And I'm nothing but a stupidly optimistic, karma-believing, delusional pacifist en route to the torture chamber, being led there by my last remaining sliver of hope.

*

The sunlight is so shockingly unexpected that I can't step through it. The absolute brightness of pure light pressing against my naked body holds me in place.

"Move!" The VC boy jerks me forward, pulling me. He is surprisingly strong for such a small boy.

I stumble to a patch of scrub, where he trips me and I drop to the dirt.

Panting and gasping, I stare at the unobstructed sky while I wait for his bullet to pierce my skull.

When I hear his feet shuffle toward me, I try not to let my heart race. I don't want my last moments laced with terror. I keep my eyes on the beautiful blue sky, and I breathe slowly, calmly, knowing that at least I will die staring into the beautiful blue of freedom.

Until black material covers my face and the sky is stolen.

Fuck you, I think, as blood pounds faster in my veins.

Fuck you, I think, as my hands begin to shake.

And fuck you, I think, as tears burn my eyes.

"Put these on." His voice is low and right down in my ear. "Hurry!" He cuts my hands free and lifts my foot. I feel soft material against my skin as he slides my leg into a pair of pants.

I rip the shroud from my face to see that it is not a death hood at all, but the top half to a pair of black pajamas. The boy smiles at me as he helps get my arms through the sleeves, and then pushes a cone-shaped straw hat on my head. Onto my feet he slides a pair of sandals with rubber tire soles and inner tube straps.

"There." He sits back on his heels and squints at me. "Now you are invisible. But we must hurry; the other guard will notice we are missing any moment. Do you think you can run?"

I struggle to my feet and limp over the uneven ground on these surprisingly comfortable sandals. Pain flashes in my thigh with every step, but I just close my eyes and keep going.

"What is your name?" I puff.

"I am Binh."

I point to myself and breathe: "Japhy."

He bows slightly as he repeats my name: "Japhy."

"You saved me." I don't say these words to him; I say them to myself, to hear them out loud. "You saved me." Because maybe hearing them will help me believe this is really happening. That I am free from my cell. That I am outside in the light of the setting sun. That I have survived.

"There is an American base not far from here," he says. "You will end up lost and maybe get caught again, so I will lead you."

"What will they do to you?" I ask. "The other guards? When they realize you let me go."

His lips press into a line. "I will say you fought me and escaped. It was not my fault. I will not be harmed." His voice wavers as he speaks and he keeps his eyes away from mine.

"Will they kill you?" I whisper.

He takes a long breath. "I owe you my life, good Japhy," he

finally answers. "And I am honored to give you back your life, no matter the cost."

"No, Binh, you can't go back there!"

But he just smiles. "I must."

When I open my mouth to argue, he shakes his head at me. "One year ago, my whole family was killed by South Vietnamese soldiers; they thought we were Viet Cong, and they wouldn't listen when we tried telling them otherwise. They burned my whole village, and I heard my mother and sisters, screaming, trying to escape the fire. I wanted revenge. I quit university, where I had been studying medicine, and signed up for the North Vietnamese Army. I thought, if I can kill enough of the South's army, eventually I will kill someone who was there when my family died." He pauses and looks up at the sky, which is streaked in a bloody red, and getting darker with every second. "But recently I was involved in an attack. I killed four American soldiers. On one of them, I found a photograph of his family: a woman and two small children. And I realized that he was a person, just like me. I realized that every man fighting in this war has a life, a family. I realized that I had become no different than the murderers who burned my village. From that moment, I did not want to be a part of it. I do not want to cause pain to people anymore. But," he sighs, "it is not my choice. I must fight in this war. My country is forcing me."

"Man, I know how that feels," I say. "Come with me to my base. They will help you; *I* will help you. I promise."

Binh raises his eyebrows. "Now *you* are the one offering *me* freedom?"

"Freedom?" I smile and wrap my arm around his shoulder. "Oh, I can tell you how to find freedom, my friend!"

It is dark now and we stumble through the trees, with Binh begging me to rest every few minutes. Every step on my wounded leg is more painful than the last. Sweat beads and falls like rain with the effort it takes to just keep on going. I huff and pant and gasp in pain. But I will not stop, I will not rest, until we reach the safety zone that gets closer with every single agonizing stride. Not until I stagger home, with Binh right beside me, not until I know he is safe too, will I rest.

And I will be taken to a hospital, and maybe even discharged as a wounded soldier. I could be home again in a matter of days! And Ray ...

"It is not much farther," says Binh. "Just through these trees."

I walk faster, suddenly numb to all the aches in my body.

Ray.

For me, this war is over. Finally fucking over. And I made it. I'm going home.

The excitement burns so brightly inside my brain that it shoots up into the night sky like a flare lighting up the entire heaven.

"Get down!" Binh pushes me to the ground, and I realize that the light in the sky, which is still falling slowly back down to earth, is very real indeed.

"It's a trip flare!" I say. "They know we're here."

I push myself up into a crouch and peer through the grass, and I hear someone shout: "There! I see them! VC!"

I struggle to get words out, but they are blocked by the chokehold of fear as I look down at myself, and at the black pajamas that clothe me. And, had I not been looking down at that precise moment, I would not have seen the grenade roll silently past my left foot.

I kick at it. Feel its solidness against my exposed toes. Hear it thunk back down in the grass somewhere that is still far too close to where we stand.

I grab Binh. I push him forward. And we run like hell.

We run until we fall.

We run until everything that is, suddenly, just *isn't* anymore.

chapter seventy-one

ray

I woke to the sound of an infant crying. To that unmistakable bleating rasp of a newborn. Jackknifing in my bed, I tried to search for her but my vision blurred; I was blinded again by searing pain that stabbed between my legs. I cried out from the shock of this severe and unexpected ache, and fell back against my pillows with my teeth clenched.

"They don't tell us how much the afterward part hurts, do they?"

I heard a woman's voice to my left, in the same direction as the crying baby.

"It gets easier, though," she said. "After a few days you'll be able to walk around almost normally. My name's Claire, by the way. And this little guy is Matthew."

Slitting open my eyelids, I turned to see a woman in a bed next to mine with a blue blanketed bundle in her arms.

"Where is my daughter?" I asked.

"Oh, you had a girl? That's nice. But when did you see her? I've been here since they brought you in. They haven't brought her by yet."

I frowned around the room. "Where is she?"

"The nursery is just down the hall." The woman nodded

her head toward the doorway. "But if you just press that button there, a nurse will come. They'll bring her in."

I threw back my covers and whimpered as I clambered off the bed. The room swayed and sweat beaded on my forehead and upper lip with the strength it took to ignore the pain.

"You should really get back into bed ..." said Claire.

"I have to stop them from taking my baby!" I staggered across the room and leaned against the door to catch my breath. Exhaustion sagged me and I couldn't take another step. The pain in my middle spread down my legs and up my spine. But then the baby, Claire's baby, Matthew, started his pathetic bleating again, and the sound was anesthesia for my battered body. That sound, that desperate cry of a child to its mother, eclipsed any discomfort I felt. My child, my *daughter*, was just down this hallway. If, I thought, she still was *my* child. How long had I been unconscious? How long had she been alive in this world, unclaimed by her mother? How long would it take before perfect Mr. and Mrs. Henshaw came and took mine and Japhy's baby to make her their own?

But, surely, they wouldn't even know she was born yet. I wasn't due to give birth for weeks, so maybe this would all be fine after all. Just like everyone had been telling me. Just like I had been telling myself. I could call Sheridan right now. Let her know I'd changed my mind. I mustn't be the first birth mother to do that?

There was a payphone at the end of the hall, beside the elevators; I'd go there in a minute and call her and cancel the whole thing. And, once I hung up, everything *would*, in fact, be fine after all.

But that could wait.

I shuffled along the corridor, taking birdlike steps. Sparrow hops. Whimpering and gasping, while my heart fluttered like a hummingbird in my ribcage.

I was about to see Japhy again.

I'd forgotten the exact angle in the shape of his jawline. The up-curved slope of his nose. The way his face softened in sleep. And now, I was only seconds away from seeing those features again. After all this time. I was so close to him. So close.

As I rounded the corner, I saw three people standing at the open doors to the elevator. Two of them, a husband and wife, stepped across the threshold, and I heard the man say, "Yes, thank you, Sheridan."

Recognition froze me.

"We just want to start our new life as a family right away."

"Of course," said Sheridan. "I'll be in touch."

"Thank you again," said the woman, adjusting the weight of the baby carrier in her arms.

"No, wait!" I said as the doors slid shut and Mr. and Mrs. Henshaw, and that baby carrier, were gone.

Sheridan turned then. She did a double take when she saw me, a statue in the hallway.

"Heather!" she said. "I didn't realize you were awake. I was just about to come and check in on you."

I shook my head. I backed away from her. I closed my eyes and leaned against the wall.

"It's all right, I've got you," she said, gripping on to my arm and steering me to a row of chairs near the elevator doors.

"How did you know I was here?" I whispered. "How did *they* know?"

"Dr. Smyth called me to let me know you were in labor. I called the Henshaws, and they wanted to come right away."

"My baby," I moaned, thinking of what Leaf had said the other night. "I didn't even get to see her."

"Why are you even out of bed so soon, anyway?" She looked around. "Are there no nurses on this floor? I should call someone."

"No," I said. "I'm okay."

But I wasn't. I wasn't okay at all. And when the tears started, and the sobs wracked me, I didn't know what else to do but surrender myself to it all. What was the point in fighting now, anyway? Who did I need to be strong for? I'd lost everything.

Sheridan draped an arm over my shoulder. She rocked me, so gently, and whispered, "Would you like to see her?"

"Who?" I gulped and blinked at her. "Mrs. Henshaw?"

"No." She smiled and smoothed my hair out of my face. "Your baby. Would that make the process easier for you?"

"My baby?" I choked on the huge possibility of that word. "I don't understand? The Henshaws ... they took her away."

Sheridan sat back in her chair and looked at me.

"I heard them," I said. "They said they wanted to start their family right away. They were holding a baby."

Sheridan shook her head. "Mrs. Henshaw had brought a capsule with her for transportation. But there was no child inside."

"So, my baby ...?"

"Is still far too small to be released," said Sheridan. "She's quite impatient. A month early. I don't even have the official paperwork ready for you to sign yet."

"But I already signed the papers ... Months ago ..."

"Didn't you read them, Heather? The papers you signed were simply to allow us to handle your case. You can not legally consent to adopt a child out until it is born. Now that she is here, I'll get the lawyers right on it. Unless," she blinked at me, "you are having second thoughts?"

"Am I allowed to do that?" I gasped.

Sheridan took my hand then. "Heather," she said, "you don't have to do anything you don't want to do."

"But the Henshaws ..."

"Will be disappointed, yes," she said, "but they will also understand. They too know what it's like to want their own baby."

I nodded and the words began to gush, unstoppable. "I'm sorry, I really thought it was best for everyone if I placed her up for adoption, but it really wasn't what I wanted, and I should have told you I'd changed my mind, and I'm so sorry for wasting your time."

"Haven't I been telling you all along that this is your decision, and no one else's? Not your mother's, not your partner's, and certainly not the Henshaw's. You haven't wasted my time, Heather, you've allowed me to place your baby in the best home possible. With you."

This time, when the tears started, and the sobs wracked me,

I didn't just surrender myself to it all, but exalted in it. I bathed in the cleansing salt of my own tangible relief.

She was still here. She was still mine.

"I thought I heard familiar voices out here."

I hiccoughed and took a steadying breath as Leaf's soft words washed over my skin, calming my racing heart.

Swiveling in my chair toward him, I felt every cell in my body buzz in anticipation. He had stepped out of the nursery doorway and walked toward me, wheeling a plastic crib. Momma walked beside him, her arm linked through Leaf's elbow. She beamed at me and then gazed down at the plastic crib again.

At the sight of that small, orange box, my fingers started to tingle, desperate to reach inside and touch the skin that was also made of Japhy's skin.

"She's real small." Leaf glowed. "But she's perfect. Absolutely perfect."

Gritting my teeth, I pushed myself up from the hard plastic seat and took a step toward my baby. My heart thumped in my ears and with every beat I heard the question: Is it Japhy's? Is it Japhy's? Is it Japhy's? Because despite all the lies I'd told myself over the last few months, despite all the reasurances that this was *his* child, I knew the reality. I'd known it the whole time. I just hadn't known how to face that truth. But the truth no longer mattered. The only thing that mattered in this world, the one thing that mattered most, was love.

Just love.

Some people say that hearing God would be like hearing every sound in the whole world at the same time. That's how I felt as I gazed down at my baby. My breath stopped and she became everything in the whole world. She was every sound, every color, every emotion, all at the same time.

She was heaven.

She was love.

And she was mine.

She blinked up at me with big blue eyes. Her skin was smooth and pale as cream. And her hair ...

"Congratulations, *Mom*." Sheridan said.

I looked up, elated by the sound of that word.

"Take good care of her." She looked from me, to Leaf. "Both of you." And she smiled. "I know you will."

"Oh, I will," I said. "Because nothing makes love grab hold of your heart more forcefully than the threat of it being taken from you."

"Wait." Leaf frowned. "You mean ...?"

"We're keeping her."

Momma gasped and grinned and held a hand to her heart.

Leaf's lips pressed together hard, and he blinked back tears. "That's wonderful," he said. "Japhy will be so pleased, so proud, to be her daddy."

"Yeah," I whispered. "I sure do hope so."

Sheridan winked her goodbye at me and pressed the button on the elevator, and when the doors slid open, Nora stepped out.

I stiffened. I didn't know what to say to her.

The two women smiled at each other politely as they swapped places. The doors closed, Sheridan was gone, and Nora filled the entire corridor with an energy that I could not place.

"Nora," I gasped her name. "I am so sorry ... about everything ..."

"Stop." She held up a hand. "It's okay. Leaf and I have been talking. He's filled me in on quite a bit. Oh, Heather, I am so sorry that you felt you had to go through the last few months alone. That you had to endure all this by yourself. I wish you had told me, but I understand why you didn't, and I am very grateful to you for allowing me the time to get well, but still, I wish you'd felt you could talk to me."

"You mean, it's okay?" I asked. "After everything I've done, it's okay? Just like that?"

"Life is too short to worry about the past, right?" She sighed.

"But ..." I shook my head. "But I lied to you!"

She shrugged. "There are far worse things in this world. I only wish your lies were the worst of them." Blinking, she looked away before she spoke again. "I want you to know that you are always welcome in my home. My door is open to you, and Leaf, for however long either of you wish to stay."

"And it won't be just *us*, now," said Leaf, grinning. "Ray is keeping the baby."

"Oh!" Nora clutched a hand to her throat as she choked on a sudden sob. "That's wonderful. Because once you have a child, Heather, the thought that they will be taken from you ..." She choked again, blinking tears, and finally stepped forward to look down at my baby, as if she'd been gathering the strength to do this ever since stepping out of the elevator. "She has Michael's eyes! She has her grandfather's eyes." She looked up at me then with gratitude spilling from her. "And what about you? How *are* you?"

"I'm fine," I said. "Everything is fine." And, oh, it felt wonderful, so wonderful, to be able to hear my own words and finally *believe* them.

"I hope I can be like you," Nora whispered. "You are so strong, Heather. Your heart is the size of the moon. And I hope that nothing, *nothing*, will ever change that. No matter what."

And that's when I noticed that she held something in her hand. A small, yellow square of paper. "What is that?" I heard the words but didn't know how I had forced that question from my throat.

Nora stiffened.

And then she crumpled.

She slid, boneless, onto the seat where Sheridan had sat only moments ago. Back when the world had been completely different. Back when everything had finally been fine.

The telegram floated to the floor, as light as a feather, and I watched as Leaf stooped in slow motion to pick it up. His mouth thinned into a line as he lifted the paper that was surely as heavy as the entire earth. And then he cleared his throat and read out the typed script. "The Secretary of War regrets to inform you that Andrew Michael Mack, Private First Class, has been killed in action."

Everything flared, white-hot, around the edges of the telegram. Deep breaths. No breaths at all. Chest tight. No air. Room swayed. And that telegram. That small square of paper.

Nausea. Dizziness. Sharp pains. Stabbing pains. Heart, lungs, stomach, intestines, pancreas, kidneys, bladder, brain. And I was nothing.

Japhy was dead?

Killed in action?

Bullshit!

"There you are, Miss Wren, and what do you think you're doing out of bed?" Oblivious to the pall of shock and grief that was filling the length of the hallway like rushing floodwaters, a nurse smiled down into the crib and said, "I see you found her, then. And isn't she a pretty one! Does she have a name yet?" She poised her hand to write on a small piece of card.

"Yes." My voice was thin, raspy, as if the words scraped my throat raw with every syllable. "Her name is Ryder. After her father."

*

"For the last time," I sighed, "Japhy is *not* dead."

Leaf slumped on the end of my hospital bed. Crying. Again. And it pissed me off. It had been a week. A whole week of people telling me that Japhy was dead, Japhy was dead, Japhy was dead, when I knew, I *knew*, that there'd been some kind of mistake and that – wherever Japhy was – he was as alive as I was. Why couldn't they sense it too?

"I *know* he is not dead." I spoke slowly, calmly. "I can still feel his presence in this world. If he were dead, I wouldn't be able to feel him anymore; he'd be gone. Just gone. But he *isn't* gone: I can still feel him, so he isn't dead!"

Leaf sighed and wiped his eyes with the paisley tie he wore.

I smiled at that. "But if he really *were* dead, he'd sure get a kick out of you wearing his threads today."

"Ray, I know what you're going through," Leaf said. "When Poppy died, I didn't want to believe it either. But you have to accept the reality of all this. His body is home. The funeral is today, and …"

"And I'm not going," I said.

"What?"

"I'm *not* going to that funeral."

"But ... you have to go."

"I don't have to do anything, Leaf. Even if it really were Japhy's funeral – which it's not – I still wouldn't go. It's just an excuse for the military to make a big show, to pretend to care that another person has died. They don't care! If they cared, they wouldn't still be sending boys Over There to be killed and have *more* military funerals!"

"If it isn't *his* funeral," said Leaf, pinching the bridge of his nose, "whose is it, then?"

"I don't know." I shrugged. "Did you see the body? Because I didn't. It could be anyone."

"It is him. He was positively identified. I don't want to believe it either, you know? I wish more than anything that he was okay, and he wasn't lying in a coffin right now, but he is! And I'm sorry for being so harsh, but this denial you are in is not healthy. Maybe if you come to the funeral, it will help you to accept ..."

"I'm not going!" I kicked at the dress that lay across the foot of my bed. It slid over the edge with a shush and crumpled to the floor like a boneless, grief-stricken widow.

"I just," Leaf shrugged, "don't want you to regret it later."

"Regret what? Attending some stranger's funeral? I'm sure I'll be fine, Leaf, but thank you for your concern." The bed groaned beneath me as I climbed down. "Now, if you will excuse me," I said, "it's Ryder's feeding time. And if you don't want to be late for this farce you're attending, you'd better leave too."

"What am I supposed to tell Nora?" asked Leaf. "I'm sure she'll be counting on your support today."

I paused in the doorway. "Tell her she shouldn't be going either because Andrew Michael Mack will be coming home." And I stepped out into the hallway leaving Leaf, and his unwillingness to believe, behind me.

I ignored the nurses as I passed by their station. Ignored the pathetic smiles they flashed at me. Smiles that dripped with venomous sympathy. Smiles that said, "Oh, you poor dear. I'm so sorry for your loss."

Completely unnecessary smiles.

In the nursery, inside a plastic crib with a card that said *Ryder Lauren Mack*, my baby girl slept. Although she'd been tightly wrapped in a pink blanket like a chrysalis, she'd managed to extract her two tiny fists, which balled beneath her tiny chin. As I stroked a finger over the softness of her cheek, something surged inside me, hot and fierce. My daughter, I thought the words with pride. My daughter, as my fingertips brushed the soft skin. Mine and Japhy's daughter, as I smoothed the thick shock of red hair. My daughter who will never again be taken from me and who will soon meet a father that is definitely not dead.

"Hey, little one." I sat in a plastic chair and stared at the rise and fall of her chest. I imagined her little heart contracting and pulsating, sending life to every cell in her body. And as I pictured that tiny beating heart, I knew that somewhere else in this world, Japhy's heart was doing the exact same thing.

Ryder stirred and yawned and opened her eyes: deep blue pools.

Gathering her up into my arms – arms that now felt useless unless they were holding her – I unbuttoned my nightgown. My breasts were hard as rocks and just as heavy, and as her rosebud mouth opened wide and she drank from me, taking love in liquid gulps right from the source, I sighed with relief as the pressure inside me released.

I couldn't believe she was all mine. That I had made a person. That I could be so in love. That I had doubted the possibility of that love.

God, I could stare at all the little details of her face for days.

And, indeed, before I knew it, hours had ticked by. It scared me how fast her life was already passing, and how hypnotized I was by her every breath.

"Excuse me? But are you Ray?"

The voice was not familiar, and I turned toward it. The speaker was a blond man who leaned on a pair of crutches.

Deep sadness darkened his blue eyes, visible even from a distance.

I stood. "Yes, I'm Ray. Do I know you?"

The man swung toward me on his crutches. "I'm sorry to drop in on you like this, but you weren't at the funeral and I wanted to meet you. They told us you'd be here."

"It's over, then?"

He nodded and held his hand out to me. "My name is Timothy Murdoch. I was a friend of Japhy's. We were in Nam together."

Instead of taking his hand, I wrapped my arms around his neck and hugged him. His warm skin muffled my words. "Welcome home."

"Yeah, well." He looked down at the floor and shrugged. "I wish we hadn't come back without him, you know?"

I ignored that.

He leaned forward to peer into Ryder's blankets. "Oh, she's beautiful. Japhy would have been so proud. He was always telling me how he couldn't wait to get home and start a family."

"He was?" I whispered, and tears prickled me.

Pointing to a plastic chair beside mine, Timothy cleared his throat. "Do you mind?"

I wished he would just leave me alone. But this man had been Over There with Japhy. Maybe he knew something. Maybe, with his help, they'd be able to find him. I scooted a chair over to him and he winced as he sat.

"What happened?" I asked, leaving my question open.

We both stared at the baby rather than at each other as if, by not looking into each other's eyes, Timothy could speak about the horrors he'd been through without me having to see those memories screened across his retinas.

He started in a whisper. "We were walking through the jungle and it was so quiet, it was almost peaceful. Then suddenly, *boom!* We walked into an ambush. They'd boxed us in. I saw three men die right before my eyes in a matter of seconds. They just fell. They were alive one second, the next they were dropping to the ground. And the way they hit the dirt, you could just tell, you know? They were ... empty. Seeing that – seeing how easy it was to go from a living being to nothingness – it freaked me. I couldn't move. My mind kept screaming at me to get the hell out, but it was like my body was no longer connected to my brain or something.

"And then I heard him. I heard him calling me. Searching for me even as the bombs and guns were going off. He came closer and closer. But I just ..." He shook his head. "I just lay there. I didn't answer him. I didn't move. If I had ... maybe ..." He looked at me then and I saw the sharp, splintered shards within him. "It was my fault. He came back to find me and the God damn asshole got himself killed. There was another explosion and the force of it threw me backwards and I couldn't hear him anymore. I got burned up pretty bad." Lifting the cuff of his pant leg, he revealed the white gauze of bandages. "One of the other guys in the squad found me. Sam. He just picked me up and carried me to where the rest of us had gathered, waiting for a chopper. I remember seeing about ten guys from our company, ten of my friends, lying on the ground, wrapped in their ponchos. All dead. The first time we saw any action and it almost wiped everyone out.

"I told Sam that Japhy was back there still. He didn't even hesitate; just turned and went straight back into the fire to look for him, but ..." Timothy shrugged. "Anyway, I thought you'd want to know that's how it happened. I never saw Japhy alive again."

"You mean you haven't seen him *since*," I corrected.

Timothy frowned at me. "That's what I said."

"No, you said you didn't see him *alive* again. But you didn't see him *dead* either, did you?"

"No ..."

"So, you can't say you never saw him *alive* again, because you will," I said.

Timothy gave one of those horribly sympathetic smiles I was used to getting from the nurses. I took a deep breath and fisted my hands, digging my fingernails into the meat of my palms; pain dammed the words that frothed like a river in my throat.

"They kept telling me I was lucky," Timothy said. "But I

lost all my friends in one fucking go. Cat. Solomon. Bricks. Lion is still missing. And Japhy. That's not lucky."

"They'll find him." I touched his arm. "Don't give up on luck just yet. Japhy is still out there somewhere, and they will find him."

He took my hand. "They found his body."

I wanted to turn away but couldn't.

"I didn't want to believe it either, Ray. I prayed there was some kind of mix-up. I prayed so hard. That's one reason I came here today. Not just to say goodbye to a good friend, but to make sure ..."

"And can you be sure? By seeing a box lowered into the earth," I said. "Can you be sure?"

"Yes." His eyes continued to hold mine, pleadingly, and he leaned forward. "He was there, Ray. I could just ... just *feel* him there."

"You're wrong." I hissed. "And you mustn't know Japhy very well, because even if it were his body in that casket, his spirit would never attend a circus that *celebrated* the reason it was there."

Timothy frowned at me.

"If Japhy *was* dead," I explained, "then his spirit would be right here, right now, in this room, with me. And I don't know about you, but all I can feel in here at the moment is an unwillingness to believe in miracles. So, I don't mean to be rude, but if you are finished polluting this room with your denial and negativity then I will kindly ask you to leave." I stood and turned my back on him, staring down at Ryder and trying to focus on her calming influence.

"I'm sorry for your loss," Timothy whispered. "I ..." He sniffed. "I loved him."

Past tense?

I closed my eyes and clenched my teeth. "Get out."

"All right, I'll go." There was a scrape of chair legs. The shuffle of shoes on linoleum. "I'll wait in the hall. There's someone else here who wants to speak to you."

Sighing, I rolled my eyes. "It doesn't matter how many of you parade through here, it's not going to change my mind about ..." I turned to see Timothy leave the room and a second man walk in. His head was dipped sheepishly, and he held his hands clasped at his chest like he were praying.

I closed my mouth tight, trapping a scream, but it clawed at me so fiercely I wrapped my hand around my throat to make sure the flesh of my neck wasn't ripping into ribbons as the cry thrashed, imprisoned, within me.

Ryder struggled as I clasped her to my heart with so much force she began to wail.

"Get away from us!" I moaned the words, pleading them. "Get away!"

The man with the blue eyes and the red hair and the white skin held a hand up between us. "It's all right, I won't hurt you." Then he closed his eyes. "Not *again*, anyway."

Tears dripped from my soul as the memory of that horrible day in the back seat of his car roared back to this present moment.

At first, I'd tried to seem interested, to play along, to make him lower his guard so I could take him by surprise and escape. But he hadn't lowered anything besides his pants, and by the time I'd tried to fight him off, it was too late. He'd pinned me down and held me there with his massive weight and I could do nothing but wait for it all to be over. It's just sex, I'd told myself, over and over. Just sex, just sex, just sex. I'd repeated those words in rhythm to his clumsy thrusts. And then he'd cried out, and shuddered, and gone limp as a blanket atop me, and I was finally free to run from his grasp and wrap myself in the warm protection of my own lies, where nothing bad had ever happened on that back seat.

"What do you want?" I said, trying to sound as strong as I could.

"I just wanted to say I'm so *sorry* for what happened that day."

I sucked in a breath. "You want me to forgive you?"

"Yes," he said, simply. "Japhy did."

I rocked backwards at the sound of such a sacred name being spoken by lips that had once forced mine open, by a tongue that had cleaved my mouth, by breath that had threatened to end me.

"You lie." I shook my head. "Japhy would never forgive you!"

"It's true." The frat boy nodded. "He told me I was a good guy. And then he punched me in the face for forcing him to admit it. He forgave me, Ray. I don't expect you to, but I guess I just wanted you to know that *he* did, before he died." He took a step backwards. "That's all. And congratulations, too. Your baby is beautiful."

My baby.

I looked down at the eyes that were just like this man's. At skin that was just like this man's. At hair that was just like this man's. And a sob of undeniable truth bloomed from my throat like a crocus flower breaking through the snow.

All this time, I'd denied the reality to myself. Ever since I'd been told I was pregnant, ever since I'd calculated the days of conception, I'd convinced myself that I could not keep this child because it would be what Japhy would want, because it was the only way to right past wrongs, because, because, because ...

But not once did I let myself think of the truth. Not once did I admit there was even a *slight* possibility that this innocent life – a life which had grown inside me, been nourished by my body, and soothed by the drumming of my heart – that this innocent seed had been planted within me by any other gardener besides love. Because how would I ever be able to love a face whose eyes blazed in my nightmares? Whose lips smiled in that same sneering curl? Whose heart was made up of the DNA cells of a rapist? How could I keep a baby when there was even the slightest chance that I couldn't love her?

But now, as I looked down into her face, as I held her warmth against my chest, how could I regret her conception? How could I hate this horrible man for what he did to me, when it has resulted in her life? How could I *not* forgive him for making me the happiest person in the world? So, yes, I realized that I did have to forgive him, but there was no way in hell I was going to tell him that.

All throughout my pregnancy, hidden way back in the dark corners of my mind, I'd wondered if a baby conceived without love could ever truly know that emotion. But I know now that, as her mother, it is my job to ensure that every single second of this beautiful child's existence will overflow with adoration in order to make up for what had been absent in the moment that her soul had curled within me.

"You can leave now," I said, "before I call the police."

"For what?" His eyes narrowed, wrapping me up in the vice-like arms of the past. "You have no proof," he hissed. "The only other person who could back you up is dead. And they wouldn't take your word over mine; I'm a decorated American soldier! I'm a fucking hero! I risked my life to save him; you should be thanking me! You should be asking *me* for forgiveness! I got *shot* because of your stupid boyfriend." Putting his hand in his jacket pocket, the breast of which glinted with a medal, he threw something across the room.

It tinkled onto the floor at my feet, but I refused to look down to see what it was; I kept my eyes firmly on the man's face and I braced myself to scream if he took just one step toward me.

"I'm sorry," he said again. "I really am." And then, like a nightmarish monster in the bright light of dawn, he was gone.

My tears splashed the floor, pooling there beside the thing the frat boy had thrown. I reached out toward it slowly, as if it might suddenly rise up like a snake and strike. And once I realized what it was, I did feel something puncture me like venomous teeth.

In the palm of my hand, gleaming in the harsh glare of the overhead fluorescents, were a set of army-issued ID tags with stamped letters that spelled out MACK, ANDREW M.

*

In the cemetery, I knelt on the wet grass. A cold wind slid its icy fingers inside the neck of my jacket and frosted my skin, but the metal of Japhy's tags radiated heat against my heart, a protective amulet that warmed me against any chill.

Closing my eyes, I placed my palm onto the dirt of the freshly covered grave. I visualized the six feet of soil beneath me. I went deeper and imagined the dark mahogany-stained casket. Inside, I pictured the champagne-colored satin that lined the walls with soft, undulating ruffles. And I saw the shadowed, faceless body, dressed in the uniform that had killed it. Breathing in, I drew up energy from the earth, and summoned any trace of familiar warmth. But I felt only cold grit beneath my skin. This was not the body I had loved. I exhaled a smile.

But, I wondered sadly, was there a family out there somewhere, waiting to hear the news of the safe discovery of their missing soldier? News that would never be delivered to them because his body had instead been mistakenly identified and buried beneath my feet? This poor unknown soldier whose small gravestone was inscribed with the lie:

Andrew Michael Mack
September 14, 1950 – December 9, 1970
Forever free

I traced my fingertips across the carved letters and numbers and I whispered, "Where are you?"

And in answer, a memory spoke. "*When the sun sets on this union, may you meet again in the one place that is sacred to both of you.*"

And that's when I knew. If Japhy really was dead, there was only one place he would go.

... Imagine we're alone in the mountains and I'll be there just loving you ...

I had to go to Matterhorn. I *had* to. There was no choice. It was our last unfinished adventure, the place that was sacred to us both, and the only place where the truth truly waited for me.

*

The Christmas tree stood naked in Nora's living room and the house smelled like pine, like the clearing Japhy and I had slept in a lifetime ago. But now, I sat beneath the boughs, not with Japhy, but with my daughter.

A box of decorations was open on the floor and Nora removed each shiny bauble and string of beads with care, only to replace them all again once she found what she was looking for. Not one item would be hung on the branches this year. No lights would drape these leaves. No tinsel would hang and dance and shine with the glorious joy of Christmas cheer.

Because in this house, Japhy had always been the one who decorated the tree. And so this year, there would be no Christmas cheer.

Finally, Nora stood and held aloft a small angel. "Here she is!"

Or at least, I think it was an angel: it was an old toilet roll holder with a frayed piece of white satin wrapped around it; the head was a ping-pong ball with a garish face drawn in blotchy paint; her hair was a nest of gold tinsel; the wings were cardboard triangles covered in real feathers. "Andy made this for me in grade school. He hated it! But it's the greatest Christmas gift I've ever received." She placed the figurine atop the tree, smiled, and wiped at a tear. "Now, we'll have *two* beautiful angels watching over us this year."

I bit my tongue. At some point after the joke funeral I had stopped trying to convince them both that Japhy was alive. So, as Nora placed a soggy, wadded tissue in the pocket of her apron, I said nothing about how there were *not* two angels watching over us, because her son was still of this world.

Tracing a finger gently across Ryder's cheek, Nora whispered, "Thank you, Heather, Leaf. Thank you for coming back and staying with me. It's so nice to have something to get up to, you know? And thank you for my ..." she paused and smiled. "Thank you for my granddaughter." She kissed Ryder's forehead. "Thank you for giving me back a piece of my son, and a piece of my husband. Michael looks at me now whenever she does. I don't know how to thank you for that."

Again I bit my tongue.

She hummed a Christmas carol as she walked to the kitchen, and there she finished filling her final pie and lined it up beside all the other pumpkin pies on the counter, making a total of ten. *Ten* pumpkin pies. Because pumpkin pie had been Japhy's favorite, and because he had always wanted a pie feast for Christmas dinner, and because Nora had never given him one.

"Do you think it's healthy to let her grieve like this?" I whispered to Leaf. "With the tree, and the pies, and everything?"

"We *all* mourn differently." He took my hand. "Ray?"

"Yeah?"

He blinked at me. Looked down at Ryder, asleep in her cradle. "You know what's crazy? I can see Lauren in her. I guess it's the red hair. And because she's so lovely." Slipping his hand into his pocket, he drew his hand out, and said, "Listen, I, uh ... I want to give you something."

"You don't want to wait until the morning?" I asked. "It's not actually Christmas yet."

"I don't even want to wait until tonight." He unfurled his fist. Between us, his fingers opened like a blooming flower, and in the cushion of his palm, Lauren's wedding ring glinted. "I spoke to Sheridan, and asked her to draw up adoption papers. I want to give you a father for Ryder. I want to give you both a home. I want to give you time to heal. I want to give you the chance to go to College and fulfill your dreams. I want to give you the life you always planned, just with one exception. I know I'm not ... him ... but ..."

I stared at Leaf. At his hand. At that ring.

"Ray?" he said. "I want to give you ... me."

I opened my mouth, but he shook his head.

"Please understand," he said, "before you answer, I don't want to replace Japhy. I don't ever want to replace Japhy. I couldn't. Just like I don't want you to replace Lauren. You couldn't. But we've been through so much together, you're my best friend, Ray. Both of our hearts have been halved. Maybe the half of mine that is left and the half of yours that is left could make a whole one, for Ryder. And in doing so, in becoming her family, we'd be remembering Lauren and Japhy. We'd be kind of honoring them, by living *for* them."

I looked down at the ring on my thumb. Japhy's ring. And I imagined how it would look against Leaf's ebony skin. Of course, that ring wasn't really mine to give away, I was just holding it for Japhy until he came home, but what if Leaf were the one to look after it, instead of me? It would probably fit him better anyhow.

"Just think about it," Leaf said.

And just then, a single white feather fell from the wings of Japhy's angel. It twirled in its descent, spinning in loops, to land perfectly in my outstretched hand as softly as a blessing.

Ryder yawned then and opened her sleepy eyes to gaze up at me.

When Nora looked at my daughter, she saw the blue eyes of her dead husband. When Leaf looked at my daughter, he saw the red hair of his dead wife. And when I looked at my daughter, I saw proof that no matter what happens, even if life holds you down and fucks you, that there will always be something good to come of it, if you only know where to look for it.

*

"Have you given any thought to what we talked about?" asked Leaf. He kept his eyes on the road ahead, frowning. "New year, new start and everything ..."

I sighed. "No."

"Oh." His forehead smoothed. "I understand. I should have expected you wouldn't really want to ..."

"I mean," I said, touching his shoulder, "I haven't thought about it. Not yet. All I can think about is ... *this*." I waved my hand toward the window, where the purple summits of the high Sierras rose in the distance like giants. The Matterhorn, hulking and terrifying, waited for me; the ability to crush me in a second lingered in its shadow.

We drove the rest of the way in silence through Bridgeport, along a dirt road under a leafy awning of firs, ponderosas and juniper trees, over a small creek, past a little wooden lodge, and finally into a clearing that opened its arms in welcome. I stared frozen at the small wooden sign before me: *The Matterhorn Pass*.

"This is so beautiful," muttered Leaf, parking the van. He placed a large hand on Ryder's chest as she slept on the seat between us. "We'll be right here," he said. "No matter what happens, Ray, I'll be right here. Now, go and find your answers."

I wanted to tell him thank you. I wanted to explain how my feelings for him had changed. That I was *not* in love with him, as my pregnancy-fueled hormones had led me to believe. I wanted to tell him that he *was* my best friend. But instead, I just nodded and got out of the car.

My heavy boots clomped and clomped over the rocky, uneven ground. As each tenuous step took me farther and farther, higher and higher into paradise, my mind cleared. To my left was a frozen lake like faceted glass, and as I trekked higher up the track, the ice spread itself out below me and said, "Look, here I am. Admire me."

Snow blanketed the ground; the rolling slopes around me resembled clouds. Resembled heaven. Japhy? Are you here?

And finally, I let myself think of him. I let myself *really* think of him, and the events that had sculpted my life and led me, alone, to this clearing at Matterhorn.

"Well, here I am, alone in the mountains, just loving you." I sighed. "I can't believe I'm finally here. I made it," I said. "*I* made it, but where are you?" I looked around me. "Where are you?" I called. "Where are you, Japhy, you fucking asshole? Why did you leave me? Why didn't you fight harder? Why did you disappear?" Tears tried to thin my words but I growled and screamed louder still. "Why did *I* let you go? Why didn't *I* fight harder? Why did *I* disappear?"

On my rocky outcrop, high above the ground, I gazed open-mouthed at the view below. The whole world stretched out before me in brilliant hues of whites and browns and grays. I could see around the entire earth, down one side of the globe and back up the other. Japhy would have dug it so much.

Would have.

Past tense.

I sat down hard as tears clawed at my insides, stinging me, burning me. From my bag, I drew out *The Dharma Bums* and pressed my face against the torn cover, once again breathing in the smell of it. The smell of *us*. The smell of our planned future.

Tears splashed the pages as I opened the book, and a single yellow dandelion fell into my lap. The stem still twisted to form a circle. I picked it up with shaking fingers and gasping breaths and slid the ring on my finger, rehydrating its dried petals with tears. Looking down at the open pages in my lap, I read a paragraph that had been underlined in Japhy's steady hand: *It was Japhy who had advised me to come here and now though he was seven thousand miles away in Japan answering the meditation bell ... he seemed to be standing on Desolation Peak by the gnarled old rocky trees certifying and justifying all that was here. "Japhy," I said out loud, "I don't know when we'll meet again or what'll happen in the future, but Desolation, Desolation, I owe so much to Desolation, thank you forever for guiding me to the place where I learned all. Now comes the sadness of coming back to cities and I've grown two months older and there's all that humanity of bars and burlesque shows and gritty love, all upsidedown in the void God bless them, but Japhy you and me forever we know, O ever youthful, O ever weeping." Down on the lake rosy reflections of celestial vapor appeared, and I said "God, I love you" and looked up to the sky and really meant it.*

I gripped the pages.

"God," I whispered, "I love you." And like Ray Smith, I looked up to the sky and really meant it.

And like Ray Smith, alone on his mountain at the end of his novel, I was also without *my* Japhy Ryder. And now, I knew, I always would be.

Because Japhy was here.

Japhy was here.

Japhy was here.

As I read these words that had meant so much to the both of us, I felt him all around me, here, now, together in the one place that was sacred to us both.

And I knew that he must be dead.

He really *was* fucking dead.

I curled in on myself, wrapping around the shards of my heart to keep the pieces in place. Wiping my eyes angrily on the sleeve of my jacket, I threw back my head and screamed. Pure, raw, bottled-up emotion erupted from my throat until I slumped, exhausted.

"I'm here, baby," I whispered. "I'm alone in the mountains. And I'm here just loving you."

As I spoke these words again, the words that Japhy had so often sung to me, James Lee Stanley began to sing, too.

And that voice. Oh, that voice as sweet as a gift. It was the one true link I had to Japhy, and the only thing that made living – in a world where Japhy wasn't – bearable.

Gently, quietly, James and I sang to Japhy, wherever he was now.

"*May I lie beside your shoulder? Let me rest my weary bones. Younger are as wise as the older. Turn off your radio; love me tonight. Tonight. Every minute and every hour, every minute, I'll find you somehow.*"

My voice cracked over the words as I remembered the way they'd sounded in Japhy's voice, the way he whispered them, the way I would never hear them again.

"*When the moon shines through your silver curtains, turn off the lights and we'll lie there still. Imagine we're alone in the mountains and I'll be there just loving you.*"

I lifted my chin and sang straight up to him.

"*There will always be a time to love you; I knew that a while ago. Now it seems the time is disappearing, so let our loving, let it start right now. Every minute and every hour, every minute, I'll find you somehow.*"

All I had left in me was an intense love. I could feel him, or more to the point, I could feel his love for me, still completely alive and untouched by death.

"I'll find you somehow, I'll find you somehow, I'll find you somehow."

Closing the book in my lap, I stood.

Despite the frosty winter air, Japhy's dog tags warmed my skin. Lifting them over my head, I walked to the edge of the plateau, opened my hand, and watched them tinkle out of my palm and glitter as they fell away into nowhere. I didn't hear them land. I just turned and headed down the path toward my new life, where maybe one day, if I was lucky enough, love would vine around me again.

It was time for me to go home. Time to let go. Time to live. And time to say yes, yes, yes.

With my face lifted into the kiss of the sun, I walked away from the Matterhorn, leaving Japhy behind me. I left Ray behind me, too. Because really, Ray had only existed when she was in step with her Japhy. So, I walked away from the Matterhorn, no longer as Ray, but as Heather.

Heather Wren.

And soon, I thought, even *she* will not exist, because Heather Williams – mother of Ryder, and wife of Gabriel – will take her place.

chapter seventy-two

japhy

The light is bright. So bright it burns my eyes. I try to squint against it, but I can't. My eyelids won't work. But then I realize that maybe I no longer have eyelids. Maybe I no longer have *anything* anymore. Nothing but this fiercely bright light that is anything but warm and inviting. After all, isn't that how death is supposed to feel? Warm and inviting, like coming home.

There are no clouds, here. There are no angels playing harps. There is no huge, bearded man with kind eyes, or Saint Peter and his gates, not even a big red dude with a pitchfork. Just light. Just this God damned blinding light.

Sorry, God. Probably shouldn't be taking your name in vain now that I'm dead and all. Sorry about that.

But, seriously, is this *it*? Is this what I went through all that God damned (sorry, again) bullshit for?

And then, I hear it. A voice. So close it must be right inside me.

"Hello?"

It's a female voice.

"Can you hear me?"

Soft, and clear, and lovely.

This must be the angel, then. About damn time.

"Yes," I whisper. When I speak, I expect my voice to be the

same as it was when I was alive: deep, and smooth. But it comes out as thin as air. Softer than a whisper. Like a ghost.

"What is your name?" asks the angel.

The bright light blinks out, and a silhouette starts to form in my blurred vision. Slowly, I see hair as golden as a halo. It falls about her smooth, flawless face in soft, cherubic curls. Her eyes are soft and blue as the sky and *warm*. There is that warmth of heaven I'd been waiting for. Thank you!

"Do you know your name?" she says.

My name? I think. What does it matter now what I was called, or who I was?

I was a draft resister.

I was a soldier.

I was Japhy.

"My name," I whisper to the angel, "was Andy. Andy Mack."

"Well, Andy," she says. "Welcome." And then she is gone.

Without her otherworldly beautiful face in my vision, I realize that I am now staring up at a ceiling. A badly painted, white ceiling with a fluorescent tube light in the center.

"Hey, Jenny!" I hear the angel call out. Her voice is screechy now, and not at all becoming of an angel of heaven. "Get the doctor in here, will you? John Doe is finally awake!"

John Doe?

What?

I blink, and yes, I *do* still have eyelids. I also still have a body, which is, all of a sudden, charring with pain. I gasp, and groan, and oh God, oh Jesus-fucking-Christ, what the fuck is happening to me?

"Are you in pain?" asks the stupid angel, who must surely be able to tell that yes, obviously, I *am* in pain.

"Fuck!" I grit my teeth but the word squeezes through into a drawn-out sob.

"Here." She places her hand on my hand, squeezes my fingers, and gasps when I squeeze them back, hard. "You should feel better soon."

How the hell is her touch supposed to make this agony go away? How the ... but then, just like that, yes. I'm floating up and away from the throbbing horribleness that coursed through my every vein. Guess those clouds finally arrived after all. Thanks, angel.

"Oh, doctor," she says. "This one is awake. Says his name is Andy. He seemed to be in quite an amount of pain so I've just upped the dosage of morphine into his IV."

"What was his story again?"

"Brought in with shrapnel wounds from a grenade," says the angel. "No ID tags. He's been comatose until now."

No ID tags? What is she talking about? I scrabble my fingers across my chest but they close over nothing. And then I have a flash of memory: I see the VC soldier pulling my tags off me and, with a grin, draping them over the faceless and unrecognizable body of Lion. I imagine Private Leon Clancy being discovered by US soldiers and identified as the faceless and unrecognizable body of Private Andrew Mack.

"All right. Good. I'll contact the board and let them know he's conscious. Hopefully we can take this kid's name off the M.I.A. list. Some people at home are about to get some wonderful news."

Home? I think, and I smile at this word. And then I smile for the simple fact that I am able to smile. Able to breathe. Able to be.

I smile because I am alive.

Because I survived.

Because I can go home now.

Home.

Home to my waiting life.

Home to my waiting future.

Home to my waiting love.

I smile because, Ray, baby, I am alive and I am coming home to you and we can pick up our lives right where we left off.